Clouds
to
Code

Jesse Liberty

Wrox Press Ltd ®

Clouds to Code

© Wrox Press Ltd

Published by
Wrox Press Ltd. 30 Lincoln Road, Olton, Birmingham, B27 6PA. UK

Printed in CANADA

ISBN   1-861000-95-2

Trademark Acknowledgements

Credits

Managing Editors
John Franklin
David Maclean

Technical Editors
Alex Stockton
Jon Hill

Cover/Layout/Design
Andrew Guillaume
Graham Butler

Indexer
Simon Gilks

Technical Reviewers
Ed Belove
Grady Booch
Michael Jesse Chonoles
Glen Clarkson
Ian Clough
Robert Daly
Richard DiPerna
Michael Howard
Mike Kraley
Ken Levine

Technical Reviewers
Brian Lyons
glenn mcdonald
Steve Rogers
Doraiswamy Thodla

Thanks To
Jay Leve
Fred Bierman
Doug Shanks
Kevin McKenna
Kevin Tillbrook
Mary Jane Jacketti
Michael Kolowich
John Sequeira

Also To
Tom Hottenstein
Murray Levine
David McCune
Sangam Pant
David Rollert
Michael Rothman
David Shnaider
Bob Spielvogel
Stephen Zagieboylo

About the Author

Jesse Liberty is founder and president of Liberty Associates, Inc. where he provides training, consulting and mentoring in object-oriented analysis and design as well as contract programming and Internet and computer telephony development. He can be reached at jliberty@libertyassociates.com.

His web site is: http://www.libertyassociates.com.

Jesse is the author of six books on object-oriented programming and C++ and was Distinguished Software Engineer and Architect for AT&T, Xerox and PBS, and Vice President of Technology for Citibank. His next book, *Beginning Object-Oriented Analysis and Design with C++* is scheduled for publication early in 1998.

Acknowledgements

Few books have owed so much to so many people. This book could not have been written, were it not for the help and advice of dozens of people who provided heroic contributions.

I honestly can't even begin to thank these people. I can only assure them that I am viscerally aware of how much they have contributed to this book.

I start with my family. My wife Stacey, and daughters Robin and Rachel, tolerated my insane working hours and provided the kind of support, and encouragement required to see an effort like this through, and then they gave me the time to get it done. I am very grateful.

David Maclean of Wrox Press is one of the most honest and reliable people I've ever had the pleasure to meet. He never wavered in his support for this book, even when I did. He helped shape the concept, embraced the changes as we progressed, offered me support in every possible way, gave the book its title and served as its midwife. The astonishing thing about Wrox Press is that his extraordinary support was matched by John Franklin, Alex Stockton and Jon Hill. They shaped this book, gave it form and substance and breathed life into it. I've never worked with a better group of editors, and I am deeply grateful to them for their help.

Jay Leve's influence on this book goes way beyond the project at hand. Jay's unwavering commitment to quality has influenced my understanding of product development, how businesses run and how great things are accomplished. His extraordinary willingness to allow me to document the process of developing his software gave life to this book and I am very much in his debt. Jay's partners, Fred Bierman and Doug Shanks provided unfaltering support, and I believe that they have designed and built a business that will define and dominate a powerful new market. I must also thank their staff, especially Kevin McKenna, Kevin Tillbrook, and Mary Jane Jacketti, who made me feel a welcome part of their organization.

Steve Rogers agreed to provide his expertise in the analysis, design and implementation of this product, and I have learned a great deal from working with him. Steve was one of the people who originally taught me C++, and he continues to teach me as we go forward. Working with Steve is a great pleasure. Steve is the president of BobCat software and can be reached at sdr@tiac.net.

glenn mcdonald and I worked together at AT&T, and he provided brilliant insight into the book and helped me redesign it for human consumption. glenn provided a course correction at exactly the right moment, and his suggestions were like small particles hitting a moving object, changing the trajectory only slightly but having an enormous long term impact. glenn lives and designs software in Cambridge, Massachusetts, watched over by hundreds of miniature dinosaurs and an enormous plastic banana slug. He is the product designer of eRoom, Instinctive Technology's web team-collaboration software. He is also responsible for a completely non-collaborative music-review column, published weekly on the web at http://www.furia.com/twas.

Mike Kraley is a friend and a mentor. His insights into the book, software development, and so much else are deeply incorporated in much of what I've written. Mike is Chief Technology Officer at Individual, Inc. in Burlington, MA.

Ed Belove provided critical contributions along the way, and it is to Ed that I must attribute my commitment to a pair of key ideas embraced by this book. The first is that software development is best done in very small teams. The second is that it is possible to make a significant contribution without managing a team.

Michael Jesse Chonoles is Chief of Methodology at Lockheed Martin. Coincidentally, Michael and I were good friends back in high school (which is longer ago than I care to think about). He was then, and is still one of the brightest people I've ever met, and his contributions to my understanding of object-oriented analysis and design and to the early iterations of this book, can not be overstated. I am very grateful to him for his help.

Glen Clarkson, Software Engineer for Fourth Shift, provided incredible help with the early analysis and design and also created many of the illustrative diagrams used in this book. Glenn read numerous drafts of the manuscript and his contributions and suggestions were enormously helpful. He is a gifted designer and his assistance is very much appreciated.

Michael Kolowich is CEO of Individual Inc., and was president of Interchange Network Company. His assistance in helping me understand what happened, and his insight into how software is built were critical to my ability to write this book. His help is very much appreciated.

Michael Howard is co-founder and VP of Technology at InterActive WorkPlace, Inc., developers of a dynamic, intranet-based sales intelligence solution. He provided enormous help in the early design and remains one of the most gifted software developers I've met.

Richard DiPerna was most recently Vice President, Business Development for Nets Inc., a start-up focused on electronic commerce in the industrial sector. Mr DiPerna was a founding director of Bain & Company, the international management consulting firm, where he led the information industry practice for a decade. Richard helped me gain perspective on a number of issues, and his help is gratefully acknowledged.

Each of the following individuals agreed to serve on an advisory panel for this book, and their patience and assistance is gratefully acknowledged.

Grady Booch - Author of the Booch Method, Principal Scientist Rational Inc.

Robert Daly - Software consultant and co-founder of NumberSix

Ken Levine - Software consultant and founder of Lekton, Inc.

Brian Lyons - Software consultant and co-founder of NumberSix

Doraiswamy Thodla - Integra Technology International Inc.

This book attempts to offer insight into the process of software development, and so I must thank a number of people who had a direct and meaningful influence on my understanding of how software gets built and businesses thrive. Among them are Tom Hottenstein, Murray Levine, David McCune, Sangam Pant, David Rollert, Michael Rothman, David Shnaider, Bob Spielvogel, and Stephen Zagieboylo.

Finally, I must thank Mr Kaufman at Lafayette High School and the folks at Community Access in New York, each for providing computers at critical moments in my life, and Danny Sachs for suggesting that computers could be great fun.

Dedication

This book is dedicated to Jay Leve. A man with a clear vision.

```
= false;                              run                CTime
                                   CTime::GetCurren
Time();                        CTime end = theJo
= now.Format("%b %d          CTime start = theJobSet.
                              CTime todayStart(start.GetYea
                         start.GetMonth(),now.GetDay(),
er = "start < '";            start.GetHour(),
day;                         start.GetMinute(),
, and enddate > '";          start.GetSecond());
oday;                          CTime todayEnd(end.GetYear(),
= '";                       end.GetMonth(), now.GetDay(),
                            end.GetHour(),
cheduleSet.m_strFilter =    end.GetMinute(), end.GetSecond());

                             end.GetMinute() > now || todayS

                              if (todayStart > now ||
JobScheduleSet.IsOpen())      now)      theJobSet.Close();
JobScheduleSet.Requery();           {     return false;
pDoc>m_JobScheduleSet.Open();                 }

llTrack* pCallTrack;                    CTimeSpan theSpan = end now
l ok;                                   int totalMinutes =
                                    theSpan.GetTotalMinutes();  //

le                                      if (end > todayEnd)  //
pDoc>m_JobScheduleSet.IsEOF())      than today
                                        {    int AdditionalMin =
     pCallTrack = new                   GetAdditionalMinutes(theJ
llTrack(m_pDoc>m_JobScheduleSet.m_
ID);  ok = pCallTrack>Initialize();     theJobSet.m_EndDate);
                                         CTimeSpan todaySp
   if (ok)                          now;    totalMinutes =
   {   Log("ok\n");                 todaySpan.GetTotalMin
                                         AdditionalMin;
m_CallList.AddHead(pCallTrack);          }
            foundJobs = true;
                                         m_min = ( ( (m_t
   }                                totalMinutes) + 1 )
   else                                  m_Priority = th
   {   Log("...Rejected!\n");            m_Tilt = theJo
        delete pCallTrack;              m_Throttle = the
                                        m_JobID = the
   }                                    theJobSet.Cl

m_pDoc>m_JobScheduleSet.MoveNext();

                                        return true
obs;
```

CONTENTS

```cpp
 false;
ime();
 = now.Format("%b %d

r = "start < '";
day;
 and enddate > '";
oday;
 '";

cheduleSet.m_strFilter =

JobScheduleSet.IsOpen())

JobScheduleSet.Requery();

pDoc>m_JobScheduleSet.Open();

lTrack* pCallTrack;
 ok;

le
pDoc>m_JobScheduleSet.IsEOF())

    pCallTrack = new
llTrack(m_pDoc>m_JobScheduleSet.m_
ID);   ok = pCallTrack>Initialize();

    if (ok)
    {   Log("ok\n");

m_CallList.AddHead(pCallTrack);
        foundJobs = true;

    }
    else
    {   Log("...Rejected!\n");
        delete pCallTrack;

    }

m_pDoc>m_JobScheduleSet.MoveNext();


    CTime
    CTime::GetCur
    CTime end = theJob
    CTime start = theJobSe
    CTime todayStart(start.Getre
    start.GetMonth(), now.GetDay(),
    start.GetHour(),
    start.GetMinute(),
    start.GetSecond());
    CTime todayEnd(end.GetYear(),
    end.GetMonth(), now.GetDay(),
    end.GetHour(),
    end.GetMinute(), end.GetSecond());

    if (todayStart > now || todayEn

    now)
    {   theJobSet.Close();
        return false;

    }

    CTimeSpan theSpan = end now
    int totalMinutes =
    theSpan.GetTotalMinutes(); //

    if (end > todayEnd) //
than today
    {   int AdditionalMin =
    GetAdditionalMinutes(theJo
t,
    theJobSet.m_EndDate);
    CTimeSpan todaySp
    now;   totalMinutes =
    todaySpan.GetTotalMin
    AdditionalMin;

    }

    m_min = ( ( (m_t
    totalMinutes) + 1 )
    );   m_Priority = th
    m_Tilt = theJo
    m_Throttle = the
    m_JobID = theJobSet.Cl
    theJobSet.Cl

    return true
```

aJobs;

Introduction

Who this book is for

Clouds to Code is written for programmers who need to build robust, industrial-strength, commercial applications, and who want to see how it is done in the real world. It is written for project managers who want to learn how the application of object-oriented analysis and design will affect their project planning, scheduling and implementation. It is written for *anyone* who wants to understand what object-oriented design is all about. Finally, and above all else, it is written for people who want to understand what it takes to build a world class application and deliver it on time and on budget.

Developers have been struggling for the past few years to acquire a suite of related skills, including object-oriented analysis and design, an understanding of design patterns and a working knowledge of client-server and Internet-based technologies. For these professionals, the real question is, "How do I bring all these skills together and *apply* them to the implementation of a great commercial program that I bring in on deadline?"

One way to acquire that knowledge is to join a project team and live through the process. That can be an expensive education, but until now, there have been few alternatives. There are lots of excellent books that describe the theory and practice of object-oriented analysis and design, but nothing can substitute for the experience of living through the effort, watching it in action, and seeing it result in working code.

The realities of scheduling, funding, coding, and managing a development project intrude upon the academic niceties of object-oriented theory. This book demolishes the ivory tower and shows you how a small team of determined developers can apply these skills to the real-world goal of shipping a quality product on time.

In *A History Of The English-Speaking Peoples*, Winston Churchill wrote, "This book does not seek to rival the works of professional historians, it aims rather to present a personal view...." I would say of *this* book that it does not seek to rival the works of those who created object-oriented design methodologies, it aims rather to present a personal view on the development of world class software.

This book is designed to bridge the gap between academic theory and experience. It invites you to join the team as a silent observer, and to watch a real-world development effort from inception to delivery.

The Case Study

Clouds to Code offers a case study, a detailed examination of the application of these skills to the production of software. This book is perhaps unusual in that it follows the development of a real project, in real time. That project is the creation of a next generation calling application, codename: *Industrial Strength Crisis•Call®*. *Crisis•Call®* has a single mission: to make hundreds of thousands of telephone calls on schedule, reliably and with no human intervention.

This project is *not* fictional[1]. By the end of this book, *Crisis•Call* will have been created by Liberty Associates on behalf of Hypotenuse, Inc. and you'll have been there to see it happen.

Liberty Associates, Inc. provides training, consulting and contract programming in C++ and object-oriented development. We are a founding company in the Digital Guild - a coordinating body of some of the best Internet development organizations in New England.

I created Liberty Associates, then known as Rational Technologies, Inc., in 1988 and have been working as a consultant off and on for the past decade. We currently focus on Internet and telephony development, and provide on-site training in C++, Object-oriented software development, MFC, COM and related technologies.

Hypotenuse, Inc. is located in Verona, N.J. and is one of the largest public opinion polling organizations in America. Currently, Hypotenuse conducts research on behalf of 80 television stations nationwide. The anchor records a message such as,

> "This is News4 New York; I'm Chuck Scarborough. We're taking a free, one minute opinion poll and we want to know what *you* think. Results will be on tonight's News4 New York. To start the poll, press 1 on your touch-tone phone."

The respondent is then walked through the poll. It is important to note that the entire process is automated; at no time does the respondent speak with a person.

---

[1] *While the project is not fictitious, the memos, interactions and dialog have been created for the purposes of this book and do not necessarily reflect the actual communications as they happened. Some of the names have been changed and characters have been created who represent a consolidation of various real people.*

2

Hypotenuse has approximately 500 outbound telephone lines, and calls thousands to hundreds of thousands of people a day. Let me hasten to add that these are *not* automated sales calls. Hypotenuse is *not* in the business of ringing your phone and trying to sell you floor wax. Rather, Hypotenuse is in the business of calling people to get their opinions or to provide them with time-critical information they've requested.

Twelve years ago, I was a Vice President in the Human Factors group of the Development Division at Citibank. I worked for a brilliant creative designer named Jay Leve, who came to Citibank from Viewtron, where he helped develop one of the first interactive online services. Jay left Citibank to found Hypotenuse, where he is currently the president and chief executive officer. While Hypotenuse is tremendously successful in its current business of conducting public opinion research, Jay now wants to refocus the company on its original mission: *calling.*

Jay distinguishes *calling* from *polling* in that calling is far simpler, and of interest to a wider audience. In calling, Hypotenuse is, essentially, dialing a number, playing a message and hanging up the phone. While some calls will be more interactive, the essence of calling is reaching a large number of people with vital and perhaps time-sensitive information using the single most ubiquitous device in America: the standard telephone.

If we're not selling floor wax, who are we calling and what are we saying when we get them on the phone? That's really up to the people that use the service: political organizations might provide get-out-the-vote reminders, the Federal Emergency Management Agency (FEMA) might use the service to provide evacuation instructions, and schools might use it to alert parents of closings and delays. But in each case, the person being called has an established relationship with the organization making the call and very much wants the information they are receiving.

In short, *Crisis•Call* will be a flexible system to allow Hypotenuse to place any number of phone calls on behalf of any number of customers, at a moment's notice.

The outcome of the design was not known when I first sat down to write the book. I developed the book in tandem with the software project, documenting the process as we lived it, and capturing the issues, concerns, technical problems and solutions as they unfolded in real time.

The project was designed and implemented with aggressive and relatively inflexible deadlines. No allowances were made for the book, and the book does not try to hide any of our wrong turns or blind alleys; it documents what we did and how we did it. You will learn a lot about object-oriented analysis and design, coding in C++ and SQL Server, implementing design patterns, and leveraging COM and ActiveX for Internet development. You will also learn about developing computer telephony applications, managing software projects, and delivering products on time and on budget.

This book will offer relatively little actual code, and most of that will be towards the end. This is not a how-to book on programming; it is a study in the application of analysis and design to the development of software. Code will be shown in the final chapters to illustrate how the design plays itself out in the implementation.

Past Experience Applied

As we progress, I'll describe a number of other projects in which I participated in various roles: as engineer, team leader, manager and architect, developing software for some of America's largest corporations. While I will touch upon many projects, I'll focus on two specific experiences. The first was developing home banking products for Citibank; the second was building an online service, the Interchange Network, initially for Ziff Davis and ultimately for AT&T. I'll describe each of these experiences in some detail, as they teach lessons that go beyond those of the Hypotenuse experience.

At Citibank, I learned the cost of trying to develop software in an organization that is insufficiently independent. We were building a new generation 'Enhanced Telephone,' a device to allow customers to access their banking services using a telephone with a small built-in screen. This was 1986, and our theory was that the personal computer had not yet made sufficient inroads into the home to be a commercially viable means of delivering home banking. We realized that for many of our customers the telephone was a more comfortable, and certainly more common, device that would receive wider adoption.

When we began designing the Enhanced Telephone, home banking was still encountering a great deal of market resistance. The idea for the enhanced telephone had been generated in the 1970s by the man who was now, in 1986, the director of the Development Division. We anticipated getting the product into the market in 18 months. It didn't work out that way, and as I discuss issues in project management, I'll refer back to some of the organizational problems we ran into.

At Ziff, and later at AT&T, I learned a lot about how much can go wrong when you put together a large group of highly talented people and give them plenty of money and plenty of time to do something new and innovative. Never before have I seen a more creative and talented group of people who were so well funded; yet despite these apparently ideal conditions, we were unable to bring even one product to market success. Five years and perhaps fifty million dollars later, all that remained were the lessons.

Learning lessons from one's past experience is a dangerous game. On the one hand is George Santayana's compelling quote that those who cannot remember the past are condemned to repeat it; on the other is Sun Tzu's observation that generals are forever fighting the previous war. This second observation is very powerful for me. While we don't want to repeat the same mistakes, neither do we want to overreact to what went wrong on previous projects.

One of the startling aspects of software development is how many projects fail. Examine the résumé of virtually any experienced software developer and you'll find one or more failed products. The senior management at Interchange had, among them, literally dozens of failed projects on their resumes — products that were well conceived but which, for one reason or another, never saw the light of day. This is sobering; few other industries would tolerate our collective rate of failure.

The difficulty of steering a project from conceptualization through commercially successful delivery will be the unifying theme of this book. This book was written before the end was known, so fasten your seat belts, it will be an exciting ride.

Software Development Philosophy

Perhaps the single most famous rabbinical story is this:

> It happened that a certain heathen came before Rabbi Shammai and said to him, "Convert me on one condition: that you teach me the entire Torah [the first five books of the Bible] while I am standing on one foot." Rabbi Shammai drove him away with the builder's measure that was in his hand. He then came before Rabbi Hillel, who converted him. Hillel said to him, "That which is hateful to you, do not do to your neighbor. This is the entire Torah; the rest is commentary. Go and learn it."

There is a good reason that Rabbi Shammai drove the heathen away; any simplification can only mislead. There is more to writing great software than a robust design, and the devil is in the details.

There is also a good reason that Rabbi Hillel did *not* drive him away: understanding the fundamental idea supplies a context for all the details that follow. This book endeavors only to supply such a framework of understanding, and will do so within the context of the case study.

So, here's my 'one foot' description of the philosophy of this book:

> Make sure you understand the problem, implement a solution using a very small group of talented people, and let your customers tell you how to improve it. That's it; all the rest is commentary.

```cpp
= false;

Time();
= now.Format("%b %d

er = "start < '";
oday;
, and enddate > '";
today;
"';

                                                    run    CTime now
                                        CTime::GetCurren
                                CTime end = theJob
                        CTime start = theJobSet.m
                CTime todayStart(start.GetYear(),
        start.GetMonth(),now.GetDay(),
        start.GetHour(),

                start.GetMinute(),
                start.GetSecond());
            start.GetSecond());
        CTime todayEnd(end.GetYear(),
    end.GetMonth(), now.GetDay(),
    end.GetHour(),

ScheduleSet.m_strFilter =
                end.GetMinute(), end.GetSecond())

                                end.GetMinute(),   end.GetSecond()

                        if (todayStart > now || todayS
                    now)
JobScheduleSet.IsOpen()             {    theJobSet.Close();
                                    return false;
JobScheduleSet.Requery();

pDoc>m_JobScheduleSet.Open();           }
                                    CTimeSpan theSpan = end no
llTrack* pCallTrack;                int totalMinutes =
                                theSpan.GetTotalMinutes();
l ok;

ile                             if (end > todayEnd) // s
pDoc>m_JobScheduleSet.m_        than today
    pCallTrack = new                {    int AdditionalMin =
llTrack(m_pDoc>m_JobScheduleSet.                GetAdditionalMinutes(the
bID);     ok = pCallTrack>Initialize();      t,
                                    theJobSet.m_EndDate);
                                        CTimeSpan todaySp
    if (ok)
    {    Log("ok\n");            now;    totalMinutes =
                                todaySpan.GetTotalMin
                                AdditionalMin;
    m_CallList.AddHead(pCallTrack);      }
        foundJobs = true;

    }                                   m_min = ( ( (m_
        else                        totalMinutes) + 1
    {    Log("...Rejected!\n");     );   m_Priority = t
        delete pCallTrack;              m_Tilt = theJo
                                        m_Throttle = th
    }                                   m_JobID = theJobSet.Cl
                                        theJobSet.Cl

    pDoc>m_JobScheduleSet.MoveNext();                   turn tru
```

CHAPTER ONE

The Business of Software

Writing software is a complicated business, and what separates the truly valuable developer from someone who is merely a skilled technician is the ability to look beyond the details of writing the program and see the entire process. In addition to writing great code, a top developer must appreciate the role the software will play in the overall business plans of his customer.

In the chapters to come I'll describe, as it happens, the process of developing the *Crisis•Call* application. I'll describe how we determine the customer's requirements, how we design a solution, and with luck how we implement the solution on time and on budget. Before we begin, however, I want to take a moment and talk about the business of creating great software. It starts with time.

Time

Perhaps the most dangerous moment in software development, both for our client and for ourselves, is when we set the initial schedule. It is all too tempting to underestimate the size of the project intentionally, and then to have to go back and adjust the numbers. After all, there is tremendous pressure to come up with a small dollar figure and a short delivery date so that the customer will say, "Yes." There is real fear that if we guess with a margin for error, we'll shut down the project before it even gets started. The last thing we want to do is overbid the project when we really could have done it for less. "And," we're tempted to tell ourselves, "surely they realize that once we understand more, we may have to 'slip' the date?"

The sad state of the industry is that so many software projects 'slip' their date, it has become expected. Developers state their schedule knowing full well they can never hit the promised date, managers set aggressive dates figuring they'll 'slip' as they need to, and customers write off published ship dates as a pipe dream.

Setting Realistic Dates

'Slip' is such a gentle word; it's so much nicer to say a project 'slipped' than that it was late. The harsh reality is that millions of dollars are lost every year, and entire projects are canceled, because of the industry's inability to deliver even relatively straightforward projects on time and on budget. Even when customers and managers allow for the inevitable schedule slips, they invariably underestimate quite how miserably late the product will be.

Large projects have been known to run to quadruple their originally estimated development time, and then to be slow, brittle and antiquated by the time they finally lumber out of the door and onto the market. In any other industry, this would spell the death of the company. Incredibly, while that certainly happens in software, the programmers and the managers typically go on to the next big project unscathed.

> **Software projects are late because they are not managed well, period.**

That is not to say that particular managers do a bad job (although that is certainly true in some cases), but rather that *as an industry* we don't yet know how to manage software projects well. This is a startling admission, but there is no other answer: one software project after another, managed by some of the best people in the industry, is miserably, inexcusably and often fatally late.

There is a joke that never fails to make software developers laugh; it is this: "If cities were built like software, the first woodpecker to come along would level civilization."

The truth is that there are a huge number of imponderables. What we are building is enormously complex, with interdependencies that are difficult or impossible to fully understand, much less predict. We are forever reinventing the proverbial wheel, and because we don't build from well-understood components, we are always working with new, and thus unpredictable, parts. None of this is a revelation; this is a well-understood and much lamented situation.

However, this sad state of affairs is finally, slowly, changing. Microsoft[1] and other large, successful organizations are beginning to spawn a literature of success that will help other managers apply best practices to their own projects. We are not helpless. We have tools at hand to help manage the complexity, and with care and skill, projects *can* be delivered on time and on budget. Sure, it takes discipline, but it can be done.

The Rules of Scheduling

So, how *do* we build a project and deliver it on time, especially given that we are frequently under pressure to create the schedule with inadequate information about what it is we'll be building? The answer is to build only what we have time to build well.

---

[1] *Those who equate Microsoft with the Evil Empire are free to substitute any number of large successful organizations with a history of turning out quality code on something approximating a schedule.*

To do this, we will need some guiding principles, or 'rules'. Rule Number One is:

> **Features will yield to schedule and schedule will yield to quality. We will slip the schedule to ensure quality, but not to add features.**

Of course, Rule Number One begs the question of what we mean by 'quality'. To ensure quality, we must define it with great precision. As the project progresses, we will gain a better understanding of what we must accomplish. As we near completion of the code, we'll be in a position to define quality in terms of the acceptable number of critical bugs, serious bugs and minor bugs (each of which will in turn be defined in detail). We will also define quality in terms of the product's robustness, extensibility and flexibility. Each of these terms must be quantified as well. It isn't enough to say you want high quality; you must say exactly what you mean by the term. And you must state your definition as something that can be *measured*. What you measure is what you get more of. If you measure robustness, you'll get more robust products.

Creating a Schedule When You Don't Know Enough to be Sure

There are two ways to build a schedule: *top-down* and *bottom-up*. Bottom-up is what we all want to do: look at the work to be done, add up how long it takes, put in extra time for problems, add 50% for wiggle room, and voilà! You have your answer. But, as Rocky used to say, "Bullwinkle! That trick never works."

The reality is that the market will dictate how much time you have, and this deadline is far more important than the one you get by working out how long it will take to do everything you *might* do. By virtue of Rule Number One, we will drop features to hit the schedule.

It is worth noting that for some products, the determinant is *not* the schedule. Performance, robustness or even safety can be key. (In the aerospace industry, for example, safety must take precedence over all other scheduling concerns.) In any case, it is imperative to identify the single most important aspect to which all other characteristics will yield. This is tricky; what senior management *says* is most important may not be what it really *believes* to be so — and it may not *act* that way, either. You'll see this in action when you are told that, for example, the schedule is a brick wall which can't be violated and then, at the last minute, the schedule is allowed to slip to accommodate a particular feature.

The most important skill of a world-class software developer is the ability *honestly* to identify the priority order. In our case, and in most cases, the top priority is time to market with a high quality product. That doesn't mean a *perfect* product, but one that won't embarrass or financially threaten the company.

That brings us to *top-down* scheduling. In top-down scheduling, you start with your completion date and work backwards. We thus create our schedule like my father's accountant figured his taxes. "So, Dave, how much do you want to pay? Okay, let's figure up from that number," and he'd fill in the blanks above the total so that they added up to the predetermined answer. In the vernacular, "Draw curve; plot points."

How, I hear you ask, can you predict with any degree of certainty that you'll be done in that time? How can you make an accurate estimate for the length of a project when you don't know exactly what it entails? From Rule Number One, it follows that we'll cut features until we have a product that *can* be designed, implemented and tested in the allotted time. This isn't as crazy as it sounds, because Rule Number Two is:

> **You're playing pinball. Get a high score, and you get to play again.**

If the first release is a success, we will have the opportunity to build the second release, and put back in the features we left out to ensure we hit our deadline. If, on the other hand, we hold the product back, trying to add all the features we can imagine, the market will shift out from under us and the product may well be stillborn. The goal is to get the product out into use, and to give the customers a chance to tell us what *they* think is missing and where *they* would like the product to be improved.

The big win with iterative development like this is that as we go along, we can confirm and adjust our scheduling assumptions. The goal is to provide the customer with as much information as we have, but to continually update the customer as we learn more. More important, not only are we informing the customer as experience gains us new insight, we are adjusting the plan and tinkering with the design itself.

To hit these aggressive dates we'll need intermediate deadlines — milestones along the way that will prove we are on track. This brings up Rule Number Three:

> **The likelihood of hitting a deadline is proportional to the number of deadlines you've already hit.**

Hitting deadlines creates an atmosphere of success and enhances the likelihood of hitting the next deadline. It follows that missing deadlines creates a culture tolerant of missed deadlines, and begins the death-spiral so familiar to the industry. Hitting deadlines also gives the customer a warm, happy feeling about the project, and reduces his stress levels. When he is sanguine, you are more likely to be given the time and room to do the job right, without having to devote resources just to managing the customer's anxiety.

This means we want to be certain to schedule our early deadlines with enough wiggle room that we are certain to hit them. Once we have a track record of success, we can become somewhat more aggressive in our estimates.

Not all managers will agree with this. I have worked with some that said, "Whatever deadline you schedule will always be the *best* you will do. No one ever comes in early."

There is truth in this. Allowing a realistic amount of time may indeed foreclose the opportunity to deliver more quickly.

The problem is that the alternative is to create what are euphemistically called 'aggressive' deadlines. Aggressive deadlines are quickly understood by developers to be fantasies. They know that no one expects them to meet these crazy deadlines, so they write them off. Of course, since the deadline was aggressive, the manager didn't really expect it to be met, so there is little pain when it is missed.

Hitting a deadline should be like hitting a brick wall. With artificially aggressive deadlines, you go through that wall and discover it is made of paper. Guess what? The next deadline is even easier to smash through; you hardly even break stride. Missed deadlines undermine self-esteem. The developer comes to believe he is a pawn in a manager's game. If he is inexperienced enough to put up with it, he probably isn't contributing much to the project. Your most valuable people will disengage and lose their internal motivation. When that happens, your product is doomed.

Just as repeatedly missing a deadline undermines commitment, repeatedly *hitting* deadlines builds up the developer's self-esteem. After a few successes, he is reluctant to lose his standing as a developer who can meet his commitments. When the deadline looms, he is ready to do whatever it takes to hit that target.

When developers create their own, realistic deadlines, they 'buy-in'. They take ownership of the dates and make a commitment. Buying-in is very important in software development; in fact it's critical. When a developer buys-in, he stakes himself to delivering a quality product on time.

When I talk about buying-in, I do *not* mean the artificial, management-fad, total-quality, high-empowerment, buzzword 'buy-in' that so many companies try to sell. In that phony buy-in, employees are offered a chance to give their opinions, which are then routinely ignored by the folks who really make the decisions. Corporate 'buy-in' is like being elected president of your sixth-grade class — lots of pomp, but no real authority. The kind of buy-in I'm talking about is like being elected to the Continental Congress in 1775: revolutionary power to take hold of your destiny.

A theme I'll return to in this chapter and elsewhere is the great benefit I see in small programming teams, and this is one of the places where their advantage is clear. When you have a small team, you can afford to hire only the very best. When you do that, you are more likely to trust their judgment about how long something will take, and then you are less likely to impose absurd deadlines.

The market may not forgive a long lead-time; that is a business decision, and you may have to cut back on features. However, no market imperative can make a programmer code any faster. I was once told a joke in which a man meets a woman at a hotel. They begin to dance and he says, "I'm only here for the weekend." She replies, "I'm dancing as fast as I can."

Apportioning the Schedule

I typically allow about 1/3 of the entire schedule for analysis and design — the process of understanding the requirements and designing the software. Let me admit that others will tell you that analysis and design should form 50%, 60% or even 75% of the project time. If you push them, however, you'll often discover that some of what they're calling 'design', I'm calling 'implementation'. During the implementation phase, you still think about and modify the design, but the focus shifts to getting the product built.

If I show a schedule to my customers with 'analysis and design' on it, they figure we're just sitting around the conference room and chatting, and they start getting nervous when they're paying by the hour and there's no code to show for it.

Remember that they are not paying for the diagrams we create in the analysis and design phase. They can't put diagrams in a box, shrink-wrap it and send it to their customers. They are paying for working code, and as far as they're concerned, analysis and design are necessary but not nearly sufficient. This brings me to Rule Number Four:

> **No one ever wanted a one-eighth inch drill bit. They wanted a one-eighth inch hole.**

Never lose sight of the customer's goals. He doesn't care about the elegance of your design except insofar as it will enhance the quality, reliability and extensibility of the product you'll create.

We all long for the good old days of late-night hacking, when we stayed up until 3 a.m. drinking Jolt and writing code without even a passing nod to formal analysis. You can still do that; in fact many folks do. What you end up with is this: you sleep real late the next day, and you feel a lot older. When you get back to the office you discover that your code is just about as good as it was back when you *were* a college sophomore. It works, but it isn't the professional grade software on which to build a company.

I believe in analysis and design. I certainly don't mean to suggest that we should abridge the analysis or design phases to placate a customer who wants his project completed in an unrealistic timeframe. As a professional, though, it is my job to listen to my customer's needs. It is my job to work *with* the customer to make sure he understands the process and, you guessed it, to get *buy-in* on my methodology. I'm going to ask Jay to trust me, and to trust me for a long time. He'll be paying out a lot of good money. All he'll get in return is my assurance that I fully understand his goals, and that I'll deliver a high-quality product on time.

He can only provide that trust based on my reputation and on his experience of me and my work. I build that reputation by taking the time fully to analyze and design the product, so that when I do deliver it, it is right. I build that trust by making sure that my customer knows that *I* know that I work for him, and not the other way around.

Money

The one question every developer wants to ask, and which no book ever seems to answer, is this: how much good money *does* it cost to get a program written? In short, what is it realistic to charge a customer for software?

There are a number of reasons we don't talk about this much. First, our parents told us it is rude to ask how much someone earns. Second, we are all afraid of providing a competitive advantage to other developers, as if the going rate were a trade secret. Third, no one wants to show off. The fact is that we're making a lot more money than we ever expected to. The market is hot, demand is high, and writing software is lucrative — at least for now.

These are the human reasons, and I won't ignore them, but there are other good reasons to avoid talking about rates. One of the most important is this: the market is volatile, and it isn't uniform. Thus, when I talk about rates I run the risk that by the time you read this it will be out of date. Further, reasonable rates in Boston are almost certainly different from what is reasonable in other cities.

As if this weren't difficult enough, it's made more complicated by how we all feel about money. Most Americans have, in my experience, a limited commitment to capitalism. How often have you heard someone say, "What a rip off. It probably costs them $1.49 to make this, and they have the nerve to charge $15." Ask that person how the price *should* be set, and you'll likely hear something like this: "They should figure out what it costs to manufacture, add a reasonable profit, and that should be the price." An interesting idea, but it isn't capitalism.

Capitalism says that a price is set like this: *maximize your profit.* If you get to the point where raising your price lowers your sales and you end up with less profit, then drop your price just enough to reverse the effect.

Here's a story from the depression: A man stops to buy an apple from a pushcart. "$500,000," says the pushcart owner. "$500,000 for an apple?" the man asks incredulously, "You must not sell a lot of apples." The pushcart owner looks at him knowingly and says, "Yes, but at this price I don't have to."

The rate for programming is set like any other, by supply and demand. However, this can be complicated to determine. The going rate in one part of the country may be quite different from that in another. Furthermore, the rate changes over time, depending on demand. For example, I do most of my work in the Boston area. Right now, we have a shortage of developers and a lot of demand. I've talked with developers with just a year or two of experience who are earning $65,000 as full-time employees, and others with more experience but less bargaining savvy, who earn just over half that.

As in other industries, the factors of supply and demand are not the only considerations. Wages vary according to a particular person's experience and ability, but these can be difficult to assess and compare. There is a particularly high variation in compensation in the software development market, in part because no one can be fully informed. You can find out the going rate for a Nissan Maxima by checking the Internet and making a few calls, but it is very difficult to find out what your buddy is earning. Harder still is to establish a going rate for a given level of expertise and skill, even assuming you could quantify such a concept.

That said, there are certain ceilings that are difficult to penetrate. For a long time, even the best developers had a hard time breaking into six figures in full-time employment. The real money, though, is in management. 'Chief Technology Officers' have been known to earn a quarter of a million dollars a year in some companies.

Then there is the question of stock. Many start-up ventures try to compensate for lower wages and higher risk by offering ownership in the company. Depending on when you join, you may receive a quarter or a half of one percent, or in some rare cases even a whole percentage of the stock of the company. Many other companies offer much smaller fractions. The ultimate value of these stocks is imponderable; most of the developers I know who take these offers consider the stock to be a quiet, long-term investment that may well come to nothing.

It is *usually* true that you will earn a lot more as a contract programmer or as a consultant than you will as a full-time employee. It is also true that you will take a greater risk, and in many cases you will have less 'ownership' of your product. Companies use consultants in different ways: many large companies treat consultants as virtual employees for the life of a particular project, while others bring consultants in only for a quick fix.

Many in the industry differentiate between consultants on the one hand, and contract programmers on the other. A contract programmer expects to be given a well-defined project and to write code. A consultant may not write code at all; his job is to help the business figure out what it needs to do and how to do it. Many of us serve both roles, sometimes at the same company!

So, how much do I charge? I don't think this book can be intellectually honest if I skirt this issue in the same way everyone else does, so here's the answer. Like many developers, I differentiate between my long-term contracting rates and my short-term consulting rates. As I write this in the fall of 1997, my rates are $1,500/day for long-term contract programming and $2,500/day for mentoring, consulting and training.

Are these rates high? I've discovered that if you can deliver the product reliably, if you can save the company money in the long run, and if you have a good reputation and your customers believe they can *trust* you, then these rates are considered reasonable. The key here, as so often, is trust.

My clients must invest a lot of trust in my work. Typically, they don't have the time (and often they don't have the expertise) to supervise a project in detail. They have no interest in micromanaging my work; what they want is to identify the goals and then to walk away, knowing that when they come back I'll have delivered what they asked for.

The cost of software is not just the initial investment. It is the cost from start to finish, including maintaining the product; not to mention building a business on top of that software. The expertise is not just in knowing how to write C++, but it is in the ability fully to analyze the business problem, design a solution and deliver that solution on time and on budget.

There is a famous story about a train that broke down in the middle of the desert. In the luxury car was the president of the train line and his most important customer. The engineer tried everything he could think of, but he could not get the train running. They discovered that the man who built the locomotive happened to be a passenger on the train, and they called him forward. He stared at the locomotive for a few minutes, picked up a hammer and hit the locomotive sharply. It started right up. Two weeks later, the president of the line received a bill for $50,000. "$50,000!" he exclaimed, "For five minutes work?" "Oh," said the engine builder, "I should have given you an itemized bill." A few days later, an itemized bill arrived:

```
         Hitting engine with hammer:               $      1.00
         Knowing where to hit engine with hammer:  $49,999.00
```

My clients (and I would argue, most clients) don't have time to become experts in software development. That's why they hire a consultant, an architect or a chief technology officer. They need someone who knows where to hit the engine, and they want someone they can trust to get the job done. In short, they want a 'fire and forget' missile. They don't want to guide me in to the target; they want to identify the target, push the button and fly off to the next problem. Fire and forget missiles are more expensive than dumb missiles, but they let you accomplish a lot more in less time.

Team Size

Development teams, like government programs, have a tendency to grow. No one knows how this happens; we all set out to keep things small, but one day when you come into the office there are people crowded two or three to a cubicle, and there's no place to put down the pizza. You will know this has happened to you when you find yourself whining about the need for bigger conference rooms.

Some years ago, I heard that the new president of a large car rental firm called a big meeting and fired all but one of his Human Resources people. Actually, the story goes, he kept them on the payroll, but they weren't allowed to go to work or to talk with any employees. As long as they followed the rules, they could keep their now totally demeaning jobs. This guy hated HR — he felt it was an unnecessary and counterproductive buffer between managers and their staff. In short, he believed that managers should hire their staff without help from isolated professionals in ivory towers. The one HR person he retained, he gave a bonus and the following instructions: "Your office will be very small. You may have one filing cabinet to keep your papers about our insurance and other benefits. The day you need a second staff member, or a second filing cabinet, you're fired." I have no idea if this story is true, but I like it. This is a man who not only says what he believes, but he acts on it.

It is hard to put your theories into practice when managing a project. There is tremendous pressure to follow conventional wisdom. Since so many software projects fail, managers find themselves planning for survival. "If this fails, I certainly don't want anyone to say it was my fault. I don't want to look like an idiot." Sticking your neck out can be a dangerous business.

Conventional wisdom holds that if you have a lot of work to do, you hire a lot of people to do that work. What alternative is there? I am convinced, however, that 1+1 is a lot less than 2 in most human endeavors, and especially so in software development. Small teams have an efficiency that is lost when the team gets big enough to need a manager. Once you have a manager you have a *lot* more overhead, because keeping the manager in the loop adds friction to the system. The more managers, the more friction, and soon you find yourself tied up in meetings and nothing gets done.

This isn't just theory. Look around. Virtually all the great products were built by small groups of highly independent, highly motivated people. From time to time, large groups *do* produce high quality products, but the overwhelming experience is that large groups eat time and money, and produce little.

If I'm right, then why are so many products built with large teams? I believe there are two reasons. First, large companies have the money to spend, but they don't trust small, unmanaged teams. Second, small teams tend to become large over time.

Here's what happens. A small cadre of motivated programmers get together with a great idea, and they bang out a killer application — instant market success. Then what happens? Often, their success takes over. They get a lot more money and they follow the obvious business imperative: they grow. The first release was great, but the market is demanding more just when they have enough money to think about investing. And they are tired; they certainly don't want to continue doing all the work themselves. Therefore, their first investment is to hire staff. The goal is to 'leverage' their time by supervising junior developers.

This same process plays itself out in larger development organizations. As the group grows, someone must supervise, and who better than the best developers? After all, the theory goes, they earned it, and they can apply their skills across a larger group. What a great idea! Take your best developer and don't let him develop any more! Only a manager could think this is a good thing. 'Promoting' your best developers out of coding is broken in three ways:

- You deprive the product of their development skills. A system that promotes the best developers is one that ensures mediocre programmers do the development. This only stands to reason, but it seems to escape many managers. The hidden assumption is that a great developer can code five times as quickly given five mediocre programmers under his direction. I reject this assumption on its face, and experience shows just the opposite. Often, you can get a lot more done with one good developer than with five crummy ones. More important, for the cost of those five, you could have bought two great developers to work with your first, and then you'd have had a hell of a team.

- You probably end up with a mediocre manager. There is a common assumption that good developers necessarily make good managers. Some do, but most don't. Knowing how to code well does *not* necessarily imply that you can manage other coders well. Of course, the alternative is worse: a manager who can't code almost invariably can't manage others who can.

- You teach the other developers that their skills are secondary in importance to those of the managers. They quickly learn that if they want to get ahead, they must move up to be managers. Guess what? They start focusing on management skills and have less time to devote to technical skills.

The system is self-stoking. There are only so many management positions with a staff of a given size, and so the best route to success is to ensure that the development team size grows. Managers are motivated to want bigger teams. The bigger the team, the more influence and importance they have, and the higher the salary they can demand. When the financial incentive is to grow the organization, reasons will be found to do so.

You'll hear managers talk about 'headroom'; this is the space they have to 'grow' into a position of more responsibility (read "of managing a larger group"). Now, managers will never admit, perhaps not even to themselves, that the reason they want a larger group is that it looks better on their résumé and demands a higher salary. They will talk about the tremendous requirements of the project, and the demands of the deadline. As I said, reasons follow incentive.

These managers will tell you that they have thoroughly examined the requirements document, and have reluctantly come to the conclusion that they need to hire more people. It's dynamics like these that make Dilbert so funny; we laugh in recognition of our own experiences. However, it is important to recognize that these managers are not necessarily being duplicitous. They honestly believe that they need a larger staff, and that it is in the best interests of the project and the company for the team to grow.

Here's what we learn from listening to scientists who work for the tobacco companies: your ability to accurately judge and assess a situation cannot remain unaffected by your own self-interest. Managers may truly believe that they need to grow their teams for all the best reasons, but the incentive structure is so powerful that we must question their judgment on this matter. When was the last time you heard a manager say, "You know, I think I could get this job done more efficiently with a smaller team. I think I'll merge my team in with Joe's, and I'll work for him."

Here's what we learned from the collapse of the Soviet experiment: asking folks to put the greater good ahead of their own needs creates a nation of hypocrites. Asking an employee to put the requirements of the business ahead of his own career is no less absurd. We can expect employees and managers to be honest, but we can't expect them to be altruists.

When a plant is germinating, it doesn't produce a flower. All of its energy goes into growth. Only when it reaches maturity can it turn its attention to producing the flowers, which attract the bees that consume their nectar. When a *company* is starting up, it doesn't produce a product. All of the energy goes into growing the team. Only once the team stabilizes are the products that attract customers produced.

All of the incentives in traditional software efforts serve to grow the team. Grow and grow. Like voracious little weeds, the team sprouts and spreads and consumes; watered with venture capital, the team keeps growing until eventually it consumes itself. Software kudzu.

Growing Too Fast

Here's an example that comes from painful experience. In 1992, I moved to the Boston area to take on the job of Team Leader for Applications Development at Ziff Davis. We were going to build a new online service, which in time became known as the Interchange Online Network.

Ziff Davis produces *PC Magazine* and a number of other highly successful computer-related publications. Our goal was to revolutionize the online industry, to provide multitasking on Windows 3.1, to support background downloading, to present a graphically rich publishing environment, and to integrate the idea of hyperlinked text and graphics. You must remember that this was before the Web, and that at the time Compuserve ruled the online industry with a service that was totally text-based.

We knew we were taking on a large development project, and as we looked at what was ahead of us, we were determined to hire the best and brightest staff to work at the bleeding edge of development. Tragically, one of our first decisions was to begin hiring right away, when what we should have been doing was analyzing the problem and designing the software.

We spent the early months of 1992 interviewing and training our teams. Before long, we had two Vice Presidents, a Director of Development, four Team Leaders and about twenty developers. In addition, we had a full staff of editorial contributors, a user interface design team, and a quickly growing QA team. We *didn't* have a coherent requirements document or a fully understood architecture, but boy, did we have fun.

Never before have I met such bright people. We were going to change the online world forever, and we set right out to get started. Unfortunately, organizing and coordinating such a large group of developers is a major undertaking in itself, and the price we paid was a tremendous overhead in keeping everyone informed and up to date with the progress of the project.

As a small example, we coordinated our conversations using Lotus Notes. This afforded us an excellent tool not only for exchanging ideas, but also for recording our discussions and documenting the resulting decisions. The cost, of course, was that the discussions themselves quickly grew into a thatch of interlocking messages, and organizing, pruning and even reading them all became a chore, and then a job, and eventually a total distraction.

How did we solve this? We asked some developers to manage each discussion. Of course, this took some of their time, and so the workload had to be spread out to the rest of the organization, increasing the need for more staff. More staff means more managers, and so the team grew.

As the teams grew, integrating the code took more and more time. We knew we wanted a nightly build, to ensure that all the pieces worked together, but the effort of checking the code in and producing a working version was consuming everyone's day. Once again, we allocated resources to the task.

Each team dedicated a junior member to managing the builds. This encapsulated the cost, but it certainly didn't eliminate it. Once every team had adopted this idea, the build managers became a 'virtual' team in their own right, and guess what? They got a manager, and they started holding meetings. That was one more manager for the Director to manage, and with all his other managers that was one too many. He broke his group in two, creating two *more* sub-managers.

Teams divide and grow like amoebae, replicating geometrically. It isn't long before a small development team has grown and split and grown again to the point where inter-team communication becomes a major task in itself.

A more subtle cost of having such a large organization was that we tried to do too much. A smaller group might have set more realistic goals. A less well-funded group might have looked over the precipice of running out of money and felt a bit more motivation to get into the market more quickly. It was suggested to me recently that at Interchange we simply had *too much* money.

Because we were so well funded, we knew we could hire whomever we needed to accomplish our tasks. That left us feeling invincible, and unafraid to try to tackle building a multi-platform product using beta-level development tools. In addition, we undertook to provide multitasking on top of Windows 3.1, which supported only cooperative multitasking and made the creation of a multithreaded program a nightmare. As icing on the cake, we tried to add graphics and links and rich text, as well as a revolutionary new way to handle online discussions. Features piled up on top of features.

We added in style sheets, a new approach to searching, and a powerful proprietary system for developing editorial content. There was no limit to what we tried to accomplish; after all, we had the staff, the management commitment, the talent and most important, the funds. If we wanted to do more, all we needed to do was hire more staff.

As the project progressed, we fell way behind schedule. (Surprise!) Of course, it was impossible to get into the market with such an enormously complex piece of software in the eighteen months we'd originally planned for. The more we slipped, the more the competition edged forward. Microsoft announced the Microsoft Network, AOL released their Windows product, and this World Wide Web thing was showing some startling similarity to what we had planned.

As the competition heated up, there was more pressure to add still more features to keep ahead of what the other services were now offering. More features just made the deadline more unrealistic, so what did we do? We added staff, of course. We felt we couldn't possibly finish without more help. The decision to grow the staff was pernicious. We spent time discussing the decision, and then more time describing to our HR department what we were looking for. More hours were spent interviewing and cajoling candidates to take the job, and finally even more time was spent bringing the new team members up to speed.

New employees feel the need to make their mark quickly. Fresh blood introduces fresh opportunities to question the decisions already made, and more time was spent either defending past decisions or, worse, making mid-term corrections. Of course, ultimately the new team members contributed code, but even when their contribution was highly valuable, it had to be coordinated with the work of all the other developers. Soon we needed more managers, and Hey Presto! The teams started to 'layer' — we created a new level of middle managers. This pulled more developers out of writing code so that they could manage sub-teams, and guess what? Now we needed more developers. When we started, we met in an office. Soon we moved to a small conference room, and then to a large one. Within a year, we needed to rent an auditorium if we were all going to sit down together.

As the size of the teams grew, the human requirements began to conflict. Some developers liked to work early, some late. It was impossible to demand that sixty developers should all show up at the same time, so we agreed that everyone would be on site between 10 and 4. This helped, but with so many developers, there were more and more meetings.

Coordinating all the meetings became a logistical nightmare, and just taking the time to accept or decline all the invitations to the meetings was itself a drain on development time. We introduced 'Do Not Disturb' hours, during which you were not allowed to call or knock on the door of a developer. If you needed anything, you sent e-mail. No meetings were scheduled during DND hours. (I'd say this was my best contribution to the project, but three other folks have told me it was *their* idea. Even here we see that while failure is an orphan, success has many fathers.)

DND hours helped screen out the interruptions, but it only increased the pressure on the remaining hours in the day. As the meetings proliferated, there was less time to write code, but the scheduling demands didn't diminish. We solved that problem by... hiring more staff!

Regression Towards the Mean

Once a staff passes a certain size, statistical distribution dictates that you will not be able to hire at quite the same quality level. All large organizations regress towards the mean — what choice is there? (Except in Lake Woebegone, where all the children are above average.) While it may be possible to hire five or even ten of the smartest people in the world, it probably isn't possible to hire seventy people and not get at least a few who are a little less sharp, or motivated, or self-directed.

As the staff grows, management is called upon to provide more direction and more help. This takes time and increases the demand for more managers. Again, these new managers typically come from the pool of your best developers. Soon you find that your best developers are not writing code, they are managing others. Worse still, the 'others' that they are managing are your newest hires, and thus your least efficient and least informed staff.

When the staff hits a certain size, and the schedule slips beyond a certain point, count on senior management to bring in a new overall director to 'take hold' of things. This new guy must be brought up to speed, and then of course he wouldn't make much of an impression if he didn't change anything.

Whatever he changes brings a cost. No change, however subtle, will be free. The later you are, the more need there is to stay the course, finish and get the product out the door. Yet the further you are behind schedule, the more likely it is that the new director will want to make significant changes. After all, if we were going to leave things as they were, why bother bringing in new management? These changes can be fatal. Even if they are 100% brilliant and in the long run will make things much better, they won't come without an organizational price.

There is much more to say on this topic, and as we move forward I'll return to it repeatedly, but the bottom line is this: I have no idea how to make an organization of fifty or a hundred developers efficiently turn out high quality products on time and on budget. Someday, I will try to do so again, and when I apply for that job I will regret putting these words down on paper. But the reality is that *no one* is doing it today. Not Microsoft, not AT&T, not Citibank, not Xerox, no one. What they *are* doing, when they are successful, is creating small, autonomous groups that are given a clear and limited goal and set free to work. Even then, most of those projects are late, and most are riddled with bugs in their first release.

Doesn't Anybody Here Know How to Play this Game?

Among other problems in the software industry are these two: we don't have a class of professional software managers, and we don't know how to reward coders properly without promoting them out of writing code. A few companies *are* learning how to train world class software managers, but it is an ad hoc business. The folks who get their business degrees don't, for the most part, have a clue how to develop software. People who *do* know how to write software don't, for the most part, know how to manage a project. No wonder so many products die before they get out the door.

One difficulty is that the managers, even if they started out as coders, tend to lose touch with the industry. When I was interviewed at Interchange, the VP in charge of development proudly pointed to the compiler on his desktop. "That's not there for display, I write code," he told me. He wasn't exaggerating; this guy was a killer programmer, and I took it as a very good sign that he, as well those who worked for him, knew how to code.

The problem was that when we got rolling, none of the managers could afford for their code to be in the critical path. They were too busy managing the product to actually contribute to it. After a few months, they gave up on trying to stay current. The software world changes quickly — blink and you've missed the newest technology — and it wasn't long before their skills were obsolete. Late in the project, I asked that same manager which of two options we ought to follow. He looked at me sadly and said, "You tell me. I haven't written any code in four years." Let *that* be a warning to you.

There isn't an easy solution to this problem, but we know where to look for help. Certainly there are other highly technical industries which have faced this problem before.

Robert Oppenheimer was a world-class physicist. Edward Teller and others have suggested he was so far ahead of his time that his contributions weren't recognized. Had he lived until the 1980s, he may well have won a Nobel Prize for his work. Oppenheimer was charged with managing the Manhattan Project, to develop the atomic bomb in time to shorten World War II. Up to that time, no science had ever progressed more quickly than nuclear physics did in the three decades immediately before the war. The physicists on the Manhattan project built an enterprise the size of the automobile industry. They went from a standing start to producing atomic weapons in three years.

Oppenheimer was not only a world-class physicist, he was a brilliant manager who understood how to keep a project on time and on course while meeting the needs of a team full of ingenious but eccentric scientists. There are lessons to be learned from his work about how to organize and manage a large group of highly creative and gifted technical people. Oppenheimer succeeded because he had the technical credentials, because he kept his teams small and sharply focused, because he kept his best physicists doing physics and not managing others, and because everyone involved knew full well they were engaged in a life-and-death struggle to save the world.

Rewarding Coders Properly

When we find a few really great programmers, we promote them to management. And they take the jobs because they look around at who is making the decisions and who is getting the money, and they can't help but notice it is the managers. Of course, the managers justify this with that magic word, *leverage*. "Well of course we're worth more," they say, "we're leveraged across so many more tasks."

This is the organizational structure in most of American industry, so it isn't a surprise that we start out with the premise that the prestige and income belongs to the managers. However, it is far from obvious to me that the structure that works well for building cars is the right structure for building software. And software isn't the only industry suffering from this problem. How do you keep your best teachers in the classroom when the prestige and authority goes to the school management?

Yes, managers have very important skills (although in truth, most software managers are actually quite weak in traditional management expertise), but no matter how good they are, the lessons of low-tech industry simply don't apply here. Perhaps a software team is more like a professional symphony orchestra. The manager of the Boston Symphony Orchestra has a very important role to play, but no world-class violinist is tempted to go into management when he can still perform. No major league baseball player hangs up his gloves while in his prime so that he can *manage*.

I had better be careful, because I'm in my forties, and who knows how long I can keep pushing out code? However, it seems to me that there must be a growth path in this industry that keeps your architects, designers and programmers happy and appreciated without giving them the incentive to go into management as the only obvious career path.

Building Teams

Managers love to build their teams. You can always tell a manager who is measuring himself by the size of his group, because he'll start each discussion by saying, "I'm not out to build an empire, but..." This is only natural: we reward folks for being managers, and we measure managers, no matter what lip service we pay to other criteria, by the size of their team. The guy who manages three developers is just not going to have the authority (or the income) of the guy who manages 300 developers.

The problem is that software development teams almost never scale up well. Keeping all those managers in the loop and all those developers working in harmony is very hard work. And unlike other industries, there are no economies of scale, though there *are* 'diseconomies'. Once the development team gets above three or four, simple conveniences like configuration management become tasks in themselves. You find yourself, for example, doing a daily merge, and much of the week is spent integrating all the new code with all the existing code. Progress slows as new interdependencies are introduced, and with a really large organization it can slow so far you find yourself slipping backwards.

Programming Without Ego

Taken as a group, programmers have healthy egos, to say the least. At times, a strong ego can be an asset: it can protect you from worrying too much about criticism, and it can encourage you to participate in the give and take of creative sessions.

Unfortunately, ego can also get in the way, and in my experience it can be a very destructive force in a technical organization. Specifically, ego can undermine quality design and programming. It is ego that causes you to disparage the ideas of others; it's ego that encourages you to over-engineer a solution; and it's ego that tells you that only custom code can solve a problem.

Customer-driven Programming

The inverse of ego-driven programming is **customer-driven programming**. In customer-driven programming, the personal politics, interests and biases of the programmer are surrendered to the best interests of the customer. The single guiding principle here is this: *the goal is not to build great software; the goal is for the customer to make money*. The developer decides what makes the software great, using whatever criteria he thinks are most important. But the customer decides what makes the *product* great and what will maximize profits; it is the customer's judgment and decision that matter when deciding whether greatness is defined by immediate commercial success, long-term strategic positioning, or any other criteria they want to apply.

Only by focusing on the customer's needs and priorities can we hope to make informed decisions when trading off flexibility, features, robustness, extensibility, time to market, performance and all the other traits of the software. If we fully understand the customer's priorities, we can help the customer to make informed decisions about what to optimize and what to forgo.

Too often, important technical decisions yield to extra-technical considerations. I have heard professional developers say with no embarrassment that they chose a particular implementation technology not because it was best, but because it was an alternative to one provided by a company of which they disapproved. There have been a number of great political wars over the years, including the desktop wars (Mac vs. Unix vs. Windows), the object wars (COM vs. CORBA), the language wars (Java vs. C++ vs. Visual Basic), the compiler wars (Microsoft vs. Borland vs. Symantec), the debugger wars, and on and on.

I have listened with chagrin while highly paid and well-respected consultants said that they go out of their way to avoid Microsoft development tools so as not to contribute to the dominance of the 'evil empire'. Setting aside the tangled and often distorted history of Microsoft's success in the market, at its heart I suspect this reveals a deep-rooted ambivalence about capitalism, and a resentment of wealth and success.

But I'm getting off-topic. Ultimately, we come to the central issue: your customer trusts you to apply your best *technical* judgment; allowing politics to enter into your recommendations is a breach of that fiduciary responsibility.

Don't Build It, Buy It

Quite often, the right answer is *not* to build something new at all. The right answer may be just to buy something that already exists and adapt it.

For most of us, this is heresy. We are programmers; we believe it is our job, even our mission, to write custom software. We are deeply and profoundly inclined to write just about anything from scratch rather than buy it off the shelf. Unfortunately, this is often exactly the opposite of what the client needs. It is in the interest of the customer to buy what he can, and only build what he must.

As development schedules shorten, and as more and more components come on the market, there will be increasing pressure to purchase the core technologies. Programmers all across the industry will resist this move, but we will be wrong to put up the fight, and we'll be wrong for a number of reasons.

First, custom software is enormously expensive. If you can buy something that will do the job, that will almost always be the cheaper alternative. The product you buy will have been thoroughly tested, both by the vendor and by the market. Overall, the cost of writing and testing the software will be absorbed by the entire customer base, rather than by your client alone. The savings, both in development expenses and in time, can be enormous.

Second, if we are going to build complicated software (as is increasingly the demand), we simply have to start from a higher level of abstraction than we've been working with before. We will never build skyscrapers if we're forever reinventing bricks and mortar.

Third, buying components and putting them together starts us more quickly down the road to getting something up and running. Software is like a small infant. The most dangerous and potentially lethal time in its life is during its gestation. If the product is born and begins to thrive, it is far likelier to survive whatever adverse conditions it encounters. If it falters during its earliest development, even small problems may be fatal.

Once the product is up and running, you'll have an opportunity to locate the weakest aspects. If you discover that the database you purchased is not up to the task, you'll have an opportunity to swap in a more robust alternative. If the memory management module you bought is inadequate, you can then write your own. Getting the product into the hands of the customer provides a greater opportunity to write the key pieces than trying to build everything from scratch and risking that you'll miss the market opportunity and never get the product out of the door at all.

When making the decision about what to build and what to buy, we must be skeptical of our own judgment. We are not disinterested parties; we have an economic incentive to believe that custom software is required. After all, building custom software is a lot more interesting and a lot more lucrative then buying someone else's finished product. That very incentive should make us question our judgment and subject it to the most rigorous examination.

Market-driven Programming

Engineers are fascinated by technology. When I worked at Citibank, the developers and I came to believe that there were five levels, or quintiles, of technology acceptance. That is, you could divide folks into five uneven groups, along a bell-curve distribution, according to how they reacted to technology:

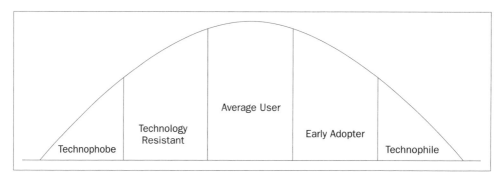

Level 1 is the technophile. That's me. Where other folks use a DayTimer, I use a Personal Information Manager — a Pilot computer that hangs off my belt. It is slower, more expensive and more difficult to use than an appointment book, but it *is* wicked cool. For the level one consumer, the technology is an end in itself.

Level 2 is the early adopter. These folks will buy technology as soon as they see *any* clear benefit. They bought CD players when they were still $500, and they're saving up for HDTV even as we speak.

Level 3 is the average user. People at level three will buy technology when the price drops and they see some real and immediate benefit. Most folks are level three.

Level 4 is technology resistant. They'll use something new, but only if they see an overwhelmingly compelling reason. These folks are just now buying CD players because nobody makes records any more.

Level 5 says, "Go ahead, pull the trigger, I won't use it." You'll find them at the bank, waiting in line to make their deposit with a teller.

The problem is that the majority of the general public is level 3 or 4, but most developers are level 1 or 2. We see a new technology and we want to find an application to put it into. "Hey, why write down a shopping list, can't we use a light pen?" "Pointers to member functions? Cool, gotta find a place to use *those*."

It is imperative to get past the ego, the self-interest, and the myopia to determine objectively if custom software really is required. Our customers count on us for this analysis because they are ill prepared to judge for themselves. If we say, "You can't use that off-the-shelf component, it will be too slow or too inflexible or too likely to break," what do they know? They have to take our word for it. This is bad for them, and ultimately it is bad for us; it drives up the cost of development, undermines the customer's trust in our judgment and often it distracts us from developing interesting new products.

It comes down to this: your software can be technology-driven or it can be market-driven. Only one of these ever produces products that anyone wants to buy.

Visual Basic is not Just for Sissies

Let's say you buy the argument that we should start with existing components when we can. Nonetheless, your requirements dictate that one or another portion of your project *does* require custom software. After carefully checking what is already out there, you conclude that your customer is best served by writing it from scratch, and (huzzah!) your customer agrees. You analyze the problem, create a design and you're ready to implement. In what language will you implement your design?

The dirty little secret that no one wants to say out loud is that most often you'll develop in whatever language you find most comfortable. Learning a language well is a difficult task, and most of us do not readily switch among a suite of alternatives. That said, different languages *do* have advantages in different situations. Coding a system-level program in HTML would be as silly as coding a static web page in C++.

I was once asked to help rewrite software for a small academic publishing company. They had their articles typed offshore, and then processed them with their filtering software to produce the final copy for the printer. Each line had a tag; one line might be tagged as the title, another as the subject, or the abstract, or the author's name. The software read through the document and massaged the data into the format needed by the typesetter.

Their programmer was a whiz with the Brief macro language, so when he was asked to write the software, he did so inside Brief. (Brief is a text editor that allows extensive customization using its C-like macro language.) They called me in when the program was taking sixteen hours each day to run through that day's work. They were about to buy a second computer because Monday's job was still running when they needed to start Tuesday's. I rewrote the program in C. When I demonstrated it to them they said, "It broke." "No," I said, "it's done." Their sixteen-hour job completed in less than two minutes.

While it's fine to write in the language with which you are most comfortable, it is imperative that you do not do so to the exclusion of all reason. Today, with just a few exceptions, you have three likely choices for producing commercial grade software on Windows: C++, Java and Visual Basic.

It's hard for many professional software developers to come to terms with Visual Basic. First of all, it looks and feels like a toy. Second, for a long time it really wasn't very useful for anything except hobbyist applications and prototyping. I must say, though, that I've never seen greater panic than I saw watching a C++ developer the first time *he* watched someone coding in Visual Basic 4.0. Here was this *designer* — not even a professional programmer mind you — turning out working code, with a beautiful user interface, in minutes. A complete program framed out in a few hours, and he wasn't *really* even writing code; he was just dragging objects onto a form and filling in tiny subroutines. This wasn't coding; it was child's play. It was infuriating.

Fortunately for those of us who have spent years developing arcane skills and who can charge a lot for our obscure knowledge, Visual Basic products still tend to be big and slow. And it's a good thing that they are, because it means we can still justify our demand that custom software be written in C++ on the grounds of performance — at least, for a while. But that is changing all the time. Visual Basic is getting better, and memory and disk storage are getting cheaper. Cheaper memory and cheaper disks mean that 'big and slow' matters less. Programming is getting expensive, which means that development time matters more. The trend is against us. We had better get on board, or we'll be drowned by the incoming tide.

Programming without ego demands that we examine our tool set, and open ourselves to using Visual Basic and other high-level application development tools when they are appropriate. One of the places you should always consider using a high-level application development tool is in creating the user interface. A skilled VB developer can bang out a UI quite quickly. Done right, you can put a C++ engine behind it, and not pay very much of a performance penalty.

On the other hand, Microsoft Foundation Classes let you build the UI quickly and easily in C++, and if you know it well you'll probably be able to produce your product at least as quickly as you can in Visual Basic. As a bonus, MFC applications are faster and smaller than VB applications. On project after project I keep thinking, "I'll just write it in VB," but somehow I can't bring myself to do it, and I write it in C++ anyway. When all you have is a hammer, the whole world looks like a nail.

Let Microsoft and Netscape Write It For You

Another strong candidate for using a language other than C++ is in the field of client-server software. Here, it may make more sense to consider HTML as your implementation language of choice for the front end. During my early research for Hypotenuse, I talked with an old friend from Interchange, Michael Howard. He said, "If you are building client-server technology, I'd advise you to stop, throw it away, and use the Web instead." These are strong words, but they are compelling.

Until recently, if I were building a client, I'd do so in C++, and then I'd have to distribute my software to all my customers. Each time I updated it, I'd have to distribute it again. Build the client software in HTML, and distribution is automatic, courtesy of Netscape and Microsoft. The browsers will even supply the core display technology, saving time and effort, and providing a well-tested, industry-standard solution.

Programming without ego is a difficult thing, and sometimes you're forced to trade away marginal features to save substantial development time. Certainly I can build a better solution if I tailor it to the precise needs of my client, but is it *so much* better that it justifies the significant cost of developing and distributing a custom solution? Can't we accomplish pretty much the same thing much more quickly using the browser, and at significantly less cost?

Subject Yourself to Supervision

Programmers believe they're the smartest people around. The last thing we are willing to accept is that Marketing or Sales or anyone else should tell us what to build or how to build it. Because what we do appears to be magic, we can usually bully them into leaving us alone. In recent years, many companies have found the tail of technology wagging the entire business.

When the development organization exempts itself from the best practices of a company, it creates a critical vulnerability. Once the technological direction of the company is set without reference to the overall business direction, there is a risk that the products being built won't be supported by a realistic value proposition.

Certainly, many products have been nibbled to death by the mice in accounting, and there is a great temptation to wave your hands and demand to be left alone to get the work done. To the extent that being a prima donna helps save you from the meddling distractions of pinhead corporate politicians, that's all well and good. But when the development organization sets itself outside the business imperative, you take a giant leap down the path of building technology-driven, rather than market-driven, software.

Subject Yourself to a Schedule

I have heard it said that great software can't be rushed, and that's probably true, but it's meaningless in a product-centered business. A flawless product delivered a year late and that no one wants any more, is a failure. A flawed product that hobbles into the market on time, and which establishes a foothold while it's improved and repaired, *may not be* a failure. A high quality product with fewer features that enters the market early has an excellent shot at success. While we can't write the code any faster just because the deadline looms, there *are* steps we can take to manage a development schedule.

Scheduling provides a discipline. It also provides a budget, which forces the difficult but necessary trade-offs in building any product: "This feature can stay in, but we won't hit the budget unless we pay for it by removing this other feature over here." Without a schedule you are like a home without a budget. You may be making more money than you ever did before, but if you're spending more than you make, it won't keep you out of bankruptcy.

Of course, over-scheduling and trying to keep detailed records of where you spend every minute is self-defeating. Only a manager could ever imagine that a programmer is able to keep track of his job hours in the way a plumber or a lawyer might. In the early days at Interchange, we tried to schedule software the way one schedules building a bridge. We put tens of thousands of lines into Microsoft Scheduler, and it ate hours and hours of our time to manage and manipulate this absurd attempt at micro-managing the process.

There were some amusing moments along the way. We each estimated our tasks in good faith, and then we added in the dependencies. The program projected our finish date early in the next century. After extensive tinkering, we rigged the books sufficiently that it spat out pretty much what we wanted it to. By this time, the data was so muddled that we couldn't get any useful information out of the system, and we eventually threw our hands up and walked away from it.

There is a reasonable middle ground. Programmers can estimate at a granularity of a week or so. Schedules can be coordinated so that deadlines are hit, and so that products ship within a week or two of their projected dates. Programming without ego demands that you create a schedule and then do what it takes to deliver the product on time.

Challenge the Requirements

If you are going to hit your deadline, you must repeatedly challenge the requirements. Programs die because they take too long to develop, and it's the responsibility of the development team to identify those requirements that are the most expensive and difficult to build. It is often the case that one or two features are driving the entire effort, and that dispensing with these requirements can cut development time dramatically. In fact, it sometimes happens that removing a single feature can obviate the need to write custom software at all!

At Interchange, we decided early on that we needed an 'offline' model. The idea was that the user could log into our network, download whatever was new, and hang up the phone. Modems of the time were relatively slow, and we guessed that our target audience would not want to tie up a phone line for hours at a time.

This was a very appealing idea, and because we came to it very early, it became an unquestioned core requirement. From this one requirement flowed many fateful decisions which may have delayed our first commercial release for a full year.

> For the want of a nail, the horse was lost,
> For the want of the horse, the rider was lost,
> For the want of the rider, the battle was lost,
> For the want of the battle, the kingdom was lost,
> And all for the want of a nail.

The entire Interchange product was not lost due to a single feature requirement any more than the kingdom was lost for the want of a nail, but the underlying lesson that small failures can lead to catastrophic consequences cannot be ignored.

Because we assumed we needed an offline model, we also needed a local database in which to store messages and documents while the user was offline. The local database was an enormously complex project in itself, but more important was that getting the database interface right was now a prerequisite to building the rest of the product. Literally everything in Interchange, from documents to mail messages to discussion notes, was an item in the database. Until the database interface was stable, it was impossible to solidify anything else.

For the first few months of the project, the database team worked hard to stabilize the interface. Of course, while that was going on we had only two choices: we could wait, which was clearly unacceptable, or we could press on and continually change the rest of the code to meet the moving target of the database interface. Deadline pressures caused us to work in parallel with the development of the enabling database technology, and we never did create a clean interface to the database layer.

Creating a local database also meant that we had to be able to map the local objects to the objects on the host. There was a need for globally unique identifiers, which we called zOIDs (**Z**iff **O**bject **Id**entification number**s**). We then needed to build a structure to map zOIDs to objects on the client and records on the host's relational database.

zOIDs needed to be unique through time and across all documents. Furthermore, objects created on one user's machine might, eventually, be available on another user's machine, and they'd have to share the same zOID. That is, the e-mail I send to you must have the same zOID on both machines (yours and mine), as well as on the host. The only place we could assign zOIDS, therefore, was on the server. The offline model meant that we had to let the customer create e-mail with a 'temporary' zOID that would be resolved when the user went online. This added to the complexity of uploading and downloading objects, and of course introduced the possibility that there would be a breakdown between updating the host and updating the client. This forced a transaction-based model across the telephone network, a tricky and difficult-to-test feature.

Because it was possible for the client to modify an object, and to do so while offline, we had the added complexity that objects might have numerous 'states of revision', all of which had to be resolved when the client went back online. Further, some objects might change on the host — documents get updated and others become obsolete — and all of this had to be resolved at each connection.

The decision to support an offline model continued to reverberate through the design. For example, we wanted to provide a significant innovation in how online discussions are conducted. The concern we had was that a few years ago, most non-technical people didn't 'get' how newsreaders worked. They felt uncomfortable with the technology, and they couldn't see the structure of the conversation. Level 1 and level 2 types (technophiles) thought newsreaders were great, but the rest of the world thought they were somewhere between bizarre and unusable.

Our solution was to break discussions out by topic, and to present the entire discussion as one large, continuous message. That is, if we were discussing which modem to buy, you would see every contribution in a single digest, one after the other:

To All, From glenn. Date: October 1 1:13pm. Subject: Modem. I'm going to buy a modem, which one do you recommend?

I have had good luck with Acme Modems. They have a 28.8 which is excellent. - Al. Date: October 1 1:17pm.

Al. Why buy a 28.8 when you can get a new 56.6? - Jim. Date: October 1 1:23pm.

glenn, think about Rtech as a good buy at less cost than Acme or Maple Modems. - Pete. Date: October 1 1:24pm.

Al, 56.6 is untried technology. I'll stick with 28.8 for now. - Al. Date: October 2 2:07pm.

The offline model made all this much more complicated. Imagine you came along after Jim recommended the 56K modem and downloaded the messages. You read Pete's note and immediately compose a reply, saying you had a lot of difficulty with your Rtech modem, and their support team refused to help. Let's also say you don't get around to connecting to the service until the next day. In the interim, the conversation may well have wandered off to new topics, and by the time you post your message it will be out of context, at best.

The offline model continued to create difficulties as we implemented it. If we were going to allow users to read documents offline, exactly which documents should we supply? It was our intention to provide tens of thousands of documents on the service, and clearly we couldn't send them *all* down. We'd have to supply only those documents requested by the user.

What did we do after you finished reading the document? A great battle raged over this issue. Some on the design team argued that users did not want to have to constantly clean up after these old documents. They were concerned we'd clutter up the user's disk with yesterday's news. Others were concerned that if we *did* delete documents the user had requested, we'd infuriate the user. After all, he had specifically paid for access time to get that article. We talked about documents expiring after an editorially determined amount of time had passed, but weren't there some documents users wanted to keep indefinitely? We could let them 'pin' these documents in place, keeping them local even after they 'expired', but now the customers would be back in the business of managing their data. The UI team felt that only geeks wanted to manage their data; most folks just wanted it there when they needed it, and gone when they didn't.

We spent a lot of time writing code to go through the user's cache and delete those documents that had expired and which weren't marked to be kept. We spent more time making sure that when we went online, we could resolve the differences between local copies and the copies on the host. Mostly, we spent time thinking about it and arguing about it and worrying about it. This ate into our schedule, and the more we argued, the less certain we were about what to do.

Keeping some documents available locally was a neat idea, but what happened if the document was changed on the server? Should we reflect the change locally? It was hard to know what the user wanted. He may have kept the article so that he could refer to a specific section, so if the update changed that section, he would be, at best, confused. On the other hand, he may want the document to stay 'current' — it would be very weird if the document had one content for him and a different content for everyone else. Think of the confusion when two members were talking about the same document but seeing different things!

We then conceived the idea of having two types of document: one was dynamic and updated by the server; the other was a snapshot or photocopy, frozen in time. Not only did our users not have a clue what we were talking about, it also set up an *expectation* that the 'live' copies would continue to change, when in fact only a small percentage would ever be updated. We went around and around these issues, eating up precious development time with endless confusion and disagreements, all of this a direct result of our one unquestioned assumption: "We need to be able to read documents offline." The complexities of the offline model piled up and piled up.

Because we had not taken the time to analyze fully the problem we were trying to solve, our requirements document was incomplete. Because we hadn't nailed down the requirements, our design was incomplete. An incomplete design left us arguing about how documents would be updated and stored, even after we had written it and modified it three times. One of our best developers finally quit in disgust after we changed the specification one time too many, forcing him once again to tear out code that he'd spent a great deal of time writing.

So, why didn't we challenge the offline assumption when the costs began to mount? One problem was that we had already invested deeply in this feature, and there was a lot of incentive to convince ourselves it was critical. If we admitted we didn't really need the offline model, we'd have to write off all that work and start over with a much simpler design. A lot of folks saw their role in the project as solving these problems, and so the offline model built up a 'constituency' — a loyal special-interest group that lobbied for it being absolutely essential.

The complexity this single requirement created was not understood at first. Only slowly, over time, did we uncover the secondary implications. There was never a sufficiently sudden revelation to force a reevaluation. I am reminded of the story about boiling a frog. If you drop a frog into boiling water, the story goes, it will hop out. But if you put it in cool water and then slowly heat it, the frog will never notice, and eventually it boils to death. The offline model boiled us to death.

The interesting question, and one we can never answer, is what would have happened if we had gone to market without it. In 1992, we believed that no service could be successful that required you to be connected any time you wanted to use it. One might argue that the revolutionary success of the World Wide Web simply proved us wrong about that. Of course, hindsight is perfect, but we ought to have understood the fundamental premise: target one or two critical features, and get into the market.

The problem *wasn't* that we couldn't see that the offline model was unnecessary for the first release; the problem was that we weren't under sufficient pressure to cut features. If we had been a very small group with very limited resources, we would never have *tried* to get the offline model into the first release. A small group would have been compelled to choose only the most essential features; and the offline model would quickly have been seen as very important, but not essential.

If we had been programming without ego, we would have surfaced this problem and jettisoned the offline model *even if* it meant that the work of some of our best programmers would go to waste. There is an important concept in business (and in gambling) called **sunk costs**. This is a fancy way of saying, "Don't throw good money after bad." It never pays to invest more to salvage a bad decision. Cut your losses, and move on.

We were like a sleep-deprived gambler at the craps table: we'd already lost our life savings, and we were now well into borrowed money. Just one more roll and our number had to come up. It just *had* to. What came up was snake eyes.

Usability Testing

A key component of programming without ego is to subject your design to review by real customers. This is very difficult to do, and it's fraught with problems.

Just having something to show users is an expensive proposition in itself. A good prototype looks and feels like the final product, even if it's all smoke and mirrors under the surface. We built our prototype in Visual Basic, and in large measure it mimicked the functionality we expected to have by the end of the project. Remember, though, that it is always dangerous to show a mock-up to senior management, because it's very difficult for them to understand how they can have something in their hands that appears to work, and yet still be a year away from release. Consciously or not, they begin to think, "We must be close, I've seen something which *almost* works."

On the other hand, a good prototype becomes a terrific functional specification; it is very easy to say what the final product should do, because you can go and see it in the prototype. More importantly, a prototype is a wonderful mechanism for getting feedback from potential customers. Showing customers pictures and describing what your product will do can't compare with letting them get their hands on and interact with it.

Even if the prototype is very limited, and can only be presented in a scripted fashion — even if most of it doesn't really work — the ability to push buttons and get a response is compelling, and helps most people think through how the product *will* really work.

Customers will surprise you. You'll show them a prototype to test the acceptability of your model for e-mail addressing, and they'll question the entire premise of e-mail in the first place. Or they'll object to where you've placed the buttons, when all you wanted to know was whether you had the wording right. You ignore these concerns at your peril, but remember that there are two dangers of usability testing:

- Danger one is that you'll ignore what your customers tell you
- Danger two is that you'll listen

I don't mean to be glib; listening is what usability testing is all about, but be careful about *how* you listen. You're dealing with a very small group of people, and it is easy to give their opinions disproportionate weight. Countless times I've heard usability testing introduced with words like, "What you are about to see is not quantitative research, it is qualitative. That means we don't have a statistically valid sample. Now, 67% of our respondents told us..."

If your research is not statistically valid, then when someone starts quoting statistics, you must stand up and walk out of the room. 67% of the respondents may mean two people. Numbers are irresistible, even to people who should know better.

Conducting quantitative research is very difficult. It involves much more than simply using a large sample; balancing and validating the research requires enormous skill. Focus groups and usability testing *can't* provide statistical or quantitative results. What usability testing *can* provide are insights from non-technical users who have no emotional stake in the process. This is also very valuable, but we should be on guard against confusing qualitative and quantitative research.

When I was working on home banking, we developed a number of metaphors for paying bills. The one that struck us as most intuitive was what we called the 'interactive sentence' approach. Essentially, the user would see a screen that said:

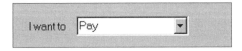

They could choose from a drop down list box to pay bills, create new accounts, transfer money and so forth. If they chose to pay bills, the sentence changed to:

Next, they could choose an existing payee. Let's say they chose Macy's. The sentence would then say:

> I want to pay Macy's $

We thought this was effortless, and that it couldn't possibly cause confusion. Everyone we showed it to in the bank thought it was a great idea. We worked up a prototype and put it in front of consumers. They hated it. They had *no* idea how to use it.

It was very difficult to accept this feedback. After all, we were the human factors experts, what did these people know? We showed it to quite a few focus groups before we finally began to believe that we needed to rethink this approach.

Get It Into Play

While usability testing is essential, the best test bed of all is the marketplace. Given the choice, I will always choose to stop testing and tinkering, and ship the product. I agree that you only get one chance to make a first impression, but that very legitimate concern is *overwhelmed* by how important it is to expose your product to a large segment of your potential audience, and then to listen to what they tell you. Get in the market. Get in the market. Get in the market. It is the market that will tell you what you need to know, and all the rest is ultimately just a distraction.

Beware the Jabberwock, My Son

Most development is done in large teams, organized top-down, with a team leader, who reports to a manager, who reports in turn to a Vice President of development. While I will argue throughout this book that you gain enormous advantages by working in much smaller teams, the reality is that most of the industry does not have that luxury.

Large teams can become far more efficient if they emulate the best practices learned at the most successful development companies. The goal is to push responsibility down as far as possible, to give your developers the room, freedom and time to write great code, and to ensure that your managers are clearing the way, not throwing up obstacles.

I was told a story about a fellow who became CEO of a Fortune 50 company. He said, "When I thought about the job, I envisioned myself as the captain of a great sailing ship. I'd stand on the bridge barking orders that would be smartly carried out by my crack management team. 'Hoist the sail! Full astern!' Each order would set in motion a flurry of coordinated activity."

"What I found," he continued, "was not that the orders weren't well executed. It was not that I was ignored. It was that I wasn't *on* the bridge. I wasn't even on the ship! I was in the water, while the ship was moving at 30 knots in the wrong direction. I was swimming for my life at the same time as I was trying to turn a six hundred ton boat by pushing on the stern with my bare hands."

The momentum that builds up in a large organization can be fearsome. You can do a lot to diminish this problem by pushing the locus of control over issue after issue down into the sub-teams, down and down until the developer and the designer have real power to make things go. To return to the analogy, it is easier for six highly motivated captains to turn their patrol boats, than it is for one commodore to turn a destroyer.

When You Must Have Meetings

Larger teams imply meetings. With that many people, communication falters, and it becomes important to get everyone into one room and let them know what is going on. Meetings build a sense of community, and they help reduce friction between sub-teams. Unfortunately, a meeting can also be a colossal waste of time. The larger the meeting, the more time is wasted. Meetings come in four types, and understanding them properly can make them more efficient.

Analysis and Design Meetings

Throughout the life of your product, you will continually analyze the requirements, and design new components. These design meetings are described in great detail throughout the rest of this book and I won't go into them here, except to say that you want explicitly to declare the purpose of such a meeting and manage the attendance carefully.

One of the great risks of a large development organization is that you will exclude your developers from the analysis and design process. On the other hand, an analysis or design meeting with 20 people is worse than useless. This argues that if you are going to grow your team, you want to do so *after* the bulk of the analysis and design has been completed. Once you understand the overall architecture, then you can, arguably, bring in developers to help you with the implementation.

The new developers in turn will need to do some analysis and design of some of the sub-components, but ownership will be clear, and thus who must attend such meetings in future should become a bit more obvious.

Issue Driven Meetings

When there is a conflict, or an issue that needs clarification, a meeting can help, but only if it is well organized. If you are going to pull developers away from their work and bring them together to think something through, then you need to ensure that someone is designated as 'owning' the meeting, and that there's a clear agenda which is published in advance.

Keep an eye on that agenda, and be careful to ask participants who are off on a tangent to take their discussion 'offline' — that is, to finish their conversation after the meeting is over. Establish the precedent that meeting time is expensive and to be kept as brief as possible. General Schwartzkopf insisted that everyone stand at his staff meetings, because he felt it kept his officers more focused and reduced the kind of side chatter that fills up so much time at such gatherings.

Issue driven meetings should have a well-understood goal, and when that goal is met, the meeting should end. Again and again you want to reinforce the message that meetings ought to be as brief as possible.

Be wary of meetings that assign tasks to each participant. Often, such assignments become ends in themselves, and these meetings can generate a lot of work, none of which is very important. One reason project teams grow is that the project leaders are not parsimonious enough in what tasks they take on. If you keep your team as small as possible, you are likelier to do only the most important tasks.

Don't be Afraid to Ask Stupid Questions

One of the great advantages that large teams have over smaller teams is the cross-pollination of ideas. The problem, however, is that you often have to ask your questions in a room with your boss. Team meetings can quickly degenerate into competitive exchanges in which each participant attempts to impress his supervisor and peers.

Junior team members are intimidated out of asking questions for fear of looking like fools, and senior team members are very careful not to allow anyone to call into question their putative expertise. As teams grow in size, factions are inevitable, and at that point team meetings can become openly hostile, with pointed questions designed less to clarify than to touch a nerve.

Smaller teams, on the other hand, can become insular, isolated from the greater development community. The Internet can help: newsgroups provide a thriving community of developers, many of whom stand ready at a moment's notice to help answer virtually any question on any technical subject.

Open, Honest and Direct

Writing software is a scientific endeavor in this way: it thrives in an open atmosphere of frank communication, and it withers and dies when politics enters the room. Nurture open, honest, and direct communication. If you are going to have meetings, instill a total disregard for rank — the lowest paid developer should be encouraged to challenge the pet ideas of the most senior architect.

I continually return to this question: would you do it this way if there were just one or two of you? If you were working with one other person, would you say, "This is true because I say so, and I have more experience than you," or, "I'm right, because I make more money than you."? Encourage all participants to keep thinking, and to surface their issues and concerns; there is no excuse for trading in your judgment for someone else's.

Team Building Meetings

Many teams find it 'useful' to meet once a week whether or not they have something to say. I've never been to one of these that wasn't an expensive waste of time. If you want to build morale, take everyone out to lunch. Piling everyone into the conference room once a week without an agenda, to review a few points that could have been distributed in a memo, just irritates everyone. If your team has 20 members, that is 40 hours wasted. Why not skip the meeting and reduce your team by one?

Design and Code Reviews

I'm a big believer in design and code reviews. They are a powerful teaching mechanism, and they can be more than worth their cost to everyone's time. Like just about everything else worth doing, though, they require careful planning.

Design Reviews

Design reviews are often frustrating experiences. The person being reviewed wants help with a particular section of the design, but gets so bogged down in explaining what he's trying to accomplish that he never gets to his real question. Further, these sessions can be quite destructive; other developers have ideas about how *they* might have solved the problem, and the person being reviewed quickly becomes defensive and angry.

Well-run design reviews are quite different. These can be very educational, and a great opportunity to broaden your perspective, but they require a lot of preparation. A well-run design review is quite a formal affair. Each participant has a clear role.

The person being reviewed must distribute a memo putting the section of the project to be discussed into perspective. He must describe what he's trying to accomplish, and what he knows about the requirements.

In the meeting, *one* person should be designated as 'facilitator'. The facilitator does not participate in the review, except to keep everyone on track and to ensure that the guidelines are followed. Another person is 'scribe', and doesn't participate in the review either; it is their job only to take notes.

One or more others are designated as reviewers. They may ask *non-judgmental* questions, and they may make suggestions. The person being reviewed does not agree or disagree with the suggestions; he simply makes note of them. He may ask questions in return, but only to clarify the suggestion, not to debate it.

At the end of the review, the scribe writes up the notes and gives them to the developer being reviewed. The developer may or may not adopt the suggestions offered, but he does *not* report back on his decisions. The design is his; the reviewers were there only to help him with the design, not to pass judgment on his decisions.

Code Reviews

Code reviews are far less formal than design reviews. They are a chance to dive into the details of someone else's implementation, and as such they are a wonderful opportunity to extend your own development skills.

Preparing your code for review by others is a great time to take a fresh look at your work and clean up those sections you've been meaning to return to. Getting ready for code review is a time to ensure that your code is readable. Well-written code has a natural flow; it requires few comments, because it hangs together like well-written prose.

Having others read your code can help you see with new eyes where your code becomes cluttered and confusing. It also presents an opportunity for cross-fertilization of ideas, something that can't easily be accomplished in any other way. In advance of the review, the code should be distributed to every participant. Each reviewer should separate their comments into the following categories:

- Design questions and issues
- Code syntax questions and issues
- Readability and comments issues
- Techniques and suggestions

The goal of the code review is to provide feedback to the developer from the perspective of another engineer who might one day have to update or even take over this body of code. Is it obvious what the original developer was trying to accomplish? Is the code laid out clearly and cleanly? A second, related, goal is to familiarize other members of the team with every section of code, so that if a team member leaves, it's possible to pick up their work and continue.

The problem with code reviews is that most developers are scared to death to let anyone else read their code. This is baring your soul in a most public way, and the fear of ridicule can be overpowering. Code reviews must be highly supportive and encouraging events; if they degenerate into competitive sessions where you ridicule the work of one another, you undermine the efficacy of these sessions tremendously.

Code reviews are particularly difficult with managers in the room. These ought to be peer reviews in which each participant feels free to make foolish mistakes. If the participants feel judged or at risk, the code review will have far less positive impact.

"And hast thou slain the Jabberwock?
Come to my arms, my beamish boy!
O frabjous day! Callooh! Callay!"
He chortled in his joy.

Hiring Great People

Whatever the size of your team, a critical factor in the success or failure of your effort will be the quality of the people you hire. Hiring great people is not easy; it is time consuming, and hard work. Think of what you will entrust to this person: the future of your company may literally be in their hands. In addition, you are making a moral, and perhaps a legal commitment of hundreds of thousands of dollars in salary and benefits. Despite this, we typically make an offer based on a handful of interviews in the course of a week or less.

In the old days, if things didn't work out, you fired the guy and moved on. You cut your losses, and ate the cost of training that person and then having to hire his replacement. In today's litigious times, however, you may pay a far higher price. The effort involved in firing someone makes cutting your losses almost impossible. Nearly every large development organization is carrying at least one or two people who management would dearly love to fire, but can't.

The cost of keeping weak people on the payroll can't be overstated. Forget their salary; forget even the opportunity cost of not having someone else in that position. Consider instead the cost to *every other aspect* of the development effort. Weaker employees become a drain on the overall system, and they breed resentment in the other developers. Further, they lower self-esteem, the core ingredient of morale. We all want to look around and say, "Gee, I must be great, I'm part of a great team." If we look around and the other guy is a pointy-headed geek who doesn't know his assembler from his elbow, what does that say about *us*?

If you *do* make a hiring mistake, you'll know about it fairly quickly. Once it is pretty obvious that things are not working out, fix it fast. You do no one any favors by dragging it out, and you can kill your development effort if you are too slow to act. If the team is large, and the person in question is very senior, the imperative to rectify the problem is only that much greater.

Keeping your team small goes a long way towards solving the problem. With a small team, you'll only be going through the hiring process a few times, so you are more likely to take the time to get it right. It's harder for a weak programmer to hide in a small team as well, so you're more likely to pull the trigger if it comes to that. A third benefit is that you reduce the statistical requirement that introduces mediocrity. Put simply, it's easier to find 3 geniuses than it is to find 30. On the other hand, with a small team you *increase* the cost of a single point of failure: if there are only three of you and one is not up to the task, then the entire team will be in serious trouble. Keep it small, but take the time to hire well.

How to Interview

Hiring great people isn't easy. You need a well-defined process, and it takes a lot of time. Given how much trust you must put into the people you hire, you must *never* delegate this responsibility. If you are going to depend on the people who work for or with you, make sure you know them well *before* they are hired. Each person you hire costs you a lot of time in searching, interviewing, checking references, and training. The best bang for your buck is to do it as infrequently as possible, and to get the very best result.

I recently served as a volunteer on the hiring committee for my daughter's school. They received over 1200 applications for their single position. The principal narrowed the résumés down to about 100, and then interviewed each for 10 minutes. We then met as a committee and chose 20 to interview. The committee consisted of the principal (manager), two teachers (peers) and three parents (clients).

Each candidate received a 30-minute preliminary interview, for which they were asked to spend 45 minutes at the school preparing a curriculum on a topic we provided. Six strong candidates were brought back for 1-hour interviews. Each of the six was asked to spend as much time as they needed to prepare a curriculum on yet another topic; typically they spent several hours doing so.

Of the six, three were asked to come back the next day and teach a class on a topic we chose, while we observed their interaction with the students. The candidate we wanted to hire went on to be interviewed by the superintendent. All of this was for a position that paid in the low $40,000 range.

Most software companies spend a lot less time hiring a lot more people and pay them a lot more money. The point is not that we should be more cavalier about who teaches our kids; it is that we must spend more time deciding with whom we will work.

If you are going to use your HR department to find and screen your applicants, don't ask them to do too much. HR personnel are pretty good at finding people, but they are terrible at screening them. One way to help them weed out the obvious non-starters is to give them a short list of questions *you* intend to ask the candidate. They can show the list to prospective candidates and let them disqualify themselves if they think the questions are beyond their knowledge. Of course, HR won't ask the candidate to answer the questions; they'll just say, "Here are some questions you'll be asked in your interview."

Plan to have more than one interview. In the initial interviews, focus less on technology and more on the person's background, ambition, interests and so forth. If you think this person may be a good fit, designate one or two programmers to determine his (or her) skill set.

I often conduct these interviews in a group. One-on-one can bog down, but a group of interviewers can keep things on track, each interviewer's questions probing for slightly different information. You have to be careful not to overwhelm the applicant, but the danger is offset by how much more efficient this technique is, and your applicants will thank you for reducing the number of interviews.

Testing for Skills

At Interchange, I was often called upon to test applicants' knowledge of C++. This is a tricky business, because it is too easy to get hung up on details and miss the bigger picture. I for one often can't remember the syntax for a pointer to a member function, but who cares? I can always look it up. The real questions are whether you know where to look, and whether you know what it's for.

Testing skills makes me uncomfortable, but if you're hiring someone to code, it's good to find out how much they think they already know. I start by asking the candidate how comfortable they are with C++. This tells me a lot about what to expect. I'm looking for candidates who know it as well as they *say* they do — I don't care about absolute knowledge as much as whether they can put their money where their mouths are.

I usually start by saying, "I've been asked to assess your C++ skills. What I'd like to do is start with some general questions, and then we'll move to specifics. Along the way I'll ask more and more complicated questions until we fall off the end of your knowledge, or I run out of things to ask." I then begin with general concepts in object-oriented programming. "Tell me about polymorphism." This is an intentionally open-ended question, and often I learn enough from this one query to get a good feel for what this person knows and how they can communicate it. We go on to discuss inheritance, encapsulation, and so forth.

Assuming the candidate has a good understanding of object-oriented programming, I'll begin asking about the specifics of C++. Along the way, I often put the following program up on the whiteboard:

```
class Animal
{
    virtual void Speak() { cout << "Animal speaks"; }
    void Move() { cout << "Animal Moves"; }
    virtual void Eat() { << cout << "Animal eats 1 ounce"; }
    virtual void Eat(int howMuch) { cout << "Animal eats " <<
                                    howMuch << " ounces"; }
}

class Cat : public Animal
{
    void Speak() { cout << "Cat speaks"; }
    void Move() { cout << "Cat moves"; }
    void Eat(int howMuch) { cout << "Cat eats " <<
                                    howMuch << " cans of cat food"; }
}
```

```
class Dog : public Animal
{
    void Speak() { cout << "Dog speaks"; }
    void Move() { cout << "Dog moves"; }
    void Eat(int howMuch) { cout << "Dog eats " <<
                                howMuch << " cans of dog food"; }
    void Eat() { cout << "Dog eats 1 can of dog food"; }
}

#include <iostream.h>
int main()
{
    Cat* p1 = new Animal;
    Cat* p2 = new Cat;
    Dog* p3 = new Animal;
    Dog* p4 = new Dog;
    Animal* p5 = new Animal;
    Animal* p6 = new Cat;
    Animal* p7 = new Dog;
    p1->Speak();
    p1->Move();
    p1->Eat();
    p2->Speak();
    p2->Move();
    p2->Eat();
    p3->Speak();
    p3->Move();
    p3->Eat();
    p4->Speak();
    p4->Move();
    p4->Eat();
    p5->Speak();
    p5->Move();
    p5->Eat();
    p6->Speak();
    p6->Move();
    p6->Eat();
    p7->Speak();
    p7->Move();
    p7->Eat();
    return 0;
}
```

This makes a very good starting point for discussing the implementation of polymorphism. I ask about which declarations will fail in the compiler, and then what behavior to expect at runtime. I hope but don't assume that the candidate will talk about how the single override of **Cat**'s **Eat()** method will hide the method that takes no parameters, and I look for an understanding of how virtual methods work. I'll also ask about why you generally make the destructor virtual, and when you might not.

Any strong C++ candidate should be able to talk comfortably about this example, and exhibit a full understanding of virtual and non-virtual methods. If we get past these issues, I continue modifying the code, making **Animal** into an abstract data type, and talking about how virtual functions work. I'll ask about implementing pure virtual functions: "Are you allowed to provide an implementation?" "Why might you want to?" I'm looking both for a familiarity with the language and an understanding of the idioms.

Another set of questions will talk about the four canonical methods: the constructor, the destructor, the copy constructor and the assignment operator. We'll talk about why you might want to provide these methods, and what happens if you don't.

If the candidate gets past all of this, they clearly understand at least the fundamentals. At this point we'll begin talking about memory management, the use of pointers vs. references, and so forth. From there we'll range into collection classes, templates and the use of exceptions. At this point I'll ask about what problems exceptions create, and how these might be solved. A very strong candidate will talk about exception handling and management of pointers, and will know what smart pointers are and how to create them.

How to be Interviewed

It is important to realize that part of doing a job well is getting the job in the first place. Here are four suggestions to consider when being interviewed.

Show That You Want the Job

If anyone tells you not to look over-eager, don't you believe it. When I'm hiring, I look for the most eager, energetic, excited person I can find. I'll take an eager novice over a bored expert any day of the week. There is always competition for the best jobs, and *wanting* the job is a major factor.

Don't be afraid that wanting the job will lower your income. The one has nothing to do with the other, and good managers know that. You have a salary requirement, but that's completely separate from whether you are eager to *do* the job. If they low-ball you, you have to be prepared to walk away, but there is never any harm in showing you are excited by the position.

Listen

This may be the single most important interviewing skill. Listen to what they want, then think about whether you can give them what they need. If so, let them know you've heard them, and how you can help. This doesn't mean parroting back their requirements, but it does mean listening hard to what they want and making sure to answer their implicit questions.

So often when I was interviewing, I'd describe what we needed and then the applicant would start talking as if I hadn't said a word. I had the sense that they had a rehearsed speech about their abilities, and they applied that one-size-fits-all approach to whomever they were talking with.

Be Brutally Honest

If you don't know something, say, "I don't know." Don't rush to assure them you can learn. It's worth making the point (if it's true) that you learn quickly, or on your own, or on the job, but don't say it defensively.

In 1983, I worked for two weeks at Citibank. At the end of the job, I talked with the Assistant Vice President in charge of the project and said, "I very much want to learn more about programming, is there a job here for me?" He said, "We are trying to hire a technical support person; you need an MBA or three years experience." "Perfect," I replied, "I don't have either of those things, but I can do the job." What a great job it turned out to be. It isn't often in history that an industry is young enough that you can come in untrained and build a position for yourself. I often felt like we were in the early days of aviation, when all you needed to jump into the plane and fly was the chutzpah to step up and ask for the keys.

In 1988, when I applied for the job at Interchange, Pat Johnson said that he was looking for someone with two years of C++, and extensive experience programming for Windows or the Mac. I told him I didn't have any of that, but there was something else I could bring to the party: I knew a lot about how people communicate online. He then said, "Okay, I understand you've not worked with C++, but how much object-oriented programming do you know?" It was tempting to lie, but I told him I didn't know any. He said, "Well, do you know what polymorphism or inheritance is?" More pressure; just a little lie here would go a long way. Say 'no' and you're dead. Say 'a little' and maybe you live another day. "No," I replied. He smiled and said, "Well, can you learn it?" Ah — now that was a question I knew how to answer.

Turn the Tables

Too often, in our eagerness to get a job, we neglect to learn enough about the position to know if we even want it. Make sure you know what kind of work you'll be doing, what you can hope to learn, who you'll work for, what your role will be, and how you can advance. This is a very effective technique because it moves your interviewer into the position of trying to sell to you, rather than deciding if you're the right person for the job. Don't use it to manipulate, though; use it to make sure you know what you're getting into.

Along the way, you need to decide if you are a development person or a production person. You need to know if you like small teams or large ones, small companies or big ones, new ventures or well-established endeavors. These preferences don't eliminate any particular jobs, but they do help you to evaluate what is most important to you.

Managing Well

Sooner or later, if you're any good, you'll get sucked into management. Watch out; it's like *Night of the Living Dead*. You see these ghouls walking around, and you will do anything not to be like them. Then one day there's a pod under your desk, and you're walking real slow. The funny thing is, once you *are* a ghoul, you think it's a good thing, and you figure everyone else wants to be one too.

What usually happens is this: you can't get any work done because the operation is going to hell in a hand-basket. The one manager who had a clue just quit, and *his* boss comes to you and says something like, "You're our best guy. We need to leverage your skills. Congratulations, you've just been promoted."

You consider the increased pay, the ability to influence the direction of the project more effectively, the opportunity to expand your résumé. You consider the alternative — they'll just hire some geek to be your new boss — and visions of Dilbert cartoons spring to mind. You mutter, "Ave Caesar, morituri te salutant"[2] and you take the job. Now what?

Give Your Developers Room

The first, best step a manager can take is to hire great people and then give them room to work. The key ingredient in building an effective small team is empowerment. No, strike that. 'Empowerment' is a term used by management to mean granting the illusion of independence. What I mean to say is, "Get the hell out of the way."

Putting three developers on a team, and then undercutting and second-guessing them at every turn, is every bit as bad as creating a team of fifty. Let me be absolutely clear about this: choose the right people, tell them what you want done, and then *close the door*. Send in food and money, and don't knock until next fall.

I have met some great managers. They believe that it is their job to *aggressively* get out of the way. In fact, they believe it is their job to get *everything* out of the way of their developers. They spend their time solving problems so that the developers won't be distracted. They buy the furniture, order the hardware, ensure that the network is working, and make sure the necessary support staff is in place. They approve the budget, watch the schedule, and run interference between the developer and upper management. This is very useful activity, and a good manager performing these tasks can greatly enhance the ability of a developer to stay focused. This job description for a manager does raise some interesting questions, however.

For example, why is it that managers are in charge? Why should the guy whose job it is to clear the way also be the guy who is setting the direction? Imagine you form a company to build the next great product. You get together with some of the brightest

---

[2] *Hail Caesar, we who are about to die salute you.*

folks you know, design the product, and start coding. Along the way, you realize you need someone to help with managing the project, keeping an eye on the schedule, and making sure things are coming together. Do you put this guy in charge? Is he now your boss? Of course not.

Is it possible to imagine a technical company, perhaps even founded by programmers, in which the managers are professional advisors to the technical staff? In such a model, the managers would keep an eye on the development schedule, and they'd advise the technical staff on which direction to take, but no one would confuse that with them being the boss.

Certainly, no one would set out with a business plan that said, "Well, I'm going to build a state of the art product. I know that the market changes quickly, and I know that my competition will be working hard to get there first, so what I'll do first is hire a bunch of managers. I'll ask them to review and question all my decisions, and to debate among themselves if we should go in one direction or another. Each time I have a schedule crunch, it will be their job to call me out into meetings to explain technical considerations that are beyond their understanding, or to tell me about new requirements."

Is it crazy to think of a company in which the most highly rewarded and influential people are those who are building the product that will be sold?

Feeding and Clothing Your Developers

People who work in large groups spend time and money in ways that are very different from how they would spend their time and money if they were working for themselves. When I worked for Citibank, we all bought DayTimers. These are wonderful calendars, and I never felt I was abusing the privilege when I bought that year's supplies. I got great use from my DayTimer, and it helped to organize my time. I believe I'm an honest person, and I would never have spent $100 on the product if I felt I was buying something I didn't truly need. When I went to work for myself, my need for such a book didn't diminish. I went to the stationary store and did a thorough evaluation of the products they had to offer. I walked out with a calendar that cost me $2.49.

Ownership

Corporate America seems to understand this premise, but it just can't live with the consequences. It talks about giving programmers a 'sense of ownership'. Giving a *sense* of ownership will get you a *sense* of commitment. That certainly isn't the same as *real* commitment.

No one works for anyone else quite like he works for himself. If you want real commitment from your developers, consider giving them real ownership — a significant and powerful stake in the company. Half of 1% is nice, but most developers are rational enough to consider that kind of stake as a bonus, not as ownership.

If you want to get someone's attention, give them 10% of the company. 10% is undeniable ownership; it provides that magnificent understanding that your fate is inextricably tied to the fate of your product and the company. When you own 10% or more of the company, you are highly motivated to do whatever it takes to make your product succeed.

One of the really nice things about giving out 10% ownership stakes is that you are forced to keep your team rather small. You can only give out 10% so many times before the lawyers become agitated. That's fine: you only need a few very motivated people for most tasks. It is my guess that 3 killer programmers, each with 10% ownership of a company, will be a lot more productive than 30 programmers that each have 1%.

Consultants vs. Employees

When I consult on a product, I usually don't get an ownership stake. What, then, is my motivation? Clearly, I'm motivated both by my internal drive, and by the need to protect my professional reputation. But hold on! Isn't an employee driven, and doesn't he have a reputation to protect?

The key difference is that I perceive myself to be working for myself. By building Jay's product, I build my company. Most employees perceive themselves to be working for someone else, and as such the product is not 'theirs'.

Reviews

Here's how to tell if your team is too large and your manager is out of touch: do you have annual performance reviews? In a well-managed team, these would be a laughable exercise. Development teams ought to be business partnerships. Imagine working day in and day out with your manager, meeting on every issue and discussing every aspect of your business. One day, your manager calls you into his office and says, "Let me tell you how you've been doing this year." If he has anything to say that you don't already know, something is very wrong, so why bother?

Taking stock once a year, setting goals and reviewing past performance, is a valuable practice. On the other hand, if it becomes an excuse to ignore problems and issues until the next periodic review, then it does more harm than good. To make matters worse, reviews are most often conducted as part of a compensation decision. The employee dutifully sits through the annual review so that he can get to the reward that's held out until the end. That reward is, in most cases, deeply disappointing. Why is that?

Managers have a dilemma. Most corporations are set up with a budgeted amount for their entire development staff. This creates a zero sum game — each person who receives above the average raise for that year must be offset by someone else receiving below the average. Thank goodness for the mediocre team members that let you properly reward your stars! I have a better idea: fire your mediocre performers, and transfer their entire salaries to your best programmers.

One of the most bizarre aspects of compensation is that new hires are often paid more than your loyal employees. Horizontal moves in the industry (changing jobs without taking more responsibility) often lead to greater increases in salary than simple annual increments. This is crazy; if you are clearing out your mediocre members, then what's left are your most experienced and most valuable people. You should be ready and eager to pay them more than you would pay anyone new.

Having a very small team puts you in a position to pay more than anyone else in the industry. Your stars should know without reservation that they could never make more working for anyone else; in fact, they should know that they are among the highest paid professionals in the industry, anywhere in the world. If the people you have working for you *aren't* worth paying more than anyone else gets, then fire them and go hire those others.

Technologist or Manager

Here's my analogy for my own attraction to management: I'm Odysseus. The sirens singing on the shore, beckoning me ever closer, are opportunities in management. The ship is my career. Strap me to the mast, and make the rope fast. Again and again, I return to the suspicion that the attraction of management is an artifact of how we organize corporations. In a company geared for building software, the job of manager would be ancillary and uninteresting.

A Radical Proposal

Ed Belove, one of the brightest guys I've ever met, became something of a role model for me while I was at Interchange, where he was CTO. He demonstrated that management is not the only path. It was he, along with the Vice President of Development, Mike Kraley, who encouraged me to give up my management position and take on a senior technical role.

Recently, Ed and I had a conversation in which I asked him the ideal size for a development team. "Three," he said without hesitation. "Small enough to work together tightly, and an odd number to break any ties. And with three people," he pointed out, "you can only have one conversation going at a time." There is brilliance in this simple formulation, but it's one that will be very hard to sell to most of the industry.

Even those who believe in small, empowered teams will balk at the idea that three developers can develop an entire project. This radical concept turns all previous assumptions upside down, and challenges the role some of the most influential people in the industry play in the development of software. With three people, what does the manager do? What does the Vice President or Chief Technology Officer do?

I am not arguing that there is no project that needs more than three developers. Three people, no matter how brilliant, can only produce so much code before they run out of hours in the day. Also, I'm not arguing that it's impossible to build a project with more than three developers. Certainly, much larger teams have delivered many solid products.

What I *am* saying is that building a great product with a large team is terribly difficult, and almost always frightfully wasteful, expensive, and inefficient — the failure rate will be very high. I'm also saying that a surprising number of projects that appear at first glance to require a very large team can really be done with far fewer developers. I'm arguing that the benefits of a very small team nearly always overwhelm the objections, and that what you lose in parallel development you more than make up in efficiency.

A Different Vision

If you take seriously the idea of a team of three, many of the principles of how to organize a software development team must be rethought. Who runs the show? Who does the hiring? Do you have formal meetings? Who talks with Marketing? Do you have a full-time Quality Assurance team?

Imagine this: you start out with a vision of a *product*, not of a team, and the vision is owned by a single person. Let's assume for now that the owner of the vision is *not* a developer; we'll just call them the 'client'. The client hires a technical lead — an architect — whose job is to get the product built. How does the architect create the right team?

The architect starts with the vision. He must understand it in some detail before he can figure out what it will take to implement. This is the **conceptualization** phase. Once the vision is understood, the architect can dimension the problem and determine a methodology.

Next, the architect works with the client to flesh out the vision, to understand its meaning and its implications. This is the **analysis** phase. To fully understand the problem, the architect may consult with domain experts, designers or other developers. How does he hire these developers, and how many does he need? For a project large enough to require a formal analysis, I suggest that one or at most two additional developers/architects is the right number. Analysis and design are a great time for collaborative effort, but only in small groups.

Once the design is fully understood, it's time to think about who will implement the product. If you are going to grow the team, now is the time to do it, but again I argue that you'll be better off with fewer developers. This may even be a good time to *shrink* the team. While analysis and design are best done in collaboration with others, it is the nature of development to be a solitary endeavor. Rather than growing the team, consider whether a single developer might be able to implement the design! If not a single developer, then consider two. Two developers can work in parallel with a minimum of distraction as they keep each other up to date. Going all the way up to three people begins to put stress on the lines of communication, but things don't really begin to break down until you have four. Once you have four or five developers working together, you need a manager, and then your effectiveness begins to plummet.

Small development teams need no managers. What a concept! All your resources are dedicated to design and implementation, with no overhead.

What About Bigger Projects?

Some projects are so large and so complex that at the end of analysis you realize that it would take *years* for three people to get it all done. Surely it's time to start hiring now?

The right answer *may* be to build a larger team, but most likely a better answer is to take a sharp knife to your requirements. Can you buy an interim solution for most of what you're going to build? Do you really need every one of these features for the first release? Aren't you better off doing a lot less and getting into the market sooner?

If you *are* bound and determined to do it all, and you manifestly need a *far* larger team, what do you do? The obvious answer is to break your project into smaller pieces and build the pieces separately.

Sub-Teams

Bigger projects come in two flavors: those that can be divided into wholly independent components, and those that just *look* like they can. While many will embrace the notion of breaking projects into smaller pieces, they will reject the idea of asking a single team to implement these pieces sequentially, and will instead attempt to create multiple teams and build the various pieces in parallel.

The problem is that the interdependencies among the pieces often make it difficult or impossible to treat the other components as 'black boxes'. While it's great in theory to say that you'll build separate components with well-defined interfaces, the trick is actually to do so. What often happens is that the interfaces are not as final as one hopes, and as they change the various teams must adjust. Coordination among these teams requires a manager and a series of meetings, and the illusion of independence is shattered.

Certainly, some projects require a number of components, not all of which can be purchased off the shelf. If time-to-market imperatives require that these be developed simultaneously, you face the difficult task of keeping changes in each component from affecting all the others. This requires a rigorous methodology, in which you fully analyze and design before you commit resources to implementation. The goal is to ensure that the interfaces are as well understood as possible, as early as possible.

At Interchange, we struggled with the question of whether to organize on vertical or horizontal lines. If we organized *vertically*, we'd have a database team, a server team, a communications team and a documents team. Each team would provide a set of skills and tools to build products, but no one would own each product. If we organized *horizontally*, we would have an e-mail team, a conferences team, an editorial and news team, and so forth. Each team would own a 'product' but there would be tremendous duplication of effort as we all implemented the underlying technologies.

This confusion resulted in large measure from trying to do too much at once, and having an inadequate analysis and design. Had we taken the appropriate time to create our core architecture, we would have built Interchange in two discrete stages. In the first stage we would have built the enabling technology; in the second stage we would have built the applications we needed on top of that enabling technology.

The advantage to such an approach would have been that the components we used to build the applications were fungible. As we created new components, they would have been available to all applications that could use them. More important, as new technologies became available elsewhere, we would have been better positioned to take advantage of them. Had we treated the communications link, the rich text editor and the database as enabling components, we would have been in a position to swap new ones in and out over time. The applications we built on top of these technologies would then have had clear, narrow interfaces to the components; changes in the underlying components would not necessarily have broken the applications built on top of them.

My conclusion is this: if you have many sub-teams, ensure that your organizational lines reflect the architecture of the product, so that there are few, if any, interdependencies among these teams. If we at Interchange had built the communications, database and rich text technologies independently of one another, we would greatly have reduced the danger that changes in one would break the others. Further, the teams could have operated independently as well. They would have needed less management, and would have remained more focused.

Some of what I'm proposing isn't the least bit new — these ideas have been tried before, and often they have failed miserably. I'm told that at one large development shop, there was an idea to make the charting group build a separate chart engine, which might then be 'sold' to the spreadsheet group, the database group and so forth. The problem was that there was no real commitment to this idea, so when the charting group began to modify their design to generalize it and make it more appealing to a wider audience, each 'client' organization could no longer get the kind of optimizations they required. They ended up building their own charting engines that did what they needed.

Division into sub-teams is doomed to failure if these teams are nothing more than a subterfuge for a larger integrated effort. If we are paying lip service to the idea of independence, but what we really have is a large organization that someone got the bright idea to break into sub-teams, then we'll spend the bulk of our time working on inter-team communication. We'll have lost all the efficiency we hoped to gain. Sub-teams only work if they are *totally* independent of one another.

Implementation Techniques

Whatever the size of your team, there are some general implementation guidelines that can contribute to the success of your project. Each of these requires programming without ego: it is imperative to program on the assumption that someone else may need to take over your code at any moment. This is for two reasons; the *less* important of which is that you may leave the project (willingly or otherwise), and someone else may be forced to pick up your work. More important, coding in this style ensures that when *you* return to the code you'll be able to pick up and continue on, rather than scratching your head and wondering what the devil you thought you were doing. (I've done this so often, I've begun to think of that earlier me as another, somewhat dumber programmer.)

These techniques include:

- Use source control
- Keep a log
- Know when to quit for the day
- Adopt a coding style and stick to it
- Use comments well

Use Source Control

Even if you are working alone, a good source code control system can save you from the single most frustrating scenario in our profession. Picture this: you get something very tricky to work, and all your tests are good. Flushed with success, you begin the next task, but something goes wrong and the system locks up. When you reboot, you're not quite sure what went wrong, so you make another change. That doesn't work, so you try to undo the most recent change, and it just gets worse. You try to go back a few more steps, but you've forgotten exactly what you've done, and now it is worse still. You begin to panic. Your eyes start flashing through the code, searching madly for the stray line that's causing the crash. You tear out everything new and try your old, working code, but now *it* crashes as well.

Now serious panic sets in. You can feel the churning in your stomach as you realize that the last time you backed up your software was two days ago. Two days isn't very long, but boy! You do *not* want to have to redo all the work you just finished. It ought to go quicker the second time around, but in fact it goes much slower. The first time was a process of discovery and revelation. The second time is pure torture; no one likes repeating work. Like Sisyphus, you may have just enough strength to roll that boulder back up to the top of the mountain, but it is no fun, and if you have to do it a few times in a row you are in great danger of the boulder rolling back down right over you.

Source code control is like putting steps into the mountain. The rock may roll back down, but it will only go as far as the most recent step, where it stops short and waits for you to come and get it. Using source code control well, especially in a team development effort, is a skill unto itself. In its most simple form, source code control just lets you mark a particular development point so that you can return to that point when things go wrong. In this sense it is like making frequent backups. Of course, a good source code control system will go way beyond this.

Using source code control, two or more developers can work in parallel and be assured that they are not stepping on each other's changes. It does this in two ways: first, it blocks the second developer from gaining write access to any file that the first developer has 'checked out' of the system. Second, if the second developer takes the file out on a 'branch', it assists in grafting that branch back onto the main trunk of development.

A good source code control system will also allow you to create 'named releases'. That is, you may ship internal version 35 to the customers as release 1.0. Typically, you'll then turn your attention to developing release 2.0. By the time problems are reported, you may be on to internal version 47. A good source code control system will let you quickly reproduce the exact code that shipped in release 1.0 so that you can find, and fix, the bugs.

Keep a Log

This is the best advice I ever received, but I've found it murderously difficult to follow. The idea is simple: each time you make a change, log it in a book. When things blow up, the log will tell you what you did, and that will help you find your way back to working code.

Here's the problem: when things are going well, who wants to take the time to write in the log? My dad used to tell me that although some houses leak in the rain, many of them never get fixed. The logic was inescapable. When it is raining, it isn't safe to get up on the roof to fix the leak. When it's a nice day, who wants to go up and fix the roof when you can be out playing in the sun?

One way to keep a log that isn't too painful is to make frequent 'check point' entries into your source control. Most modern source control programs let you set a switch so that each check in automatically checks the code right back out. This lets you leave a version in the source code control while continuing on. These systems typically let you annotate your check in with a note; make use of them, because they'll help you a lot when you have to unwind your most recent changes.

I also keep a log when I'm *about* to make a significant change, but before it is working. Writing it down forces me to think it through, and helps me find my errors when things don't work out quite as I intended.

Here's another piece of advice: buy a bound notebook for the log. Don't use a pad, and never use a spiral notebook or (worse still) a loose-leaf. You don't want to be tempted to throw these notes away; they become critically useful exactly six hours after you crumple them up and toss them in the recycling bin. Your best bet is a ledger book. A 150 page Avery Archival Paper book is fairly inexpensive, and it is nicely bound, *and* the pages are numbered. I mention this because I use them, and they're getting harder to find because so few people do their accounting on paper any more. I'm hoping you'll adopt them so that there will continue to be enough of a market that I can still get them. They work just great. I number mine and keep them forever.

Know When to Quit for the Day

The single best bit of advice for a professional programmer is this: know when to stop pounding on the code and take a step back. Despite our training and experience, when things start to fall apart we're all tempted to try rapid code/compile/test cycles to see if we can't bang the thing back into shape. Most often, we break it beyond repair.

This is particularly acute when you are under pressure and you are tired. 11 p.m. is often a great time to unravel all the progress you've made that day. You are almost done, and it would be so great to quit for the day when it is working — just one more change ought to do it. Then it breaks, but how hard can it be to fix? You *really* want it to work before you go home. Suddenly, it's 1 a.m. and you're still tinkering, but now you're simply making things worse and worse.

During World War Two, some of the greatest atomic physicists in the world were brought together to build an atomic weapon. They believed their work might bring a quicker end to the war and save hundreds of thousands of lives. They spent billions of dollars and put their careers on the line. Every day of delay meant more risk to Allied servicemen. On the day of the Trinity test, they were to set off the first atomic device the world had ever seen. They were excruciatingly careful in their preparations; there was real fear that if they got it wrong, they might detonate the device prematurely. Or *worse*, it would fizzle out and they'd lose the support they required to finish the project.

The bomb was cylindrical in shape. The plutonium and the initiator were kept separate until the last moment. The cylinder was engineered with a small space into which the plutonium and initiator would be inserted. To maximize blast efficiency, the tolerances were a few thousandths of an inch; it was a very tight fit, but in previous testing it had slipped in cleanly. On the day of the test it jammed. President Roosevelt was at Potsdam, meeting with Stalin. Ending the War, the future of American/Soviet relations, and perhaps the future of Western Europe depended on news of a successful test. The pressure on these scientists was enormous; everything depended on their making this test succeed *today*.

The engineers were frantic. Was it possible they brought the wrong plug for this bomb? Why didn't it fit? They were afraid to force it; they might set the bomb off in their faces, or break the delicate assembly and render the bomb unusable. They were afraid to leave it alone, and they were afraid to touch it, but delay was unthinkable.

Finally, their training as professional scientists took over. They pulled the assembly out, took a deep breath and sat down to *think*. Of course! The Trinity test site was in New Mexico, and temperatures that day were near 100 degrees. The plutonium and initiator had heated in the sun and expanded. The core of the device was insulated, and therefore much cooler. They laid the plug on top of the cylinder and went off to have lunch. When they returned, the temperatures had equalized and the plug slipped in easily.

You will often find a bug that will not yield — that is deep and devious and impossible to find when you are searching late into the night — will transmute itself into a tiny, obvious little flaw the next morning. When you are stuck, walk away, get dinner, and come back to it the next day; you will often find it is easy to solve after a good night's sleep.

Adopt a Coding Style and Stick to It

When you write code, you have two audiences: the compiler, and other programmers. The compiler doesn't care at all about your coding style. As far as it's concerned, white space is meaningless. Your peers, however, will curse your soul if you make your code unreadable. Write every line as if someone else will maintain it. When you return to it a few months later, you'll be glad you did.

Let's start with braces. Deciding how to align braces can be the single most controversial topic between programmers. Whatever style you adopt, use it consistently. In this section, I'll list my personal preferences.

Matching braces should be aligned vertically. The outermost set of braces in a definition or declaration should be at the left margin, and then the statements within the block are indented. No code is on the same line as a brace. Thus:

```
if ( condition == true )
{
   a += b;
   SomeFunction();

   if ( c == d )
   {
      SomeOtherFunction();
   }
}
```

switch statements get special indentation, as they can otherwise waste a lot of space:

```
switch(variable)
{
case ValueOne:
    ActionOne();
    break;

case ValueTwo:
    ActionTwo();
    break;

default:
    assert("bad Action");
    break;
}
```

Keep all lines fairly short, and break the line if it will scroll off to the right. If you do break a line, indent the following lines. Try to break the line at a reasonable place, and if there is an operator, leave it at the end of the previous line (as opposed to the beginning of the following line). This way, it is clear that the line does not stand alone and that there is more to come.

Strive to make your code easy to read, because code that is easy to read is easy to maintain. Use a lot of white space where it will help to make things clear. As a rule, I treat objects and arrays as a single thing, and I don't put space before the references (e.g. **myObject.SomeMethod()**).

Unary operators are associated with their operand, so I don't put a space between them. On the other hand, I *do* put a space on the side *away* from the operand. When it comes to binary operators, I put a space both sides. Here are some other suggestions:

Don't use spaces to indicate precedence (**4 + 3*2**).

Put a space after commas and semicolons, not before.

Parentheses should have spaces on the inside, and keywords should be set off with a space:

```
if ( a == b )
```

Place the pointer or reference indicator next to the type name. Don't put it next to the variable name or place it with a space on either side. In other words, do this:

```
char* foo;
int& theInt;
```

And not this:

```
char *foo;
int &theInt;
```

Only declare a single variable on any line. Combining this rule with the last one will prevent you from writing

```
int* varOne, varTwo;
```

when you mean to declare two pointers. In fact, if you were to write this you would have declared one pointer and one integer variable.

Be careful about how you name identifiers. The name should be long enough to be descriptive; it is worth the extra effort to spell names out. Consider limited use of Hungarian Notation; for example, prefix pointers with **p** (**pSomePointer**) and references with **r**.

The length of a variable's name should be proportional to its scope. Within a **for** loop, it is fine to have a variable named **j**, but if the variable is going to live for any time at all it should have a more descriptive name.

Avoid having two variables whose names differ only by capitalization. While the compiler won't be confused, you certainly will. Adopt a capitalization strategy: variables begin with a lower case letter, and methods begin with an upper case letter.

Consider making variable names abstract nouns (**theCount**, **windSpeed**, **windowPosition**), while methods should be verb/noun phrases like **Find()**, **ShowButton()**, and **MoveWindow()**. We used to call this **kill dwarf notation**, from the old interactive computer games where you specified a verb (move, lift, kill) and a noun (scroll, wand, dwarf).

Use Comments Well

I was watching a ball game on TV, and the pitcher was really struggling. He had walked the last two batters, and the manager and catcher went out to the mound to talk with him. It was obvious that the manager wasn't ready to take the pitcher out of the game, but he was going to give him some advice. The play by play reporter asked the color commentator what was going on. "You were a catcher; what does the manager say when he gets out there?" The color commentator thought a moment and said, "He says, 'Throw strikes.' And the pitcher says, 'I'm trying to throw strikes.' And the manager says, 'Yeah, but throw strikes.'"

Telling you to comment well is rather like telling the pitcher to throw strikes. It's a great idea, but how *exactly* do you do it? Well, your comments should never speak for the code. For example:

```
myCounter++;  // increment myCounter
```

This is worse than useless. The code speaks for itself, so get rid of the comment. There is always the danger that the comment will get out of date and you'll end up with:

```
myCounter += theNewValue;  // increment myCounter
```

Now instead of being just obvious, it is plain wrong. Comments should only be used to clarify obscure code. Ideally, of course, you should endeavor to make your code less obscure, not paper it over with a comment. Don't comment:

```
a = j / 60; // compute how many minutes
```

Instead, make the code clearer:

```
howManyMinutes = howManySeconds / SECS_IN_MINUTE;
```

Comments should be used to explain what a section of code is *for*, not what it is *doing*. Use complete English sentences; the extra effort involved is paid back in having much clearer comments. By the same logic, try to avoid abbreviations. What seems exceedingly clear to you as you write the comment will seem cryptic some months later. Use blank lines and white space to help the reader understand what is going on. Separate statements into logical groups.

Organizing the Source Code

Each source and header file should have a consistent layout; it makes finding and managing the code much easier. The way you access portions of your program should also be consistent.

Always use **public**, **private**, and **protected** specifiers; don't rely on the defaults. List the public members first, then protected ones, then private ones. List the data members in a group after the methods. This is trickier when using classes built by the Microsoft Wizards, but it is worth the time to rearrange these files and get it right.

Line up function return types, names and parameters. Consider these two listings; which do you find easier to read?

```
bool GetStartFromEnd (CTime& start, CTime end, int nSizeOfList, int
nAudioDuration);
int GetWhichList (CCaller* pCaller, CString customerID, bool onlyOne);
void GetWhenToCall (CCaller* pCaller, CString customerID, bool& alwaysNow,
CTime& start, CTime& end, bool& useTimeZones, int& whichTilt, int& nIsCrisis);
void GetStartTime (CCaller* pCaller, CString customerID, CTime& start,CTime&
end);
void GetEndTime (CCaller* pCaller, CString customerID, CTime& start,CTime&
end);
```

```
  bool    GetStartFromEnd     (CTime& start, CTime end, int nSizeOfList,
  int     GetWhichList        (CCaller* pCaller, CString customerID, bool onlyOne);
  void    GetWhenToCall       (CCaller* pCaller, CString customerID,
                               bool& alwaysNow, CTime& start,
                               CTime& end, bool& useTimeZones,
                               int& whichTilt, int& nIsCrisis);
                               int nAudioDuration);
  void    GetStartTime        (CCaller* pCaller, CString customerID, CTime& start,
                               CTime& end);
  void    GetEndTime          (CCaller* pCaller, CString customerID, CTime& start,
                               CTime& end);
```

Put the constructor(s) first in the appropriate section, followed by the destructor. Alphabetize the rest of the methods, both in the header file and in the implementation file. Or, rather than alphabetizing, consider grouping your methods by sets of functionality. This gives you a quick view of what your objects do, and is a good check on whether you are asking any one object to do too much.

Alphabetize the **#include** directives at the top of your implementation files (be careful about order dependencies, but to the extent that they are under your control, consider an order dependency to be a bug, and fix it). Comment each **#include** statement if it isn't obvious why you needed it. And be sure that *every* header file has inclusion guards to protect against multiple includes.

Join a Community

One of the downsides of small development teams is that you work in isolation. Larger teams provide access to a greater pool of talent, and there is usually someone around who has already been there and done that. When coding in a smaller team, expand your horizons using the Internet and journals.

When I began the Hypotenuse project, I thought a lot about which newsgroups might provide useful information. I already participated in comp.lang.c++ and comp.lang.c++.moderated, but I expanded my participation to include comp.databases.ms-sqlserver, and a few of the Microsoft newsgroups as well.

In addition, I kept up my subscription to *C++ Report*, *Microsoft Internet Developer* (MInD) and *Microsoft Systems Journal* (MSJ), which keep me up to date on the latest developments. Finally, I subscribe to a number of mailing lists (e.g. **mfc@listserv.msn.com** and **otug-owner@rational.com**), which extend the community and bring important issues to light.

Both Wrox Press (http://www.wrox.com) and Liberty Associates, Inc. (http://www.libertyassociates.com) will offer ongoing support and related information for this book.

Object-oriented Analysis and Design

The remainder of this book describes the analysis, design and implementation of a computer telephony project. It will be written in real-time, as it happens. Nothing will be hidden; you'll join me as I figure out what the customer wants and how to deliver it. You'll see every wrong turn, every mistake, every insight, every success.

What I hope you'll walk away with is this: object-oriented analysis and design is a process. It is a skill, not unlike programming. What is needed is experience and insight. But there is no magic here. It doesn't take a Ph.D. to do it well. In fact it isn't an academic exercise at all, it is a practical tool to manage the complexity of modern software development. It is only worth doing if it helps you create better programs: more robust, more reliable, more extensible. It is my experience that it does just that, and over the next few months, I'll endeavor to prove the point.

```
= false;

Time();
= now.Format("%b %d

er = "start < '";
oday;
. and enddate > '";
today;
"'";

ScheduleSet.m_strFilter =

JobScheduleSet.IsOpen())

JobScheduleSet.Requery();

pDoc->m_JobScheduleSet.Open();

llTrack* pCallTrack;
l ok;

ile
pDoc->m_JobScheduleSet.IsEOF())

    pCallTrack = new
llTrack(m_pDoc->m_JobScheduleSet.m_
ID);    ok = pCallTrack->Initialize();

    if (ok)
    {   Log("ok\n");
    m_CallList.AddHead(pCallTrack);
        foundJobs = true;

    }
    else
    {   Log("...Rejected!\n");
        delete pCallTrack;

    }
m_pDoc->m_JobScheduleSet.MoveNext();
```

```
                        CTime::GetCur
                    CTime end = theJo
                CTime start = theJobSet
            CTime todayStart(start.GetYe
        start.GetMonth(), now.GetDay(),
            start.GetHour(),
            start.GetMinute(),
            start.GetSecond());
            CTime todayEnd(end.GetYear(),
        end.GetMonth(), now.GetDay(),
        end.GetHour(),
        end.GetMinute(), end.GetSecond());

            if (todayStart > now || todayS
        now)
            {   theJobSet.Close();
                return false;

            }

            CTimeSpan theSpan = end no
            int totalMinutes =
        theSpan.GetTotalMinutes();

            if (end > todayEnd) // a
        than today
            {   int AdditionalMin =
        GetAdditionalMinutes(theS
        t,
        theJobSet.m_EndDate);
                CTimeSpan todaySp
            now;    totalMinutes =
        todaySpan.GetTotalMin
        AdditionalMin;
            }

            m_min = ( ( (m_t
        totalMinutes) + 1
        );   m_Priority = theJo
            m_Tilt = theJo
            m_Throttle = the
            m_JobID = the
            theJobSet.Cl
                    return tru
```

```
m_pDoc->m_JobScheduleSet.

_Jobs;
```

CHAPTER TWO

Conceptualization

The Inception

Liberty Associates Inc. provides training, consulting and contract programming in C++ and object-oriented development. It is early in December 1996, and we've been contacted by Hypotenuse Inc., Verona, N.J. who are interested in having us build their next generation, industrial-strength, out-calling program. To get us started, I go to New Jersey to meet with Jay Leve, the president of Hypotenuse. Our goal in this first meeting is just to flesh out the initial concept.

Leve explains that Hypotenuse will sell a *Crisis•Call* Notification Service to governments, non-profits and corporations. Political organizations might use the service to provide get-out-the-vote reminders, FEMA might use the service to provide evacuation instructions, schools might use the service to alert parents of closings and delays. In each case, the person being called has an established relationship with the organization making the calls and very much wants the information he's receiving.

He wants the software to manage the client accounts, and to allow designated representatives of these clients to call in, record audio, supply lists of phone numbers and order the calls to begin. In short, *Crisis•Call* will be a flexible system to allow Hypotenuse to place any number of fully automated phone calls on behalf of any number of customers, at a moment's notice.

In Jay's vision, the software will manage the calls and report on each job, providing summary and detailed information about what numbers were called, which calls were answered and potentially what choices the recipient made.

Jay's brief description of the product forms the core of the initial conceptualization phase. In his book *UML Distilled*, Fowler calls this the **inception**. By either name, the goal is to establish what we are doing and why, and to determine the scope of the project.

A key goal of the conceptualization phase is to determine which aspects of this solution will be in the software and which are external to the system. Our focus at this point is to think about how the system will be used, and by whom. At this early stage we're not looking to build a product specification or a requirements document, we're simply trying to understand how Jay and his customers will interact with the system.

The Road Map

Hypotenuse has asked us to tell them what this project will cost, and how long it will take to deliver. Of course, in an ideal world we would fully analyze the problem before setting the delivery date. Further, this analysis would last as long as was needed to fully understand the problem. But this is not the ideal world, and in *this* world — the real world — customers are under tremendous market pressure. They have budgets to create, as well as partners, bosses, and sometimes spouses, to assuage, not to mention customers of their own to serve. In short, we need to help set their expectations, and we need to respond to their need for a schedule based on the information they've provided at any given moment.

The reality is that if we can't give them an informed estimate of the scope of this project based only on the summary they've provided so far, they may not be able to *afford* to let us move forward with a full analysis. They understand that we don't know enough to pinpoint our schedule, but we can certainly help them to differentiate a project that will take eighteen weeks from one that will take eighteen months.

The Right Size for this Job

The *Crisis•Call* project fits right in with my growing conviction that great software can be written by small teams. I approach team size with the strong bias that smaller is better. In any given project, there is always the opportunity for someone to prove that a larger team is required. To do so, however, they must show both that there is too much work for the project to be completed by a smaller team, and also that adding more people will actually get the job done on time. It is my experience that most projects are done most efficiently by very small groups of highly motivated people.

In this case, the project as initially conceptualized does not strike me as requiring all that much development. We have good reason to believe, based on Hypotenuse's experience in telephony and my understanding of the industry, that we can *buy* much of what we need, and we'll only code those aspects of the project that are unique to the needs of Hypotenuse. It is my preliminary estimate that, while I will need some help with the analysis and design, the actual implementation will be kept to one or two developers with support from Hypotenuse's Operations department.

The initial design team will negotiate and settle upon the interfaces between the various modules before the code is written. The interfaces will be narrow, well defined, and more or less immutable. At least, that's the theory. As we progress, we'll see how theory plays out in practice.

The days when a project could last two to three years are pretty much over. Such projects exist, and some take 100 developers, but among these it is the exception that ever gets finished. The fact is, with 3 developers you can build a first version of almost anything, and you can get it done a hell of a lot faster if you don't have to take up a large percentage of your available resources with managing (as opposed to implementing) the project.

This is a controversial opinion. In fact, I may be in the minority on this one, but the more I see of large and small projects, the more I'm convinced:

> **If you want to get something done, hire a few very bright folks, lock them up with the tools they need, and stay the hell out of the way.**

The First Schedule

The first schedule *must* be preliminary; after all, we don't know exactly what we're about to build. On the other hand, this schedule will take on a life of its own; and the project will forever be evaluated in terms of the promises we make today, so we want to think carefully about what we say. I propose the following general guidelines as a rough starting point:

Phase	Preliminary Completion
Conceptualization	December
Analysis	January
Design	February - March
Implementation	April - August
Alpha	September
Beta	October

At this point, I meet with Jay and explain my initial assumptions about team size and the overall schedule. He immediately embraces my suggestions, as they fit in well both with his own financial requirements and with his extensive experience managing the development of software projects. Jay is eager to have me manage my own time, turning to him only to explore and understand his vision of the end product. That said, delivery in this calendar year is obviously a high priority for him.

Conceptualization, Analysis and Design

The outcome of the conceptualization phase will be an understanding of the functional requirements of the system from the perspective of the business. We will identify how the system will be used, and we'll describe, but not detail, the customer interactions and screen designs (visualization). We will conclude the conceptualization phase by detailing how the system will be used and how it responds to requests and events. We'll create use cases to describe how the system is used, along with a full functional description.

The analysis phase uses the high-level conceptualization to formalize the exhaustive set of requirements. We will revisit the use cases, this time detailing the high-level objects in the system that respond to the user's requests. We'll also create both a dynamic and a static model of the system. In short, by the end of this phase, the requirements document will be complete and we will know what the principal objects are.

The design phase transforms the requirements into an **architecture** — a set of diagrams and decisions that enable a talented developer to render the concept in code. In the design phase, we'll identify all the classes and detail their interfaces. This phase is divided into high-level design, where we'll examine how the pieces fit together, and low-level design, which lets us take into account the actual platform and implementation technologies we'll use.

How the Initial Phases are Sequenced

These phases are not discrete. We can identify each activity and separate them in our minds, but in a healthy project the process is iterative and incremental. *Iterative* in that each phase is repeated as subsequent phases change the assumptions; *incremental* in that each phase builds upon the previous ones. Analysis lays the groundwork for design, design decisions impact analysis, and analysis, in turn, causes modifications to the design.

Booch methodology talks about **micro-cycles** — quick tight phases, in which you conceptualize and analyze part of the system and then design for that part. It would, in fact, be accurate to collapse the first three months into a single 'conceptualization-analysis-design' phase. We break these out to indicate that as we move through this time, the *emphasis* shifts; more of the time is spent on the detail level as we ready ourselves for implementation.

In a note to the OTUG (Object Technology User Group) mailing list, Robert C. Martin said, "The problem cannot truly be understood until the solution exists." What a great quote!

Here's what I think he meant: the process of solving the problem and designing the implementation helps refine not only *our* understanding of the problem, but the solution we provide helps *the customer* modify his own understanding of what he needs, and thus change the requirements. Seeing the solution modifies the customer's understanding of his own requirements — now that *is* a powerful idea.

I call this the Martin Uncertainty Principle — it suggests that the problem and its solution are always in motion with respect to one another. It is imperative to keep this in mind. What does it imply for the day to day plan? It says that we must keep the customer engaged and fully informed. The goal is to invite the customer into the process, so that his understanding of what he needs can evolve as our understanding of the solution solidifies.

Implementation, Alpha and Beta

Implementation is the longest phase, but it is at least partially constrained by the design created earlier in the process. As implementation proceeds, the design (and perhaps the analysis) will be modified; but we don't expect the class interfaces to change; they will remain immutable right up until the time it is stupid not to change them. And then we'll change them on the spot and figure out what went wrong.

During alpha testing, the code will be feature-complete and we'll concentrate on identifying and fixing bugs. When we believe the rate of finding bugs has dropped to a point where the gain from finding more overcomes the risk introduced by letting friendly users see the product, we'll subject the code to beta testing.

What I mean is, at some point we'll feel confident that any remaining bugs are unlikely to aggravate our friendly users, and we have a good chance that they will find the few remaining problems before we ship the product. In the case of Hypotenuse, we won't so much be 'shipping a product' as exposing an increasing number of people to interaction with the system, but the principle holds: only a limited number of folks will use the system until we are sure it is reliable and robust.

This risk-based perspective will drive all of the decisions as we go forward. Every decision will be evaluated against the alternatives to determine which presents the greater risk and which provides the greater benefit. A risk/benefit analysis is implicit in every decision, but it will be my job to articulate these trade-offs, so that the client can be clear about what he is getting and what he is paying.

As beta testing continues, the bar for fixing bugs will rise — that is, the bugs will have to be more significant to warrant the risk of changing the code. Once again, the risk of leaving the bug in will have to outweigh the risks of fixing the bug and thus introducing new problems or schedule slips, which bring their own risks.

Visions and Roles

Someone must own the *vision* of the product. This cannot be a committee; it must be a single individual. No great software has ever been created by committee; ultimately it is always one person with a clear and unwavering vision who delivers the next killer application. VisiCalc, 1-2-3, Word, Notes... each was owned by a single visionary. The visionary should participate in every meeting in the early days of the project; it is their job to keep the project moving forward.

At times, organizations want to build software, but the requirements are poorly understood. The company knows it needs *something*, but it's trying to solve a number of ill-defined problems. This is a recipe for disaster in software development. The job of the software architect in such a situation is to refuse to rush to design until the problem has been clearly articulated. As a purely practical matter, you will never know for sure if your product is a success unless everyone agrees on what you were trying to accomplish in the first place.

There has been great discussion over recent years about what you call the person responsible for the overall design of the software. Some people call this person a software analyst, a designer, or a systems analyst. I tend to use the term 'software architect', as it evokes the right metaphor — it's the person responsible for creating the structure and integrity of the software.

In every project there is a single product visionary and a single software architect. Each may have other people providing expert advice and guidance, but someone must own the vision and someone must own the software.

In very large projects the visionary may draw upon the help of a number of technical experts who will provide guidance when thinking through how the product will be used. Typically, these domain experts will work for the visionary, but it is the visionary who will own responsibility for the direction and overall quality of the product. The experts will provide testimony, but the visionary will provide leadership.

In a similar way, the software architect may have a number of software analysts and designers who make significant, perhaps even majority contributions to the project, but ultimately the design and implementation of the software must be 'owned' by a single individual. This level of accountability is essential to ensure that the product will be delivered on time and to the client's specification.

In our case, Jay Leve owns the vision in its totality. He has had it in his head for ten years, he knows exactly what he wants, and my job as architect is to get it down on paper and to flesh out the details. But the devil is in the details.

Jay has a clear picture of much of the project, but there are some things he hasn't thought through fully. I will work hard to force these issues to the front *before* they become a problem. Customers invariably focus on those parts of the project that are essential to their business model, and ignore everything else. That is fine and good, but it's important to help them think about all the tiny little rat's nests they might otherwise pass over with a hand wave. When the customer says, "So, we'll find out who the customer wants to call *<hand wave, hand wave>*, and then when he wants to make the calls *<hand wave, hand wave>*, and then we'll just make the calls *<hand wave, hand wave>*," alarm bells better go off. Who we call? When we call? How we call? These are probably pretty complex issues, and we'd better nail them down early in the process.

Once I know what we need to build, it's my job to reset the schedule, guide the analysis and design, lead the implementation, and deliver the product on time and within budget. On a larger project, some of this would be done by a technical manager. As you can imagine, the relationship between the technical manager and the architect can be complicated if they don't know and trust each other well. Any project larger than a few developers requires these roles to be carried out by different people; it quickly becomes impossible for one person to do both well at the same time. This is another advantage of a very small team: the architect *is* the project manager, as well as the lead developer.

The Role of QA

A Quality Assurance engineer should be in the room for the first meeting. Too often QA is isolated; at the end of development they are given a finished requirements document and a body of code, and are expected to certify that the code meets the requirements. Testing at that point is expensive and often inadequate; more importantly it often misses the larger picture of whether the code does what the client intended it to do.

That isn't to say that there's no role for such testing. Once we believe the product is solid, it makes all the sense in the world to give it to a QA engineer who has *not* been part of the process to see if it does what we think it does. Such an independent observer is more likely to be objective and less likely to bring preconceptions to the testing.

Testing must be an integral part of the design and development, so problems can be identified early. Study after study has demonstrated that the earlier in the life cycle of the project you catch a bug, the easier it is to fix. The overhead of forcing a developer to go back and fix a bug caught months after he wrote that section of code can be crippling; far better to have the developer and tester working together from the start.

This is a place where *larger* projects have a huge advantage. When you have fifty developers on a project, it's a relatively small additional expense to assign a full-time QA person to the team. In a smaller project such as this one, we can ill afford to keep a QA person in the room for the whole nine months of the project.

On the other hand, we know that Operations will need to test and accept the code when it is completed, so we *can* keep the VP of Operations in the room. Further, my wife (and the Vice President of Liberty Associates), Stacey Liberty, has ten years of quality assurance expertise, and Jay asks that she stay at least marginally aware of developments as we move forward.

Who Designs the Interface?

I've never met a developer who wasn't convinced he could do an excellent job designing the user interface, and I've never met one who actually *could*. The presence of an interface design specialist during the analysis and design phase can make the difference between creating an adequate product and shipping a killer application.

Once again, with a smaller team we need to be quick on our feet. Just as Liberty Associates will provide the QA for *Crisis•Call*, Jay himself will provide the UI requirements for now. Jay was the Vice President in charge of the human factors group at Citibank, and is well qualified to serve in this role. Later, when we are ready to design screens, we may want to add a graphic artist.

What do you do if you don't happen to be a user interface expert? As with any good object-oriented design, your first approach is to encapsulate the risk. To the extent you can design your interface separately and independently from your code, you have a better chance of fixing one without breaking the other.

That said, sooner or later you may want to bring in professional expertise. This presents a problem. There are a lot of folks offering UI expertise, but few of them are very good at it. Even more than software and business expertise, creating a great user interface is more of an art than a science. You will want to make sure you know who you are dealing with, and you will of course want to see a full portfolio before even considering bringing someone into your project.

First Meetings

The core analysis team will consist of five people:

- Myself, acting as system architect
- Jay, the customer and owner of Hypotenuse
- Kevin, the head of Operations at Hypotenuse
- Steve Rogers and Glenn Clarkson, working for me as OOA&D experts

Before this first team meeting begins, I distribute the preliminary conceptualization and an initial schedule. It's time to sit down together to finalize the conceptualization.

The very first step is to document the concept — what the system will do, and what it won't do. We want to make sure we are all in agreement about what we'll be providing. Further, we want to *identify,* but not detail, the use cases; we are laying the groundwork for the formal analysis phase. In turn, the analysis phase will culminate in a suite of documents that will constitute the complete requirements documentation, and lead us cleanly into design.

We begin our first meeting in Jay's office at Hypotenuse at 9:30 in the morning of December 1. I begin with a review of the schedule. Hypotenuse wants this product in the market by next fall. I love natural boundaries. Seasons, rivers, mountains — they all provide a nice solid wall against which I can throw a schedule.

It isn't a coincidence that St Louis has its border at the Mississippi River; natural boundaries have enormous psychological impact, and you ignore them at your peril. We'll divide our work on seasonal boundaries: design in the winter, implementation in the spring and summer, delivery in the fall. It's arbitrary, of course, but it fits with our general guidelines, and it makes it easy for the client and for us to keep an eye on our progress.

Fleshing Out the Conceptualization

It's time to flesh out the initial idea for *Crisis•Call*. We start with this straw-man summary of what we'll build:

> *Crisis•Call* will be an integrated, modular, reliable, secure, scaleable, flexible system to allow Hypotenuse to call any number of phone numbers on behalf of any number of customers, at a moment's notice, and to track the results of and provide reports on these calls.

The Phases of Calling

Jay thinks about calling in four stages:

- Customer sign-up
- Preproduction
- Production
- Post-production

Customer sign-up is the entire process of adding a new customer to the system. At this stage we need to learn a bit about who they think they might be calling, when they might call, and so forth. We also need to get whatever information we'll need to handle billing.

Preproduction is the time when the customer tells us to start calling for any particular job. At this point they must supply both audio and a list of people to call. When they give us audio, a schedule and list of people to call, they've created a **job**.

Audio may be shared from job to job, or it may be different for each job. Similarly, it is possible that a customer will reuse their phone list from job to job, or that each job will mean calling a new list of recipients.

Production is the time when we actually make the calls. We can anticipate initially having 500 to 1500 telephone lines available for outbound calls, but the system must be able to scale well beyond that.

We must balance the load, manage the priorities so that important, time critical calls go out first, and we must capture the user's responses, if any. We broadly differentiate between *Crisis•Calls*, which, by definition, go out immediately, and *Flash•Calls*, which go out at a scheduled time.

An example of a *Flash•Call* might be a school calling parents to notify them of a Snow Day closing, or CNN calling particular viewers (who have asked to receive these calls) to alert them that a particular guest is going to appear on air. An example of a *Crisis•Call* would be calling everyone within 5 miles of a nuclear power plant and telling them to evacuate the area.

Finally, **post-production** encompasses all the reporting we'll do on the calls we've made. We can anticipate two types of reports: pre-canned standardized reports, and dynamic reports. Further, there are two audiences for these reports: Hypotenuse's clients who want to know which of their customers were contacted, and Hypotenuse's management, which needs to know how effectively the system is being used.

Perishable Data

Jay points out, again and again, that in essence this is a very simple business. It is the transmission of valuable but perishable information. One person has information that has high value to another, but the value diminishes greatly over time. It is the job of Hypotenuse in general, and *Crisis•Call* in particular, to deliver that data from the source to the recipient while it is still fresh. It is imperative to realize that data can 'spoil' in a matter of minutes.

Calling vs. Polling

When Jay founded Hypotenuse in September 1990, he imagined calling tens or hundreds of thousands of customers to deliver timely information. In 1992, he found he was able to use his technology to conduct public opinion polls in response to breaking news, and have the results air on television on the same day. This is a highly successful business model that has made Hypotenuse one of the largest public opinion polling companies in the world. On the other hand, there are only so many television stations out there. Jay wants now to return to his fundamental premises about calling. Fortunately, calling is simpler than polling.

Jay identifies this difference in our earliest meeting:

> "In a call, you wait for the person to answer the phone. You *may* then ask that person to identify himself, either by pressing 1 (to indicate that a person, not a machine, has answered) or by entering a password (to ensure you have the right recipient). You can imagine the latter like this: the phone rings, someone answers and they hear a voice saying, "This is *Crisis•Call*. Please ask the Indian Point Power Plant employee to come to the phone. If you are that employee, press 1. If you will get the employee, press 2. If the employee is not available, press 3." This repeats until you get a 1, 2 or 3, or the person hangs up, or we time out. When you get a 1, you say, "Please identify yourself by entering your password and then press pound," or whatever.

> That is the most interaction there is in calling. In fact, in the simplest case, there isn't even that much — just call the phone, wait for an answer, play the message and then hang up.

> But polling is different. Polling is, first of all, a much more complicated interaction on the phone. You must qualify the user, like asking if the user is an adult. You must also filter out the right segment, like asking if they are a

registered Democrat. Sometimes your call flow branches based on their answers. If they are pro-death penalty then you might ask if they would apply the death penalty in cases of rape, but if they are anti-death penalty you never get to that question. Finally, you must 'balance' the result set so that you are sure you are getting a representative sample of the population.

Calling is much simpler: you just call, play the message, hang up and move on. As such, I'd expect the program to manage calling to be all the simpler as well."

This is the magic and the danger of this enterprise. The customer, Jay, envisions something quite simple. How hard can it be? Why would it take so long? I stand warned — my customer thinks that what he wants is easy.

The good news is that the vision is clear in his head. There are details to uncover, but a motivated, excited client with a clear idea of what he wants is always a wonderful thing. I can manage his expectations as we go along, but I'd far rather work with someone who knows what it is he wants, than try to build software for someone who has only a vague understanding of his product and a hunger for quick profit.

Hypotenuse's Software

So if Hypotenuse is already making hundreds of thousands of calls to support polling, how are they doing it? With commercial strength, but not *industrial* strength code. Their existing software runs on DOS. The original programmer wrote his own multitasking and networking layers to support the production-level software, and the preproduction, sign-up and post-production software either don't exist or are independent of, and not integrated with, the production software. In short, they're getting it done, but sub-optimally.

Not unlike many other projects, *Crisis•Call* will be written not only in the shadow of the existing software, but in many ways in reaction to it. In the earliest meetings, Jay's description of what he needs is often framed in terms of what he already has. In Jay's eyes, this is very much Version 2.

Version 1 was written in 1992. The world has changed since then. Hypotenuse is now eager to use industry standard solutions to multitasking, networking and telephony. This is smart; leveraging the work of others both reduces the development time and reduces the risks involved in the project. In addition, using industry standard solutions allows Hypotenuse to transfer the cost and effort of maintaining large aspects of the system to the vendor. If we use Microsoft's networking solution, then *they* maintain that software, rather than Hypotenuse having to keep it current. This holds down long-term maintenance costs over and above the initial development costs. We have many more options today than in 1992, and part of the design process will be understanding and choosing among an embarrassment of riches.

While we don't know what the platform will be for the final product, it is clear from the outset that it must provide native support for multithreaded applications, that the networking software must be independent of the application, and that the database layer must be fully abstracted out so that we can swap in new databases as needs and competitive advantages change over time.

Okay, this is a lie. We don't *know* what the platform will be, but there are only two realistic candidates: UNIX and NT. UNIX is the telephony industry standard, and it offers a well-established, hearty and robust environment. No one ever gets fired in telephony for choosing UNIX.

NT offers a better set of tools and also offers the Microsoft muscle. Microsoft has made a big commitment to Internet and telephony development, and they are the big guns in software development. Going where they go may be a lot easier than blazing our own trail.

On a more practical note, it has been five years since I developed for UNIX, and I'm more comfortable with NT. Oh, did I just say that out loud? Most of us never admit that we choose our tools from those with which we're most comfortable, but it is the reality of software development — and why not? If we already know the tool, we'll save all that learning time, and we'll be that much more productive.

Of course, it would be a mistake always to choose the same tool no matter what the problem; clearly, some problems are better solved with specialized tools. On the other hand, it would also be a mistake to ignore your existing skill set; after all, why not leverage your invested experience? NT clearly has the inside track, but I endeavor to keep an open mind. An open mind, however, is not necessarily an empty one.

Jay stated on the first day that the project must be fully documented. He set as a requirement that any experienced, intelligent programmer should be able to come into the company and, using only the documentation, be up and running and ready to maintain the code in a week. This strikes me as entirely reasonable. He is a bit fervent about it, based on his prior experiences, but that is understandable.

The amount of documentation appropriate to a given project is a product of many factors. Chief among these is the number of developers who will need to write or maintain the system. At a minimum, this project will need a requirements document, an overall architecture document and a guide to the source code. Given Hypotenuse's sensitivity on these issues, we may well decide to flesh out these documents a bit more than we would otherwise do for a product of this scope.

This book will serve as extraordinary documentation; you may not always want to go quite this far.

Understanding the Use Case Model

We anticipate that customers might use *Crisis•Call* in a number of different ways. Understanding these will help us both in creating the preliminary requirements, and in creating the use cases. While it is tempting to build the functional requirements document on the strength of Jay's instincts about the project, it will help me to get a handle on what we are building if I can understand in some detail how the customers and staff will interact with it.

Thus, before beginning even a high-level functional requirements document, we take the time to work up use cases. A **use case** is a description of an interaction between an **actor** and a **system**. At this stage, we don't care how the system works, and we treat it as a black box — the actor sends messages and the system responds.

In this context, an actor is anyone or anything that interacts with the system. Thus, the customer, the administrative assistant, the salesperson, and the owner's accounting system are all candidate actors.

Use cases describe the interaction between a particular actor and the system, surrounding a single event. For example, our first use case might be, "The customer initiates a job," where a job is a set of outbound calls. This might give rise to further use cases where the customer calls into the system, picks out the list of people he wants to call, records audio, and tells the system the calling parameters, such as when to start calling and the acceptable hours of the day to make the calls.

When creating use cases, the first question that arises is, "What is the appropriate level of detail?" For example, which of these is best:

- The customer starts a job
- The customer calls in, chooses phone numbers and audio, sets the date and time and other calling criteria, and starts a job
- The customer calls in, chooses his list of managers and his inspirational sales audio, sets the system to start calling on Monday between the hours of 9 a.m. and 4 p.m., and starts the job

I'd suggest that the second use case hits the right granularity. We don't expect to design the system to handle calls on Monday differently from calls on Tuesday, so the level of detail in case three is just a distraction. On the other hand, fleshing out some of the details of a particular use case can help uncover hidden details in the requirements, so the first use case is too vague.

We start with a brainstorming session. A number of years ago, I took a three-day course on Synectics. Synectics was a technique for generating and nurturing ideas; it was targeted at marketing professionals who wanted help with thinking through business proposals. One of the techniques I liked was that at the early stage, ideas were generated but not commented on. The goal was to give the idea time to flower before examining it too closely.

This applies well to the brainstorming of use cases. Each participant articulates a use case and we write it on the whiteboard. We don't edit the list, we don't even comment on each proposal; we start by writing them all down. If it turns out that there are duplicates or marginal suggestions, we can eliminate those after we have the list.

Our preliminary set of use cases looks like this:

1. A potential customer calls and talks with a salesperson to gather more information

2. In a sales conversation with a salesperson, the customer decides to sign up

3. A potential customer logs in to the Internet to sign up

4. A potential customer calls into our phone mail system to sign up

5. The potential customer needs more information or clarification

6. An existing customer calls in, chooses phone numbers and audio, sets the date and time and other calling criteria and starts a job

7. An existing customer prerecords audio for future use

8. A customer uploads a set of phone numbers for use with an upcoming job he has already scheduled

9. A customer calls in to cancel a job scheduled for the next day

10. A customer calls in an emergency cancellation of a job already in progress

11. A customer calls in a crisis call. The audio and phone list have already been selected, the calls are to begin instantly.

12. A customer has scheduled a job to begin now, but the audio is not yet available

13. A customer needs to send us phone numbers but doesn't have access to the Internet, so he sends a list on a disk via Federal Express

14. A customer needs a detailed report of everyone called, differentiating between those who answered, those where a message was left on an answering machine and those that couldn't be reached at all.

15. The owner wants to know whether he has enough lines to handle every emergency

16. Operations wants to be certain the system is secure

17. Operations wants proof the system is reliable

18. The manager of Sales wants to know if he can sell a job calling 250,000 people in the first week of May.

19. A customer wants to deliver one message to registered Democrats and a different message to everyone else on his list

20. A customer wants to offer the recipient of his call the opportunity to bridge the line to someone else

21. We place a call and get a person on the line and play the appropriate messages

22. We place a call and get a machine and play the appropriate messages

23. We place a call and think it is a person but it is a machine

24. We place a call and think it is a machine, but it is a person

25. We place a call and get a busy signal

26. We place a call and get an operator intercept for a number no longer in service

27. We place a call and get a ring but no answer

28. A call recipient returns our call and asks never to be called again

These use cases are not exhaustive, but they give us a starting point on describing the kinds of interactions we need to plan for. Representing them in diagrams will help us to flesh out the interaction and capture it in a way we can refer to and discuss.

We begin by focusing on what the customer wants to do with the system. Use cases 1 to 4 imply a customer will want to 'sign up', use cases 6 to 13 involve managing jobs, and use case 14 indicates that the customer wants to get reports out of the system (the remaining use cases describe other aspects of the system). All of these top-level needs are captured and summarized here.

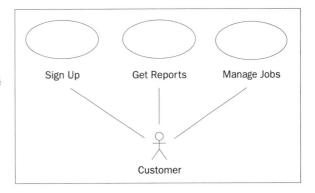

This simple diagram illustrates the principal interactions and keeps us grounded in our understanding of the customer's primary uses of the system.

Creating the Context Diagram

The next thing we can extract from this list is that the primary actors who will interact with the system are the customer, the administrative assistant, the salesman and the owner. While these roles are not precisely defined yet, we know what we mean to a workable approximation, and they serve to help us to understand the interactions.

Capturing this relationship in a context diagram lays the foundation for the work to come. In the original Booch notation, both the system and the actors were represented as clouds:

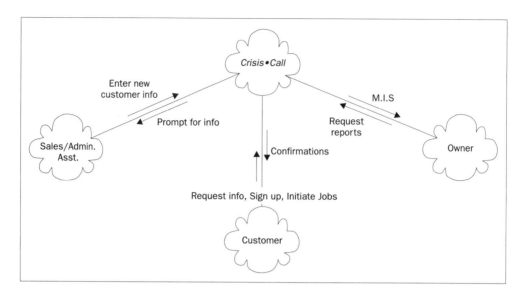

The lines between the clouds represent relationships; the arrows indicate significant messages between the actors and the system. Thus, when the customer asks the system to provide information and to sign him up, the system comes back with a confirmation, such as an account number. The customer initiates a job (calling a set of numbers, playing a specific audio), and the system issues a confirmation number.

In the same way, the salesman or the administrative assistant may sign up a new customer, and the system will prompt for the required information and confirm the new account. The owner might request reports on usage, and the system will reply with the correct reports.

There is a lot of detail not shown in this diagram, but the essential relationships between the actors and the system have been established. Most important, the distinction between what is *in* the system, and what is an actor interacting *with* the system is shown.

Here is the same diagram in UML notation:

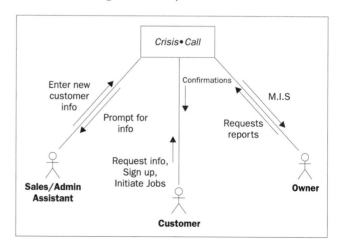

Note that we've captured the same information, but the notation better distinguishes between objects (rectangles) and actors (stick figures). I lament the loss of the clouds — *Rectangles to Code* isn't quite as snappy a title — but otherwise believe the new notation is superior. If nothing else, rectangles are easier to draw. Throughout the rest of the book I'll use the UML notation, except where the Booch or OMT notation is superior, in which case I'll show both.

Use Case Scenarios

Each of these use cases can be described in more detail. An anecdotal telling of how such a use case might play itself out is a **use case scenario**. We start by creating a few scenarios based on a single use case:

> An existing customer calls in, chooses phone numbers and audio, sets the date and time and other calling criteria and starts a job.

One scenario that we may be able to build on this use case is:

> The customer is Edison Electric. They have to plan for emergencies at their nuclear power facility, which might include the need to call in all their managers and support personnel. In this event they want to call the right houses, but ensure that only the right person receives the message and that they know who got the message and who didn't. When the request comes in, the system must fulfill it immediately. By its nature, this will be an unplanned and unscheduled event.

There is actually a series of interactions implied by this use case. First, there are the interactions associated with setting up the lists, audio and calling parameters. Second is the initiation of the sequence in the event of an actual emergency. Third is the interaction between the system and the recipient of the call. Last comes the return of the report on who was called and the outcome of these calls.

We can create a **message trace** or **sequence diagram** to capture these interactions:

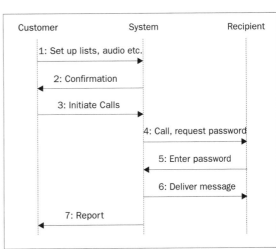

We continue to add to our collection of use cases, building examples that describe all the interactions between the actors and the system. At this point we are not decomposing the system into objects; later we'll revisit these use cases and determine the high-level objects, but for now we're simply examining how the system is *used*, and how it is required to respond.

We try to work methodically through the use cases, making sure we examine those that are sufficiently different from one another to reveal all the interesting interactions with the system. In fact, most of the interactions at this level are pretty straightforward. Putting them into message trace diagrams clarifies the sequence of events and helps tease out the details of how the actors will interact with *Crisis•Call.*

Creating a Requirements Document

As the concept of *Crisis•Call* becomes clearer, and as we get a better handle on how the actors will use the system, it is time to start documenting the preliminary requirements. We start with *functional* requirements — that is, what the system must be able to do, not how it will do it.

How big is a requirements document? What is in it, and how is it organized? I don't have an ironclad rule. For some projects, it's a formal document complete with **visualizations** — pictures of what the product will look like. For others, it consists of a series of notes and some sketches. In a large project, I'll often ask someone to take ownership of the functional specification and keep it up to date. I've seen projects large enough that just maintaining the documentation was the full-time job of a small team. Most often, the ideal person to take charge of the requirements document is the QA team member.

Writing a good specification is hard work. Doing it well, so that a developer can work from the specification without ambiguity is a special skill that is not easily acquired. A good specification is complete: it not only tells you what the product does, but also details how the product will react to any stimulus — what happens when the user clicks, changes, edits, presses, connects, disconnects and so forth.

As the developer writing the code, the specification ought to leave me in no doubt about what it is I'm to create.

Requirements at Interchange

At Interchange, our requirements document was 250 pages long. It went through eight full revisions (and hundreds of minor revisions) in four years. I have picked an example more or less at random from a section of the specification that I was responsible for implementing. This is not an especially complicated section, but it does give a flavor of the level of detail provided.

This section describes how Interchange determines the domain of a search. That is, when a user presses FIND, what area of the service is searched? Note that this is just a small section of a much larger description of the 'Find' dialog itself. This particular section merely explains what goes in the 'Domain' drop down (a drop down in the lower right hand section of the Find dialog). I quote at length to give you a sense of the level of detail that a specification might include.

The find dialog also includes a drop-down list allowing you to change the **domain** of the search. The drop-down lists some or all of the following five entries, as appropriate, in the reverse of the following order:

1. The selected item or items that are service folders, sections or discussions — in short, those that can contain other items. If one item is selected, the drop-down entry will display the title of the item; with multiple items selected, it becomes "n selected items." If no items are selected, this entry is not present in the drop-down list.

2. The window that was active when you initiated the find...command — it is a section highlights window, service-folder browser or discussion. If a section highlights window is the active window and you choose its entry from this drop-down the search receives as its domain the entire section associated with the highlights window.

3. The service folder in the context of which the current item was opened. This is defined in the following fashion: if the active window contains active Previous and Next buttons, this domain entry contains the name of the folder over which they operate. If the active window doesn't contain Previous and Next buttons, if these buttons are inactive (which they might be if the item in question was opened from a highlights page or an embedded link) or if the current item was opened from a user folder, this entry in the domain drop-down list is skipped.

4. The section that the item being viewed in the active window belongs to. If this entry already appears in the domain drop-down by virtue of one of the previous entries, Interchange does not repeat it.

5. The directory that the aforementioned section belongs to. If this entry already appears in the domain drop-down by virtue of one of the previous entries, Interchange does not repeat it (This is the only entry that is <u>always</u> present; if the Directory window is active and no items are selected, clicking Find brings up a Find dialog whose domain drop-down includes only this entry).

If multiple items are selected, the default domain is the selected item and their content (the first entry above). When one item or no items are selected, the drop-down defaults to the second entry above the window that was active when you executed Find. If that entry isn't available (if the active window contains an article, for example) then the default becomes the highest choice in the above list that is available.

If any of these domain entries would refer to items only available locally (such as the Inbox or any of its system folders, the customer Directory, user-created folders, any item in Archives and so forth) that domain is skipped. If doing so excludes all possible domains from the drop-down list, Interchange presents you with an error message.

If a section highlights window is active, and you select two of its index folders and then begin a search, the domain drop-down includes: the selected index folders; the section itself; and the directory that contains that section. If while browsing a folder of discussions, you select one discussion within it, the domain options resulting from beginning a search consist of: the selected discussion; the active window; the section that contains it, and the directory containing that section (In both of these cases, the list is actually presented in the reverse order: the most general information — the directory involved — goes at the top of the drop-down list, and the most specific — the selected item or items — goes at the bottom).

If you use this drop-down to change your domain, the query manager used in he Find dialog changes appropriately. This guarantees that your choice of attributes is always accurate relative to the current search domain. When the header of a folder is brought to the local machine, its query manager accompanies it, thus ensuring that the appropriate query manager can always be found locally. If by some chance a folder's query manager is missing, the folder in question may be treated as if it were remote — or the folder may be considered local but does not allow a search to be conducted on it. *Developer note: whichever of these two is easier to implement is fine.*

You can change the domain via the drop-down even after you have selected attributes and entered values to search for; if this is the case, those attributes not included in the new query manager are immediately removed from the Find dialog. These attributes are retained in memory so that if you switch back to the previous domain before executing or canceling the search, as many of them as can fit are restored within the dialog.

As you can see, the specification leaves nothing to chance; every detail is specified. This functional specification was the collective wisdom of a large design team, and was the road map for an even larger development team.

You Don't Need it All at Once

The specification for *Crisis•Call* will start out fairly simple. To get a handle on the functional specification for *Crisis•Call*, we subdivide the calling process into four principal stages: account sign-up, preproduction, production, and post-production. In addition, the requirements document must capture the needs of Operations, Management and Sales.

It is not necessary to get every conceivable feature into the requirements document before you begin the design phase. As we proceed we'll flesh out the requirements. In all likelihood, the requirements will evolve as we learn more.

Crisis-Call Account Sign-up Functional Requirements

At the time a new customer signs up for the service, we will record their first and last name, address, phone numbers, fax numbers and so forth. We will also 'validate' the user to make sure that we can legally make phone calls on their behalf.

There are strict regulations on outgoing calls. By federal law, if a customer of Hypotenuse wants to use Hypotenuse's technology to make fully automated calls, the customer must be able to certify that they have a pre-existing relationship with the people to be called. They can not make 'cold calls' to potential customers; they must be calling existing clients, or members of their club or organization. In short, the customer must have a demonstrable existing relationship with the recipients of the call. If it weren't for this legislation, everyone's phone would be ringing night and day with unsolicited advertising. Hypotenuse does *not* use its technology to do so-called 'telemarketing'.

At the time a customer signs up, they will also tell us how they are going to pay for the service. There are three models we'll want to explore as we go forward with the system:

- Credit card customers. For smaller accounts this may be realistic.
- Payment in advance, purchase orders, and so forth.
- Payment via phone bill.

This last option will require more research, but the new telecommunications bill allows vendors, under certain circumstances, to have their bill included with the customer's local phone bill. This is a powerful and attractive option, as it enlists the local phone company in the collections process.

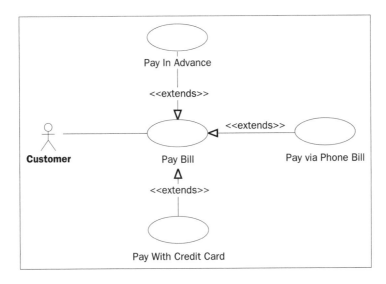

Jay anticipates allowing the user to sign up in a number of ways. Here is a classic analysis dilemma. On the one hand, the methodology dictates that it is too early to consider these issues in detail. On the other hand, telling the client to wait until we get to that stage of analysis is a losing battle. First, it convinces your client that you're overly focused on a theoretical process and not sufficiently focused on his problem. Second, when you tell someone to 'hold that thought', they do — to the exclusion of all other thinking. It is much better to get it out, write it down and then come back to it at the right time.

Some people may sign up to become a customer by calling in to Hypotenuse and speaking with one of the salespeople. The sales staff will need access to the system from their desktops, and the system will have to ensure that all of the right data is collected.

Jay anticipates that other potential customers will sign up over the Internet. He envisions a form they might fill out at Hypotenuse's web site.

Finally, it may be possible for customers to sign up over the telephone. The technology for interacting with a customer over the telephone is variously called IVR (Interactive Voice Response) or Audiotex. By any name, this is the familiar phone-mail menu system, "To learn more about *Crisis•Call*, press 1. To sign up to become a customer, press 2."

Jay anticipates asking the customer to predict his usage of *Crisis•Call* at the time he becomes a customer. We might ask questions like, "How many different sets of people might you call?" Some customers will answer one, some will answer a few, and some will call dozens or even hundreds of different lists of people.

We'll want to go on to ask how many numbers might be in each list, when the list might be called (for example, only in emergencies, weekly, monthly and so forth) and when these calls might be initiated (unpredictable, weekends, workdays, summer only, etc.)

Load Management

All of this is to help Hypotenuse plan for its peak-load management. This is a significant topic, and one to which we will return many times over the course of the project. Hypotenuse will always have a finite number of phone lines, and its ability to fulfill the customer's expectations will most often be limited by the number of calls Hypotenuse can generate in any given period of time.

A restaurant typically finds that it is crowded during the lunch hours and dinner hours, and much less crowded at other times of the day. They must staff accordingly, making sure they have enough waiters for the afternoon rush, even if that means some waiters will sit around idle during some hours of the day. They must have enough tables to handle the dinner demand as well (remember what Yogi Berra said: "Nobody goes there no more. It's too crowded."). However, they don't want those tables sitting empty for much of the day, because they represent an expense.

Hypotenuse's problem is not dissimilar. They want to be sure to have enough phone lines that the sales force never has to turn down a job, and so that they can always handle their emergency calls, but not so many that the phone lines are sitting unused. Phone lines are leased, and every unused minute represents unrecoverable costs. *Unlike* a restaurant, however, if Hypotenuse needs to expand its capacity, it can do so fairly easily. While a restaurant might have to break through walls or even move to a new location if it wants to double the number of customers it can seat at dinner, Hypotenuse can bring in twice as many phone lines with just a few weeks' notice.

In one sense, this issue of how Hypotenuse will handle its peak load is similar to issues faced by every software project. Virtually all software is used unevenly throughout the day, or from day to day. It is a common mistake to design either for the minimal load case or for the peak load case, but optimizing for either of these extremes can be an expensive error. The goal in the analysis phase is to determine what the distribution of load will be, and to make the necessary design tradeoffs to ensure that the 90% case will be optimized, but that the software won't break under heavy load. To determine the distribution of load, we will look at our use cases — they will help us get a fix on how the system will be used, and that will tell us what we need. During preliminary testing we'll revisit these assumptions based on real-world experience.

Preproduction Functional Requirements

In the preproduction phase, the customer initiates a job. A job is defined as a set of calls to a list of phone numbers, all of which share a common **call flow** (interaction with the customer) and use the same audio. A job may start and stop over the course of a number of days, but it is continuous over time. That is, while we may suspend a job between, for example, 10pm and 10am, we immediately resume when the calling window reopens.

Preproduction begins when an *existing* customer contacts Hypotenuse with the intention of scheduling a job, and ends when we begin calling. Thus, preproduction includes the tasks of generating a job ID, asking the customer for a list of numbers to call, recording audio and detailing the call flow. Finally, preproduction ends by scheduling the new job and verifying that the system can handle the load given all the existing commitments.

Detailing the call flow includes telling us if we must ask for a key press to distinguish a person from a machine. In other cases, we must ask for a password; in still others, we just play the message when the phone goes off hook.

Scheduling the job includes telling us the start time and end time (when we say 'time' we always mean date and time) and the calling constraints (e.g. call only between 9 a.m. and 5 p.m. local time).

Jay imagines preproduction will be accomplished using IVR, the Internet, or both. Sending us phone numbers will of course be easier using the Internet than using the telephone. Conversely, recording audio is probably much easier using IVR. Most customers will want to take advantage of both, recording the audio using IVR but sending us phone numbers and scheduling the job over the Internet.

Preproduction, by its nature, involves the customer calling *in* to Hypotenuse. Thus, the system must be able to answer the phone and interact with the customer appropriately. Further, if the customer is to contact us via the Internet, we have to assume a home page on the Web, and all the security implications that brings with it.

Production Functional Requirements

The production system needs to be able to call any number of recipients reliably. Hypotenuse currently has over 500 phone lines available and we anticipate scaling this up to more than 1500 in the first 18 months. To get us started, however, we're figuring on supporting 288 lines via 12 T1 connections.

T1 connections provide digital telephone access. Each T1 connection provides 24 'time slices' or virtual lines. Thus, 12 T1s provide 288 virtual phone lines. For version 1.0 we must support 12 T1s, active simultaneously, handling both inbound and outbound calls. During the analysis phase we must also establish the likely scale for the system. In the next six months, will we grow to 24, 48, 96 or 144?

Continuing with the requirements, Jay points out that the production system must know exactly who has been called at any given moment. In the event of a system crash, we must be able to resume where we left off, neither missing any calls nor duplicating calls already delivered.

Further, the production system must be able to call back to recipients whose phones didn't answer or were busy. We'll want to do this in an intelligent way, backing off the recall schedule as we try repeatedly, calling busy numbers more frequently, and waiting longer to retry those numbers which are not answered. In any case, we do not want to spend all our time trying to reach someone who isn't home, while failing to try others for even the first time.

In addition, we can anticipate that we'll need a number of different calling computers, each managing a subset of the outgoing lines. These lines must be coordinated so that we can arbitrarily spread our calls out across the system, as demand requires. The current Hypotenuse software can't do this, so if calls are made on a machine with 48 lines, they can be in the position of having one job of ten thousand calls stacked up waiting for a single block of 48 lines, while another 300 lines remain idle.

In addition, the system will often be juggling any number of different jobs with different priorities, and while we may not want to starve medium priority jobs of access to the phone lines, we must ensure that high priority jobs are getting out as quickly as possible.

Jay anticipates offering at least two levels of service. For now we are thinking of these as *Crisis•Calls* and *Flash•Calls*. *Crisis•Calls* must go out instantly, while *Flash•Calls* come in a variety of price brackets depending on how quickly the customer requires that the calls be made.

Each of these priorities is priced appropriately. Jay points out that FedEx now sells second day delivery. Often, if they are not too busy, your second day package will be there in one day, but FedEx has bought itself the flexibility to manage its peak loads by pushing some packages off a day. They buy this flexibility by offering a discount to those customers who don't absolutely, positively *need* it there the next day.

The airlines have taken this idea to its logical conclusion. They are so aware of the load on their system overall, that at any moment they can determine the fair market price of a particular seat on a particular flight. Thus, they may discount a seat either because it is bought well in advance (helping them with their planning) or because it is bought at the very last minute and would otherwise go empty.

Each of these models has its analogy in how we will, eventually, want to manage the load on the Hypotenuse calling system. For version 1.0, however, peak load management will probably be managed by purchasing so many phone lines that we are never near the practical limit.

Post-production Functional Requirements

There are two types of report that the system will be required to provide. One is management information needed by Jay and the sales force and directors of Hypotenuse. This is covered later under the headings of *Sales & Marketing Requirements* and also *Management Requirements*.

A second set of reports will be provided to the customer. These will detail or summarize the calls made on any particular job. Typically these will include aggregated or detailed information about each attempted call: whether it was answered, whether we detected a human or a machine, how many retries were attempted, and so forth. These reports can include the times we called and the duration of the call.

If the call flow requires feedback from the customer, this can be captured in the report as well. Further, the report can be sorted by phone number, recipient name (if we have that), time and date or success type.

We can imagine any number of reports the customer might like, but for version one we expect to provide only a limited number of canned reports. The design must anticipate, however, that over time our customers will have access to dynamic reports, which we will supply over the Internet.

Operations Functional Requirements

The Operations department is responsible for keeping everything going. They are particularly sensitive to 24x7 availability and reliability as well as security.

Given the literal life-and-death nature of some of the calls Hypotenuse anticipates being responsible for, the Operations department needs to set realistic yet aggressive requirements for availability. In addition, they will need a plan for disaster recovery, which includes the ability to be back in business quickly in the event of any anticipated (or unanticipated) loss of service.

These disasters include the server or database crashing, the phone lines crashing, a fire, an earthquake or some other natural (or unnatural) disaster. Depending on who the clients are, and what they require from Hypotenuse in the way of guarantees, we may want to have fault tolerant systems, backup systems, or even a 100% replicated system offsite.

Operations needs to query the system at any given time to determine the current status of the system, receive reports on what is in progress, find out the load on the machines, line usage and so forth. In addition, there are summary and detail reports that Operations will need in order to make recommendations to management. These might detail the usage of the system over time, showing the mean, high, and low usage points and the distribution from the mean.

In our early meetings I ask Operations to start thinking about what they'll require from the system and what reports they'll need. Once we understand the functional requirements from the customer's viewpoint and the managerial requirements, we'll want to be sure to spend a lot of time reviewing the operational needs as well.

There's Nothing New Under the Sun

These considerations are not unique to Hypotenuse. Again and again I'm reminded that the issues we're considering here apply to many other applications. Fault-tolerant systems and redundant applications are the norm in mission-critical applications. The questions we're asking have been asked dozens of times before.

The software industry is in its infancy, and nowhere is that made clearer than in how often we find ourselves solving a problem that we absolutely *know* others have solved before us. Certainly in other industries one could go to the literature and look up how dozens of others have gone about the same task. This is much harder to do in the software industry. We don't even share a common vocabulary for many of these issues. Each problem is handled as if it were unique, as if we were the first ever to confront building a system with such requirements.

The good news is that this is changing. We're developing a literature of best practices; but it is a slow and painful process. There is no governing agency responsible for sifting the wheat from the chaff, so even when you *can* find a book or an article on your problem, there is no assurance that the solution offered will be valid, let alone coherent.

That said, an ad hoc movement to uncover 'patterns' in design and organization processes is taking hold. The seminal book *Design Patterns* set the stage for this understanding and many of the industry periodicals, led perhaps by *C++ Report* and *The Journal of Object-Oriented Programming*, have devoted lots of space to discussing these issues.

Sales & Marketing Functional Requirements

The Sales and Marketing teams have two fundamental requirements of the system:

- They need to enable relatively non-technical people to be able to add new accounts
- They need to be able to check availability of port minutes in anticipation of large sales

Adding New Accounts

From a marketing perspective, the ideal system would allow an administrative assistant to access the system and to be able to provide prospective customers with all the information they need to make a decision to become a customer of Hypotenuse. Further, the system ought to prompt the administrative assistants through the account sign-up process, so that they are certain to gather all the required information. The system should also return a new customer identification number so that the customer can immediately begin ordering jobs.

Administrative assistants would thus mediate the customer-system interaction in a way that will mimic what the customer would otherwise do directly with the system. Hypotenuse might take advantage of this to give better service to large potential customers, or to help sign up customers who are reluctant to sign up to a costly new service using IVR.

This idea builds on one I discussed with Jay over a decade earlier. At the time, he and I were working for Citibank. We were asked to make recommendations on what the branches could do to improve customer service. We learned that Citibank, like so many other banks, had a hard time getting the highest possible level of customer service from the people who worked in the branches. Everything in the system conspired to ensure that these folks were unable to help a customer with the simplest tasks, like opening an account, getting a loan or investing.

While everyone paid lip service to how important these jobs were, the line staff who had the job of working with customers were certainly perceptive enough to recognize that the prestige positions were those with the *least* interaction with the customer. Over time, the very best customer service people were culled from the ranks and promoted into other positions. What was left were those who were least able to provide good customer service. Yet these were the very folks who were talking with the customers and creating Citibank's customer service reputation, for better or worse, and mostly for worse.

Citibank funded a study of customer satisfaction. What they discovered was this: their customers were not happy. Many customers reported that they had complained about a problem but that it was not resolved to their satisfaction. Many of these were now banking with another bank.

Interestingly, the group that was most satisfied with Citibank, in fact their most loyal customers, were those who said they *had* reported a problem, but that problem had been handled well. These customers were measurably happier with the bank than even those customers who had never had a problem at all!

The implications were stunning: the bank had a tremendous opportunity either to solidify or to destroy their relationship with their customer each time there was a service issue. Managers are fond of saying that every problem presents an opportunity; in this case, the research showed there was truth in this trite expression.

One of the most significant problems affecting the quality of customer service was staff turnover. Two decades earlier the average branch personnel had, to pick a number, a decade's experience. Today the average branch officer has no more than a year or two of experience, after which he typically either quits or is promoted to a back office position. There simply was not enough time to teach the branch personnel everything they needed to know about the expanding list of bank products and policies, and also to teach them how to provide excellent service. In fact, it has become overwhelmingly expensive to try.

I proposed that we divided the two tasks. I proposed that Citibank focus all its training on customer service. This in itself would be an enormous job. I referred to this as recreating the *Myth of America That Never Was*. Entering a branch would evoke Jimmy Stuart in *It's A Wonderful Life*, where the local branch officer knew you by name and inquired after your business and your family. Suddenly, the indifferent, isolated, hostile city would be left behind, and you'd be greeted by a person whose entire life was devoted to helping you find what you needed and get your banking done quickly and effortlessly.

The trick, of course, was ensuring that this embodiment of altruism was also reasonably well informed about the bank's offerings. No small issue, however, as Citibank had literally dozens of investment options and hundreds of procedures and regulations.

In order to enable the customer service people to concentrate on creating a startling level of customer service, we had to free them from learning the myriad details about the ever-increasing number of accounts and products offered. I suggested that we migrate this knowledge into the computer system. The customer service staff would know only two things:

- How to make customers feel warm and welcome
- How to use the system to get answers

The rule I proposed was that no one would *ever* refer a customer to someone else; the person who greets you at the door would answer all your questions. To perform this magic, they would sit down with you, in comfortable leather chairs, both on the same side of a desk with a computer terminal on it. Together, you and the bank officer would work your way through an interactive banking session.

In short, the customer service staff would become guides, experts in how to work with the system. They would be customer advocates, assisting customers in finding the answers to their questions, opening accounts and planning for the customer's financial needs.

The essence of this idea, to which I remain committed, was that the system would know better than any staff member ever could, what information was required and what feedback to supply. The system would know the order in which to ask questions, the interdependencies in the information flow, and the details necessary to complete a purchase.

In the same way, if Hypotenuse is going to drive down its customer support costs, it must invest the system with the knowledge of what information we need from the customer, freeing their sales and customer service staff to focus on customer relations.

Checking Port Minutes

When Jay is selling a job to an important customer, he has two great fears: will he sell a job he can't deliver, or will he turn down a job he could have taken? These are two sides of the same coin: limited resources. No hotel wants to leave rooms empty, but much worse is to have a customer arrive and find that there is no room at the inn.

Jay told me a great story. One day, he showed up for a convention and waited in line to check in at the hotel. A well-dressed representative of the hotel approached him in the queue and asked about his reservations. "Well sir," the hotel employee said, "we'd like to offer you a free night's stay at our sister hotel just down the road. On us."

The next thing Jay knew, he was in a cab, fare paid, on his way to a different hotel. Sure enough, the room was free. What happened? The hotel had overbooked its rooms. Clearly, they looked up and down the line of customers waiting to register and picked him out, correctly, as attending a convention. This and his age at the time (early twenties) suggested that he was unlikely to be someone who would return to the hotel. Playing the odds, they opted to send him away and keep a better candidate. It was less expensive for them to pay for his stay at another hotel, than to tell another customer that they had overbooked.

At any given time, Hypotenuse will have a finite number of ports. Since each call takes a predictable amount of time, on average, the system should be able to examine all its commitments, factor in the available time windows and the relative priority for each job, and report on whether a proposed job can be accommodated.

For example, suppose that in February, Hypotenuse is projected to have 1000 phone lines. Examining the planned jobs for February 13 reveals that there are five jobs that *might* be handled on that date, and three more that *must* be handled on that date. Analyzing the length of the anticipated phone calls, and factoring in the number of people called and the hours they can be called reveals that, between 9 a.m. and 5 p.m., the system will be running at 50 to 70% capacity, depending on whether the optional jobs are handled at that time.

Further, suppose that a salesperson is trying to sell to a florist who wants to call 50,000 previous buyers on the day before St Valentine's day, to offer them a last minute special. Can the system handle these calls? Each call is projected to take 1 minute, so the system will need 50,000 port minutes between 10 a.m. and 4 p.m. During that window there are six hours, which is 360 minutes; we have 1,000 lines, so that's 360,000 port minutes. Since the system will be no more than 70% utilized, there are at least 108,000 port minutes available, and the system can easily accommodate these 50,000 calls.

A more sophisticated system would also factor in the possibility of a crisis arising during those particular minutes, and would want to report on the relative risk against the projected likelihood of any or all of the crisis customers activating their system at the time in question.

In any case, from the perspective of the sales force, the system will provide the ability to verify that the port minutes are available. In fact, depending on the lead time, the sales team could use this information to make a sale even if the minutes are not available — given a sufficiently lucrative contract, Hypotenuse could use this report to purchase more access to the network.

Management Functional Requirements

The functional requirements for Management overlap those of Operations and Sales. Management needs to be able to query the system as to its current status, available port minutes, and its performance over arbitrary periods of time.

A typical management report might show the utilization, described in various ways, over the past month. This report might be used to call out idle time on the lines, times when Hypotenuse was perilously close to running out of ports, jobs delayed because of lack of access to the network, and so on.

Various reports might be used to plan for future expansion and to document Hypotenuse's success in meeting the needs and expectations of its customers.

Visualization

Now that we have a good idea of how the system ought to behave, it is time to create some pictures of what the system will look like. These early demonstration programs or drawings will help us discuss the detailed requirements with the customer and will breathe life into the project, providing a focus for analysis and design.

This particular project has a number of front-end systems:

- The IVR component for account sign-up
- The Internet component for account sign-up
- The IVR component for preproduction
- The Internet component for preproduction
- The IVR component for production
- The printed reports for post-production
- The Internet component for post-production
- The client-side access for account maintenance and operational reporting

While it is premature to decide at this point, there is a strong inclination to avoid creating a standalone client component at all, but rather to provide all access through industry standard Internet browsers.

This particular customer has a lot of experience with IVR and can easily visualize what the dialogs might be like for the IVR components. Rather than mocking this up, we decide to begin the analysis phase by charting the flow of these interactions.

The browser screens that will handle account sign-up and preproduction are another matter entirely, and we will want to consider creating some of these early in the process to give the customer something to react to. Screens such as these can germinate ideas and can help ensure that we are in sync with the customer.

Jay downplays the importance of these screens for now. He understands that HTML is flexible, and we can work out the exact details of how these screens are presented when the time comes. This does, however, raise the issue of what else might be provided on the Internet, once Hypotenuse has a presence.

Let me be clear, in most applications I would spend some time at this stage building mock-ups of the front-end screens. These are critical to helping the customer clarify his thinking, and can reveal lacunae in our understanding of the problem. In this particular case we made a conscious decision to skip this step for three reasons:

- This particular software presents its most important aspects via IVR, and so has no visible interface
- For those places where there is a visible front end — the Internet access — we'll almost certainly use simple forms whose layout will be relatively unimportant, at least in version 1.0
- Our client is a user interface expert, and nothing we show him will teach him anything he doesn't already know

This last point is the clincher for me; Jay has a much clearer idea of what he will want than I can ever suggest. We'll learn as much from examining flowcharts and requirements as we will from mockups, and here is an opportunity to save a bit of time on the schedule.

This provides an important lesson in design methodology: find the right balance between following the methodology and not doing anything stupid. You don't want to toss methodology out the window without a good reason, but when you *have* a good reason, don't hesitate to adapt to the situation at hand.

Internet Functional Requirements

The discussion about Internet pages and Internet interaction causes us to realize that there is another component to this application we hadn't originally considered: the Hypotenuse Home Page. Until this point, we'd been considering the Internet to be a front end for the system, but the Internet offers marketing opportunities that can be leveraged once we're in the process of creating the browser pages.

In addition to providing front-end access to various components of *Crisis•Call* (account sign-up, preproduction and post-production, as well as Operational, Sales and Management access to the database and the *Crisis•Call* system), the Internet provides an opportunity to offer marketing material and related information to customers.

The Hypotenuse requirements can be divided into three logical groups:

- *Crisis•Call* front end for customers
- *Crisis•Call* operational access for staff
- Marketing material for customers

It is this last possibility, a set of marketing pages on the Hypotenuse web site, which suddenly becomes very exciting. Marketing on the Web may dramatically shorten the time between a potential customer learning about Hypotenuse and that customer signing a contract. The online service can provide not only marketing brochures, but also explanations of the legal requirements and a copy of the contract.

In addition, the web service can provide technical support to customers who are experiencing difficulties accessing the system, or working their way through the preproduction interactions. Finally, the web page may, over time, allow the customer access to real-time information about the progress of their jobs.

Getting Ready for Analysis

At this point, we have a requirements document, which tells us what the system can do, and we've validated this document based on our use cases. We've also created some preliminary visualizations to help understand how the system looks and feels. It is time, therefore, to open the black box and begin to analyze the system itself. This leads to the next phase, **analysis**.

```
= false;

Time();
= now.Format("%b %d

er = "start < '";
oday;
' and enddate > '";
today;
"'";

bScheduleSet.m_strFilter =

JobScheduleSet.IsOpen())

JobScheduleSet.Requery();

pDoc>m_JobScheduleSet.Open();

llTrack* pCallTrack;

l ok;

ile
pDoc>m_JobScheduleSet.IsEOF())
{
    pCallTrack = new
allTrack(m_pDoc>m_JobScheduleSet.m_
bID);
    ok = pCallTrack>Initialize();

    if (ok)
    {   Log("ok\n");
        m_CallList.AddHead(pCallTrack);
        foundJobs = true;
    }
    else
    {   Log("...Rejected!\n");
        delete pCallTrack;
    }

    m_pDoc>m_JobScheduleSet.MoveNext();
}
```

```
run
CTime::GetCurren
CTime end = theJobSet.
CTime start = theJobSet.GetYea
CTime todayStart(start.GetYear(),
start.GetMonth(), now.GetDay(),
start.GetHour(),
start.GetMinute(),
start.GetSecond());
CTime todayEnd(end.GetYear(),
end.GetMonth(), now.GetDay(),
end.GetHour(),
end.GetMinute(), end.GetSecond());

if (todayStart > now || todayS
now)
{   theJobSet.Close();
    return false;
}

CTimeSpan theSpan = end - no
int totalMinutes =
theSpan.GetTotalMinutes();

if (end > todayEnd) //
than today
{   int AdditionalMin =
GetAdditionalMinutes(the
t,
    theJobSet.m_EndDate);
    CTimeSpan todaySp
now;    totalMinutes =
todaySpan.GetTotalMin
    AdditionalMin;
}

m_min = ( ( (m_t
totalMinutes) + 1
);
m_Priority = t
m_Tilt = theJo
m_Throttle = the
m_JobID = the
theJobSet.Cl

return true
```

Analysis

In the analysis period I have two significant goals:

- Turn the functional specification from a narrative of general principles into a specific and detailed list of requirements

- Begin to identify the high-level objects and understand their relationships in terms of the business model

Drilling Deeper

I convene the first analysis meeting early in January. The meeting gets off to an inauspicious beginning; we are confused and ill focused. One moment we're talking about business requirements, the next we're deep in the mud, arguing over operating systems. Before long we're talking about how we're conducting the meeting, and rather than getting anything done, we're tied up in knots about what we should be doing.

What we need to bring order to this discussion is a formal process. We don't have to become academic and rigid about it, but using a process will help us focus on the business problem and free us from having to worry about how we get from here to there. We decide to make an informal but meaningful commitment to a process. The Three Amigos — Booch, Rumbaugh and Jacobson — have agreed on a process called Rational Objectory, which details the development lifecycle. We will follow this method, using the Unified Modeling Language as our notation.

In the conceptualization phase we paid attention to the external view of a system. We started talking about how the system will be used, and from those use cases we were able to create a domain model. We treated the calling system as a black box and focused on how it would be used by the various 'actors', including the sales force, the customer, Management and Operations.

Now, in analysis, we'll construct a logical class model and extend the use cases into the system as object interactions. A logical class model is not constrained by language details. While I expect that most of the classes in this model will eventually translate more or less directly into C++ classes, I'm not focusing on the language at this point; I am more concerned with the logical entities and how they interact.

This model will detail how the system will deliver the functionality identified by the requirements model. We won't consider implementation details such as language, class libraries, distribution, or database. These decisions belong in the design phase, which will follow the analysis.

This approach allows us to turn our attention to those aspects of the problem we've not yet modeled: the network, the Internet, the IVR application, and the reports we want to generate.

To make progress and to avoid being overwhelmed, we go back to our earlier strategy of breaking the problem down into segments: sign-up, preproduction, production, and post-production. In conceptualization we discussed the functional requirements of each of these aspects of the project; now it's time to tease out the exact specifications and to begin thinking about how to model these needs.

Sign-Up Analyzed

Analysis meetings are intense efforts to get past the simple description and find the hidden details. Jay joins us to consider, in detail, what information we want to gather at sign-up time. This information will not only identify the customer, but will help us with capacity planning and overall customer service.

To get a good picture of what this meeting is like, let me take a moment to describe Jay Leve. Jay is a couple of years younger than I am; he is a short, enthusiastic, excitable guy with a clear vision of his world. Jay thinks big, and he talks in grand themes; he is an expansive man who insists on doing things 'right'.

The Viewfinder

My picture of Jay can only be understood by an analogy. This is more than appropriate, as Jay is the king of metaphors; he believes firmly that we only learn new things in terms of things we already understand, and if you want to get a point across to Jay you had better come up with a compelling metaphor. (I can hear Jay in my mind's ear hollering, "Right! Without a metaphor, nothing can be understood.")

Here's my analogy for Jay. I used to have a single-lens reflex camera with a range finder in its center. When you looked through the viewfinder, you would see two images. You'd then turn the focusing ring until the two images were brought together into a single image. If you turned the wrong way, they moved apart. As you approached focus, the images moved closer and closer together. If the target was out of range, the two images never fully converged.

This is how Jay sees *everything*. One image is the way he believes the world should be, the other is the way things are. He will do absolutely anything to bring those images into sharp focus, and he won't be comfortable until there is only a single image in his viewfinder of the world. Be on guard if you or your work is the ring he has to twist to bring things into focus; he'll break the lens before he'll leave things askew.

The Vision

Jay opens the meeting by describing his grand vision. His understanding of his product is all of a piece, and it is my job to help him break it down into its constituent parts, and then to distinguish which of those pieces are essential. I mean to use the literal definition of 'essential'; I want to know which of the elements of calling are of its essence, and which are just artifacts of the ways Jay has come to think about the problem.

When we were at Citibank, Jay and I worked with a fellow named David Rollert. David was a graphical artist by training, and one day he related to me this story: he was talking with a customer who said, "Dave, use more red here." David asked him what he wanted to accomplish. "I want it redder." "Why?" David asked him. "Well, it is too impersonal like this, I want it to be warmer, friendlier." "Great," David replied, "then tell me that. You want it warmer and friendlier. I can do that. Leave the color choice up to me, that's what you pay me for."

It is Jay's tendency to say, "Use more red." It is my job to get him to tell me what he wants to accomplish, and I'll pick the right tool to make that happen. It may well be that the right shade of yellow will make the reds already in the picture stand out in just the right way to make the overall effect much warmer and friendlier.

The Customer

We begin by thinking about the customer. Certainly we need to know the customer's company name, address, and other company details. In addition, we want to capture information about each **contact** at the company who might be authorized to trigger a job.

For each of these contacts we'll want to capture daytime and evening phone numbers, daytime and evening fax numbers, and an e-mail address. For marketing purposes, we also want to ask the customer how they heard about the service.

Jay wants the new customer to project his usage of the system, because such information will be vital to capacity and port planning. We will ask the customer to guess about a number of different ways they might create jobs. For example, will they always call the same list of phone numbers?

We start sketching out what a form might look like. This is *not* the design of the final form, but rather a technique to help Jay think through the issues and determine what information is critical.

After we establish whether the customer will use a single list or more than one, we can ask how big the lists will be. We decide to ask the customer a series of questions for each list they anticipate using. We'll start with the size of the list. We agree that the customer can't know in advance what the precise numbers will be, but they can tell us an estimate, probably based on sensible ranges that we'll provide to prompt them:

How many numbers will you call?

- Less than 1K
- 1-5K
- 5-10K
- 10-20K
- More than 20K

Asked in this way, and imagined as an item on a form, we can't help assuming that this is a drop down list box, but in the analysis stage we hold such a decision in abeyance. It may be that by the time we get to design, this question is quite different, and a list box will no longer be appropriate.

We will also ask the customer to give us a sense of when they'll be making calls to that list. Some customers will use the list once and throw it away. Others will create lists used only in a particular emergency, and still others will call particular lists on a regular or episodic basis.

Now we move on to consider the audio used for each job. Some customers know they'll always play the same audio on every list for every job. Others will change their audio, perhaps for each job. We also want to ask them to estimate how long their audio will be, as this will help us estimate how many port minutes they'll need:

About how long will you talk?

- Under half a minute
- Under a minute
- One to two minutes
- More than two minutes

Finally, some customers do their calling seasonally or on particular days of the week. We can ask them to guess about that and also to tell us which time zones they'll be calling into. Most of the calls will, no doubt, be on the coasts, as that is where the population centers are, but some customers will be more evenly distributed, and knowing that may help us plan.

We also agree that at sign-up time, the customer will have the opportunity to review the contract if the sign-up is being conducted through our web site. This raises the issue of security and encryption, but we put off these considerations until design time.

Preproduction Analyzed

In our next analysis session, we tackle the details of the preproduction phase. Jay prepares for this process by creating a flowchart of how he would interview a customer to get the information required to make a 'flight of calls' — that is, to run a single job.

We start by defining more terms. In sign-up we defined a **customer** (or **account**) as a company with a contract with Hypotenuse, and a **contact** as an individual at a particular account.

A **call** is a single phone number to which we'll play some audio defined by a **call flow**. A **job** is a set of calls and a particular schedule. Thus a job in its totality is a set of phone numbers, a set of audio to play, a call flow that defines the interaction with the customer, and a schedule that details when to call.

At this meeting we discuss the fact that preproduction can be accomplished either via IVR (Interactive Voice Response — phone mail in which you are prompted, "Press 1 if you want to schedule a job.") or over the Internet. The IVR format, by its nature, lends itself to a flowchart. The Internet application will more likely be a smart form, and thus somewhat more event-driven.

We agree, immediately, that capturing the phone list will be easier over the Internet, and capturing the audio will be easier over the phone. While it is possible to upload `.wav` files (audio files) over the Internet, it's far easier simply to record your messages as part of the IVR interaction. Similarly, while it is theoretically possible to key in all the phone numbers you want to call, the 99% case will be to upload the phone numbers, either through our web site or via e-mail.

It is Jay's instinct that the majority of jobs will be launched in one of two ways. Either the customer will call into our IVR system, or the customer will call a salesperson. In either case, the trick will be getting the phone list, and we agree that this will be a separate step, accomplished through e-mail or by uploading via a web browser, FTP or other Internet-based technology. In the worst case, the customer can always send a diskette by FedEx. Jay begins laying out a common use case:

> "The customer calls in and we ask if he wants to get information, sign-up, or trigger a job (Jay's *flight of calls*), wording to be determined. Let's concentrate on triggering a job. The first thing we do is ask for his social security number."

We discuss why we might use the social security number. The goal is to uniquely identify a particular contact, so that if a customer complains — "Hey, who told you to call 10,000 of my customers at 4 in the morning; we never asked for that!" — we can say, "Well, Joe Smith, social security number 000-00-0000 called at 3:15 p.m. on January 12th and asked us to make the calls. This was confirmed by him entering his secret password."

If each person has a unique identification number (and social security numbers are guaranteed to be unique), then we're all set. We not only know which client company placed the order; we also know which individual at that company was on the line.

Once we have the ID, we then ask the customer for their password. What if the customer doesn't want to have a password? We discuss this at some length, considering the advantages and disadvantages of forcing customers to choose a password. Finally we decide that it is the customer's choice. If the customer *has* a password, we'll ask for it at log-in, otherwise we won't.

Design for the 90% Case

This is a fundamental premise of design that I learned from Jay a decade earlier when we worked together at Humanware — design for what 90% of the people want to do 90% of the time. Only when you have that clearly understood, implemented, and working do you allow yourself to be distracted by the boundary conditions of what the other 10% of the people want to do the remaining 10% of the time.

If you handle the boundary conditions in the middle of designing your program, you'll get so hamstrung by these difficult but obscure problems, that you'll lose sight of your original goals.

Next, we need to find out what phone list the customer will be calling. Some callers, especially 'crisis callers', won't have more than one list. There is no reason to force them through an extra step, and by the nature of a *Crisis•Call* we want to streamline the process. Ideally, when a crisis arises you call in, enter your ID and password and hear, "To confirm that you want to begin making your emergency calls, to your predefined list, using your prerecorded audio, press 1 now. To review your audio, press 2..."

Thus, when we know who the caller is, we'll look up the account. If the customer told us at sign-up that he always uses the same list, we won't ask which list to use, we'll just go on to the next step: when to call.

In a crisis, we don't want to put the customer through the step of telling us when to call, so *at sign-up* we'll ask the customer if all calls are always to go out immediately. If this is chosen, then at preproduction we won't have to ask.

If the customer has *not* told us to always start immediately, we must find out if *this* call is a crisis, or if the customer wants to schedule the calls. We must then find out what audio to use. The customer may have only one audio he uses all the time, or he may record a set of prerecorded messages. If he has a set, he will want to choose, at preproduction, which one to use for this job. Other customers may want to record new audio on the spot.

Again, we decide that the customer will be asked, *at sign-up*, if they *always* want to use the prerecorded audio. If so, we won't ask any questions, we'll just use it. Otherwise, we'll check how many audio segments have been recorded and ask the customer if they want to use one of these or record new audio.

Finally, we'll confirm the user's choices and start calling. As you can see, a customer can tell us at sign-up that they always use the same audio, always call the same list, and always want the calls to go out as a crisis. For this customer, preproduction goes like this:

- Call in
- Confirm the calls
- Hang up

It is possible that at preproduction time the non-crisis customer will not yet have given us the phone numbers. In that case, the system will instruct the customer how to provide the phone numbers, and will remind them that calling can't begin until the numbers are received. Similarly, the customer may want to delay recording or sending the audio until a later time, after setting up the job but before the job is run.

Numbers

As a result of this analysis we've identified a few identification numbers:

- Account number
- User Identification (UID, most commonly the social security number)
- Job number
- Phone list number
- Audio segment number

In Jay's existing software, ranges of numbers are used to identify different types of customers. Assigning an account number is a non-trivial effort, requiring someone in Operations to spawn a new number for each account. In addition, passwords are used to identify particular phone lists to call. All of this was an attempt to organize the numbers and to reduce the number of numbers a person must recall.

I argue that account numbers and passwords should be divorced from each other and should be as simple as possible. Further, each number should do exactly one thing: a password should provide security and no other information. After some discussion, we agree on the following design:

Account numbers will begin at 10,001 and count up from there. Phone lists will be tied to the individual account, and will start at 1 and count up from there. Thus, if the Democratic National Committee is account 10003, its fourth phone list will be 10003-L004. Audio will be identified in the same way, but with the key letter A, thus audio five for the DNC will be 10003-A005.

Long after we put this into place, I realize that I should have avoided any numbers with ones or zeros in them as the numeral 1 and the lowercase letter l are often confused, as are the numeral 0 and the letter O.

Production Analyzed

At first glance, production is very straightforward: go off hook, play a message, hang up. I ask Jay if there is more to it. His answer is classic: "Nope, that's it; except for when it isn't." He then goes on to describe any number of variations.

There are three major issues in production:

- Call flow
- Picking the next phone number to call
- Picking the right phone line to call on

Call Flow

In the initial conceptualization, we assumed a number of different out-calling patterns, or call flows. The simplest call flow is: *detect answer, play message, hang up.* Somewhat more complex is: *detect answer; if person, play message 1; if machine, play message 2; hang up.* The call flow could get a lot more complex when there is an interaction with the recipient, for example: "If you are the Federal Marshall, press 1. If the Federal Marshall is on the way to the phone, press 2. If the Federal Marshall is not available to take this call, press 3. If we've reached this number in error, press 4."

Delivering many of these more complex interactions hinges on our ability to differentiate reliably between people and answering machines. To do this, I need a better understanding of what the telephony cards can provide.

Detecting People vs. Answering Machines

Call centers are very big customers for voice processing card manufacturers like Dialogic, Rhetorex, and Natural Microsystems. The feature most in demand from call centers is the ability to distinguish, very quickly, between answering machines and people. Here's why: a typical call center has a pool of sales people. Before automated dialing, these sales people would each dial on their own phone and try to reach potential customers. The problem was that a large percentage of their calls resulted in busy signals or no-answers. Call centers automated their systems so that a computer made the calls, and only when they reached someone did the call switch over to a salesman.

This was fine, but with the increasing popularity of answering machines, very often the salesman found himself talking to a machine and not to a human being. The telephony card manufacturers added the ability to distinguish between people and answering machines in response to demand from these call centers. With today's technology, the computer places the call, and only when a person is detected is the call switched to the salesman.

Typically, the salesman may not even hear the customer say, "Hello." His computer lights up with the customer's name and he just says, "May I speak with Mr. Liberty?" Now in some cases this is a bit silly, as I may have just answered the phone, "Jesse Liberty," and yet the salesman didn't hear that, so he just asks for me anyway. Of course, this causes no real harm, and in compensation for this trivial inconvenience, the salesman never has to wait for a phone to be answered, and never hears a busy signal or an answering machine.

We can piggyback on this ability of the card to distinguish humans from machines, but we're still not fully out of the woods. When a telemarketing call center gets an answering machine, it is free just to hang up and try another number, but many of Hypotenuse's *Crisis•Call* applications require that messages be played accurately to answering machines.

This is trickier than it sounds. Although the card can tell us that we've contacted an answering machine, it *cannot* tell us if the machine is recording our message. Perhaps the outgoing message has been played ("Hi, we're not at home, please leave a message after the tone.") but the tone hasn't sounded and the machine isn't recording yet.

We could of course wait for the beep before playing our message, but there are two problems with this. First, beeps come in many flavors, many tones, and many sounds. Some machines don't beep; they warble. Some use one beep, some a series of beeps. Second, the calling card can be fooled, and it may be that we're not really talking to a machine after all, we're talking with a person. In this case the beep will never come.

Stepping Outside the Envelope

Audiotex Service Bureaus have spent a lot of time trying to figure out what to do about this, and Jay and I review the body of knowledge. We realize that to solve this problem we must think about it in new ways. What is the trouble with answering machines? Why do we need to treat them differently?

One big issue is this: we can't know how long the answering machine's outgoing message is, so we don't know when to start playing our own message. If the customer misses part of the message, what do we have them do?

We decide to solve the first problem through Jay's idea of a 'signature' opening. Every message will be prefixed with a bit of audio. This announces the call, and tells the customer that what is coming is important information (rather than a sales pitch). In those rare cases where the state of the art telephony technology is wrong, and we're talking with an answering machine, the worst that will happen is that the signature opening won't be recorded, but the customer's message will be. Thus, each call might begin with distinctive music or tones, followed by an announcer saying something like, "This is *Crisis•Call*! An important message follows..."

Originally, Jay thought he might end his messages with something like, "If you missed any part of this message, please call 1-800-555-1111." The number provided would vary from job to job, and would be the phone number of the customer who had ordered the call.

There were problems with this idea, however. Not every Hypotenuse customer would be prepared to answer these calls, and relying on them to do so would significantly reduce our ability to meet their needs. I suggested instead that Hypotenuse keep a bank of incoming lines. When the customer calls in, we'll analyze the incoming number using ANI, often called Caller ID. We'll determine who the caller is, figure out what message we left on their machine, and play it again. In those cases where we can't determine who is calling, we'll ask the caller to enter their 10-digit phone number.

Now our signature idea is complete. We play a signature opening that is long enough to cover any answering machine's message, but if the customer *does* miss any of the message, they can hear it again by calling in to Hypotenuse.

A complete *Crisis•Call* might sound like this:

> <Sound Signature>. This is *Crisis•Call*! An important message follows. If you miss any part of this message, you can hear it again by calling 1-800-555-5555. John F. Kennedy Junior High School will close one hour early today, at 1:30 p.m., due to the inclement weather. Please make appropriate arrangements to pick up your child at 1:30 p.m. today. If you missed any part of this message, you can hear it again by calling 1-800-555-5555. Thank you.

We'll work to develop empirical experience on what percentage of calls are followed up with an inbound request to repeat the message, and we'll tinker with the duration of the messages and other factors to reduce this number over time. The big 'win' here is that we now have only one call template — one generalized path for all calls.

Jay refines this idea. We'll *try* to differentiate between machines and people, but we'll set things up so that our interactions are acceptable even when we get it wrong. For example, if we think we have a person, we can play a different introduction — one that may be shorter than the introductory message we play for machines. In the event we are wrong (it is a machine, after all), that will be okay, as we'll be repeating the 800 number at the end of the message. Similarly, if we think we have a machine but in fact we have a person, they won't hear the ideal interaction, but they'll hear an acceptable message.

Handling Key Presses

We revisit this solution a number of times. I still don't get it, though, as I don't see how we'll ask the user to press a key. Since we're not relying on differentiating machines from people, how can we ever ask for a key press? Won't there be a similar problem if the user has a rotary dial phone? Jay reminds me of an idea he has articulated a number of times before, but which didn't sink in until today.

"We'll say, 'Press 1 to talk with an operator...' *<pause>* 'If you are listening to this on an answering machine, please call...'"

The penny finally drops. We'll pause long enough for the user to take an action, but then we'll go on to handle the answering machine or a rotary dial user. This gives us only one message to record, yet handles the answering machine well. Over time, we can refine the exact length of that pause. When the rotary dial user calls in, we will note their originating phone number and play the appropriate message. No key press will be required. In the event that we *do* need interaction, we can pass the caller to a line with more expensive hardware that supports voice recognition ("Press or say '1' to continue").

This simplified flow affords us the ability to handle, "Press 1 if the person we're looking for is on the line," as well as call bridging, and does it in a way that also works for answering machines. We know that shortly after version 1, we'll need to expand to somewhat more complicated call flow templates, but this will give us a solid foundation.

I bookmark the idea of additional capabilities, such as asking the recipient to enter a password before we play the message. This is a logical extension to the work we'll be doing. Conversations with Doug, the VP of Marketing, expand this idea to inserting the recipient's name in the audio. "This is Boston Gas calling for <inserted name>. When <inserted name> is on the line, please press 1... Please enter your password..."

This is a classic example of feature creep. One idea spawns another. Noting these features and coming back to them in a subsequent version is a great way to extend your product and keep it alive. Cooking every great idea into the first release, on the other hand, is a great way to kill a product before it ever comes to market.

Since I expect this particular application to have frequent releases throughout the year, there will be plenty of time to add these features back into the product once we have a stable first version. The goal is to create a solid foundation on which we can build a very robust and flexible set of applications.

Prioritizing the Calls

The second significant issue in production is picking which telephone number to call next. Each job will have a priority assigned to it. Jay thinks about it like this: there are *Crisis•Calls* and there are *Flash•Calls*.

Crisis•Calls must be handled immediately by their very nature. It is possible that there are relative priorities among crises but in the 99% case these are not meaningful; we'll need to use every available phone line for any crisis.

Flash•Calls will be sold with a promised schedule. We imagine two types of contracts. One says that we will call the numbers provided, starting on this date, at this rate of calls. The second type is more akin to Federal Express's second day delivery. With second day delivery, your package *may* be delivered the next day, or it may take two days. In exchange for charging you less money, FedEx buys a bit of flexibility. If they are busy on the first day, they have the right to push your package off a day. If they are not busy, they can send your package through, and you get a bargain. In a similar way, we may sell a lower priority *Flash•Call* that often *will* go out the same day you contract for, but may be delayed if we are busy. In exchange for that flexibility, the customer will receive a discount. While we can imagine any number of possible priority-based contracts, the details are more of a business decision than a design decision.

We also imagine that some customers will have a wider or narrower window during which they are willing to have their calls delivered. One thing they are buying is port minutes (how many numbers to call, times how many minutes each call takes) but a second, more subtle, purchase might be the *rate* of calls — that is, how many port minutes per hour they want to buy.

Imagine that Hypotenuse has 1,000 lines. They can then sell 60,000 port minutes per hour. Now imagine two customers, Company A and Company B. Each wants to call 120,000 phone numbers, and each will play a one minute message. Company A needs its numbers called between 5 p.m. and 8 p.m. on Monday; Company B needs its numbers called between 9 a.m. Monday and 5 p.m. Friday.

A one-minute message is a simplification to keep the math easy. In fact, we'll measure the duration of the audio and add additional time for setting up the call, dialing, ringing, connecting and so forth. There is also the time required to tear down the connection and recycle the line. When we talk about a call taking a minute, we mean the sum of all of this. We will give the name **cycle time** to the length of time between starting one call and being ready to start the next.

Let's continue with the example. Company A wants to spend 120,000 port minutes in three hours, or 40,000 port minutes/hour. Company B wants to call during an 8-hour time frame over 5 days, or a total of 40 hours. Thus, Company B wants to spend 120,000 /40 or 3,000 port minutes/hour. Clearly, Hypotenuse can afford to charge less for 3,000 port minutes/hour than for 40,000 port minutes/hour, even though both customers are calling the same number of recipients, and talking for the same duration.

How much less to charge is entirely a business decision, but the system must support the option. It would be bad if Jay booked both customers and couldn't make Company A's calls during its critical three hours, because the system was in the middle of making Company B's calls and was too stupid to realize it should suspend Company B's calls for three hours in order to make Company A's calls.

The system, therefore, must support the idea of prioritizing calls in subtle and complex ways. Initially, this will mean assigning relative priorities to each job, but the system must also be able to analyze the requirements of each job and schedule accordingly.

Managing Simultaneous Calls

Once calls are scheduled, some jobs will inevitably overlap. If the system is smart, it will not *allow* jobs to be sold that require more resources than the system has. Imagine that Company A wants to make 50,000 one-minute calls between 8 and 9 p.m., and thus requires 50,000 port minutes. Company B wants to make 400,000 calls between 6 and 10 p.m., and so requires 100,000 port minutes per hour. If Hypotenuse only has 100,000 port minutes per hour to sell, one of these jobs will not complete (unless Hypotenuse has time to buy more phone lines). This is a physical fact of life, and the system must respond to it.

Similarly, the system needs to find the best calling schedule for jobs that have been sold. Assume, for the moment, that Hypotenuse can support 200,000 minutes of dialing per hour. Company A requests 50,000 calls between 8 and 9 p.m. Company B requests 300,000 calls between 5 and 9 p.m. Company C requests 80,000 calls between 7 and 9 p.m. How do we schedule the calls between 8 and 9 p.m?

Company A needs to call 50,000 people during that hour. Company B needs to make one-fourth of its calls, or 75,000 calls. Company C needs to make half of its calls, or 40,000. In total, 50+40+75 or 165,000 calls must be made. Company A's percentage of that is 50,000/165,000, or 30%. Company B requires 75/165 or 45%. Company C will require 40/165, or 24%. (The exact percentages are more complex and will solve the rounding error.) Thus, if we apportion the requirements, we know how to apportion the lines.

The system will want to make these calculations pretty frequently. After 10 minutes, these requirements may have shifted slightly, and the system can stay in tune and in balance by rechecking and reapportioning periodically. The calculations will become even more complex as we consider other scheduling requirements.

Understanding Schedules

As we discuss scheduling calls, more detail emerges. This is a classic example of where analysis can help avoid design pitfalls. Had we stopped with the customer's first explanation of the requirements, we'd surely have painted ourselves into a corner. Only by rigorously examining the exact requirements in detail were we able to fully understand the problem.

Tilt

It turns out that some customers want to tell us, "Start calling at this time, and call as fast as you can," but others want to say, "Call 50,000 people at exactly 8 p.m." They realize we can't do this, but what they'll settle for is something like, "Call these 50,000 people as close to 8 p.m. as you can, but not one minute after 8. Perhaps a product is going to be offered for sale in a TV auction, and they have 50,000 customers who have asked to be notified in advance, "Turn to channel 28 at 8 p.m. to make your bid." They'd like to let folks know about this at the last possible minute, but there is no point in telling anyone about it once the bidding is over.

The preference as to which end of the calling window is to receive most calls is called the job's **tilt**. This use case is back-tilted — we want to tilt as much of the work towards the end of the job as possible. The vast majority of jobs are front-tilted; that is, we begin calling at the appointed time and call as quickly as we can.

Throttle

During our discussions, another scheduling requirement also comes to light — some customers will want to limit the number of calls made in an hour.

Suppose an insurance company has the phone numbers of 10,000 customers whose automobile insurance policies are delinquent and will expire tomorrow. The company may wish to call all of these customers and tell them that their insurance is about to lapse. The company may want to offer customers an option to be connected to a representative so that they have no interruption in coverage, but the insurance company knows that it has only enough staff to handle 50 inbound calls simultaneously. By calculating the anticipated throughput, Hypotenuse is able to 'throttle' the number of calls it makes. The insurance company can set the throttle to ensure that its customer service representatives always have someone to talk to, at the same time ensuring that no policy holder is on hold for too long.

The **throttle** of a job is therefore the maximum number of calls to make in an hour.

We establish the following atomic pieces of scheduling information that a customer *may* specify for a particular job:

- What is the earliest time and date this job can start?
- What is the absolute latest time and date this job must end?
- During what hours may we make calls?
- Do you want to throttle the calls?
- Do you want to tilt the calls?

Thus, if you wanted to start on January 1 at noon, and call weekdays between 9 and 5, but make no more than 500 calls per hour, you would set the earliest date as 1/1/98 noon, the latest date as unspecified, the hours as M-F 9-5, and the throttle as 500. You would also use front-tilt, which is the default.

Don't Crush the Central Office

The customer will, as we discussed, provide a number of constraints on their calls. We must start after the earliest start time, be sure not to finish after the latest stop time, and make no more than the allowed number of calls per hour. There is one additional constraint of which the customer may be totally unaware, but which Hypotenuse must take very seriously.

If Hypotenuse were to start calling thousands of numbers in a tight geographical area, they could well flood an exchange or even an entire central office, taking every available circuit and leaving the town without telephone services. Imagine the publicity that would result when the chief of police, the local fire department, and the school system suddenly found themselves unable to make or receive phone calls.

The problem is made a bit more complicated because many towns have a number of exchanges, some of which are not contiguous numbers. For example, one town may have the exchanges 372 and 373, but also 996.

Schedule Monitoring and Adjustment

As we discuss scheduling with Jay and Kevin, his VP of Operations, we discover a significant assumption on their part that hadn't made it into our analysis to date. While Jay agreed that the system would need to schedule the majority of the jobs, he felt strongly that the system would never get it right the first (or even the 10th) time, and that human intervention will always be required for some jobs.

Operations will, therefore, need to be able to monitor what the system is doing now, what it anticipates doing in the future, and will also need the ability to manipulate jobs to make way for other jobs that the system otherwise couldn't 'fit'.

Ultimately, we will need to design and implement *SnapShot*™ — a graphical, networked tool to see (and perhaps to manipulate) the calling schedule. We agree that *SnapShot* will be able to recreate the calling pattern for days in the past, anticipate the calling pattern for days in the future, and will provide a real-time, up-to-the-minute picture of what the system is doing *right now* while it is running.

Jan	Feb	Mar	Apr	May	Jun
Jul	Aug	Sep	Oct	Nov	Dec

S	M	T	W	T	F	S
26	27	28	29	30	31	1
2	3	4	5	6	7	8
9	10	11	12	13	14	15
16	17	18	19	20	21	22
23	24	25	26	**27**	28	1
2	3	4	5	6	7	8

The exact design of *SnapShot* will be worked out as we get closer to its implementation, but we agree on some general design ideas. An authorized user will open a dialog box that will present a calendar:

Double clicking on a day will provide a 'snapshot' of that day's scheduled calls:

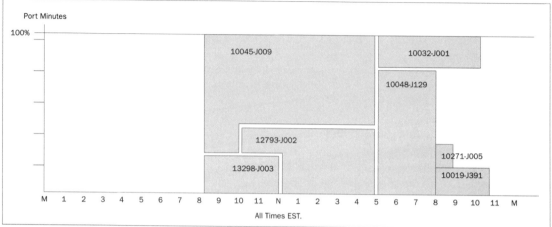

In the final version, each of these blocks would be drawn based on information in the database. If *SnapShot* were to be used for editing (as well as viewing) the schedule, then each block would be movable and resizable, and the act of resizing and then saving the changes would cause updates in the database to the affected jobs (which may well be all the subsequent jobs for that day!).

Note that in this chart, job 13298-J003 begins at 8 a.m. and runs until noon. At the same time, a second job (10045-J009) starts, and two hours later a third job (12793-J002) begins. The ports are shared based on priority, density, etc. Jobs ebb and flow, depending on what other jobs are demanding ports.

This application is non-trivial, and involves these challenges:

- Computing the resource allocation
- Drawing the chart
- Computing the changes based on manipulation

Computing the resource allocation *must* be done by the system if we are to project whether or not we can sell new jobs. Drawing the chart should be fairly straightforward. Computing what must change in every job to accommodate direct manipulation may be much more difficult. If Operations shifts these boxes around and then says, "OK," the system must figure out how to set throttle, priority, etc. to accommodate that. This can be simplified as follows: each job will have two sets of settings: the first (set by the user) involves values like throttle; the second, set by the administrator, involves absolute values. When the administrator adjusts a job, perhaps it stays adjusted (and maybe displays in a different color) no matter what else changes.

In addition, this application does not scale well as currently conceived. While this is a good way to view half a dozen concurrent jobs, it will become unreadable when we look at 50, let alone 200 concurrent jobs. Our tentative plan to manage this issue is to aggregate all the smaller jobs into a single representation.

For version 1.0, we need a way to make this information available. It is possible that it won't be graphical, and it's similarly possible that it will be read-only. This will be determined as we move forward. Kevin also points out that we'll need an audit trail that logs every change (when it was made, and by whom), and which offers comments explaining why the changes were made.

As we consider this in greater detail, we note that the only use for the editing facility we're postulating is this: Hypotenuse wants to sell a job, but the system reports there are insufficient resources. The guess here is that a person can move things around and make room. We will test, empirically, whether we can build an automated system that is at least as good as any human operator might be at scheduling jobs.

Analysis vs. Design

At this point we note that we are delving fairly deeply into the design in our attempts to understand the requirements. It is tempting to rigidly reject these design considerations, but that would be foolish. My rule of thumb is to make sure that we are catching these design ideas as they come along, but not to go fishing for them. The focus of this stage of the effort is, and remains, understanding the requirements; certain design considerations will fall out of the process, but that is serendipity.

Picking the Right Phone Line

In addition to scheduling calls using complex algorithms, the system must also choose the right phone line on which to place each call. Once again, there are some subtleties. First of all, not every port will have all the capabilities of every other port. For example, for some purposes, notably incoming lines, we'll need to have voice recognition.

The people we call may call us back to hear the message again. When we ask them to tell us their phone numbers, we'll need to support speech recognition for those who do not have touch tone phones. Telephony cards that support speech recognition are expensive, and we can assume that not every port will support this ability. We'll want to protect these lines and not tie them up with outgoing calls unless either the outgoing calls are sufficiently important, or our estimates tell us these lines won't be needed for incoming calls any time soon. In any case, we'll need to dynamically allocate various ports to various uses as the calls progress.

In addition, not every port will be tied to the same outgoing long distance service. Hypotenuse buys its long distance lines in bulk, and so gets a competitive rate. It is prudent, however, not to hand all of one's eggs to the same vendor, so Hypotenuse also buys from a second vendor, though in smaller quantities. These second lines are thus more expensive to use on a minute by minute basis, and we'll want to be careful about which calls are assigned to those lines. If we are making calls that have plenty of time to complete, there is no sense in paying a premium on fulfilling the calls, and we can wait for the less expensive lines to free up. On the other hand, if we are on a deadline, or are making *Crisis•Calls*, then we will want to use every available line.

Call Bridging

Many potential customers will want to offer their call recipients the option to take an action. You can imagine calling on behalf of a political action committee and saying, "Your senator is about to vote on an issue you care very much about. Tell him what you think. To be connected with his office, press 1." In a previous example we considered the insurance company which wanted to say, "To talk with a customer service representative and ensure there is no lapse in your coverage, press 1."

When the customer presses 1, we will make an outgoing call (to the senator's office or to the insurance company) and then bridge the two calls together.

Post-production and MIS Analyzed

In version 1.0, we will provide the customer with summary and detail information about who we called and what the results were. This will include our best guess as to whether we spoke with a recipient or left the message on a machine, as well as whether the person called into our system to have the message repeated.

The trickier and more interesting question is what MIS, Jay, and Operations will need from the system to better manage the business. It is imperative that we get a good understanding of what is required, recognizing that these needs will evolve, so that we can make sure we're capturing the right information at the right granularity.

We now make a decision that violates an 'ivory tower' understanding of the process, but which is entirely correct from a real-world development viewpoint: we decide to postpone the analysis of post-production until after the design and at least the partial implementation of the rest of the system. There is already plenty on our plate, and we think we understand enough of the MIS requirements to move forward.

The single greatest risk in this decision is that our database may not reflect the information we'll need if we don't understand, in advance, what reports we'll be generating. I ask Jay and Kevin to spend some time thinking about what reports they'll need for their customers and to manage their business. They promise to get back to me very soon, and we move on for now.

Actors and Use Cases

We return to our use cases with the goal of filling in the details. We now understand a lot more about how the customer interacts with the system. In our first use case diagram, we stay at the top level. The customer can sign up and 'become' a customer, he can manage his jobs (start them, change them, etc.) and he can ask for reports on the work we've done.

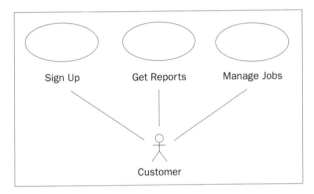

Each of the uses (Sign Up, Get Reports or Manage Jobs) can now be broken down further. For example, based on our use cases, 'Manage Jobs' can be broken down to include 'Start a Job', 'Initiate a Crisis Call', 'Cancel Jobs', or 'Change Job Parameters'. I capture these possibilities in this figure:

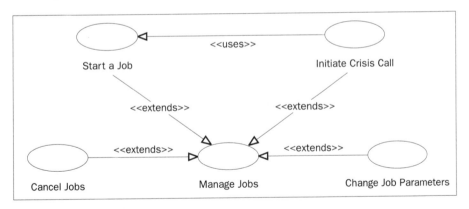

In a use case diagram, the designation <<extends>> indicates that one use case is a specialization or variation of another. For example, 'Cancel Jobs' is a special form of 'Manage Jobs'. This is very similar to inheritance in C++ — the idea is to factor out commonality into the base class or use case, and then to add additional functionality or specialization in the derived class. In C++ we say the derived class inherits from the base; with use cases we say the derived use case <<extends>> the base use case.

The <<uses>> designation indicates that one use case subsumes everything in another. This is simply a shorthand way to avoid cut and paste — much like a function call in C++. For example, when you create a job you must choose the phone numbers and also choose the audio. Since other scenarios will also need to choose audio and phone numbers, we break these operations out into their own use cases, and then we say that 'Create a Job' <<uses>> 'Choose Audio' and 'Choose Phone Numbers'.

At first glance, 'Start a Job' appears to be atomic. Of course, on closer examination we realize that to start a job you must have first created a job, and to have done that you must have chosen your audio and phone numbers. 'Start a Job' also involves whatever it takes to log into the system and to select among *Crisis•Call, Flash•Call* and so forth. All of this is captured in the figure:

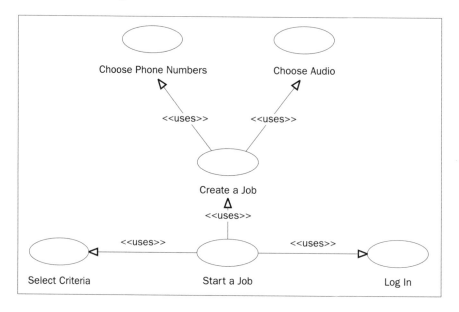

We continue generating these diagrams until we have a set we consider more or less complete, which captures most of the interactions with the system. We continually refer back to the original set of use cases to make sure we've captured what we know.

Objects

We are now ready to begin thinking about what high-level objects we'll be working with. We start by brainstorming: writing down *every* potential object to give us a running start. For this exercise, the whiteboard is particularly useful. We'll add a 'notes' section, so that we can capture ideas about how the object is used, but we don't want detail at this time.

At first, nothing is rejected; we'll write down every candidate object. Also, we won't differentiate between objects and attributes for now — we can worry about collapsing some of these objects into attributes of other objects once we've created a fairly exhaustive list. If we get stuck, we can **highlight** words in the 'notes' section that may themselves be candidate actors or objects.

As a next step, we parse the use cases to see if we can extract any additional candidate classes. We start with the nouns, both explicit and implied. These include customer, system, job, call, phone list, and audio.

Candidate	Type	Notes
Customer	Actor	
Owner/Manager	Actor	
Operations	Actor	
Sales/Admin. Asst.	Actor	
Job	object	A **job** is a **set** of **phone numbers** associated with **audio**, a **call flow** and a **schedule**
Call	object	A **call** associates a **single phone number** with a **job number**
Flow	object	Describes the **IVR** interaction for an **outbound call**
Schedule	object	Describes when a **job** is to begin, end and what hours it can be performed
Phone number	object	
Phone list	object	
Audio	object	The entire **set of audio** for one **job**
Audio segment	object	A **single audio piece** to be played
Prompt	object	**Audio** requesting **key strokes**
Response	object	**Keystrokes** entered by the **customer**
Account	object	Represents the **customer's company**
Contact	object	An **individual** at an **account**
Result	object	Encapsulates **report** on a **single call**
Port	object	Represents a **single phone line**
Web page	object	
Form	object	

While this list is preliminary, it is a good starting point for identifying the principal actors and objects, and lays the groundwork for the creation of a **model dictionary**. The model dictionary will manage the definitions of every object in the system.

One problem with assigning a type to a noun like this is that nouns that are actors are often also classes or objects. For example, 'customer' is an actor, but will probably be represented in the system as a class, so that the system can record details of a particular customer. Later on it can sometimes be helpful to adopt a naming convention to avoid confusion, e.g. CustomerActor, CustomerInfo.

With these classes and the use case diagrams, we can begin to think about the relationships among the objects. Examining the use cases for managing a job, and this list of objects, we generate a preliminary sketch of what seem like the most important classes:

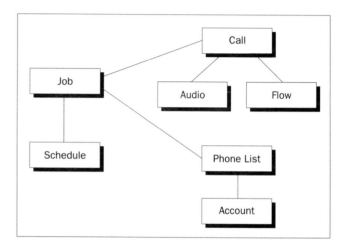

From this sketch, we can begin to consider how these objects interact. One way to lend order to this consideration is to consider the sequence of interactions among these objects, which you can see on the page opposite.

We are beginning to capture the interactions and the complex relations in a series of useful diagrams. These will be particularly helpful later in the process as we work through the design, and then test that design against the use cases that we've identified.

The next step is to work on the list of classes. We'll want to differentiate more clearly between those that are objects in their own right, and those that are best represented as attributes of objects. We'll want to eliminate redundancy, and begin the process of creating a more detailed definition of each of the objects. Finally, we'll want to begin the work of detailing the responsibilities of these objects and their collaborations.

CRC Cards

CRC (Class-Responsibility-Collaboration) cards are nothing more (and nothing less!) than 4x5 index cards. On each card you write the name of the class; beneath the name you may want to write its subclasses and superclasses. The rest of the face of the card is divided in half. On the left side, you write the word *Responsibilities* and on the right side, you write *Collaborations*. Finally, on the back of the card you write a brief description of the purpose of the class.

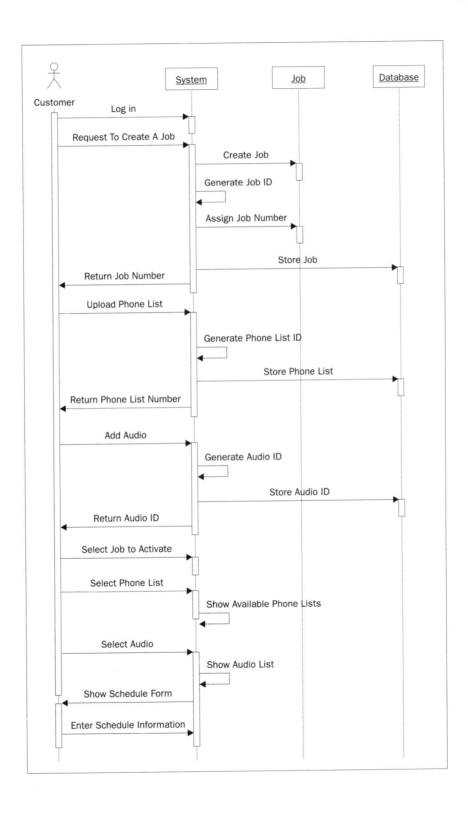

CRC cards are low-tech tools to help understand the principal classes and how they interact. They encourage role playing, which can be a powerful technique for understanding how the design will fulfill the use cases.

Filling in the CRC Cards

We create CRC cards for each of the principal classes. We start by putting the class name on the top line and taking a preliminary guess about the responsibilities and collaborations.

Class:	Job
Responsibilities	**Collaborations**
Knows list of phone numbers	
Knows audio to play	
Knows flow to use	
Knows schedule	

Class:	Call
Responsibilities	**Collaborations**
Knows phone number to call	
Knows job it is part of	
Knows current status	
Knows number of attempts	

Class:	Flow
Responsibilities	**Collaborations**
Knows interaction between recipient and IVR	

Class: Schedule

Responsibilities	Collaborations
Knows when to begin calling or when calls must end	
Knows what hours calls may be made	
Knows if hours are local time or EST	
Knows tilt	
Knows priority	

Class: Phone List

Responsibilities	Collaborations
Knows what phone numbers to call	

Class: Audio

Responsibilities	Collaborations
Knows all segments for a job	

Class: Account

Responsibilities	Collaborations
Knows contact information	
Knows contractual information	
Knows list of contacts	
Knows A/R & credit status	

Rather than creating cards for all the objects we've identified, we fill out only those cards we think we understand on inspection, and which we think will help with understanding the use cases. In the first attempt, we do *not* fill in the collaborations; they will come as we use the cards to work through the use cases.

We start by examining the scenario we identified in the last chapter:

> The customer is Edison Electric. They have to plan for emergencies at their nuclear power facility, which might include the need to call in all their managers and support personnel. In this event they want to call the right houses, but ensure that only the right person receives the message and that they know who got the message and who didn't. When the request comes in, the system must fulfill it immediately. By its nature, this will be an unplanned and unscheduled event.

The first object involved is the Account. It must know how to reach the right folks at Edison Electric. Therefore, we also need the Contact object, so we create a Contact card and add it as a collaboration on the Account card:

Class:	Account
Responsibilities	Collaborations
Knows contact information	Contact
Knows contractual information	
Knows list of contacts	
Knows A/R & credit status	

Class:	Contact
Responsibilities	Collaborations
Knows name	
Knows phone numbers	
Knows addresses	
Knows unique identification number	

Note that while the Account class has Contact in its collaborations, the Contact class does not reciprocate. The collaborations are typically recorded only one way: if Account needs information from Contact, the former makes the entry.

> "They have to plan for emergencies at their nuclear power facility, which might include the need to call in all their managers and support personnel."

We have handed the CRC cards out to the design team, and the engineer holding the Phone List waves it in the air and says, "I have the list of who to call." Do we need to create a Contact object for each person on the list? No, the Contact object is for contacts at our Account, not for those who are called. In fact, the system doesn't need an object for the people who are called, other than the Phone List.

> "In this event they want to call the right houses, but ensure that only the right person receives the message and that they know who got the message and who didn't."

This immediately changes the previous assumption. The system *does* need to know at least some information about each person called. We need to know, at a minimum, how they identify themselves.

The engineer with the Call card waves it in the air and says, "The Call can be tied to a password or other identification string. It can even be tied to the recipient's name if the customer needs that."

Class:	Call
Responsibilities	Collaborations
Knows phone number to call	
Knows job it is part of	
Knows current status	
Knows number of attempts	
Knows password if any	
May know recipient's name or ID	

> "When the request comes in, the system must fulfill it immediately. This will by its nature be an unplanned and unscheduled event."

This creates a lengthy discussion. Is a Schedule object needed in this case? We agree that it is, although it will need to accommodate the idea of calling *now*, with no limit on when it is finished or what hours the calls are made. We imagine this being, perhaps, a derived type of Schedule object called a Crisis.

We take a moment to translate the CRC cards back into UML class descriptions, so that we can begin to examine the relationships among these classes. We begin by entering the classes into Rational Rose, and continue translating CRC cards into class specifications until our principal classes are all represented:

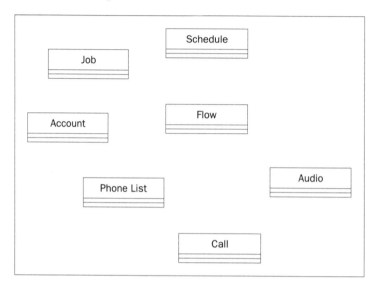

At this point it is time to begin thinking about how these classes relate to each other. We know that a Job has one or more phone lists, so we pick up the appropriate tool in Rose and draw that relationship. By double clicking on the line we can enter the **cardinality**, or in UML terms the **multiplicity**, which in this case is n to 1 (each job has only one phone list, but each phone list may be used on many jobs).

We continue laying out these preliminary relationships until the diagram represents what we know about these classes and how they relate to one another:

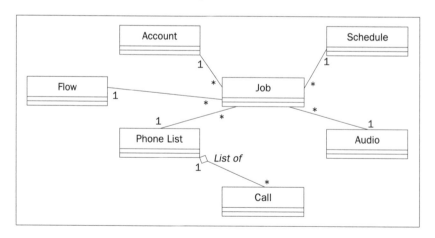

As we draw the relationships, we realize that some of the responsibilities that we initially thought were attributes of the class are best shown as relations. Thus, rather than telling Rose that Job has a Phone List (as an attribute), we show that as a 'has-a' relationship between the two classes.

CRC cards are an excellent tool for answering the common question, "What is an attribute, and what is a class?" A class owns a responsibility. CRC cards can help you differentiate which objects own the responsibilities implied by your use cases. Going back to our table of prospective objects, we see immediately that our 'phone number' class has no notes. When it came to creating a CRC card, we couldn't provide it with any responsibilities other than knowing its own intrinsic data (the phone number itself). This led us to decide to make 'phone number' a simple attribute of the Call class rather than create a Phone Number class and link them with a has-a relationship.

CRC cards can also help you find those classes to which you've assigned more than one responsibility. Each class should have either a single responsibility, or a small set of closely related responsibilities. If you find your class has two or more highly disparate responsibilities, it may be time to break it into two or more classes.

The power of UML diagrams is now clear. In this single, small diagram we can see a lot about these seven classes and how they relate to one another.

Generalizing the Process

During analysis, we worked hard to tease out the details and to distinguish between those features which are absolutely required in the first release, and those that can be held back.

By talking through how the system will interact with the actors, we are able to detail what it must be able to do. In this case the actors include the customer setting up jobs, the people we call, and Management.

This essential point cannot be overemphasized: by examining how the system will be *used*, we get a much more detailed picture of what it must be capable of doing. The use cases imply the responsibilities of the system.

We achieved this level of detail by moving back and forth between a deep but narrow discussion of a single feature, and a wider and more generalized discussion of the entire product. During analysis we were careful to challenge Jay's assumptions about what he required continually, and to explore creative solutions that redefined the problem into something we could solve.

A classic example of this latter approach is how we solved the issue of differentiating calls answered by people from those answered by machines. We started by understanding, in detail, the technical obstacles. The solution was not technical, however; it was achieved by redefining the problem so that it didn't much matter whether we were accurate in this detection; we found a solution that worked best when we could differentiate, but worked acceptably well when we failed.

Moving on to Design

At this point in the analysis we begin to approach the asymptote, where continued analysis will yield only marginally greater understanding of the project. The tendency to continue analyzing and reexamining the issues indefinitely is called 'analysis paralysis', and can be just as dangerous as under-analyzing the system. Watch for the warning signs of diminishing returns on your investment of time and energy, and don't be afraid to get going on design; you can, and will, return to analysis once you've designed for a while.

In fact, we begin the design phase knowing that the design process itself will tease out more requirements, which will need to feed right back into the analysis. That is fine and as it should be. As I said at the beginning, the process is an iterative one.

```
m false;
Time();
= now.Format("%b %d

er = "start < '";
oday;
' and enddate > '";
today;
= '";

ScheduleSet.m_strFilter =

JobScheduleSet.IsOpen())

JobScheduleSet.Requery();

pDoc>m_JobScheduleSet.Open();

llTrack* pCallTrack;

l ok;

ile
pDoc>m_JobScheduleSet.IsEOF())

pCallTrack = new
llTrack(m_pDoc>m_JobScheduleSet.m_
bID);
ok = pCallTrack>Initialize();

if (ok)
{    Log("ok\n");

m_CallList.AddHead(pCallTrack);
foundJobs = true;
}
else
{    Log("...Rejected!\n");
delete pCallTrack;
}

}

m_pDoc>m_JobScheduleSet.MoveNext();


run
CTime
CTime::GetCurren
CTime end = theJob
CTime start = theJobSet.
CTime todayStart(start.GetYear(),
start.GetMonth(), now.GetDay(),
start.GetHour(),
start.GetMinute(),
start.GetSecond());
CTime todayEnd(end.GetYear(),
end.GetMonth(), now.GetDay(),
end.GetHour(),
end.GetMinute(), end.GetSecond());

if (todayStart > now || todayS
now)
{    theJobSet.Close();
return false;
}

CTimeSpan theSpan = end no
int totalMinutes =
theSpan.GetTotalMinutes();

if (end > todayEnd) //
than today
{    int AdditionalMin =
GetAdditionalMinutes(the
t.
theJobSet.m_EndDate);
CTimeSpan todayS
now;    totalMinutes =
todaySpan.GetTotalMin
AdditionalMin;
}

m_min = ( ( (m_t
totalMinutes) + 1
);
m_Priority = theJo
m_Tilt = theJo
m_Throttle = the
m_JobID = the
theJobSet.Cl
return true
```

CHAPTER FOUR

High-Level Design

Exploring the Platform

In theory, one might complete the high-level design without considering the implementation technology. Many experts in object-oriented design recommend this approach, and it makes a certain amount of sense. The idea is to avoid overly constraining your design. This theory would also argue that you ought to decide on your hardware only when you know a lot more about what it must do.

That said, it isn't how I'll do it here, and it isn't how I *would* do it on just about any real project. The reality is that I can't sleep at night until I know, deep down in my heart of hearts, that this project is technically feasible, and I can't know *that* until I understand a lot more about how we'll implement it.

There is a 'chicken and egg' problem here, of course. How can I know if I can implement something, if I don't know what I'm building? The answer is that even before we begin the formal design, we have enough from the analysis to make some sharp guesses, and to begin making some tentative assumptions.

As we sit down to begin the discussion, we agree to take the time to prove to ourselves that we understand enough of the implementing technologies to believe in the schedule, and then we can turn our attention to the high-level design. Once we understand the design at a high level, we can dive into the details and work through the implementation. Only once implementation is well under way will we consider optimizing for performance.

Again, this is the theory. I can tell you that from time to time we'll go into the details to make sure that we've not designed something we can't implement, but we'll only far go enough to reduce our anxiety. Then we'll back off and save the real low-level details for the next round of design.

Platform Decisions

The most important decision is this: every component of the system will be sufficiently encapsulated that if we decide later in the process to change these decisions, or to re-implement parts of the system with newer technologies, we can do so without breaking the rest of the system. For example, if we decide to use SQL Server now, but in a year or two realize that Informix or Oracle is a better solution, we'll just unplug one and plug in the other. None of the rest of the code should be affected by that decision, if we design it right.

Telephony Card

The first question we need to address is the easiest: which telephony cards to use? Hypotenuse has already answered that question to its own satisfaction, many times over. They are well invested in Dialogic cards, and Dialogic is the leading vendor in the field. There is little reason to spend a lot of time wringing our hands over this decision; we'll stay with Dialogic until and unless we see a compelling reason to change. Dialogic cards are supported on just about every conceivable platform, and so choosing Dialogic doesn't seriously constrain our other platform decisions.

Telephony Software

The question of which tools to use to write the telephony components is much more difficult. Our choices come down to three general approaches:

- Use an application generator
- Write to the Dialogic API
- Use a toolkit or class library

Application Generators

We spend a lot of time on this question, as the decisions we make will have far reaching consequences. I was skeptical of application generators right out of the gate: I worried they wouldn't scale, wouldn't be sufficiently flexible, and that we'd pay a significant performance penalty. I spoke with and visited a number of vendors who were *convinced* that each of these objections could be overcome. They pointed out that building telephony applications was all they did all day, and they promised to shorten my development time and reduce my risk.

It is always very difficult to evaluate the long-term limitations of a suite of tools. You can ask a vendor, "What might I want to do with your product that I won't be able to do because of its limitations?" but they are disposed to overcome objections, not to provide a frank appraisal of why their tool won't do what you need. They just aren't prepared to think about the question in those terms. Further, without objective comparison testing, it is hard to quantify the price you will pay for any tool, and especially for an application generator, where you are buying a single, integrated approach.

I have no real prejudices here. I know that many C++ programmers think that such programs are for wimps, and that real programmers always write source code. For the moment, they are right, but only because the application generators are not yet up to the job. The day I become convinced that an application generator can do the job will be the day I switch over. After all, I don't write in assembler, I use the Wizards whenever I'm writing Windows code, and I have no desire to spend my time in the mud when I can be soaring in the clouds.

The fun in an application like the one we're creating is in conceptualizing the pieces, and building an efficient application that meets the customer's needs. If an application generator can shorten that process, then great! The problem is this: how do you determine the price you'll pay? Robert Heinlein coined the acronym TANSTAAFL — There Ain't No Such Thing As A Free Lunch — and I don't expect to find one here.

Before investing a lot of time in determining the efficiency or flexibility of the code produced by the various application generators, I start by examining the actual monetary costs. The Dialogic API and the class libraries I'm considering have no run-time licensing fees; the leading application generators do.

The most promising application generators I can find have a *per port* run-time fee of $300. Even with intense negotiation, we realize this will never fall below $150. For 500 ports, that adds $75,000 to the cost of development, and as we scale up the operation, our costs will scale up dramatically. The combination of run-time licensing and my own skepticism about flexibility and performance leads me to set this option aside while I pursue other approaches.

Writing to the API

The other extreme of the software development curve is to eschew all help and write directly to the Dialogic API. This is an attractive alternative; the API is well supported and documented. It is, however, a C-style library of function calls.

The first thing I'd do would almost certainly be to write a class library to wrap these function calls and to provide an object-oriented interface to the boards. The question then is whether I'd be better off writing this myself or buying it from someone who has already provided a class library for this purpose.

Visual Voice

We identify the Visual Voice class library as a viable alternative to writing our own class library for the Dialogic cards. There are one or two other class libraries available, but they appear to be targeted at smaller applications. Visual Voice is an industrial-strength alternative that doesn't try to do too much or second-guess your development effort; it simply provides an object-oriented interface to the Dialogic API.

Visual Voice ships with three interfaces:

- The Visual Voice ActiveX control
- The Visual Voice class library
- The Visual Voice DLL

The first of these is most often used in Visual Basic applications. Drop the control into your form, and Hey Presto! You have control over the telephony card. The problem is that you can't easily write a multithreaded application using Visual Basic.

Artisoft, the company that produces Visual Voice, strongly suggests setting the ActiveX control aside, and using either their class library (if you're a C++ programmer) or the DLL (if you're not). We decide to go with the class library.

A limitation of Visual Voice is that each application written using it can handle 72 lines at most, and then only when running on NT. After some discussion with them about our application, we decide to scale this down to 48 lines, and to build the calling machines on Windows NT Workstation. The folks at Artisoft felt that using a lower number of lines (48 rather than 72) would optimize their use of memory and greatly increase the absolute reliability of the system. The 48-line limitation isn't significant for us because this is a *per machine* limit. The overall system can grow as large as we need.

The decision to go with Visual Voice has enormous implications for the design, and makes me uncomfortable. Using Visual Voice will dictate that we will need a series of stand-alone calling machines rather than an integrated array of virtual ports. Visual Voice will dictate the operating system (Windows NT) and, inevitably, it will dictate some of the core architectural relationships. In exchange for this, however, Artisoft will apply *their* resources to managing the Dialogic API, and will ensure a clean and painless class library for us to work with. On balance, this seems like an acceptable trade-off, and we decide to move forward with this decision.

This 'build or buy' dilemma is classic. In the past, the default solution was to build your own custom solution from scratch. These days, with more rapid development and more high-powered components available, the correct solution is more often to assemble your application out of existing pieces. The problem is that the existing pieces don't always fit together, and don't always do exactly what you want.

Finding the right balance between writing from scratch, and building on the working (if limited) solutions you can buy, is often one of the most difficult, and certainly one of the most important, decisions you'll make. In this particular case, there were three options open: writing code directly to the Dialogic driver, using the Visual Voice API, or going with an application generator. While I spent some time thinking this through and making sure I understood the trade-offs, once the costs/benefits of each were pretty well understood, the decision to go with Visual Voice was relatively easy.

Operating System

The only realistic operating system choices for a telephony/Internet application are UNIX and Windows NT. The primary considerations in deciding between these operating systems will be:

- Suitability to task
- Performance, security and scalability
- Availability of tools
- Integration with the other parts of the system

Both UNIX and NT are particularly suitable to Internet and telephony applications. UNIX has had the edge over the past few years, but this is changing rapidly.

It is difficult to get reliable statistics for performance differences, but a review of the literature shows that either should be fine. Security is excellent on both platforms, and they both scale well, although UNIX may have a short-term advantage in building fault-tolerant redundant systems.

The picture is in flux, however, because Microsoft needs to solve every problem we'll be confronting if they are to take the lead in Internet development (as is their clear intention). Every issue we'll face in the development of *Crisis•Call*, with the exception of the particular manipulation of the Dialogic cards, will be confronted by everyone developing Internet applications.

As part of Microsoft's commitment to become the premier platform for Internet development, they are releasing literally dozens of tools over the next few months. Our design phase is scheduled to end in April, which is concurrent with the release of Microsoft's new tools, including Visual InterDev. We will leverage these tools in the development of the web pages and are counting on these technologies to make delivery of database information quick and easy.

The net result of this is that, once coupled with a suite of tools that will simplify development, NT appears to offer the performance, security and scalability options we require. We will ride Microsoft's shirttails as they solve the very problems we'll be confronting in implementing this system.

The remaining question lies with the telephony piece, but all the options we are considering — application generators, class libraries and writing to the Dialogic API — have implementations on NT that are either as good as or better than those on UNIX. Our decision to use Visual Voice is the final compelling reason; Visual Voice only runs on NT.

A reasonable and defensible argument can still be made for UNIX, but the combination of available tools, Microsoft's commitment, and the other, interdependent platform decisions we've made, leads us to choose NT.

Programming Language

I know a lot of programmers who tell me that their decision about programming language is made in response to the problem they are trying to solve. They imagine their development choices as a series of tools, and the craftsman picks the right tool for the right job. It is a great image, but it isn't how most of us work.

While I have programmed professionally in Assembler, Pascal, BASIC, Visual Basic, C, C++, Java, and a number of scripting languages, I don't move among them freely if I can help it. Generally, I work with the language I'm most comfortable with unless there is a compelling reason to do otherwise. There are times when you *absolutely* want to choose, for example, HTML over C++, but there is almost never a time when I'd choose Pascal over C++. Once I moved from Pascal to C, I never went back; when I went from C to C++, another door closed behind me.

Visual Voice supports three programming languages: Visual Basic, Delphi and C++. As I said, Visual Basic does not easily support multithreading, and we know that an application of the scale we're proposing would never work without such a feature. As well as providing support for multithreading, C++ has the advantage that it is a cross-platform development language. While it looks like we're settling on Windows and MFC, if we change these decisions in the future, C++ gives us the flexibility to maintain our code across platforms. Visual Basic and Delphi are Windows-only.

> *Visual Basic and Delphi are usually best for rapid development and proof-of-concept work, although in skilled hands, building an application with MFC and the Visual C++ Wizards can be almost as quick. However, when you're considering the more general case, the **big** advantage of going with VB is that VB programmers tend to be less expensive than C++ programmers, and that brings down the long-term maintenance costs of your project.*

Our decision turns on the performance requirements: C++ will give us smaller, faster code. Thus, given the practical programming realities, the requirements of the task at hand, the tools and components we have decided on, and my own skill set, the choice is pretty easy: we'll write the telephony application in C++ using the Visual Voice class libraries.

Having chosen our language, we must now choose among the available application frameworks. I have programmed extensively with MFC, and I'm reluctant seriously to consider Borland's alternative, OWL. I've read nothing to convince me it offers a significant advantage. Microsoft's Active Template Library *does* have some significant advantages in the way it works with DCOM, but my reading of the literature suggests that it is targeted at applications that have no UI, or at building controls that will be used by other applications. We anticipate having a UI, at least in the early stages, and MFC offers the ability to get the UI up and running quickly.

We decide to move forward with MFC, but to work hard to encapsulate it so that we can migrate to ATL if that becomes appropriate down the road.

An All-Microsoft Solution

While we could easily spend a lot of time deciding on the right database to use, the truth is that our database requirements are fairly simple, and any industrial-strength, multi-threaded relational database should be fine. SQL Server has the advantage of being manufactured and supported by the same folks who provide the operating system, and of integrating well with Microsoft's Internet Information Server.

There are two Internet servers to which we give serious consideration: Microsoft's and Netscape's. The single great advantage of choosing Microsoft's Internet Information Server is that by coupling IIS with SQL Server, Microsoft's database solution, we can use a suite of integrated tools that are known to work well with one another. This, coupled with the Visual InterDev toolkit, makes for a very powerful combination.

This (nearly) all-Microsoft solution has great appeal — when we call for help, we will not have to chase from vendor to vendor as we try to track down the specific areas we're having trouble with. When we call Microsoft with a question, specifying the application as one running on NT, using IIS with SQL Server as a back-end, offers far greater likelihood that they will be able to provide the help we need.

Lessons Learned

Choosing your programming language and application framework can be one of the most critical development decisions of the project. In this particular case, given what we needed to accomplish and the other tools chosen, Visual C++ and the Microsoft Foundation Classes were the obvious choices for the primary tools. Less clear is the degree to which we should try to take advantage of the relatively new tools available to support ActiveX and DCOM. You can't miss that Microsoft has heavily invested in this technology, and that ultimately we'll want to take advantage of some of what DCOM has to offer. The question is whether the technology is ready for primetime, and what the cost will be to learn what I need to know to use it well. I still see DCOM as 'bleeding edge', and I'm gun-shy after previous experiences with similarly young technologies.

In 1992, when we set out to build the Interchange Online Network, C++ was a relatively new language, with few compilers and only the most sparse of application frameworks. Senior management dictated that Interchange would be a cross-platform product, running equally well on both the Mac and Windows. This requirement drove many of our subsequent decisions.

We were wary of attempting simultaneous cross-platform development, but seduced by a new class library that promised to hide the details. Apple, in cooperation with Symantec, was developing a killer cross-platform application development framework. They agreed to bring us into the beta program for what they were calling 'Bedrock'.

Originally, they intended that we should work with Bedrock without access to the source code. This was unthinkable; it is nearly impossible to work effectively with a class library without access to the source code, and this beta product was barely documented. They subsequently agreed to supply a copy of the source code stripped of the semicolons. This was a clever solution to their concern that we might violate our agreement not to recompile their product, but it immediately established a lack of trust that, at least for me, always marked the relationship.

The decision to go with Bedrock was fateful in many ways. Bedrock only compiled with Zortech, which even then was an old compiler with problems of its own. C++ was still evolving, but Zortech had stopped at a previous version of the language. Further, since we were restricted to Zortech, we were constrained in which debugger we could use, and were forced to work with a beta copy of the very promising but not yet fully implemented Multiscope debugger (which was later absorbed into Symantec's compiler).

This left us in an awkward position. When a program failed, we had to ask ourselves, "Is it my code, the class library, the compiler, or the debugger that's broken?" It was impossible to tell. The cost to the schedule of the resulting confusion is incalculable.

Encapsulation

The net effect of my experience with the class library decision at Interchange is this: I'm reluctant to live on the bleeding edge of development. If there's a way to accomplish all I need to do without using DCOM and ActiveX, I'm inclined to set them aside for now. That said, there are times when there simply is no choice: your customer is demanding that you include a feature that is only supported by a new, possibly beta-level, product.

In this case, object-oriented technique comes to the rescue with **encapsulation**. When there is a dangerous aspect of your code, built on a shaky foundation, the single best defense against having your entire edifice collapse is to ensure that the questionable technology is isolated from the rest of the product.

This is nothing more than the logical continuance of the overall commitment to building components. A component-based product consists of small isolated units, which can be plugged in and out of the product without breaking anything else. This is achieved by creating narrow and well-understood interfaces; any component that supports a given interface is interchangeable with any other component that supports the interface. This is one of the fundamentals of object-oriented programming, and its importance can't be overstated.

Patterns

There are a number of design patterns to support multi-platform development. The **abstract factory** pattern supports the idea of abstracting out object creation, and dynamically creating the right object based on which system you are developing for. As an example, we might create an abstract base class called `Button` and then implement a `MacButton` and a `WindowsButton` as derived classes.

Creating the **MacButton** using the **new** operator would hard-code the decision, which is exactly what we're trying to avoid. The abstract factory pattern solves this by abstracting out the process of object creation. Here's the problem. If we were to write:

```
MacButton* pButton = new MacButton;
```

then when we wanted to change it to

```
WindowsButton* pButton = new WindowsButton;
```

we'd have to find every instance of the former and change it to the latter. In traditional programming, we'd solve this with **#ifdef** statements, which make for very ugly and hard-to-maintain code. With the abstract factory pattern, we write instead:

```
Button* pButton = myFactory->CreateButton();
```

At compile time, we simply ensure that **myFactory** is an instance of a **WindowsFactory** or a **MacFactory**, and the rest follows from that one, highly encapsulated decision. In fact, if we later decide to support a third platform, we need only create, for example, a **UnixFactory**. To make this work, of course, all three factories must derive from the abstract base class **PlatformFactory**. For example, we might have:

```
class PlatformFactory
{
    virtual Button*   CreateButton   () = 0;

    // ...
}


class WindowsFactory : public PlatformFactory
{
    virtual Button*   CreateButton   ()
        { return new WindowsButton; }

    // ...
}
```

It's worth noting that you often need to implement your multi-platform solution in terms of an existing and immutable class library that you obtain from a vendor. In this case, the **bridge** pattern can help 'bridge' your code to theirs, using a set of classes that provide the interface between your platform-independent code and their platform-specific class library. Both of these patterns are described in detail in *Design Patterns, Elements of Reusable Object-Oriented Software* by Gamma et al.

Internet Application Development

At this point in the project, I don't need to know how I will implement each component in detail, but I do need to assure myself that I am taking on a manageable effort. I drive over to SoftPro in Burlington, where I pick up books on NT Server and Workstation, Microsoft Internet Information Server, Microsoft SQL Server and ActiveX. I also bought *Instant Active Web Development Programming* by Alex Homer — a terrific introduction to many of the implementing technologies I'll be using.

The following week, I order a 2-line development package from Visual Voice; it is time to install the software, fire it up and figure out just how difficult this is going to be. On all counts, I am pleasantly surprised: none of it looks like being all that hard. There are a lot of pieces to bring together, and some of this technology is new to me, but it is all quite manageable, and the tricky parts of Internet development will be made easier by some of the new tools about to be released by Microsoft.

Focus on the High-Level Design

I convene the first, formal high-level design meeting bright and early in mid-February. We've spent the past six weeks nailing down the specification requirements with Jay, and exploring the implementing technologies to prove to ourselves that this is an entirely manageable project. Now we're ready to begin designing the major components.

"So," I ask, "where do we start?" We quickly agree that the most effective thing will be to tackle a specific chunk of the design, and we zero in on the out-calling process. How will this work?

Outbound Calls

One significant issue we immediately identify is, "How will the system figure out which phone number to call next, and which line to call it on?" To get us started, I propose these high-level components: a database, a call server and a series of calling machines.

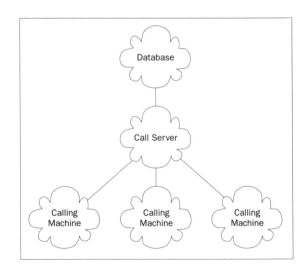

The machines are connected on a local area network. The call server is responsible for feeding each of the calling machines. The calling machines may present themselves to the call server as a single bank of phone lines, or may each present a subset of the total number of lines independently.

Getting a Number from the Database to the Calling Machine

We initially imagine that the calling machine will ask the database for the 'next' number to call, but there are a number of problems even with that apparently simple picture.

First, determining the correct 'next' number is non-trivial; there are many factors to consider. Some jobs have a higher priority than others do, some are tilted towards the start (or end) of the allotted time, and some are throttled to limit the number of connections per hour. We agree that the call server will need a scheduler object, whose job will be to determine the right mix of phone numbers from the 'current' jobs.

> **This is a general pattern in object-oriented analysis and design. If there is a discrete job to do, then we look for an object to do that job. This division of responsibility creates a cleaner and more extensible design.**

A second problem is that we will have a number of calling machines, and each will be asking for numbers from the scheduler at the same time. A list (or queue) will allow us to serialize these requests, so that we can fulfill them in a reasonable and reasoned order. Scheduling is a big enough job on its own, so we'll want another object to handle the fulfilling of requests from the calling machines.

Steve points out that much of what the call server must do is similar to what an operating system must do: match jobs with available resources. The power of this observation is that it supplies a metaphor for the task at hand. By comparing each sub-task to those done by an operating system, we can quickly understand what must be done. He goes on to point out that many of the algorithms are already well understood, and we can build on the lessons learned by the people who build operating systems. For example, drawing on his understanding of how modern operating systems work, he proposes we divide the call server into two objects: a scheduler and a dispatcher. These objects will work in tandem, sharing a call queue.

The scheduler will work with the database to determine which calls must be scheduled, and to order those calls. It will feed phone numbers into the call queue. The dispatcher will take numbers off the queue and give them to the calling machines. This division of responsibility is desirable for a number of reasons. Most important, each object should do one thing and only one thing. The scheduler is responsible for knowing what must run next; it shouldn't know anything about fulfilling requests from clients. The division also gives us the flexibility later to add more schedulers. Each scheduler may add to the queue, but only one object will take things *off* the queue, which will help with data integrity.

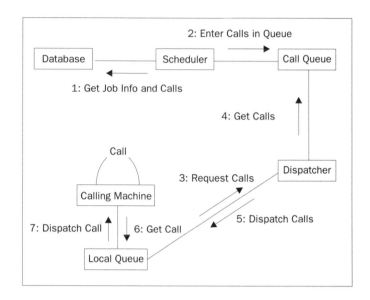

We create an 'object interaction' or 'collaboration' diagram to capture these relationships.

The calling machine's responsibility is *only* to manage the call. It doesn't know or care anything about the schedule of calls, or the order in which calls will be made. The dispatcher gives it a call object, and that object associates a phone number with a flow. The flow in turn associates audio and a sequence in which to present the audio to the recipient.

At first, we imagine that the calling machine requests a call from the dispatcher each time a line opens. This will involve considerable inefficiency for the calling machine, however, due to network latency. The imperative is to keep the calling machine 100% busy. Every time it completes a call, another one should be there, waiting to be called.

We agree that, *as an optimization*, the calling machine will keep a queue of its own. This is the 'local queue' object you can see in the above diagram. Since each machine will handle 48 lines, and the fastest a call can be completed and the line recycled is 1 minute, the machine will consume at most 48 calls per minute. We need there to be enough phone numbers in its queue to ensure that the queue can never be emptied. To play it safe, we decide to provide three sets of 48 calls, which we name 'chunks'. One chunk contains 48 phone numbers; each calling machine will keep a queue of three chunks.

When the queue drops below the 2-chunk mark, the calling machine will request another chunk from the dispatcher. In this way, the machine will be calling one chunk, holding a second chunk and receiving a third chunk at any given moment. Even if the network slows for a moment, the calling machine should never notice. We generalize this idea to say that the local call queue will have a 'low-water mark', and when the number of calls waiting drops below that mark, the local call queue will request more numbers (in a batch) from the dispatcher.

Scaling the Architecture

It is imperative that the architecture scales cleanly. While the first release may handle only 288 lines at a time, we must anticipate scaling the service to handle as many as 20 times that. There isn't much need, however, to scale beyond that point. 5,760 lines would give us more than perhaps any other calling center in the world. To ensure that we'll be able to scale, I'll repeatedly ask, "What happens when we go to 1,000 lines? What happens when we go to 5,000 lines?"

One advantage of grouping the calls into batches (of, say, 48) is that each calling machine will make requests across the network less frequently. If we imagine that the dispatcher can handle at least one request per second (and it should handle many more than that), it can therefore handle 60 machines each requesting 48 calls, or a total of 2,880 lines in the proposed configuration of 48 lines per machine.

When we grow beyond this size, it will be time to create a second scheduler. At that point, we'll need a 'balancer', whose job it will be to keep the various schedulers evenly balanced, based on the sizes of their call queues. We want to spend enough time thinking through how this will work to ensure that the architecture scales, but we don't need to fill in all the details since it will be quite a long time before we get up to 3,000 lines. We certainly won't implement this design until we need to, and in fact this becomes a rule of development:

> **Design for the future, but code for immediate needs.**

If our estimates are empirically shown to be conservative — if a scheduler can handle not just 1 dispatch request per second, but three — then we can stay with one scheduler for 8,640 lines, and that's well beyond what we ever anticipate. Of course, if we are wrong in the other direction — if handling even a single request per second is too taxing — then we'll need to add new schedulers more quickly, but that would surprise me very much.

If, ultimately, we do need to create more than one scheduler to handle a very large number of calls, we must decide how to split up the calling machines. Which machines will be allocated to each scheduler? There are two obvious alternatives: divide the calling machines among the schedulers, or have every scheduler talk to every calling machine.

At first glance, it seems the easiest path is to divide the calling machines by profile, so that one scheduler handles calls for the calling machines with 'inexpensive' phone lines, and another handles scheduling for the calling machines with 'premium' phone lines. There are a number of problems with this approach, however.

The first problem with linking schedulers to profiles is that there will be an uneven distribution. We will not, for example, have the same numbers of inexpensive and premium phone lines. The second problem is that we'll need the 'balancer' to figure out which machines are *eligible* for a given job. For example, some jobs will require any available line, but other jobs will be designated to run only on inexpensive lines. This increases the complexity of the overall approach.

The third, and perhaps most significant problem, is that there will be a combinatorial explosion of profiles. If we have machines with *three* levels of expense (differing phone lines with differing price plans), and only some machines have voice recognition boards, and only some have, for example, the ability to conference call, we quickly find ourselves with 27 combinations or profiles.

Considering the second alternative, the issue here is how we'll handle record locking so that two schedulers don't access the same queue at the same time. This isn't a very difficult problem, however, so we decide this will be the route we'll pursue when it is time to worry about more than one scheduler. Convinced that we *can* scale (and thankful that we don't yet *have* to scale), we set this issue to rest.

Scheduling Calls

In our next design session, we are almost ready to move on. What shall we tackle next? The calling machines, perhaps, or the database? Before we start, however, we confess to a nagging concern about the calling architecture: what exactly will it take to schedule calls?

The scheduler must take into account the myriad factors of:

- Earliest date we can begin calling
- Latest date we can end calling
- Times of the day we are allowed to call
- Tilt
- Priority
- Throttle

We agree that, strictly speaking, this is a matter for low-level design and it is premature to focus on it now. On the other hand, the design depends on knowing that this can be done efficiently, and none of us is comfortable just to leave it as is. We agree to take a temporary digression into this topic, arguably a bit early, so that we can assure ourselves we fully understand the issues.

The highest-level description of what we want to accomplish is this: "For every eligible job, create an allocation of the available phone lines."

Eligibility to Call

A job is eligible for calling if the current time under consideration is after the job's absolute start time, before its absolute end time, and within the boundaries of the time it is allowed to make calls. We acknowledge that we'll have to handle time zones, but we leave that as a detail for later in the process.

Tilt

To keep the problem simple, for now, we assume all calls will tilt towards the front. We will set aside the impact of scheduling jobs that tilt toward their end time; this will, we hope, turn out to be a special case of the more common scheduling problem of calls that tilt to the front.

Priority

We have been talking about the priorities of the various jobs without establishing a definition. I submit that priority reflects a relationship between various jobs, and determines their relative access to the available ports. Thus, if one job has priority 3 and a second job has priority 2, the first job will place three calls for every two placed by the second job, all other considerations being equal.

This is consistent with how operating systems deal with relative priority, it is easy to capture in code, and it's easy to explain to the client. Hypotenuse will probably not deal with raw numbers; they may establish, for example, three levels of priority: 'low', 'medium' and 'high'. All they need to do is tell us their relative weights. For example, if they tell us that high priority calls ought to be made at four times the rate of medium, and that medium should be at twice the rate of low, we can easily translate 'low' into priority 1, 'medium' into priority 2 and 'high' into priority 8. Of course, they can establish any arbitrary number of priorities they like, and we'll use configuration files to allow them to change these ratings at will.

Throttle

Throttle establishes an effective *maximum* number of calls to make per unit of time. The customer, however, does not want to specify throttle in terms of calls to *make* but rather by the number of *connections* per hour. I propose that we handle this by establishing an initial ratio of attempted calls to successful calls. That ratio will be applied to the requested number of contacts to guess at how many calls we'll need to schedule to meet their constraint.

In fact, we'll keep a global ratio and a per-job ratio. The per-job ratio will be modified as we progress, as a result of experience in the single job, while the global ratio will be modified by our collective experience in all jobs. Thus, over time, the system will get smarter about its starting point, and as a job progresses we'll get smarter about that particular job.

For example, we might start out by assuming that 70% of all calls will result in a contact with a person. The global constant is set at 0.7, and the per-job constant starts at 0.7 as well. If a customer asks for 70 contacts per hour, we'll schedule 100 calls per hour. As the job progresses, we may adjust the constant to reflect our actual success rate. As many jobs feed back into the system, the global constant will be modified, so new jobs will *start* with a better guess.

To summarize, the system will first determine which jobs are eligible. It will then establish the relative priorities among the various jobs, and will assign the total set of available ports by the relative values.

The Calling Architecture

The picture we are working with now looks like this:

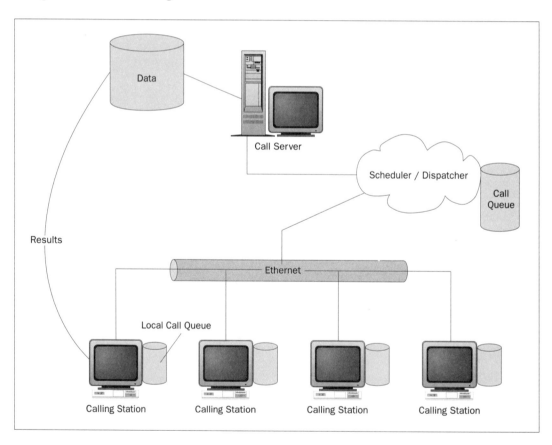

On one side of the network is a database. There is also a call server, which consists of a scheduler and a dispatcher. The scheduler fills the call queue, and the dispatcher draws from the call queue to feed the calling stations. Each station keeps a local queue, the purpose of which is simply to manage the network latency so that the calling stations are never without calls to make.

As we consider the call queue on the server, a number of options are discussed. We might put all the anticipated calls into the queue, and reorder them as the system reassesses relative priority. The idea would be to stack the calls up into one long virtual list, and then paw through it, reordering it as we go.

This has a number of problems, the most significant of which is that the list might be very long. There may be many jobs running at any given time, and each job could have hundreds of thousands of numbers. Managing such a list and reordering it may be very difficult, not to mention time-consuming.

An alternative is to keep the call queue rather short. When we assess the relative priority of the calls, we fill the queue with just enough to handle the load for a few minutes. When the queue falls below a preset amount, we reassess and refill. As the calls work their way through the queue, the relative order is maintained not by reordering the queue itself, but rather by reordering what we put in. If the queue is short enough, it will take only a few minutes for the effect of these changes to be felt. On reflection, I believe this to be a superior design.

Whither the Queue?

The next question about the queue is whether it is simply a table in the database, or it's a data structure in the call server application. The argument for putting the queue in the database is that we get transaction safety and ODBC support for free. The argument against is that we'll be hitting the database a lot more. Also, the queue is a relatively simple structure, so there may be no reason to over-engineer it as a table in the database.

We make the tentative decision that the call queue will be held outside the database, probably as a linked list. An added advantage of this is that we anticipate reusing much of the code that manages the call queue when we write the code to manage the *local* call queues on the calling machines.

Handling Retries

A related question is what we'll do with retries. When the calling system can't contact a recipient, either due to a busy signal, a no-answer or a busy circuit, we must reschedule the call. Jay has required that all calls in a job be tried once before any calls are *re*tried. Further, we don't want to busy the system by repeatedly trying someone who isn't home; it would be smarter to move on to other jobs and return to that call periodically.

We imagine a lot of smart 'back off' algorithms. In such a scheme, we will decrease over time the frequency with which we try a number. The assumption is that if they're not home an hour later, it's even less likely they'll be home an hour after that. For the first release, however, Jay prescribes a rather simple algorithm: we'll retry busy signals every 20 minutes and no-answers every hour, for a total of ten retries per phone number. For *Crisis•Calls* we'll retry busies every 2 minutes and no-answers every six, for a total of 20 retries. These numbers are arbitrary, so they will need to be parameters that Operations can set, and that will ultimately adjust themselves heuristically.

Where do these retries go? Are they held in the queue or in the database? We know we'll need to revisit these questions once we understand the calling client, but before we leave the call server we want to consider how we'll handle *Crisis•Calls*.

Handling Crisis·Calls

When a *Crisis•Call* comes into the system, it will take over all the lines. We discuss how this will actually be implemented. My suggestion is that the scheduler registers a *Crisis•Call*, and then immediately dumps its queue of calls waiting to go out. This implies that the queue must be rebuilt at the end of the crisis.

The scheduler will inform each of the calling machines that a *Crisis•Call* is in the pipe, and the calling machines will flush their call queues as well. They will complete whatever calls they are in the middle of, but their queues will immediately be filled with the *Crisis•Call* phone numbers, so the next calls they make will be for the *Crisis•Call*.

Once the crisis has been handled, the queues will be reinstated, picking up where they left off. To accomplish this, the database will need to know what calls are currently in the queue. We decide that the system will not distinguish between calls in the call queue (on the call server) and those that are cached at the local machines. This will be considered one large, virtual queue.

Calls will be marked 'enqueued' when they are added to the call queue. They will next be updated in the database at the conclusion of the call attempt. The calling machine must report back to the database for each call attempted. At the conclusion of a *Crisis•Call*, the queues are rebuilt as follows:

1. Each calling machine reports on all successful calls
2. Any calls that remain marked as 'enqueued' are then restored to the queue.

We note that this process should be very similar to how the system recovers from a failure. If the calling server, for example, is temporarily shut down (by a catastrophic loss of power) it will restore itself by asking all the calling machines to report on their successful calls, and then to dump their queues. When the system settles out, any calls marked 'enqueued' will be restored to the call queue.

This will ensure that we never fail to call anyone, and as long as the calling machines are able to report on their successful connections, we'll never call anyone twice. The one exception would be if the calling machine itself were to fail before it could report on its successes.

Designing the Call Client

We've already said a lot about types of calls, and retrying calls, but nothing about how the calling client actually accomplishes its tasks in the first place. We have agreed that the calling client has a local queue, and that when the queue falls below a low-water mark, it will request a new set of calls from the dispatcher. This will ensure that the calling machine is never starved of numbers to call, and that each port can be kept busy at all times, when there are calls to make.

At the conclusion of each call, the status of the call object must be updated to reflect the outcome of the call. Possible outcomes include a successful connection, failure due to busy signal, no answer, operator intercept, busy circuits and so forth. The calling machine must update the database with these results.

We discuss and debate how this update will be accomplished. If each call is updated immediately upon its completion (successful or otherwise) then the system has minimal vulnerability to a crash. On the other hand, updating the database after each call may involve literally thousands of updates per minute, and we speculate that this may be a lot of network traffic, and a lot for the database to handle.

The alternative is to store up a set of calls and update them all at once. For example, we might update the database once a minute, or once every 48 calls, or on some other batched basis. We agree that the calling thread won't concern itself with these details. Each call will be updated at the conclusion of the attempt and then it will be handed to a 'reporter' object. The reporter will be in the same process space as the caller, but its job will be to interact with the database, presumably using ODBC. There will be one reporter per calling station.

The next question to arise is this: to whom should the reporter report? It might hand the call back to the database, but if the call needs to be *retried*, does it get put back in the database, or should it be handed it to the scheduler?

We discuss this for some time. The advantage of handing it to the scheduler is that we save database traffic. The scheduler, after all, is the one that must retry the call after enough time has passed. The problem is that this makes the scheduler's job much more complex. It is possible that by the time the call is ready to be retried, it is past the calling window for that job, and so the call must wait until the next day. Also, different calls may have different retry intervals depending on the reason they were incomplete and the number of previous attempts.

We agree that the right answer is to put the unsuccessful call back in the database. The database handles records for a living, the call may not be retried for some time, and the scheduler shouldn't be busy with managing and juggling the hundreds or thousands of calls waiting to be retried.

Subsequent to the design meeting I talk with Kevin (the VP of operations) and then with Jay. They tell me that not only must every phone number be fully accounted for, but every *attempt* must be fully logged, including what time we started the attempt, what time we ended the attempt, and what the outcome was. This implies that each call attempt is actually a record in the database, and *that* validates our design in which the reporter updates the call record in the database.

In fact, a natural outcome of that requirement is this: when a call is rescheduled, what actually happens is that a new call record is generated! The original call record is then allowed to live in the database, holding the record of the first attempt, and the new call record is added to the database for another try according to the retry parameters of the job and the system.

This produces a lot more records for the database, and we try to dimension what we expect. Given 1,000 lines the system could, theoretically, make 60,000 calls per hour. This gives us an absolute maximum of about 720,000 calls per day, or 260 million calls per year.

There are two false assumptions in these numbers. The first is that we'll be limited to 1,000 lines, when it's quite possible that we'll have thrice that number. That would imply nearly 800 million calls per year! The second mistake, however, is assuming that we'll run at maximum capacity day and night. We agree that we need to plan for peaks of 1,000 or even 3,000 calls per minute, but Jay estimates that the largest number we need to plan for over the course of a year is about 50 million calls, *including* retries.

While 50 million records are certainly a lot, it isn't really all *that* much. Each call record is pretty small: a job number, a telephone number, a start and end time, a code for success or failure type, and perhaps a bit more information. We estimate each record at about 30 bytes, or a total of 1.5 gigabytes of information per year. This is an entirely manageable amount of data, though we'll want to work with Operations to ensure we can 'dump' this data out to tape at least once a month.

Handling Catastrophic Failures

The next step in testing the design is to ensure that we can recover if any of the significant machines fails: the database, the call server, or a calling machine. In each use case, we need to understand what happens to calls that are in the database, in the call server queue, in the calling machine queue, or completed but not yet reported back to the database.

The Call Server Fails

If the call server fails, our goal is to reestablish it in exactly the same way we recover from a *Crisis•Call*:

1. The calling machines are told to dump their queues
2. The calling machines finish their calls and report back to the database
3. The call server queue is flushed
4. The call server is refilled with any calls marked 'enqueued' in the database
5. The calling machine queues are replenished from the call server

As long as we give all the calling machines sufficient time to finish their calls and report back to the database, we can be assured that any completed calls have been recorded, and that any calls still marked 'enqueued' have not yet been called and should be put back in the queue.

The Database Fails

Database failures come in two flavors: a temporary loss of power without loss of data, or an unrecoverable hard disk crash.

In the first case, the restoration process is identical to how we recover from failure of the call server. The second case should be much rarer, and we'll use RAID level 5 to ensure we can recreate the data in the case of any single disk failure. In the unlikely case that more than one disk fails, or that the entire database bursts into flames, we'll have no choice but to restore from backup. We must ensure that this is viable, and that we have a plan in place to handle this contingency.

The Calling Machine Fails

This is much like the call server failing, except that our optimization, where we cache some of the call reports and update the database less frequently, means that we *can't* know which calls on the calling machine were completed and which were not. If the calling machine were to fail, it may well be holding some completed calls that will never be reported to the database. In fact, if we need to ensure *absolute* data integrity, then even if we are updating the database with a call report after each call, there is a small chance that the calling machine might crash in the time between finishing a call and the reporter updating the database. While the odds are minimal, if we want to be absolutely certain of 100% data integrity, we must design for that possibility, no matter how remote it may be.

To know which calls are suspect, we require a slight variant on our recovery scheme for the call server. After a crash, we must bring the call server to a steady state, flushing the queue and waiting for all the calling machines to finish their calls. Once this process has completed, and the database has been updated accordingly, any calls left marked 'enqueued' must be the ones that were on the crashed calling machine. These calls were either never tried, or never updated in the database, but we can't know which. Jay has suggested we then call *all* these numbers, but prefix the messages with an apology, "Due to a system failure, you may have received this call already, in which case we apologize for disturbing you again..." Wording, of course, to be determined. Again, this will only be needed if we are *not* updating the database after every call.

In short, we feel confident that this design ensures that we can recover from any anticipated failure of any of the machines. We particularly like the idea that recovery from a machine failure follows the same course as the normal recovery after a *Crisis•Call*; this is clean, elegant and likely to stand up well to changes in the system.

Designing the Call Flow

In our next design meeting, we turn our attention to the call flow object. To understand what this object must do, we examine the various call flows that may be expected, both for incoming and outgoing calls. A typical, though simple call flow for outgoing calls is illustrated below:

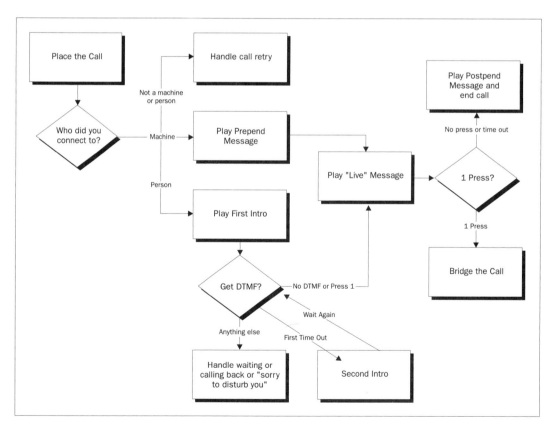

The acronym DTMF stands for 'Dual-Tone Multiple Frequency', which is how the telephone companies describe touch-tones.

We've recognized from the beginning that handling many different flows might be complex, and that for version 1.0 we may want to choose a simple solution that will meet 90% of the customers' requirements. The flow in the diagram was the result of Jay thinking through *his* minimum requirements. While it looks fairly straightforward, it has some difficult features. Before we examine them, though, let's walk through the flowchart.

The flow begins in the upper left-hand corner, in the box marked 'Place the Call'. The system goes off hook and tries the number. If it fails to connect to a machine or to a person, we handle it appropriately, rescheduling the call for a retry later.

If we think we got a machine, we play the prepend message, something like, "Stand by for an important message from *Crisis•Call*. If you miss any part of this message, you may dial 1-800-555-5555 to hear it again." This prepend message begins with a sound signature and is designed to identify the call, give information about hearing the message again, and to fill the time while the machine is playing its outgoing message. In the event that we really connected with a person, this message is designed to be sufficiently inoffensive that no harm is done.

If, on the other hand, we think we reached a person, we play the first introductory message. This is where we might ask the person to press 1 to hear the important message. If we get a 1 press, we have confirmed that we have a person. Additionally, we might offer other choices, such as, "If you are the NYNEX employee, press 1. If you will ask the NYNEX employee to come to the phone and we should wait, press 2. If the NYNEX employee is not home and we should call back later, press 3. If we have reached you in error, please press 4."

If we are talking to a person, we'll get a 1 press. If we are talking to a machine, we'll time out, and in the second introduction we can say "If you are listening to this on your answering machine, please ask the NYNEX employee to call 1-800-555-5555 to hear an important message from NYNEX. Otherwise..." at which point we repeat the menu choices. Again, the goal is to handle the case where we think we have a person, but in fact we have an answering machine.

Once the person presses 1, indicating that we have our man, we play the live message. If they press 1 again (to bridge the call to their office), we handle that request. Otherwise, we play the exit message and we end the call.

The truth is that even though this is a single flow, it implies that we may or may not bridge the call. Many customers won't even offer the option of bridging the call, so there are really at least two flows implicit in this one. Further, some customers won't have introductory messages, though that can be accomplished very easily by having an empty file for that message.

Going with the Flow

Inevitably, our attention is turned to the call flows themselves. These will control the interaction between our system and the recipient of our calls. In effect, they are the 'user interface' for calling. How are we going to manage these flows? Will they be scripts in a scripting language, like Visual Basic for Applications or JScript, or will they be hard-coded in C++?

"Well," I begin, "we can design this so that each flow is hard-wired, or we can make the flow be data-driven. Data-driven is obviously more flexible, but it's also more difficult to implement. The question is whether we need that much flexibility."

Glenn and Steve both suggest we consider a scripting language. The client would specify the flow in this language, and an interpreter would handle the flow at runtime. While the flow described above will handle many of the outgoing calls, we realize that Hypotenuse will soon want to do something different, and it would be unfortunate if they had to get a programmer involved for every change.

Steve asks, "What are the primitives? Let's figure out what it has to do before we try to figure out how to implement it." The primitives are things like 'go off hook', 'dial', 'wait for tones', and so forth. The system must recognize specific tones and branch accordingly. These are exactly the primitives provided by the Visual Voice class methods. We'd like the scripting language to allow us to map to these specific class methods, and to introduce programming logic as required. (If you get back a '4' press, call method `PlayMessage()` with the message, "Sorry to disturb you.")

Steve suggests that Tcl would be the ideal candidate language for this job. A Tcl interpreter would be supplied as a DLL. Each calling thread would instantiate its own interpreter, which NT would handle cleanly using reference counts on the DLL. Hypotenuse would write Tcl scripts with a simple editor, and we'd set up a table mapping Tcl commands to Visual Voice class methods. The only tricky part is that we'd need to create an external C interface for Tcl, but essentially each Tcl command will invoke a class method, get back a response, and branch accordingly.

We call up the Tcl home page, http://www.sunlabs.com/research/tcl/docs.html, to take a look at what's available about Tcl. It turns out that this is a very well supported product, with a comprehensive guide, John Ousterhout's *Tcl and the Tk Toolkit*, published by Addison-Wesley.

Glenn suggests taking a look at Visual Basic for Applications. This is Microsoft's solution to scripting and has, again, the advantage of being adopted by many applications and thus a lot of market support. I contact Microsoft to learn that VBA is licensed through Summit Software. I speak with a salesperson there, who tells me a number of interesting things. First, they *do* license VBA, and they have an additional product that integrates VBA into MFC. The pricing on the license is confidential, and they only reveal it under non-disclosure. He also points me to VBScript, which is a limited version of the same product that's free, but less powerful.

So far, we have identified three candidate approaches for writing these flows:

- They can be Tcl scripts
- They can be VBA scripts
- They can be hard-coded in C++

At the next design meeting I ask, "Can we encapsulate the flow so that we can choose among these scripting options, perhaps even switch between them as we go along?" In the end, we set this discussion aside for a while; Steve and I will investigate each option and return to make a decision when we know more about the relative costs and difficulties that will result from each. For now, we simply don't know enough about what is involved to make an informed decision. Further, we don't have a firm enough understanding of how many flows we'll need to support, or how often they'll change.

Designing the Caller

We agree to take a step back from this issue and examine the calling module from a higher-level design perspective. We take a clean sheet of paper, and rethink the objects that will implement the calling machine requirements.

"What are the objects?" asks Steve. "We should have a local call queue manager that manages the calling machine's list of calls. It has to take calls from the dispatcher and ensure that the flow and audio it requires are available."

Is this one object or two? Perhaps the local call queue manager works with a flow manager, which would be responsible for ensuring that the flow object is available, and for getting it from the server as needed.

How would this work? The local call queue manager examines a call object, which contains a job ID. It then tells the flow manager to make sure that everything for that job (that is, the flow and the audio) is available. The flow manager checks its local cache to see if the call flow and the audio are available — you could think of this as a sort of 'flow queue'. If necessary, the flow manager will make a request to the database to get the call flow and the audio.

In addition to the local call queue manager and the flow manager, each calling machine has a number of 'callers' (we've been using 48 in our calculations so far). The job of the caller is to get a number from the local queue and to call it, using the flow from the flow queue. When completed, the caller updates the call and hands it to the reporter.

We capture these relationships in a UML diagram. Note that all the callers on one machine share the same local call queue and flow queue, but that there is only one of each queue per calling machine.

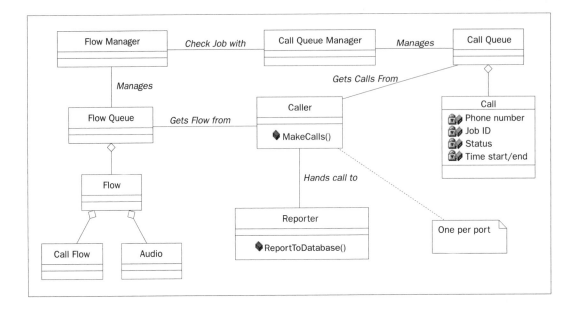

The Call Object

Conversation turns to the call object itself. The call object knows when we are supposed to call, and what number to call. It has a job ID that lets us find out what audio to play and what call flow to use. When a call completes, we need to create a call result object to capture the result of the call. This object will know when we actually placed the call, whether we connected, whether we received a 'busy' tone, and so forth. If we *do* connect, it will know at what time we connected, and at what time we disconnected.

The first question on the table is this: "Is the call object the same as the call result object?" To answer this, we need to decide what information both objects contain. The call object certainly needs to know the phone number to call and the flow to associate with that call. It also needs to know when the call can be made, based both on the original call schedule as well as on any retry parameters, current status and so forth. The call object looks like this:

```
class CCall
{
public:
    // member methods

private:
    CString     m_CustomerID;
    long        m_CallID;
    CString     m_PhoneNumber;
    CString     m_JobID;
    CTime       m_TimeWeShouldStart;
    CTime       m_TimeWeMustEnd;
};
```

The call *result* object is a product of the customer's requirement that we keep a record of every call Hypotenuse makes, whether or not it succeeds. Each call result object must know what number we called, when we started the call, when we connected, when we ended the call, and the outcome of the call. The call result object looks like this:

```
class CCallResult
{
public:
    // member methods

private:
    CString    m_CustomerID;
    long       m_CallID;
    CString    m_PhoneNumber;
    CString    m_JobID;
    CTime      m_TimeWeStarted;
    long       m_NumberOfAttempts;
    CTime      m_ConnectionDate;
    long       m_ConnectStatus;
    CTime      m_TimeWeEnded;
    long       m_EndStatus;
    int        m_FinalResultStatus;
    long       m_LineNumber;
    long       m_VRU;
};
```

Here, **m_EndStatus** tells us how and why we disconnected (finished the call, customer hung up, etc.), while **m_FinalResultStatus** tells us if the number was connected, busy or not answered. **m_VRU** is the identification number of the calling machine that placed the call.

As a matter of high-level design, these objects are clearly related, but they're not the same. At implementation time, it may be convenient to merge these into a single class to make manipulation in and out of the database simpler.

Designing SnapShot

Operations has requested we build a graphical, networked tool to view the calling schedule, which we are calling *SnapShot*. *SnapShot* will be able to recreate the calling pattern for days in the past, anticipate the calling pattern for days in the future, and will provide a real-time, up-to-the-minute picture of what the system is doing *right now* while it is running.

The *SnapShot* module will consist of two significant components:

- The scheduler
- The displayer

The scheduler's job is to determine, for any given time period, what the distribution of calls will be. The scheduler's job is frighteningly close to that of the call server's scheduler, and we discuss whether additional high-level design is required for this aspect of *SnapShot*. Our goal is to re-use the call server's scheduler as much as possible to handle this aspect of *SnapShot*, and we believe any differences are certainly at a lower level of design, or even just implementation details.

> *Go to any design meeting and you're sure to hear someone's voice dripping with derision when he sneers, "Yes, but that's an implementation detail." They say this much as a Victorian woman might have said, "Yes, well, she is a servant." The only things lower than an implementation detail are optimizations.*

The displayer's job is to map these decisions to a visual display. We want to isolate the display aspects of *SnapShot* from its engine, so that we can modify the display as the requirements change. In our initial visualization of *SnapShot*, the displayer's job is fairly straightforward: it will create a graph of a day, dividing the *y*-axis into segments of 15 minutes for each of the 24 hours, or 96 segments. It will divide the *x*-axis into one segment for every ten phone lines. In a system with 480 phone lines, that will create a graph with 48 * 96 or 4,608 squares. Each square will be filled in based on which job is running on those lines in that time slice. These numbers should fall out of the scheduling algorithm discussed earlier.

Notice how quickly and easily we've slipped into discussing implementation details. The high-level design of *SnapShot* is so simple that we can't help sketching out how it will actually be done.

The tricky part of *SnapShot* is implementing the ability to reschedule by directly manipulating these representations of the jobs, and we've decided to delay designing this feature, as we suspect it will never be needed. The only reason for such direct manipulation would be to override the system's ability to schedule, and we expect the system to be quite good at this task.

If the *customer* wants to manipulate the characteristics of a job, however, that will be possible through the forms we'll provide through the standard Internet access.

Handling Inbound Calls

At any moment, the system must anticipate a number of inbound calls. These will come in two flavors: customers calling in to schedule jobs or launch *Crisis•Calls*, and call recipients calling in to replay messages they want to hear again. As a design goal, we would like dynamically to allocate the phone lines to accommodate these incoming calls, so that no one receives a busy signal, but at the same time no lines that could be making calls are idle.

The system will estimate how many lines must be kept open at any time so that, as they become used, there will be sufficient time to allocate more lines. If, for example, we kept only one line open, and there was an incoming call, there could be a delay before we could open another line. It is possible that every other line would already be in use making outgoing calls.

The system will therefore designate inbound-sensitive machines, and will tell each machine how many lines to keep open. In the majority of cases, it will designate only one machine, telling that machine to keep, for example, ten of its lines open.

As that machine's lines cycle through their calls, they will check their count of open lines. If the count is below the designated number, the lines will not be used for outgoing calls, but rather will wait for inbound calls. Once ten lines are open, newly opened lines can be assigned outgoing calls. If the machine finds that so many of its ports are in use supporting inbound calls that it can't keep ten open lines, it will inform the call server. The server, in turn, will ask another machine to keep ten of *its* lines open, at least until the original machine informs the server that it can once again handle the load.

Let's take an example. Assume we have ten calling machines, each with 48 lines. The call server decides that given the current volume of calls, ten lines must be kept open for inbound calls. The call server tells machine number one to keep ten of its lines open.

Machine one's first line becomes available, and it looks at the number of open lines: zero. It keeps the line open, and registers that one line is now in this state. This is repeated nine more times. At this point, the machine has ten open lines, and 38 in use making outbound calls. Then, an inbound call takes up one of the lines, decrementing the number of open lines to nine, and incrementing the count of inbound calls to 1. As one of the 38 lines that had been handling outbound calls cycles, the machine notes that only 9 lines are open, and it keeps this line open for incoming calls, incrementing the number of open lines back to 10.

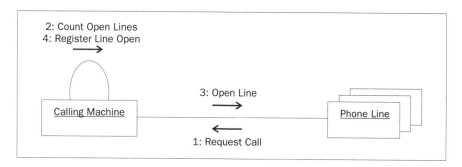

The situation now is that ten lines are open, one line is handling an inbound call, and 37 are handling outbound calls. If five inbound calls come in before any further lines become open, the outbound reserve falls to five. This ebb and flow continues. If the inbound traffic begins to pick up, more and more lines might be consumed, forcing more and more lines to remain open. At some point, the machine notes that fully 39 of the 48 lines are handling *inbound* calls, and only 9 lines can remain open. It informs the call server that it needs help, and the call server asks machine two to keep ten lines open.

The two machines operate independently of one another. The call server knows it needs ten lines open, and that it has two machines working on it. When machine one falls back to an acceptable level of inbound calls, it tells the call server it is back in business, and the call server tells machine two to resume full outbound service. We'll want to build some hysteresis into the system so that we're not bouncing back and forth to the call server asking for help. For example, machine one might not signal the call server that it is out of the woods until it has fewer than, say, 20 lines handling inbound calls.

This design allows for a reserve to compensate for network latency, and keeps the outbound machines independent of one another. They don't have to share a common count of reserved lines; they only need to know their own state. The call server doesn't need to know about the internal workings of the calling machines; it needs only to know how many lines it requires and which machines have been asked to handle that load.

This design requires that the ability to roll inbound calls to the next available line is managed externally to the system (in the T1 circuit itself) and that the call server has an implicit awareness of how these inbound calls will be assigned.

Preproduction

Having spent a lot of time designing the call server, the call stations and so forth, we think we understand how outbound calls will be made. All of the work done so far has assumed, however, that the customer has successfully scheduled calls in the system.

It's time to examine how that is done. At a very high level of abstraction, we know that the customers will call into the system, and work their way through a call flow if they dial in, or fill out forms if connecting via the Internet. One way or the other, they will tell us what they want us to do.

But how is that interaction managed, and how is the information captured? Steve suggests we create a 'job manager', whose responsibility is to take the output of either the IVR interaction or the forms filled out on the Internet, and create a job in the database.

I question this, stating that I had been working with the assumption that the Internet form will be nothing more than an IDC script that uses the controls on the form to create a fairly straightforward SQL statement for adding jobs to the database.

Steve's objection to this approach is that we ought not to have more than one point of entry into the database. If the forms are entering information on jobs, and the IVR preproduction code is also entering that information, we've duplicated the work and we risk letting them get out of phase with one another as the requirements change. He proposes instead that both the IVR and the form feed a job manager.

Using the Observer Design Pattern

There are many objects in this design that will want to know when a job is added to the schedule. Certainly the scheduler will want to know, as might *SnapShot*, and perhaps also the flow manager. An obvious solution would be to put a notification method into the job manager. However, notification is not an intrinsic part of managing jobs, and the complex code for registering those classes that need to be informed when a job is added doesn't really belong in the job manager.

More importantly, once you work out the logic of registering those who are interested in these changes, and then notifying them, you'd like to abstract this out into a class of its own and be able to reuse it with other classes that might be 'observed' in this way. Similarly, the classes that want to be informed may want to abstract out their ability to observe into a reusable class as well.

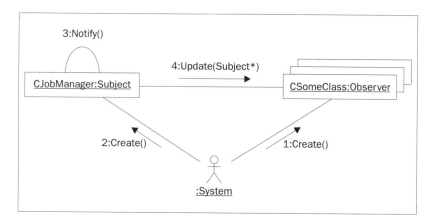

The **observer** pattern says that you can meet these needs by creating an 'observer' class. In our example, the scheduler might be an observer of the job manager. **Observer** will be an abstract class with a pure virtual function, **Update()**.

We'll then create a second abstract data type called **Subject**. This keeps an array of **Observer** objects, and also provides three methods: **Register()** (which adds observers to its list), **Notify()** (which is called when there is something to report), and **Unregister()** (which removes observers from its list).

Those classes that wish to be notified of jobs registered with the system will inherit from **Observer**. The job manager will inherit from **Subject**. The **Observer** class registers itself with the **Subject** class, and the **Subject** class calls **Update()** each time a job is registered with the system.

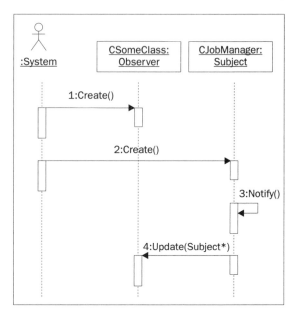

So that we can better focus on the sequence of events, we convert the collaboration diagram into a sequence diagram:

If **CJobManager** were a class we expected to reuse, we might note that not every class derived from **CJobManager** necessarily wants to be observable. To get around this, we could create a new class called **ObservedJobManager**, which would inherit both from **CJobManager** and from **Subject**. **CJobManager** would then no longer inherit from **Subject** directly. This would separate out the observer pattern aspects from the job management responsibilities, and thus we could reuse either or both.

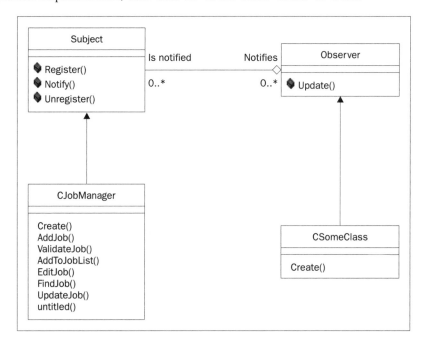

Debating the Job Manager

The ability to make the job manager an observed object is compelling. The problem is that doing so will make the Internet access a lot more complex. The forms must now interact with the database up to the point where they are ready to add a job to the system, but instead of adding that job, they must open a connection to the job manager object (which, presumably, is running in its own process space) and send it the job request instead. The job manager, in turn, will add the job to the database and inform any observing objects of the change.

This additional complexity buys us the ability to have a single point of entry into the database, and arguably reduces the number of transactions in the database, both of which are good things. In addition, the observer pattern allows every interested object to be informed when new jobs are scheduled.

Steve suggests we think about how *Crisis•Calls* will be scheduled. One option is for the job manager to feed the crisis directly to the scheduler. More likely, the job manager enters the job into the database and *then* informs the scheduler, which immediately acquires the job from the database and swings into action, purging the server's queue and telling the calling machines to flush their queues and get to work on the *Crisis•Calls*.

Certainly all of this can be done with database triggers, but that puts still more of the work into the database, which Steve argues is short-term profitable but long-term foolish. The system will scale a lot better if we can distribute more of this responsibility out of the database and into other systems.

Validating Jobs

Once again, it's time to take a step back and consider the job manager from first principles. "What," Steve asks, "are the reasons for having a job manager in the first place? The primary responsibility of the job manager is to own the policies about whether or not a job is valid. Forget implementation for now, this is the reason to have such an object."

"In order to accomplish this primary goal, the job manager must know about each job that is added or removed from the system. This enables the job manager to handle a second goal: informing interested objects when jobs are added, edited, or removed." This is a compelling argument, and we are all persuaded that the job manager's responsibility warrants complicating the interaction between the Internet form and the database.

In the classic observer pattern, we would derive the job manager from an abstract data type (ADT), the **Subject** class, and we would derive each of the interested objects from an ADT **Observer** class. We will not do that for now, as there is no need to do so in our design and there is little likelihood that we'll have other objects that need to share this functionality. If, later, we decide we need to abstract this capability out of the job manager, we can always do so. In that case, as objects register themselves with the job manager, it will in turn delegate this responsibility to the new **Subject** class.

An important result of the fact that the job manager will own the policies on what is a valid job, is that we can make the assumption that any job in the database is known to be valid. This is a *very* big assumption — it follows from having an object that owns the policies, but *only* if we agree that no job gets added to the database without the express approval of the job manager. Having this rule enforces database integrity, which is in itself a Good Thing.

If the job manager is going to validate jobs before they are added to the database, perhaps it makes sense for the job manager to be the object that does the actual update into the database? This is not the only alternative. As we discussed, the database might do the validation itself, or it might trigger the job manager when the job is added, and ask the job manager to validate it. There are any number of permutations on this, as databases can capture rules, trigger events, and so forth, but we are in agreement that this validation is best done in an external C++ program. And if we're making such a program, and these are its responsibilities, we agree that it ought to be the responsibility of that program to add the object to the database once it is validated.

The next question is whether the job manager receives a fully formed job object, or just the raw ingredients. I propose that once you have the raw ingredients you must pass them to *some* function, so rather than passing them to the job manager, why not pass them to the job's constructor? Thus, to add a job, you instantiate a job object and then call something like **myJobManager.Add(thisJob)**. What happens when you delete a job? We postulate that you just send a job ID, and the job manager does the rest.

Editing Jobs

A harder question is what happens when jobs are edited. We discuss two general approaches. In the first, you send the job manager an edited job, and it begins a transaction. It deletes the old version of the job, then validates the new version against the database. If it is valid, the job manager adds the job and commits the transaction; if it is invalid, the job manager rolls back the transaction. The reason to start with the delete is that the job manager must evaluate this job in the same way it would if the job were new.

The alternative is that the client of the job manager hands the edited job to the job manager and requests the edit. The job manager validates the new version before deleting the old version of the job. If the job manager must consult with the scheduler, it indicates that this is an edit, so the scheduler makes the necessary internal adjustments to consider the edited, rather than the scheduled, version of the job. This pushes that responsibility over to the scheduler, but avoids a large transaction.

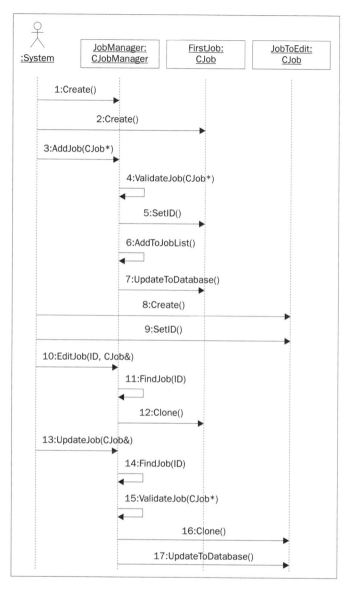

This use case raises the question of **record locking**. We don't want to be in the position where two people or processes are editing the same job, because the first one saved will be overwritten when the second one is saved. This is normally solved with record locking, but in this case it may not be a problem, as jobs are not frequently edited, and never by two processes or people at the same time. At least, that is our assumption.

But won't the scheduler modify the job when it is rearranging things to accommodate large new jobs? Actually, no — the job *only* captures the contracted requirements; the scheduler handles the actual scheduling of times to make calls. Thus, if the job allows us to make the calls over a six-hour time frame, the scheduler is free to bunch up towards the front (usually desired), but can push calls out anywhere in the six hours, so long as the calls complete in time. Changing the job is changing the contract, and the scheduler is not authorized to do that.

A new wrinkle is introduced: what do we do with invalid jobs? It is certainly possible for a customer to fill out a job request but for that job not to be fully valid. Perhaps they've not yet sent us the phone numbers or recorded the audio. Perhaps they want to specify the exact start date at a later time. This would indicate that it should be possible to add jobs to the database and for them to have a status flag. It would be the job manager's responsibility to decide if (and when) that flag can go to 'ready', based on validating the job.

Now that the sequence is understood, we can look at this using a collaboration diagram to understand the relationships among the objects. Note that this captures *exactly* the same information as the sequence diagram, but moves the focus from events over time to interactions among objects:

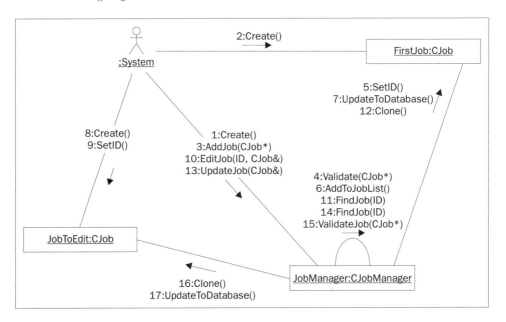

This means that the forms and the IVR flows can both add jobs to the database (and edit them as well), but when they are submitted — that is, when the customer indicates he wants the job scheduled — it will be the job manager's responsibility to decide to set the job's status to 'ready'.

In any case, the job manager must be prepared to answer the question, "Can this job be ready?" To say yes, the job manager must prove that the job is internally consistent, that we have all the necessary information (e.g. phone numbers, audio, schedule, etc.) and that we have the necessary phone lines available. It may take a while to determine whether or not we have sufficient phone lines, but on the other hand most of the time we won't be very close to the limit. We consider having the job manager keep a snapshot of the entire calendar. After some discussion we think this is a good idea; the job manager can cache an approximation of the current commitment of resources expressed as a percentage of the available resources.

Thus, the job manager would know, at any time, that for a particular date the system is currently committed to (say) 40% of capacity. When it is asked to validate a job, if that job will not take up too much of the remaining resources, the job manager can approve it without consulting with the scheduler. For example, the policy might be that as long as the job won't push past 75% of capacity, the job manager is free to validate the job. If the new job *will* push past 75% of capacity, then the scheduler must be consulted to ensure we can work all the requirements out before we make a commitment. Such a scheme will require that the job manager update his calendar each time a job is added or removed from the system or is edited, but the job manager is well situated to do just that.

Active vs. Passive Objects

All of this brings up the question of which object should be 'active'.

Steve tends to think of the job object as relatively 'passive'. It knows what a job is, but it doesn't know what a *valid* job is; that task is given to the job manager. Further, the job doesn't know how to get to the job manager; it is handed over. I challenge this approach, offering that perhaps the job should validate itself. Steve counters that doing so binds together the job with the policies, and that is bad design because the policies can be expected to change over time. In fact, under some circumstances, we might keep multiple policies in effect.

I find that compelling, but question why the creator of the job doesn't just instantiate a job and then tell it to validate, at which time the job can pass itself off to the job manager. This is a small, almost religious point, and one that has little practical impact, so of course we dig in and fight it out as if it were the most important question of the day. Steve believes that the job shouldn't need to know where it gets validated, and that this won't scale well. I contend that the objects creating jobs shouldn't need to know about the job manager, they should just create a job and set it spinning. I'm reminded of that old Tom Lehrer song, "'Once the rockets are up, who cares where they come down? *That's not my department*,' says Wernher von Braun!"

We finally agree that the job should know how to add itself to the database, and I agree to accept the premise that the job is handed to the job manager, secretly figuring that I'm the one writing that part of the code, so I'll decide later how I want to do it!

In the middle of that tangent, we did uncover an important issue. The policies may well change over time, and it may make sense to capture the policies not in code but rather in a scripting language. We can use the same mechanism we'll be using to capture the call flow, probably a Tcl script. And we can use the same expedient of encapsulating this area of the object so that we can hard-code the first version, and then swap in the more flexible solution as we move forward.

Designing the Internet Site

The Internet site nags at me. On the one hand, we've done very little to design it, but on the other it seems to me to be a fairly straightforward exercise. The pages on the site will be strictly utilitarian for a while. We won't invest time or energy in making them attractive or snazzy at first; we'll just offer the customer a home page, and pages for sign-up and preproduction. There will also be pages for administrative work on the database.

Using Forms

Our assumption is that the first version of the pages will use straightforward HTML forms, though we hold out the possibility of greatly enhancing the usability by adding ActiveX controls as we go forward. *SnapShot*, for example, may use an ActiveX control to create its display, as might many of the other administrative pages.

IDC

One of the easiest and most straightforward ways to handle forms is with Microsoft's Internet Database Connector (IDC). The form is written in HTML, but its 'Action' statement points to an IDC script. The script manages the database connection, issues SQL statements and retrieves records. The output is then returned to the user via an Extended HTML template — an HTX file. HTX files are just like HTML files, except that we add tags that act as placeholders for the data returned from the database query.

Because the HTX files act just like HTML files, it is possible for the HTX file to contain more controls, which in turn call more IDC scripts. In this way, we can gather information, display results, gather more information and interact freely with the SQL database along the way. The IDC scripts and the database communicate via the **O**pen **D**atabase **C**onnectivity (ODBC) protocol. ODBC is an open standard supported by virtually every major database in use on Windows platforms.

Having identified IDC as a viable approach, I decide to examine this issue when we are closer to developing the Internet piece of the application. In a larger project, we might designate an Internet developer who would go off and work on this design in parallel. Another choice — the one we are making for this project — is to sequence this issue, pushing it out to later in the process so that we can make better progress in building the underlying database technology and getting the telephony piece up and running. Microsoft is due to release a number of new tools for Internet development during the time we'll be finalizing the design, and it makes sense to leave this issue open for now.

Wrapping up the High-level Design

It is late March, and there is good news and bad. The good news is that we've taken tremendous strides, and the high-level design is almost done, to a first approximation. The bad news is that we'll certainly need another round of high-level design when we know more about the implementing technologies. We'll want to revisit some of our thinking about the database, and we'll certainly want to spend more time thinking about the Internet application as we move forward.

To some degree, the schedule is driving us off the high-level design and into the details, but that isn't a bad thing. I'm much more inclined to get the telephony and database pieces up and working quickly, and fill in the details of the Internet application as we go along, than to succumb to the temptation to spend another month working through all the theory before we write any code. We agree to move on to low-level design and then to begin implementation, holding out the assurance that we'll revisit these topics once we know more, and have built some of the core modules.

Validating the Use Cases

Before we can put the high-level design to rest, however, we must prove to ourselves that we've at least covered the most important use cases with what we have. We schedule a session with the following agenda:

1. Identify a small number of key use cases and create use case scenarios
2. Walk through the scenarios and 'prove' the design against them

Identify the Key Use Cases

We return again to our list of use cases, and identify the key uses of the system. These are the *sine qua non* of what we are building, and we want to ensure that we now understand them and can support them with the model we've built. After much discussion, we agree that the principal uses can be categorized as:

- Customer signs up
- Customer initiates and manages jobs

- The system makes the calls
- Customer or management can get reports

The Customer Signs Up

Customer sign-up will be accomplished entirely on the Internet. We have envisioned a series of simple forms, which interact directly with the database via ODBC. This of course is quite different from preproduction, where the job manager will mediate the interaction. Sign-up will have no impact on the scheduler, and so if an invalid customer record is added to the database, it won't break the system — it will just require customer service intervention to get it straightened out.

We have intentionally delayed in describing the sign-up mechanism in any significant detail for a number of reasons. First, we've focused on out-calling, as we think that is the harder problem. While there are some issues in building the call flows, this pales next to the complexity of scheduling the calls and implementing the call stations.

Second, it will be possible to sign up the first few customers by directly manipulating the database using SQL Enterprise Manager. Even if we don't get the Internet piece working for a while, we know we can get customers into the database. As long as we can generate and fulfill call requests, we can delay implementing the ability for customers to sign themselves up in the system.

Third, and almost equally important, Microsoft is releasing a suite of new tools this month for building Internet applications. This is a classic example of how the real world intrudes into theory. While in theory it might make sense to nail down these pieces, we don't really *need* to understand the Internet piece in detail yet. We are under pressure to move on, and by waiting a month, the job will be much easier and we'll have more resources to bring to bear.

Even if we are going to enter the customer information into the database manually, however, we do need to know what information to capture and what tables to enter them into. In the analysis phase we discussed these requirements in some detail. The tables are pretty straightforward, and we're confident we know enough to postpone this issue until we get to the low-level design of the database itself.

Customer Initiates and Manages Jobs

This is what we've been calling preproduction: the ability to schedule a job, and to change that schedule as needs change. In the final version, the customer *or* Hypotenuse staff will be able to manipulate these jobs through either the Internet interface or the IVR interface.

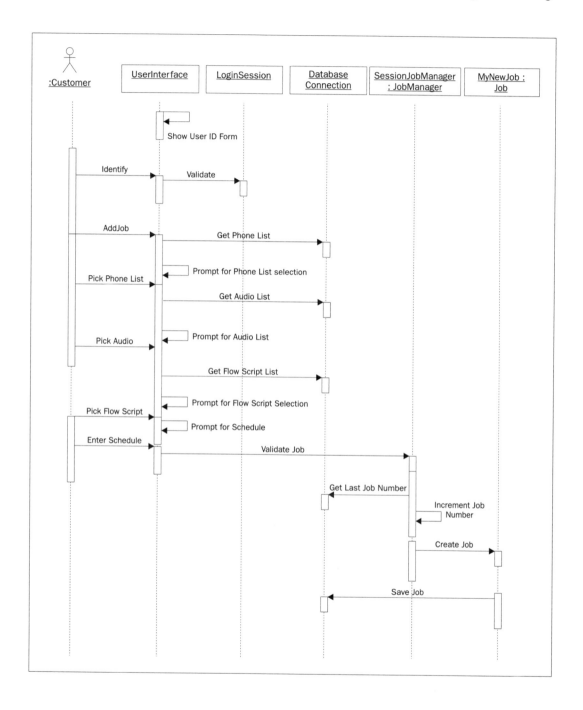

Again, we've delayed worrying about the Internet interface, though we now know this won't be as straightforward as sign-up. In sign-up, the Internet form will communicate directly with the database via ODBC. In preproduction, the Internet form will talk with the job manager, which will validate the job and then put the job into the database. The communication between the Internet form and the job manager will not be via ODBC, but rather by another method of interprocess communication, still to be determined. When we get to the low-level design, we'll need to tackle this question, for now it is enough to say they will communicate over a reliable, high-level protocol.

The IVR interface for preproduction is fairly well understood. We intend to develop this initially as a C++ routine, but eventually we'll reimplement it using the same scripting language we'll use for outbound calls. We spent a fair amount of time thinking through how to keep some phone lines open for inbound calls, so that our customers can get through to schedule jobs. We also gave long consideration to how, when they do request a job, we'll validate that there is enough bandwidth to fulfill their request.

Because both the Internet objects and the IVR must go through the job manager, there is a greater imperative to get the preproduction components working sooner rather than later. The only other way to add jobs to the system will be to bypass all of these mechanisms and directly manipulate the database using SQL Enterprise Manager. That would clearly be undesirable, as it bypasses the job manager and could introduce database corruption.

The customer must provide audio, a list of numbers to call and the characteristics of the schedule, including start and end dates and times, as well as the tilt and throttle, if any. The system must also allow the customer to initiate *Crisis•Calls*.

While the mechanism for the delivery of *Crisis•Calls* is different from that for *Flash•Calls*, the ways they get initiated are almost identical. In a *Crisis•Call*, many of the parameters can be assumed. Thus, we don't ask for the start time (it's now) or the end time (it's as soon as possible), there's no throttle (by definition), and the tilt is towards the beginning.

For both *Flash•Calls* and *Crisis•Calls*, preproduction involves the Internet application (filling out the form and providing the data) or the inbound IVR application. The latter will use the same calling machines as the outbound application. Are the same objects (callers, reporter and so forth) in use? We decide to review the outbound use cases, and then return to this nagging question.

Editing and Deleting Jobs

The system must also support editing and deleting jobs. To get a sense of how these tasks will be accomplished, we build sequence diagrams. Here is the diagram for deleting a job:

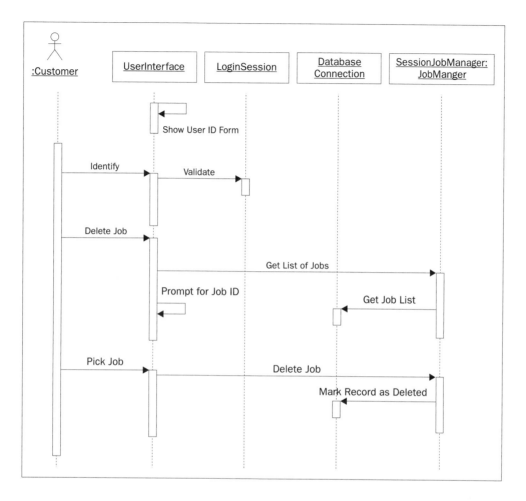

Certainly, the high-level design at this point handles these manipulations without trouble. The job manager's responsibility is to broadcast the change to interested objects so that they can take the changes into account. This will certainly affect, for example, the scheduler, which may have to take action if a currently running job is deleted.

The System Makes the Calls

This is where we spent the majority of our design time, and not surprisingly it is the aspect of the system we understand best. The picture we started out with has stood up surprisingly well under fire:

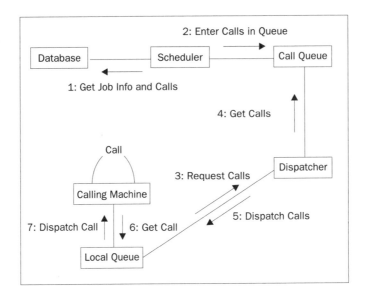

The scheduler will query the database each time its call queue falls below a low-water mark. It will establish which jobs are 'current', and will allocate resources appropriately among the jobs. It will then fill its call queue. The local calling machine's architecture is also well understood:

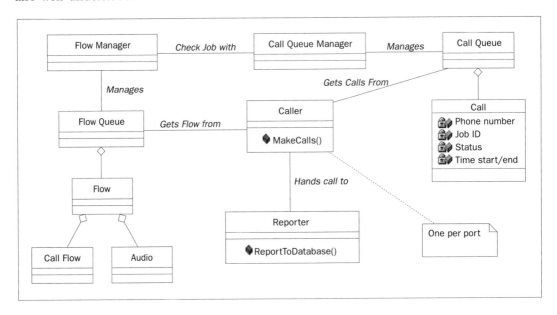

Each calling machine's local queue manager will request a set of call objects from the dispatcher each time its local call queue falls below the low-water mark, and the dispatcher will draw from the call queue that the scheduler filled. As calls are delivered to the calling machine, the local flow manager will ensure that the call flow and related audio are local to the calling machine. If they are not, it will request them from the database via ODBC.

Once the caller places the call, the call result is handed to the reporter. If the call was successful, the reporter places it back in the database. We've not decided whether this is the same table (or even the same database) whence it came, but that is really an optimization to reduce the load on the database, and doesn't change the design. If the call was not successful, it is cloned, the start time and a few other fields are updated, and it is placed back in the database awaiting recall.

Crisis·Calls

What happens with a *Crisis•Call?* Our design indicates that the queues must be flushed and the calling machines redirected to handle the crisis:

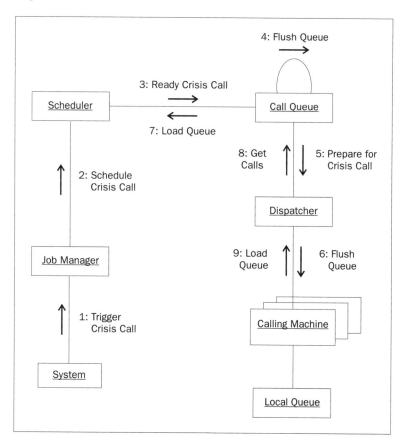

The customer will trigger the call, and the job manager will validate it. The scheduler will flush its queue and tell the calling machines to flush their queues. The *Crisis•Calls* will then be loaded into the call queue as the next job, and the normal mechanisms for filling the calling machines' call queues will in fact load the *Crisis•Call* numbers.

Re-examining Preproduction Calls

Can this design support incoming calls? Certainly a call flow and a set of audio can be created for the incoming call. All the interactions are identical, and they've been well documented in Jay's flowchart.

The flow manager and call queue managers will not be used for incoming calls, and we'll need to create a class derived from the reporter, whose job will be to interact with the job manager to provide the outcome of the incoming call. Our working assumption is that the result of this preproduction call will be the creation of a job object and a set of call objects, but that won't happen at the client side; that will be the responsibility of the job manager. What *is* created at the client side, and how that is conveyed to the job manager, is an open question that we can't ignore for much longer. Before tackling this, however, we complete our survey of the primary use cases by considering post-production.

Customer or Management Can Get Reports

We have intentionally avoided designing this part of the project. We've asked Jay to provide a comprehensive list of the MIS reports he'll require, so that we can make sure our design of the database will allow us to capture the required data. His preliminary list matches the data we're already planning to capture in the job, customer and call tables.

Delivery of MIS will be through the Internet, and it is on my list to look for ActiveX controls that can help us generate and format summary and detail reports, both for our customers and for Management and Operations. I'm not very worried about this however, because SQL Server is a popular high-end database product and I'm certain there are many products we can buy off the shelf to meet this need.

Design Review

This review of the high-level design by examining the use cases has been very productive. While our design is not riddled with holes, there are a few omissions that appear quite startling this late in the project:

1. The Internet design, and how it supports sign-up and preproduction

2. The inbound IVR design, and how it interacts with the job manager

3. MIS reporting

We reaffirm our decision not to worry about the Internet design or the MIS reporting for now — these will be handled in good time. The inbound IVR design works well enough with the existing calling design as long as we understand that the reporter must be sub-classed to a preproduction reporter, whose job is to interact with the job manager.

There comes a time in every design when it is time to move on. While we don't feel at peace with every aspect of the high-level design, real-world scheduling considerations combine with my need to sink my teeth into the details, and we call an end to the high-level design process. There are issues we'll revisit, but it is time to get down to the nitty-gritty. We open a virtual bottle of wine, salute our design, and call the first meeting of the low-level design committee.

```
= false;                                          CTime
                                    CTime::GetCur
Time();                          CTime end = theJo
                                CTime start = theJobSe
= now.Format("%b %d          CTime todayStart(start.GetYea
                           start.GetMonth(), now.GetDay(),
                           start.GetHour(),
er = "start < '";           start.GetMinute(),
                            start.GetSecond());
oday;                          CTime todayEnd(end.GetYear(),
, and enddate > '";          end.GetMonth(), now.GetDay(),
                             end.GetHour(),
today;
                              end.GetMinute(), end.GetSecond());
= '";

ScheduleSet.m_strFilter =                                  now || todayS
                                      if (todayStart > now ||
                               now)
JobScheduleSet.IsOpen())                 {    theJobSet.Close();
                                              return false;
JobScheduleSet.Requery();
pDoc>m_JobScheduleSet.Open();          }
                                     CTimeSpan theSpan = end no
lTrack* pCallTrack;                    int totalMinutes =
                                    theSpan.GetTotalMinutes();
l ok;
                                       if (end > todayEnd) //
JobScheduleSet.IsEOF())            than today
ile
pDoc>m_JobScheduleSet.m_            {    int AdditionalMin =
                                  GetAdditionalMinutes(the
     pCallTrack = new
allTrack(m_pDoc>m_JobScheduleSet.Initialize();       theJobSet.m_EndDate);
bID);     ok = pCallTrack>Initialize();          CTimeSpan todaySp

    if (ok)                        now;      totalMinutes =
    {   Log("ok\n");              todaySpan.GetTotalMin
                                  AdditionalMin;
m_CallList.AddHead(pCallTrack);     }
        foundJobs = true;
                                     m_min = ( ( (m_t
    }                              totalMinutes) + 1
    else                           );      m_Priority = t
    {   Log("...Rejected!\n");         m_Tilt = theJo
        delete pCallTrack;             m_Throttle = the
                                       m_JobID = the
    }                                  theJobSet.Cl
pDoc>m_JobScheduleSet.MoveNext();

                                       return true
pDoc>m_JobScheduleSet.                 obs;
```

CHAPTER FIVE

Low-Level Design

With the high-level design in place, it's now time to turn our attention to how we'll implement this design in code. Low-level design bridges the gap between the theory of the high-level design and the reality of the implementation. In the low-level design, we must nail down the classes and design their interfaces. We must also plan the database tables, work through the scheduling algorithms and finalize all the remaining details before beginning implementation.

As we progress with the implementation itself, we may need to tinker with the decisions we make here. We will set the bar low for changing how we implement functionality, but we'll set it high for changing the class interfaces, so we intend to spend a fair amount of time getting those right. Our first low-level design meeting sets the agenda for the weeks ahead. We make a comprehensive list of what things have to be designed, and then we separate them along the spectra of difficulty and importance.

We agree to begin our efforts by understanding how the scheduler builds its call queue. This will force us to design the SQL statements, and will open discussion about queue management in general, and about the clients of the various queues, including the dispatcher, the local queue manager and the flow manager. It will also force the issue of the database and table design; we don't expect this to be very complicated but we must make sure we spend the necessary time to get it right.

We will then turn our attention to the call reporter and the preproduction reporter, and to how the latter interacts with the job manager. This will force us to finalize the low-level design of the job manager, and cause us to examine how we'll implement the remote procedure calls.

Along the way we must detail how we'll handle multithreading and the related issues of locking records and critical areas of the code. We will also need to talk about how we'll segment our components, what objects will share thread or process space, and so forth.

Getting Started

We begin the low-level design by organizing our effort. We identify a number of areas of principal concern:

- The call server
- The call client
- The class interfaces
- The database design
- The reporters and queues
- The Internet

We decide to start with the call server, as this is the central piece of the calling software. The call server is divisible into the scheduler and the dispatcher, and it is the scheduler that will require the most thought. Once we understand how the calls are selected and made available, it follows naturally to think about how the calls are actually made, and so we will turn our attention to the call client. With these modules fully designed, we can stop and flesh out the public interfaces of the principal classes, and from there we can design the database tables.

When these features are fully designed, we'll start to look at the supporting classes, such as the reporters and the queues that will hold the phone numbers. That will complete our design of the IVR aspects of calling, and we can turn our attention to the Internet components.

The Call Server

The call server will function as a **service** under NT. This is not unlike a daemon in UNIX; it's a program that runs either when the system starts up or when started manually, but which does not require a user interface. An NT service can run even when no one is logged into the system, which is perfect for our needs. Calling can be fully automated and need not be thought of as an interactive program.

We agree that we'll implement calling first as a simple executable program, and then eventually as a service conforming to the NT standard. The service will not be the scheduler, but it will launch the scheduler as an object within its own process space. In essence, the service will house the scheduler, the dispatcher, the call queue, and the job manager. That is, the service itself will get things started by instantiating these objects at startup.

The Scheduler

There will be only one scheduler in the system. The scheduler maps well to a design pattern known as a **singleton**, which enforces the idea of a single instance of a class for an entire application, or in this case for an entire system of applications. In the classic example[1], a singleton class declares a static **Instance()** method, which is called to access the single instance of the class.

The declaration is:

```
class CScheduler
{
public:
    static CScheduler*      Instance          ();

protected:
    CScheduler();

private:
    static CScheduler*      theScheduler;
};
```

And the corresponding implementation is:

```
CScheduler* CScheduler::theScheduler = 0;        // Initialize the static member

CScheduler* CScheduler::Instance();
{
    if (theScheduler == 0)
       theScheduler = new CScheduler;
    return theScheduler;
}
```

Adding Calls to the Call Queue

In the high-level design, we identified the following steps the program will follow in order to add a call to the call queue:

1. Determine which jobs are eligible
2. Establish the relative allocation of lines
3. Add calls to the queue based on the allocation

[1] *Design Patterns, 1995*

Determine Which Jobs are Eligible

We decide to encapsulate the question of, "When is a job eligible to be called?" into the more general idea of a 'policy'. Policies may be implemented in a variety of ways. At times we'll create full-blown policy objects, at other times a class method or even class data may encapsulate a policy. The logical entity *policy* serves to capture the rules and procedures for a particular situation; the implementation details will vary from object to object.

In this particular case we have a good idea what the policies are (a job must have audio, phone numbers, a start date and so forth), but spend some time thinking about which class will enforce this policy.

It is the scheduler's responsibility to identify which of the jobs are eligible, but the scheduler should not know anything about the details of jobs, and that includes these policies. We already have a class that's responsible for much of this: the job manager. The original high-level design created the job manager specifically to decide when a job was valid.

The specification states that the customer can add jobs to the database even if they don't have the audio or phone number at the time they call. The database must be able to store these incomplete jobs so that the customer can update them at a later time. The job manager, therefore, is called upon to validate these jobs and decide when they are complete, so it will be the job manager that owns the policy. The scheduler will delegate responsibility for answering the question of 'readiness' to the job manager.

When is a Job Ready?

The wonderful thing about low-level design is that we can finally sink our teeth into the details, and the first thing to delineate is the exact policy on job readiness. We agree that for a job to be ready the following must be true:

- The job must have a set of phone numbers to call
- The job must have audio to play
- The job must have a flow
- The start date and time must be earlier than now
- The end date and time must be later than now
- The customer's account must be 'current'
- The job status must be 'can-be-run'

We have not defined what it means for a customer's account to be 'current'. This will be a business policy issue outside the domain of this software. We need only check whether or not the account *is* current, however defined.

Another requirement is that the job status must be 'can-be-run'. Again, we have not defined all the possible alternatives, but we suspect other statuses might include 'canceled', 'incomplete' and 'completed'. We have also intentionally not defined what the criteria are for a job to be set to 'can-be-run'. It is important to separate these concerns: the job is ready when the status is 'can-be-run' *and* the other criteria are met. What it takes to earn that designation is another matter. It is as if a professor said to you, "You may take my class when you pass the introductory course." He isn't telling you what it takes to pass that other course, only that you must do so before starting his.

Establish the Relative Allocation of Lines

The allocation of available phone lines to current jobs is one of the scheduler's two principal and related responsibilities; the other is to determine whether we have sufficient resources available to accept a job proposed for a future date.

The scheduler will keep a reference to the call queue (as, incidentally, will the dispatcher). The call queue will be instantiated by the call server, and again, the call queue and dispatcher will both be singletons.

The Scheduler's Interface

With this design, we have sufficient information to write the public interface for the scheduler. We agree that we'll note some methods in the private interface as we think of them, but they are implementation details that may change as we implement the class. It's the public interface that we want to get right as early as possible, though again, realistically, we know this is just the first attempt.

```
class CScheduler
{
public:
    void              Begin             ();
    void              End               ();
    BOOL              DoesThisJobFit    (job&);
    static CScheduler* Instance         (CCallQueue&);

protected:
    CScheduler(CCallQueue&);

private:
    List<Jobs>        GetEligibleJobs   ();
    void              ChartSchedule     ();
    void              FillQueue         ();

    static CScheduler* theScheduler;
};
```

The call server will call **Instance()** to instantiate the singleton, passing in a reference to the call queue object. The principal public methods are **Begin()** and **DoesThisJobFit()**. **Begin()**'s job is to start up the scheduler; **DoesThisJobFit()** will encapsulate the decision as to whether there is time in the schedule to handle this job. Note that the **FillQueue()** method is not public, because filling up the queue is an implicit part of the scheduler's behavior. Instead, the call queue will own a synchronization object that the scheduler will block on. The synchronizing event will signal the scheduler to fill the queue (by calling its private **FillQueue()** method), and this will happen each time the queue falls below its low-water mark.

The scheduler won't know where the low water mark is, but it *will* know how many calls to add to the queue each time **FillQueue()** gets called. This will be based on two system policy attributes.

The system policy object will be persistent, stored in the database, and instantiated by the call server on startup. It will contain a number of system-wide attributes, including **SizeOfCallQueue** and **NumberOfLines**. The system policy object is another good opportunity to use a singleton, and doing so neatly avoids creating a global variable and helps control access to this important object.

SizeOfCallQueue will tell the scheduler how many calls it ought to add to the queue per available line. Thus, if the system has 100 lines, and **SizeOfCallQueue** is 5, then the scheduler will add 500 numbers to the queue each time its **FillQueue()** method runs.

NumberOfLines will be the current number of phone lines available for calling out on all the calling stations combined. This number will be made available to the call server and updated as calling machines come online and go offline. When the call server starts, this number will be set to zero; as calling machines register themselves with the call station manager, **NumberOfLines** will increase. The call station manager will be defined below, but its principal job is to allow the call server sufficient knowledge of what calling resources it has available.

Therefore, when the queue signals that it has hit its low-water mark, it will signal the synchronization object. This will cause the scheduler's **FillQueue()** method to run, which will multiply **NumberOfLines** by **SizeOfCallQueue** to determine how many phone numbers to add to the queue. We'll call this number the **RefillSize**; the next question is then how the scheduler should allocate it among the eligible jobs.

Priority and Throttle

The relative allocation of lines is a function of the number of calls each job wants to make, how much time each job has in which to make the calls, the relative priorities of the jobs, and each job's throttle and tilt. We start by factoring in the relative priority of each job. This will be assigned as a business decision, based perhaps on the type of contract sold to the customer. All things being equal (and they never are), a job with priority three will get one half as many lines allocated to it as a job with priority six.

Let's examine what happens when we have four jobs with various priority levels. Assume job A has priority 1, job B has priority 3, job C has priority 4 and job D has priority 2. Further assume we have 1,000 lines, and that all four jobs are making calls which each take one minute.

If all our assumptions hold, the 1,000 lines will be allocated in the proportion 1:3:4:2. Thus, job B should get 30% of the allocation, or 300 lines. The other jobs will also be allocated appropriate numbers of lines:

Job	Priority	Allocation
A	1	100
B	3	300
C	4	400
D	2	200

We next decide to take throttle into account. Throttle acts as a maximum number of lines. If C is throttled at 300 lines (per unit of time) what will we do with the remaining lines? Clearly, we want to reallocate these lines among the other jobs, and we'd like to keep the relative priorities intact. Further, we want to ensure that the order in which we do the evaluation will not change the allocation — it ought not matter if we figure out how many lines to assign to D before or after we allocate to B.

Originally, I was quite worried about what I've been thinking of as 'fixed window' calls: that minority of calls in which the customer dictates both a starting date *and* an ending date. Steve points out that the idea that other calls don't have a fixed end date is an illusion; as a matter of quality of service, *every* job must have a fixed end date, even if the customer doesn't specify one. After all, if a customer asks us to make 10,000 calls and it takes us four months, he is hardly likely to be satisfied!

We agree that each job will have an end date. That date will either be explicitly specified by the customer, or it will be *implicitly* specified by the system based on policies that are set (and can be changed) by Hypotenuse.

Handling Back-Tilt

Back-tilted jobs want to run continuously right up to their deadlines, but making as few calls early in the process as possible. These are *very* difficult to schedule. At any given point in time, the system knows what jobs it has, and might allocate all the remaining lines to the back-tilted job. This would optimize our promise to make the calls as late as possible, but it significantly reduces our flexibility as new jobs are added to the system.

We work hard to come up with a simple, iterative algorithm, but this problem doesn't yield so easily. I propose that we preprocess the back-tilted job so that we can treat it as a front-tilted job. To do that, we have to give it a fixed starting point.

I propose that we start by setting a policy on what the maximum percentage of available lines we want to devote to back-tilted jobs is. This number might be captured as a system-wide policy, or it might be captured on a job-by-job basis. When the job is proposed, we use this number to establish how long the job will take. For example, if the job will be allocated 50% of the available lines, we might compute as follows:

1. We expect to have 100 lines available.

2. Make the allocation based on 80 lines to allow for *Crisis•Calls* and calling machines that are out of service for repairs.

3. Determine how long each call will take and how many calls there are to work out the number of port minutes required.

4. Divide port minutes required by available lines (50% of 80 lines = 40 lines) to determine the total number of minutes required. If each call is 1 minute and there are 4,000 calls and 40 lines, then we need 100 minutes.

5. Back off that many minutes from the end time to establish the start time.

Now we have a start time (100 minutes before the end time) and a minimum (40 calls per minute), and we can put this job into the system. If the scheduler rejects the job because we don't have sufficient resources to allocate the minimum, we can try again with a smaller percentage (e.g., drop to 40%). This preprocessing of the back-tilted job simplifies the scheduling, but at a price.

If, when we are ready to run the job, we discover that not 50% but 75% of the lines are open, then the system *might* want to delay the run and reschedule based on this greater availability. That would better meet the needs of the customer, but it would constrain us from taking new jobs in that limited time frame. This is a business issue, not a technical one, but the implications are that the system might want to reschedule based on new information as it approaches the start of a back-tilted job. For release one, we'll preprocess the back-tilted job, put it in the schedule and leave it alone. Later we may want to adapt the back-tilted job based on evolving knowledge of system resources.

Handling Crisis-Calls

Hypotenuse must balance three needs. We must instantly respond to a crisis with every available resource. Second, we wish to keep all lines active and in use as much as possible. Finally, we must be sure that even after we handle a crisis, we can still meet our deadlines on other calls.

Crisis•Call customers subscribe to the service much as one might purchase insurance. You hope never to have to use it, but you pay cheerfully each month for the peace of mind it provides. *Crisis•Call* customers don't just pay for the calls they make, they pay for having the system standing by ready to meet their needs in the event of a crisis.

We agree to under-schedule the system sufficiently that should a crisis arise, we will still meet our other scheduling commitments. Hypotenuse anticipates that most *Crisis•Call* jobs will actually contact a relatively small number of people, and so even a significant crisis will disrupt out-calling only briefly.

This under-scheduling doesn't stop us from utilizing all available lines — all the calls continue to run as fast as possible, using 100% of the available resources — it just means that we don't make commitments that we can't keep.

We agree to start by scheduling to no more than 80% of our capacity. As the system gains experience with *Crisis•Calls*, that number may be adjusted over time.

Add Calls to the Queue Based on the Allocation

Once we know the job allocations, the next trick is to get the call objects into the queue. To do this, we need to generate a SQL **SELECT** statement against the call table in the database. The scheduler will have an ODBC connection, wrapped up in an MFC recordset object. The **SELECT** statement will want to select only eligible calls.

This naturally brings us to the question of finding out exactly which calls are eligible to be made, and that must include calls that have already been tried unsuccessfully. We note that the retry time may vary, both for different types of failures (we may wait longer after a 'no answer' than after a 'busy') and for different jobs (Job A may wait longer after a busy than Job B does).

We can capture the retry policy in a policy object, but how do we create a **SELECT** statement that isn't overly complex? After some discussion, we hit on the idea of tagging each call with the earliest allowable retry time. This will allow us to issue a very straightforward **SELECT** statement: "Select all calls whose retry time is before now."

I go on to suggest that each call object will hold a start time and an end time. That time will be initialized to the start and end time of the job. Once the call is made, the start and end times will record the actual start and end times of the particular phone call. If the call fails, the call record will hold the start and end time of the attempt, and the *new* call record (to be used for the retry) will hold the earliest time we can retry as *its* start time. Thus we'll use the same field for two purposes.

The *job* start and end time will provide us with information about what time of day and what dates we can call any number in the job, but each *call* will also tell us when we can retry. This allows us to say, "Give me all calls for this job whose start times are before now."

Once we have this **SELECT** statement, we'll also want to order the results by the number of attempts. Thus, for any given job, calls that have never been attempted will all be tried before we begin any retries. This will create a very natural reordering. For example, if there is an eligible retry of a 'no answer' that has been tried only twice, it will come before an eligible retry for a 'busy' that has been tried three times. Of course, if the 'no answer' isn't ready yet, it won't pass the filter, and so won't be in the sort order at all.

ODBC & MFC

The scheduler will connect to the database using MFC support classes. Because SQL Server is not a Jet database (as Access is, for example) we'll use the ODBC rather than the DAO classes. Microsoft provides a nice MFC wrapper for ODBC, so much of the complexity of ODBC is hidden from us, simplifying our database code.

The application will have one or more **CDatabase** objects, which each represent a connection to a **datasource**. An ODBC datasource comprises a database, the information the system needs to access that data, and the location — essentially, the database name.

All of this is a way to abstract out the details and generalize database access, but for our purposes, the **CDatabase** object simply represents the call database itself. The connection across the network is handled by ODBC, and is invisible to the application.

Once we have the database object, we'll create a **CRecordset** object to represent the set of records we'll be selecting from the call table. We get the recordset by setting up a **SELECT** statement, filling in the filter and sort clauses and so forth. Once the recordset is established, it will be pointing to the first record in the selected set of calls, with each field in the database represented by a member variable. Obviously, we can read values from these variables, or update the current record by setting them. We can **Move()** to the next record, and iterate through the records as needed. The task of getting each record and marking it 'in the queue' is fairly straightforward, and ClassWizard will help with creating the necessary mapping between the **CRecordset** member variables and the fields in the database.

An optimization will be to set the size of the **CRecordset** object so that it fetches more than one record from the database at a time. Doing so should improve performance at the cost of making the code somewhat more complex. Initially we'll just get one record at a time; once we understand where the performance bottlenecks are, we can return to this area of the code as an opportunity to improve performance.

Central Office Protection

An obscure but critical requirement of the application is that we don't call too many numbers within a single central office in too short a period of time. We want to avoid having folks in the town unable to get a dial tone because we've used up all the lines — it wouldn't be good for our corporate image!

The COP (Central Office Protection) object will enforce this policy. Before any numbers are added to the call queue they will be submitted to the COP object, which will keep a dictionary as a member variable. In this dictionary, the key will be the area code/ exchange combination, and the value will be the central office. The COP will also keep a table, with one entry per central office, of how many calls can go to that office per minute. (This table will be implemented as yet another dictionary, but this time the key is the office number, and the value is the maximum number of calls per minute). Finally, the COP object will keep a running total of how many minutes' worth of calls are already in the call queue for a given central office, and it will know how many minutes' worth of calls it is now proposing to add to the queue.

The scheduler will hand a call object to the COP object by invoking the **OkayToAdd()** method, which returns a Boolean. A **TRUE** value means it's OK to add this call to the queue; if it's **FALSE**, the scheduler will throw the call away and get another. Since the update to the call will happen *after* this test, the call will not be marked enqueued, its status and attempt count will be unchanged, and thus it will be eligible in the next round.

This is a simple and elegant solution that can be simplified further in V1 by keeping a fixed limit on the number of calls to *any* area code/exchange pair, and ignoring the central office question altogether as a first approximation. In subsequent releases we will build a table of area code and exchange pairs mapping them to central offices, and then mapping central offices each to maximum calls per hour.

The Dispatcher

The dispatcher is a frighteningly simple object. Its job is to manage the requests received from local queue managers on the various call stations. The dispatcher will provide a connection *for* the queue manager, and will keep a connection *to* the queue manager. This will allow the request to get more calls to be asynchronous. In other words, the local queue manager will request calls and return immediately. When the dispatcher is ready to send the calls, it will call the queue manager back with the calls it has retrieved from the call queue. A quick sketch of the dispatcher class in pseudocode helps us capture these essential characteristics.

```
class CDispatcher
{
public:
    void                    Begin               ();
    void                    End                 ();
    void                    GetCallsFromQueue   (int n);
    static CDispatcher*     Instance            (CCallQueue&);

protected:
    CDispatcher(CCallQueue&);

private:
    static CDispatcher*     theDispatcher;
    CQueueManager*          theQueueManager;
};
```

The Call Queue

The call queue will be created when the call server starts. It will own a synchronization object on which the scheduler will block. When the call queue 'notices' that the number of calls it contains has fallen below the low-water mark (held in the system policy object), it signals the synchronization object, which causes the scheduler to fill the queue.

The queue itself is a very straightforward encapsulation of an STL object. We'll implement the queue as a singleton to ensure that there is only one in the application.

The Call Station Manager

The call station manager is a simple object in the call server that is responsible for keeping track of how many lines we are currently keeping open for incoming calls. It coordinates this effort among the call stations, as I'll describe in a forthcoming section. This object too is a singleton.

The Job Manager

The job manager is responsible for determining which jobs are valid. It owns a policy object that delineates what makes a valid job, but typically a job is valid if it has a valid start date and end date, and if it has a list of phone numbers, the necessary audio and a flow.

The job manager is also responsible for breaking jobs down into sub-jobs to handle time-zone dependent calling. Finally, the job manager is responsible for reading the file containing the phone numbers associated with a job, and for populating the call table.

Rethinking Queue Management

In a subsequent design meeting, we rethink the queue management. There are a number of problems that become evident when we discuss the dispatcher, which will be providing service to a large number of calling machines (perhaps as many as 200) and will need to be able to respond pretty quickly. The current algorithm has the queue setting a low-water mark when it needs to be filled, at which point the scheduler will need to compute the call distribution and then fill the queue. This could take a while.

What are the specific areas of concern? First, the current design has the scheduler sitting idle until the refill is needed, and then just when it has to be quick, it has to do all its work. This is not a great solution.

Second, the scheduler is throwing away its recordset after each refill, which will no doubt cause the database to be hit more often than is necessary. The scheduler will refill the queue quite often, but the set of jobs from which it will pull calls will change only infrequently. If the scheduler can hold onto the recordset, it can go to the database with an expensive **SELECT** statement less often.

Finally, it's *only* getting a new recordset after each refill, and when there are busy calls that need to be retried, that may not be frequently enough. Once we are retrying numbers, the recordset *will* change often, as new numbers become eligible for retry after waiting an appropriate amount of time. Thus, if 100 numbers were busy, and if the policy is to wait 10 minutes before calling again, then the set of which numbers we should be dialing will change every few minutes.

We redesign, but in fact we only have to redesign a small piece. Rather than revealing a weakness, this is actually dramatic confirmation for our design. When a change has a very localized impact you know that you've succeeded in encapsulating your various objects cleanly; the time to worry is when one small change begins to unravel the fabric of the entire product.

The first change is that we want to increase the frequency with which the dispatcher and the scheduler remove calls from and add calls to the queue. This will keep the scheduler busy when it might otherwise be idle, and thus reduce the load at any given time. It also affords greater opportunity to pick up calls to be retried. In short, the two need to relinquish their locks frequently, to increase the throughput of the machine. The second change is that we don't want to throw away the recordset until we have to, and further, we want to build the recordset *before* we acquire the lock.

There are two ways to decide when to fill the queue. We can have the queue set a pair of low-water mark events (fell below and rose above) and a pair of high-water mark events (rose above and fell below). The scheduler can then add to the queue with granularity that is adaptive based on when it falls below or rises above these marks, shooting for a steady state between them. The alternative is that every time the scheduler gets an opportunity to own the queue, it can top it off, asking the queue how many it needs to be filled. This approach seems simpler and more straightforward, and it's the one we'll use.

The scheduler must know when it is time to throw away its recordset and get a new one. At first we thought that this was only when a job started or ended, and thus it wasn't very frequent. However, we now realize that we'll need to reset the recordset whenever we have calls eligible for retry. This isn't a problem, however. When we are retrying calls, we'll want to refresh the recordset to ensure that we are getting all the retries as quickly as possible. When we are not retrying calls, we can hang on to the recordsets until we are notified by the job manager that a job has become active or been canceled.

In fact, MFC provides the option of performing a 'requery' on a recordset, which is much quicker than closing and reopening it. Here's how it works: each time we want to pick up the calls that need to be retried, we'll modify the filter string to reflect the new time constraints (all calls whose start dates are after *now*), and then call **Requery()**.

The MFC documentation suggests that some of the optimization gained by using **Requery()** on a recordset is lost if we change the filter string. At the moment, however, I'm not focusing on database optimization. I suspect strongly that the effective throughput of the database will be so fast, and we'll tax the system so little, that it won't be an issue. The gating factor on performance will almost certainly be dialing out and interacting with the customer. Rather than optimizing the database, I'm more inclined to get it all up and running, and *then* take a look at where the real performance issues are.

So, here are the changes in this redesign. First, we'll no longer throw the recordset away unless we have to, and we'll only have to when jobs move in and out of being current. Second, we'll top off the queue every time we get the chance, so that we minimize the time for which the scheduler must lock the queue. Last, and perhaps most important, we'll compute the distribution percentages *before* we need to add to the queue. Thus, the routine for the scheduler is this:

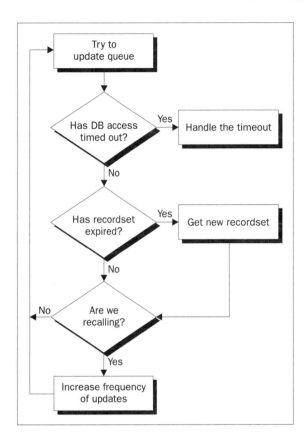

The determination of whether the recordset has expired is that a job has been added or removed. Each job goes through all its first attempts before it starts retrying. Once you are in retry mode, you need to requery the recordset every two minutes or so to pick up the newly available retry numbers.

Updating the queue is slightly more complicated, because we'll want to put the locking mechanism into the queue itself. By the time we hand calls to the queue, we want them fully created. The queue doesn't want to be waiting around while the scheduler is computing the right calls or creating the right mix. To deal with this, the scheduler will create a list of calls, which it will fill up while not talking with the queue. Periodically, it will hand that list to the queue, which will take as many calls as it needs and return the shortened list back to the scheduler which can, in its own time and on its own nickel, fill it back up.

This way, the scheduler can go to the queue quite frequently (say, between 1 and 10 times a second) and ask, "Here, would you like to fill up?" Every once in a while, the scheduler will need some time to rebuild its local list, but when it does the queue can live on the numbers already provided. In the unlikely event that the scheduler doesn't get back to the queue before it's fully depleted, the dispatcher must be able to handle the situation of an empty queue, relinquishing its lock frequently so that the scheduler can get back in there and fill it up.

When the call queue is taking call objects off the list passed in by the scheduler, it must update the database, marking these calls as enqueued. Updating the status of each record in the recordset individually would be rather slow. Instead, we decide that there will be an identifier field in the call table, which we'll use to update the records as a batch. The identifier is a unique number that will be assigned to each record by SQL Server, and I make room in the call object for this number. As calls are added to the call queue, I catch this number and build up a SQL statement in a string variable **strCmd**. This string reads:

```
"UPDATE CALL SET Status = ENQUEUED where CALLID = <callid> AND <callid>..."
```

Every 500 calls or so, I send that SQL statement to the database, by writing:

```
theDatabase->ExecuteSQL(strCmd);
```

Thus, in a single SQL statement, all 500 records are instantly updated. Since this happens while the call queue is locked, there is no danger, even if the call server should crash at any point immediately before or after this statement is executed. The key requirement is that the record be updated before the call is dispatched to the calling machine, and this fulfills that requirement.

The Call Station

While the low-level design of the call server was relatively straightforward, the call station presents a more difficult challenge. During high-level design, we didn't fully think through how the call station will handle switching back and forth between making and receiving calls.

Our first thought is to kill the calling object when the line must be switched over. We even consider making the calling object and the receiving object inherit from a common base class and transmuting one into the other, but this seems too clever by half.

Finally, we hit on the idea of abstracting the port out of these objects and into a 'line' object. The line will have knowledge about the port and its current state. More precisely, the line manager will know, for each port, which of the following states it is in at any moment: waiting to receive a call, receiving a call, waiting to make a call or making a call. All of the line objects will be owned by the line manager, which will apportion lines to either callers or receivers depending on what it needs to accomplish.

When the line manager is 'born', it will create a circuit to the call station manager and be told how many of its lines should be kept open for incoming calls. The line manager will assign that many line objects to receivers, and the remaining line objects to callers. When a receiver gets an incoming call, it will inform the line manager so that the latter can keep track of how many incoming lines are available, and reapportion lines as needed.

For example, if the line manager is told to keep 10 lines open for incoming calls, it will begin by handing lines 0-9 to receivers and the rest of the line objects to callers. If receivers 5 and 7 report that they are taking incoming calls, then the line manager will flag lines 10 and 11 to be handed to receivers when they become available.

When a line becomes available, the line manager will start a thread for the appropriate object (receiver or caller). When the line manager needs to change the state of that line (i.e. change it from 'receive' to 'call', or vice versa) it will set an event. Each time a caller or receiver completes a call it will wait on that event. If it gets the event, it will let the line manager know that line is being returned to its control, and the thread will terminate.

The receiving thread cycles through answering calls, reporting on the results, and waiting for more calls. It informs the line manager every time it starts or ends a call, and it watches for the 'change status' event whenever it isn't in the middle of a call.

The calling thread cycles through making calls as long as there are calls in the local call queue. After each completed call, it hands the result to the reporter and checks the status of the 'change status' event synchronization object. If that object is signaled, it lets the line manager know its line is now available and terminates its own thread.

The calling thread gets calls from the local call queue by watching a semaphore object. When there are no calls to make, the calling thread will block, waiting either for a call to become available or for the event signaling that it ought to give its line over to a receiver.

If the line manager runs out of lines to assign to receivers, it will inform the call station manager, which will assign another machine to the same task. More specifically, the line manager will keep high-water and low-water mark synchronization objects. When the high-water mark signals, it will tell the call station manager that it needs help, and clear the low-water mark. When the low-water mark signals, it will clear the high-water signal and let the call station manager know it no longer needs help.

In addition to instantiating the line manager, the call station service will instantiate the local call queue, the local call queue manager, the flow manager and the call reporter.

Local Call Queue and Local Call Queue Manager

The local call queue keeps a synchronization object tied to a low-water mark. When the queue signals the synchronization object, the local call queue manager will request more calls from the dispatcher. This design still makes sense, even though we got rid of the low-water mark on the call queue on the server. The reason is that the network latency involved in filling this queue means that we *do* want to ask for objects in a batch from the dispatcher. Also, since we're only filling enough for one calling machine, these are fairly small batches.

After it has made its request, the function will return and the local call queue manager will wait for calls from the dispatcher. The dispatcher will send calls when it has them to send.

Outgoing Calls

When we get into the mechanics of calling, we decide to produce a quick drawing to show the principal objects involved in the process, and the relationships between them. There are a lot of object interactions going on at this point, and it's helpful to be able to be able to 'see' everything in one place:

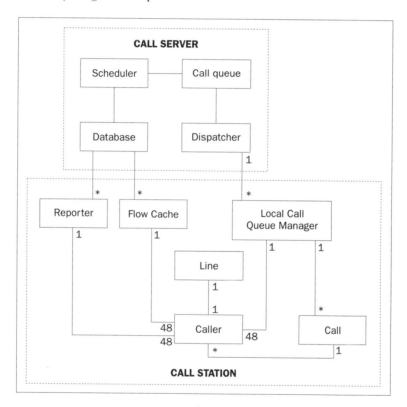

The Callers

When a caller is handed a line object, it asks the local queue manager for a call object. The call object includes a reference to the flow, which the caller then asks the flow cache for.

If the flow isn't available, the flow cache will request the flow from the database. This is how new flows are distributed through the system. Rather than proactively distributing a new flow to every call station, the stations request them as needed.

In the meantime, while waiting for the flow to be delivered from the database, the caller marks the call with the status 'flow not available', but does *not* increment the count of attempted calls. It hands the call to the reporter, which will hand it back to the database for rescheduling.

If the flow is available, the caller is now ready to place the outgoing call. When the call is completed, it updates the call object, increments its count of attempts, and adds the call to the reporter's report queue. The caller then returns its line to the line manager.

The only complex or interesting thing the caller object does is to make the calls, which is to say it executes a Tcl script and interacts with the Visual Voice class library.

The Call Reporter

The reporter is the only reader of the report queue, and this is the only place in the design where we have multiple writers and a single reader. Still, the 48 writers (the receiving and calling objects) will only be adding small objects, and they'll only be doing so around once a minute. Contention for this queue will therefore be fairly low.

In the first release, the reporter will read each record out of the call report queue, and will immediately place the call into the database. If the call was not successful, it will also create a *new* call record, setting the retry date and placing that record into the database to be retried.

Because this process involves a write (and possibly two writes) to the database, we become a bit concerned about database traffic. Early prototyping and preliminary testing show that the database can certainly handle at least 6,000 updates per minute, with no optimization at all. While this is enough for what we want to do, it is only so by a narrow margin, and we begin to think about where we might reduce network traffic.

Database Issues

We note that the database must be updated each time we add a call to the call queue, as well as once after each call (or twice if the number must be recalled).

We consider a number of potential optimizations. We might, for example, decide not to create two records in the event of a recall. The current design says that the original call record represents a single attempt, and that retries require the creation of a new call object. We challenge this, but the truth is that it's a pretty clean design, and we're reluctant to abandon it.

A second suggestion is that we reconsider updating the database each time a call is added to the scheduler. We're keeping the 'enqueued' flag only so that we can recover from a crash. Perhaps there is a better way. I speculate that we could keep a log on the local machine. Each time a caller is about to make a call, it can record that fact to the disk. When the call finishes, it can update that record. In the event of a crash, we have only to look for those calls that were begun but not completed.

The objection to this, of course, is that the record is stored on the very machine that we are concerned might fail. We amend this idea to suggest that rather than recording to disk, a message is sent to a logger object on a central machine. This logger can keep track of calls that begin but don't end, and can take preemptive action when necessary, alerting Operations when lines seem to have gone dead.

This seems clean, and it will reduce database traffic, but it makes the application more complex and may not be needed. Steve suggests we hold off on this until we can prove we need it. After all, the database access may be fine, or we may be able to optimize it in a number of ways. For example, we may be able to improve performance by caching, or by using larger recordsets, or by adding memory, or by upgrading the hardware. Any or all of these could well turn out to be cheaper and easier than the proposed logger object.

Incoming Calls

The receiver is to incoming calls what the caller is to outgoing calls.

There are two flows (one for replay requests and one for preproduction calls), and both are cached on every call machine. These flows don't change very often. When we add a new flow to the database, we'll need a way to broadcast the information to all the calling machines to update their caches; the call station manager seems ideally suited to this task.

When the line manager hands a line to the receiver, the latter waits for an incoming call. It examines the number the user is *calling* to determine whether this is a request for a replay or a preproduction call, and then invokes the appropriate flow.

If the request is for a replay, the receiver tries to determine the number the call is coming from. If it can pick this up from the ANI number (the digital equivalent to the caller ID), it can immediately ask the database for the most recent call to that number. If not, it will have to ask the caller to give the right phone number.

One way or the other, the receiver will ask the database for the appropriate call object, and then ask the flow cache for the associated flow. It's entirely possible that flow will no longer be cached, and there will be a brief delay while the cache retrieves the flow from the database. Once the receiver has the flow it must begin the flow from the point of recognizing that it has 'connected' with a live person. At the conclusion of the call, the receiver will update the call object and hand it to the reporter, which will store it in the database.

If the receiver is handling a preproduction call, it interacts with the user based on the preproduction flow it received when it was created. The data gathered during the preproduction call is formatted into a job object that the receiver hands to the preproduction reporter.

The Preproduction Reporter

The preproduction reporter will place that job into the database via ODBC. The database will then inform the job manager that a new job has been added, and the job manager will attempt to validate the job, setting its status accordingly (pending, ready, incomplete, etc.).

Prototyping

There are a number of details to be worked out about the call station implementation that will be greatly clarified as we begin prototyping. I am reluctant to flesh out too many of the details of the flow cache, for example, as we don't yet know for sure how we'll implement the call flows. Will they be scripts interpreted at runtime? Or might we hardwire the flows for the first version?

The call station is awash with objects, each with its own narrow area of responsibility. While this is a powerful model, before we spend a lot of time detailing the responsibilities of the reporter or the line manager, we may want to start with a simplified approach which gets us up and running and making phone calls.

It is time to begin prototyping. In a prototype, we can experiment with the interaction between the Visual Voice library and our design, and we can begin better to understand the interactions among the various objects we've conceptualized.

Monitoring the Systems

Operations will want to watch the call server and the calling stations in action. In addition, the developers will need to be able to monitor these objects to ensure they are working as expected. The requirements document does not detail what information is needed, and I ask Jay and Kevin to start thinking about what they might want.

During one of the low-level design meetings, we discuss how we might make this information available while the system is running. Each machine might provide summary or detailed information of its progress, but it would be great if this could be consolidated on a console, and even better if it could be available over the Internet.

Our initial thought is to build an Automation object that will expose the data. Jay could hire a Visual Basic programmer to write a VB application that displays the information in whatever format he prefers. Before going down this path, however, I'd like to look into putting the information into a set of forms available through the web server. We decide to look into using ASP, which may allow us to take both of these paths together. Thus, we can massage the data using a component built by a Visual Basic programmer, and then export the results to the Web. This would allow us to monitor the performance and state of any part of the system from anywhere in the world. Given that Hypotenuse is in New Jersey and I'm in Massachusetts, this has a lot of appeal.

The Database Tables

It's finally time to take a first stab at detailing the principal database tables. The first thing to know when building these tables is that we won't get it right at the first attempt. Building the database may be the most difficult thing we'll have to do in the whole project. The difference in performance between a well designed database and a poorly designed one can be orders of magnitude, so we'll work on this for a while, and then we'll try to bring in some serious expertise to review our design.

The first table to design is the job table. The job objects will be stored here, and each field in the table will correspond to a member of the object. We want to be sure that the information in this table is only that which is specific to the job, and is not stored anywhere else.

The Job Table

Name	Type	Notes
Job ID	int	The unique ID of this job or sub-job.
Parent Job ID	int	The parent job (or zero if no parent)
Call ID	int	Foreign key into the call table
Audio ID	int	Foreign key into the audio table
Flow ID	int	Foreign key into the flow table
Customer ID	int	Foreign key into the customer table
Start date	Date	Date and time to start. Time is also earliest time of day
End date	Date	Date and time to end. Time is also latest time of day
Throttle	int	Maximum number of contacts per hour
Tilt	Boolean	TRUE = front tilt. FALSE = back tilt.
Retry Policy ID	int	Foreign key into the policy table
Date entered	Date	
Date last modified	Date	
Who modified	int	Foreign key into the customer table
Who requested	int	Foreign key into the customer table (original request for job)
Priority	int	Relative priority among jobs
IsCrisis	Boolean	Is this job a crisis?
TheCount	int	Total count of calls for this job

The job ID is required to identify this job uniquely. It is the key that relates jobs to calls — each call record will be tied to a single job. The parent job ID allows us to break up a job based on time zone, but still aggregate the results. We decide to include a number of additional foreign keys to facilitate relating the job records to the various other records (such as which audio is to be played for this job).

The essential scheduling characteristics are captured here as well, such as the start and end date, and the throttle and tilt. We discussed breaking these out into a scheduling table, but we believe there is a one-to-one correspondence — that is, each job would relate to exactly one scheduling record, so nothing would be gained by putting these in a separate table.

We add a couple of fields to track when the job was created and when it was last modified. If a complete audit trail will be required, we'll take these fields out and create a new table that will have one record for each modification, keyed to the job ID.

Of equal significance is the call table. The call represents the information we need to call a phone number or to record an attempted call. We tie each call back to the job table to find out the audio, the flow, and so forth. The start and end fields in the call are different from those in the job. The job knows the minimum start date and the maximum end date for the entire job, whereas the call knows either when we tried or when we may next try this particular number.

The Call Table

Name	Type	Notes
Call ID	**int**	Unique primary key
Job ID	**int**	Foreign key into the job table
Phone number	**String**	
Start	**Date**	Start time or earliest retry time
End	**Date**	End time or time of last attempt
Number of attempts	**int**	
Status	**int**	Flag (not tried, busy, no answer, etc.)

This initial set of data is just enough to uniquely identify each call. We will need to flesh out the right fields to capture the data required by Jay for his MIS without so bloating the table that the database swells up and keels over.

Designing the Other Tables

While there are certainly other significant tables, their design can wait until we are implementing them. The job and call tables are the driving forces in the database. We decide to hold off designing the other tables, or even identifying which fields (other than the primary keys) will be indexed.

SnapShot

Just what is *SnapShot*? Is it a stand-alone executable, or just a set of methods in the existing call server? I propose that we extend the call server to include the *SnapShot* object, which remains dormant until its **GetSnapShot(Date)** method is invoked. Calling this method causes the *SnapShot* object to interact with the scheduler.

We believe we have the fundamental building blocks to create *SnapShot*. The *SnapShot* object is responsible for drawing the graph, and delegates to the scheduler the responsibility for providing the distribution of jobs, in 15 minute increments, throughout the day in question. The scheduler must be extended to include a *SnapShot* method, whose job is to run these numbers in a low priority thread. The scheduler isn't being asked to do anything new; it just runs the methods that establish the relative allocation of lines, but rather than going on to allocate the lines, it just reports back to the *SnapShot* object.

Interprocess Communication

Until now, we have been treating interprocess communication with a bit of a hand wave. We've been able to do this because most of the interprocess communication will be handled by ODBC. Each time an object talks with the database directly, we'll create an ODBC connection using the MFC **CDatabase** and **CRecordset** classes, and this is pretty easy to do.

The tricky part is working out how to connect the dispatcher with the call stations. The simplest approach is probably to connect the server and client together using Windows Sockets. This has a lot of appeal, as it's a tried and true technology. It has been well tested, and there is a lot of experience in how to make it work well.

A more complicated approach, but one that may provide far more flexibility, is to use DCOM. DCOM is an extension of COM, the underlying technology for OLE and ActiveX. The advantage of DCOM is that it functions at a higher level of abstraction than does Windows Sockets. All of the connection details, along with marshaling objects across process boundary, are handled by DCOM. In addition, Microsoft has positioned COM as its interprocess communication solution, and thus more and more of the tools emerging from Microsoft are based on COM.

COM supports the notion of component based programming, and this is a powerful idea that we'd like to integrate into the design. The problem is that despite the enormous help afforded by the compiler, building a COM-based MFC application is still more complicated than building an MFC application without COM.

Initially, I'm inclined to go with Sockets: they are simpler, and they'll get us where we need to be quite quickly. The more I learn about DCOM, however, the more convinced I am that it's the right long-term solution. The question is now whether to try to build a COM application from the start, or to add it on later.

I spent 15 minutes on the phone with Richard Grimes, the author of *Professional DCOM Programming*, which was then still in the middle of its editorial process. I learned more in that phone conversation with Richard than I had in several days of reading other people's books. He was very generous with his time and as you might expect, he felt that DCOM was a far superior solution, and that it wouldn't take very long to get it up and running for this application. I then read a preview copy of his book; no surprise, it was terrific.

Before leaping headlong into the DCOM pool, there is one additional approach worth considering, and that's to use the database itself to manage the call queue. Since all the other objects are using ODBC to handle their interprocess communication, why not consider letting the queue do so as well, or more accurately, why not move the queue into the database, and let the client communicate with it via ODBC?

There is a lot to be said for this approach. In this model, the call server becomes a somewhat simpler object. In fact, there will be no need for the dispatcher, because the call stations will just open recordsets on the call queue itself. Thus, the synchronization between the scheduler and the dispatcher is no longer needed. The scheduler can be put on a timer and simply top off the queue once a minute. (We could be more adaptive and update on any number of criteria, but why over-engineer this?)

When the call stations want to take a call from the call queue, they will open a dynaset on it, and iterate through the records. For each call they find, they'll make a copy and call **Delete()** (to delete it from the call queue). This gets a bit complicated, as other call stations may include the same record in their dynasets. Thus, they must *attempt* the delete and catch the exception that will be thrown if another machine attempts to delete the same object. If the delete attempt succeeds, they can add the call to their local call queue. If it throws an exception, someone else has deleted that record, and they must throw it away and get the next one. The logic is represented in the flowchart on the next page.

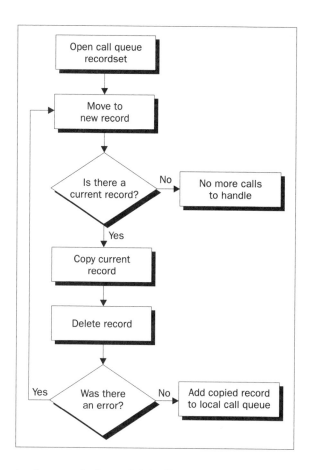

We are concerned that pushing the queue into the database will be like killing a fly with a nuclear weapon. The biggest issue is that we could be adding an intolerable load onto the database, thus slowing down the system.

At the conclusion of this discussion, we decide to hold off making this decision. We're all convinced that DCOM is the right long-term solution, so the question really boils down to this: Do we start with something easier? Are Sockets a better first step? Should we push the queue into the database just to get it up and running quickly? The best way to approach a problem like this is to prototype some simple solutions. I set out to build the scheduler and the dispatcher. Within a few hours they are up and running, sufficient to test how they'll share the call queue.

Segmenting the Components

Steve identifies our need to delineate the various components. What modules will we be working with, and what machines will they reside on? Which objects share thread space, which share process space, and which must be on the same machine?

For example, while the scheduler and the dispatcher will almost certainly be in their own, separate threads of execution, it's hard to imagine that they won't be in the same process space, at least initially. These two objects are very tightly coupled. While DCOM will afford 'location transparency', network latency will almost certainly be an issue when the dispatcher and scheduler have to constantly communicate with one another. In any case, it is not an issue at the moment, as there is little downside to keeping them within the same process.

Similarly, the local call queue manager and the caller objects will be in the same process space. Less tightly coupled are the callers and the reporters, but we'd be surprised if they too weren't in the same process. Even the flow manager and the local call queue manager, which are very loosely coupled, are likely to be in the same process, as they are probably implemented in the calling executable.

Of course, the callers and the call server can't be in the same process, as they will be on different machines. They will communicate across the network, using ODBC to talk with the database and DCOM to talk with one another.

Many of these initial decisions about which objects will share process space were made more by gut instinct than by careful review and discussion of all the options. I am reluctant to rely too heavily on DCOM as it is new and I don't understand it fully. Where it is easy and clean to keep objects in a single process space, or to use ODBC for interprocess communication, we will do so. Where DCOM offers an obvious improvement, we'll use that.

Because each of these objects will be well encapsulated, we can revisit these decisions as the needs change, but our imperative at the moment is to get the system up and running with a fairly straightforward and simple model.

Revisiting the Use Cases

Before completing the low-level design, we agree to identify the key use cases and to test the low-level design against representative scenarios. We start by making a list of the critical use cases:

1. Create a new customer

2. Add a job to the system via IVR

3. Add a job to the system via the Web

4. Prerecord audio for future use

5. Upload phone numbers

6. Send in phone numbers on disk

7. Cancel a job

8. Edit a job to reschedule it

9. A *Crisis•Call* arrives

10. Stop the system

11. Start the system from a full stop

12. Examine the schedule

Returning to the CRC Cards

We will test our design against the use cases by fleshing out the CRC cards and making sure we understand how the objects will interact to fulfill the requirements of particular scenarios. Steve will hold the CRC cards relating to the call server, I will hold the cards relating to the calling machines, and Glenn will hold the cards relating to the rest of the system.

1. Create a new customer.
Jim Baker of the Coyote Lobbying Group wants to sign up to call his 50,000 members every time Congress considers laws that will adversely affect the coyote. He speaks with Mary Helpful, the sales clerk at Hypotenuse, and agrees to the terms and conditions of membership. Mary fires up her browser and brings up the page for signing up a new customer. This page is designed to walk a Hypotenuse employee through the process. There are a number of questions the employee must ask the prospective customer, and links to follow based on the customer's answers. When the form is properly filled out, the customer is given a customer ID number.

This is a natural, but unfortunate, first scenario. It's natural in that it puts us at the sign-up stage, a reasonable starting point for considering the system as a whole. However, it's unfortunate because so far we've consciously sidestepped both the Internet design issues and the sign-up process.

We've done this because we believe these aspects of the system are among the most straightforward and need little advance design. We'll build the forms using FrontPage, and we'll handle the database interaction using either IDC or one of the new technologies supported by Visual InterDev. We intend to build the sign-up piece only on the Internet (not on the phone system at all) and we'll probably build it last. Feeling slightly uncomfortable that our very first scenario went unanswered, we move on to use case number two.

2. Add a job to the system via IVR.
Now a fully registered user, Jim Baker calls in the following day to launch a new job. He puts in his social security number and the system prompts him for his password. Having entered his password, the system asks which list he'd like to call. Jim enters 005. The system determines that he doesn't always place the

calls immediately, and asks whether he wants the calls to start immediately or to schedule them. He schedules them for the next day, starting at 9 a.m. The system asks if he wants to record audio or to use one of his prerecorded messages, and he decides to record new audio. The system prompts him through the recording, and tells him the new audio will be saved as audio number 008. He is asked to verify his order, which he does, and that concludes the call.

We begin the walk through. When Jim calls into the system, the call is routed to the next available incoming line. I hold up the receiver card and say, "I'm the receiver. I answer the line and examine the DNIS (Dialed Number Information Service) number, which is the number the caller actually dialed. He called 1-800-PRE-PROD, and so I know this is a preproduction call and I need the preproduction flow. I got that from the flow cache and I begin to interpret what it says. That causes me to play the right prompt message. The rest of the scenario is just Jim interacting with me, while I gather information and branch based on what he tells me."

We discuss this and realize that it's actually a bit more complicated than it seems at first sight. The receiver is also interacting with the database, checking repeatedly to see if it's supposed to prompt for a list number, or if there's only one list, and so forth. This immediately suggests that what we want is to talk to the database *once* and get a copy of the customer's record, so that we know the answers to all these questions without having to go back to the database. The second use case has revealed an important design consideration that we hadn't incorporated yet. The receiver object will want to request a customer record from the database, and it will want to hold that record for the duration of the call.

I continue on as the receiver. "Now that I have all the information for the job, I can break the connection and hand the information to the reporter. But shouldn't I just go ahead and make a job object and hand *that* to the reporter?"

A discussion begins about where the knowledge about creating a job object should reside. I suggest that the receiver *must* have that knowledge. If I *don't* create the job object, then I have to give the appropriate information to the reporter. The only reasonable way to do that is in some predefined order, otherwise it's just so much meaningless data. If I have a predefined order, I'll want to build a structure to hold the data as I gather it. The best structure for that would, of course, be the job object itself.

The CRC card is updated to reflect the fact that the receiver will create the empty job object at the beginning of its interaction with the customer, and will 'fill in' its parts as the flow proceeds.

Each customer will have told us a lot about how he'll use the system when he first signed up. We capture this information in policy objects, and at preproduction time we'll check the customer's records and modify the questions we ask based on the information we find there.

This rings true. It is clean, elegant and consistent with the rest of the architecture. Use case number two now works, and has contributed to the overall design. We go on to number three, but back away immediately. The only difference between use cases two and three is the way in which we gather the information, and we've already agreed not to examine the Internet piece yet. We go on to use case number four.

Use cases 4, 5 and 6 can, I suggest, best be seen as the partial creation of jobs, and thus work exactly as use case 2 did. We talk about whether this is reasonable, and realize that what's missing in 2 is some acknowledgement not only of the creation of the job, but also of its validity. We agree that as a result of adding the job to the database, a SQL Server trigger may be fired that submits the job to the job manager, which in turn validates the job and sets its status.

7. Cancel a Job.
Jim calls back later in the day to cancel the job. Once again, the system recognizes the number he's calling and the receiver invokes the right flow. This time, he asks to edit his job and then on the edit menu he asks to cancel it. The system cancels the job.

Again I hold up the receiver card and say, "This is identical to number two until we get to the point where he goes into edit mode. When he indicates he wants to edit the job rather than create a new one, we get the job number. Instead of getting a new job from the customer database, we actually get the job from the job database. He indicates he wants to cancel, so I mark the job canceled and put it back in the database. Adding it back to the database causes the trigger to fire again and the job manager to be notified."

Steve holds up the job manager card and says, "I confirm that the job is still valid, but now I mark it canceled. I then notify all interested objects that the job has changed." We spend a bit of time discussing whether it is the job manager who cancels it or the receiver. We agree that the job manager owns that responsibility.

Steve then holds up the scheduler. "OK, the scheduler is certainly interested. The first thing I do is to update my list of jobs so that I know what is supposed to be running. Then I have two choices: I can flush the queue to get rid of the calls from this job, or I can let them play out for a minute or two but not add any more."

This is a tricky question. On the one hand, we don't want to keep calling if the customer has asked us to cancel; on the other, flushing the system sounds expensive. All other jobs will be slowed down if we flush the queue and then refill it, but by how much? We should be able to flush the main queue, ask the calling stations to flush theirs, and then refill fairly quickly. Do we have to wait for all the current calls to complete? We shouldn't; they'll finish and report. The recycle time should be very quick, so there is no reason not to flush the queues. The minute lost is almost certainly worth it to provide near-instant cancellation. We will want to subject these speculations to empirical testing.

Use case 8 is a variant on number 7. Use case 9, however, warrants a full discussion.

9 A *Crisis•Call* arrives.
Joe Obfuscation, the chief engineer at Mission Point Nuclear Facility, calls into the system while four jobs are making calls. He punches in his social security number and password, and the system realizes that any call from this account is a *Crisis•Call*. We already have the phone numbers and the audio, so we play the verification message, "Your request for crisis calling has been received. We are beginning our emergency calls now. If this is an error, please press star now, otherwise hang up and we will continue calling." He hangs up, and we begin calling.

I hold up the receiver card. "Right until he hangs up, this is just like the previous preproduction calls. I had less to do, but it was along the same lines, with no changes in responsibility. In fact, even when he hangs up, I just do the same thing. I hand the job to the reporter, which puts it in the database. We should make a note, however, that if the reporters ever decide to hang on to some reports for a while to batch them up, they should treat crisis requests as a flush of that cache. They should report them to the database immediately."

The job is added to the database, triggering the job manager. Steve holds up his card, "I validate the job and notify interested parties." He puts down the job manager card and picks up the scheduler card. "I realize it is a *Crisis•Call* and I pull the emergency switch. That is, I flush my queue and ask the call station manager to instruct the calling machines to flush theirs."

Glenn holds up the call station manager card and says, "I send a *Crisis•Call* alert message to all the line managers, because the line managers already have a connection to every calling machine." Does this make sense? We agree to live with it for now, but to work on whether it's really the best possible connection between the call server and the calling machines. Glenn then holds up the line manager and says, "I pass the message along to the local call queue manager."

I hold up the local call queue manager card and say, "I dump all my calls." This is just like what happens when a job is canceled.

Steve holds up the scheduler, but immediately steps out of character to raise a concern, "As soon as I dump my queue, I fill it with the *Crisis•Call*. I could just fill it with the entire job, but there are two reasons not to. First, there might be hundreds of thousands of calls, and while we're handling them, a second crisis might arise! Second, it's a more elegant solution if I just do my normal job. Each time I hit the low-water mark, I'll ask the database for all eligible jobs. The highest priority jobs when there are any *Crisis•Calls* are the *Crisis•Calls* themselves, and I'll handle those as usual. As long as the queue stays full, there should be no problem getting the calls made as quickly as possible."

I point out that while *Crisis•Calls* are to be handled first, the queue will fill with all eligible jobs; thus if there are only a few *Crisis•Calls* to make, they will go out first but the system will remain fully engaged.

I hold up my local call queue card, "As soon as I dump the queue I'll ask for refills, which the dispatcher will give me from the *Crisis•Calls*." This seems clean and well designed. A good example of where the design stood up under scrutiny.

Use case 10 examines what happens when we shut down the system. This seems pretty straightforward, and we talk through how the queues are emptied and the various components shut down safely and write their data to the database. No new issues arise examining the shutdown scenarios.

Use case 11 examines a cold start. The trick here is to make sure you have eliminated any dependencies *between* processes, and that you understand the order dependencies *within* each process. We decide to set this aside for now, as we'll understand these issues better once we have more of the system up and working.

Use case 12 essentially describes *SnapShot*. Steve holds up the *SnapShot* object and says, "I am called through the Internet and I open a connection to the scheduler. I pass in a request for *SnapShot* information for 9:00 am, 15 minutes, for April 10. The scheduler returns an array of job *SnapShot*s. These are data structures that identify a job and its allocation of lines. I plot these onto a chart, and ask scheduler for the next set."

"My interaction with the scheduler will be asynchronous, so I'll give the scheduler a callback to let me know when it has the answer." He puts down the *SnapShot* card, picks up the scheduler card and says, "I'm the scheduler and I don't have anything new to do here, except to be sure that I'm fulfilling the request in a low priority thread, so as not to interfere with my day job."

Getting Ready for Implementation

The review of the use cases confirms our impression that the design is solid, and sufficiently comprehensive to begin coding. There are still minor details to work out, but we can make a lot of progress with the code and revisit the design based on what we learn. The next step, just before we fire up the compiler, is to create a plan of attack.

A small group of designers still needs coordinating to handle source control, merging, testing and so forth. Implementing *Crisis•Call* is a fairly small job, however, and budget considerations and my general unwillingness to expand a team beyond the absolute minimum combine to dictate that I'll do the implementation alone.

Think of the benefits of working on this as a one-man team! No need to integrate the work of the various developers, no meetings to catch each other up, and no distractions as we get out of sync with each other. The coordination between the work I do on one part of the code and another should be about as good as it can get — I hope there isn't too much chance of my getting out of touch with myself!

The question of source code control is thornier. With more than one programmer it wouldn't be a question at all, it would be a necessity. With a single programmer, however, there is more of a trade-off. On the one hand, I've little desire to be hamstrung by the need to check out and check back in each source file as I use it. On the other hand, I've been saved more than once by the ability to roll back to a previous version. As I start handing over the interim versions to the customer, source code control *will* be a necessity. After all, if I can't recreate the version of the program the customer is working with, I'll be lost.

The development environment I've bought is Visual Studio, part of the Microsoft Universal MSDN package. Included in this package is SourceSafe, and I make a tentative decision to use it for version control.

The requirements are well understood, the high-level design appears to be robust and extensible, and the low-level design has covered the details. We understand the database tables, and we have mapped the interactions among the objects. The only thing left is to write the program.

The problem, of course, is where to start. There is a bootstrapping issue when writing a large application: you can't build it all at once. Personally, I like to code incrementally: I get a small piece working, and then build up from there. The question is, which small piece do I begin with?

All of this is made much more difficult by inertia. My brain is a heavy, lethargic, inert mass that's at rest. Getting it rolling along the path of building this project won't be easy, and it will take a lot of energy in the early days just to build up a bit of momentum. If I must ask it to scale a difficult incline, I can be certain it will roll back to its starting point and crush me underneath. The trick is to get something fairly easy working right away. I decide to start by creating tables in the database and filling them up with some test data. I can then begin writing the call server software to fill up the call queue, and from there I can go on to write the calling stations. Piece of cake.

```
= false;
Time();
= now.Format("%b %d

er = "start < '";
oday;
  and enddate > '";
today;
= '";

JobScheduleSet.m_strFilter =

JobScheduleSet.IsOpen())

JobScheduleSet.Requery();

pDoc>m_JobScheduleSet.Open();

pDoc>m_JobScheduleSet;

llTrack* pCallTrack;
l ok;

ile
pDoc>m_JobScheduleSet.IsEOF())

      pCallTrack = new
llTrack(m_pDoc>m_JobScheduleSet.m_
bID);   ok = pCallTrack>Initialize();

    if (ok)
    {   Log("ok\n");

  m_CallList.AddHead(pCallTrack);
          foundJobs = true;
    }
    else
    {   Log("...Rejected!\n");
        delete pCallTrack;
    }

    }
m_pDoc>m_JobScheduleSet.MoveNext();

CTime::GetCurre
  CTime end = theJob
  CTime start = theJobSet.
  CTime todayStart(start.GetYear(),
    start.GetMonth(),now.GetDay(),
    start.GetHour(),
    start.GetMinute(),
    start.GetSecond());
    CTime todayEnd(end.GetYear(),
  end.GetMonth(), now.GetDay(),
  end.GetHour(),
  end.GetMinute(), end.GetSecond());

      if (todayStart > now || todayS
  now)
    {   theJobSet.Close();
        return false;

    }

    CTimeSpan theSpan = end no
    int totalMinutes =
theSpan.GetTotalMinutes();

    if (end > todayEnd) // s
than today
    {   int AdditionalMinutes(theJ
GetAdditionalMinutes(theJ
t.
        theJobSet.m_EndDate);
        CTimeSpan todaySp
    now;   totalMinutes =
    todaySpan.GetTotalMin
    AdditionalMin;
    }

        n_min = ( ( (m_t
    totalMinutes) + 1
    );   m_Priority = t
        m_Tilt = theJo
        m_Throttle = t
        m_JobID = the
        theJobSet.Cl
            return tru
```

CHAPTER SIX

Implementation

It is early April, and we have a sufficient design to begin coding. The use cases for how customers and Hypotenuse staff will interact with the system are fairly well understood, and they constitute the bulk of our requirements document. The high-level design describes a solid client-server architecture with clean distribution of responsibilities among the principal classes. The high-level design appears to have translated cleanly into the low-level design, and we are confident in our choice both of NT as a platform and of C++ as a development language. In short, we're ready to begin coding and to see how the design plays out when we actually start building the product.

Along the way I expect to follow the design closely, but I do not necessarily expect to implement it all in the first version. There may be opportunities to simplify the implementation without undermining the fundamental architecture as described in the previous chapters. The key is to get something working and to keep it working as we add features. This process of iterative, successive approximation will give us the greatest likelihood of success as we move forward.

Laying the Groundwork

Before beginning the implementation of this project, I identify a number of areas in which I need to achieve expertise quickly:

- Programming with Visual Voice
- SQL Server 6.5
- Microsoft Visual C++ 5.0 and MFC 4.21
- WinSock Programming
- Tcl programming

I approach these tasks as I usually approach learning new technology and begin with a few trips to the local bookstore, where I buy two books on SQL Server, and a book each on WinSock Programming and Tcl.

There are no commercial texts that I know of on Visual Voice, but I have their manual and I'm pretty confident that will do. I've spent a lot of time using and teaching MFC, so I don't need much extra help there, except to catch up with the newest developments. For that I use the MFC online documentation, the Microsoft Developer Network and an early peek at the latest revision of Mike Blaszczak's fantastic book on MFC (now titled *Professional MFC with Visual C++ 5*).

Next, I will buy a few days of consulting time. I find that spending one day with someone who knows a subject cold can save me many days of thrashing. I always approach it the same way: I read a book on the subject before they show up. I then spend an hour with them checking my understanding, and explaining the piece of the problem I'd like to solve. Finally, we spend the rest of the time *writing* the application together. By the end of the day I'm almost always ready to carry on by myself. That one day is well worth the cost; it often saves me a week of work.

Preliminary Tinkering

During the design phase I'd done some preliminary work with SQL Server. I created a few test databases and began thinking about how to manipulate the data. Microsoft Visual C++ 5.0 Enterprise Edition now includes a very cool new product: the Database Designer. Within this GUI environment, you can create tables, generate indices, and establish relationships and constraints between various keys and among tables. With five minutes' tinkering, I had a reasonable working model of my most important tables:

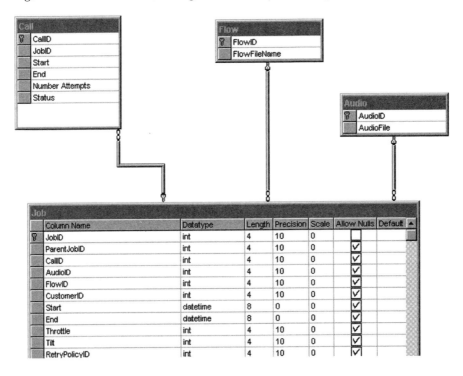

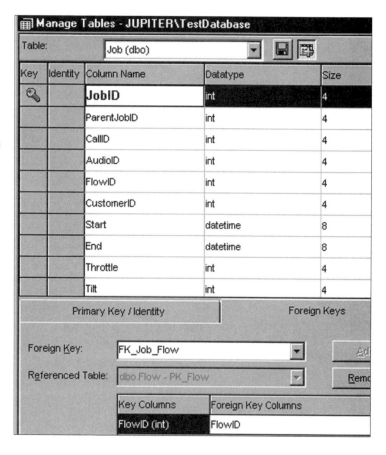

This tool is quick, intuitive and easy to use. Creating table relations is literally drag-and-drop, and couldn't be much simpler. I must admit to being a bit of a skeptic, so I quickly opened the SQL Enterprise Manager to inspect these new tables, indices, and relations:

Sure enough, it had built the right tables, created the appropriate foreign keys, and established the referential integrity. Very nice.

I should say that my normal inclination is to avoid changing tools just before starting a new project. While new products may bring significant improvements, they also introduce great risk. By their nature, they must be less familiar, they are almost certainly less reliable (at least at first), and there has been little opportunity for the market to shake out critical bugs. There was a rule of thumb in the industry, which programmers used to quote more or less seriously: never use a 'dot zero' product. That is, wait until at least one minor release (e.g. 5.1) has surfaced the most obvious and egregious bugs.

There is strong motivation for me to eschew moving to Visual C++ 5.0 in favor of staying with MSVC 4.2, especially since it is a dreaded dot zero release. In this case, Microsoft did a great job crushing my resistance. The new, integrated Visual Studio is perfect for what we need to do in this project. The confluence of Visual C++ 5.0, Visual InterDev, IIS, SQL Server, and the Database Designer was just too good to turn down. Microsoft was offering a totally integrated solution, and I couldn't help but jump at the chance.

Creating the Infrastructure

On a larger project I'd spend a month prototyping, with the explicit understanding that all of it would be thrown away when I started over. On this project I don't feel I can afford that luxury, so I want to be a bit more careful that what I write now will have a high likelihood of surviving into the final product.

On the other hand, I have to start some 'proof of concept' experiments with the tricky issues of flows, interprocess communication, database access, and making the calls. I decide to start by banging together a single executable that will create the call objects *and* place calls. The advantage of building a single executable is that I can get the interactions working using ordinary function calls, and confront the remote procedure calls later. My current plan is to use DCOM to get the local call queues on the calling machines to talk with the server call queue, but that can wait while I get things more or less functional on one machine.

The User Interface

Before I can start even this simplified task, however, I need to consider how much infrastructure to put in place. When I sit down to write the program, the very first question I ask myself is what kind of user interface to supply. In the long run, I'd like the program to be able to report on its state and progress to any interested observer. The right way to do this is to provide a web-based front end.

From any browser anywhere in the world, I'd like to be able to log in and ask the system to report on what it's doing. The job manager would report which jobs are current, *SnapShot* would report on the current and planned schedule, and each calling machine might report on how many calls it has made recently, what is in the queue, and so forth.

For the short term, I'll need the ability to track the behavior at the console. That is, while I'm developing the software, I'll want to be able to see the progress of the various components. I know from experience that my needs will change as development progresses, so I start with the decision to create a **log** object, which will manage reporting. Initially, it will just wrap the **TRACE()** macro provided by MFC, which simply writes a formatted string to standard output.

The **log** object will do no more than pass arguments to the **TRACE()** macro. I start by giving **log** a number of simple constructors, each of which will manage a formatted string. Its definition is on the next page.

```
class log
{
public:
    log     (CString theString, CString theParam);
    log     (CString theString, int Val1, int Val2);
    log     (CString theString, int theVal);
    log     (CString theString);

    ~log    ();
};
```

If I need to print a value, I can pass in a string and the value. For example, if I want to show the return value from a method I might write:

```
log("Here's the value %d", val);
```

This will invoke the constructor that takes a **CString** and an **int**. The implementation passes this along to **TRACE()**:

```
log::log(CString theString, int theVal)
{
    TRACE(theString, theVal);
}
```

Later, as the program evolves, I can use the **log** object to do more sophisticated reporting — the trick is to be able to turn it on and off. I'll add some Boolean values to the document for the various areas of the program I might wish to log. Each object will then implement a **Log()** method that will create a **log** object if the right flag is set. For example, the line manager's **Log()** method looks like this:

```
void CLineManager::Log(CString theString, int theInt)
{
    if (m_pDoc->bLogLineManager)
        log(theString, theInt);
}
```

This is a method of **CLineManager** that takes a **CString** and an **int**. If the Boolean flag **bLogLineManager** is true, a **log** object is created. For now, that does nothing more than pass the string and integer along to **TRACE()**. Later, we may have it write to the database, to a logging file on the local machine, or even to a stand alone trace utility. The log object separates the interface (keep a note of this activity) from the details of its implementation (how and where we store this 'note').

Clearly, I'll want the ability to turn logging on and off, and so I'm inclined to create a dialog-based interface. Since I'm pretty sure I'll want to have a document to maintain the state of the various objects, my best bet is an SDI application whose primary view class is derived from **CRecordView**. **CRecordView** is similar to **CFormView** in that it allows you to create your user interface in the Visual C++ resource editor, but it adds the ability to link up to a database. This will come in very handy.

Populating the Database

There are a host of 'boot-strap' issues with this project — things that really need to be done before I can get started. For example, it's difficult to work with the data until it is in the database, but it is difficult to get data into the database until I understand more fully how I want to work with it. I decide to start by writing a simple program to create jobs and lists of phone numbers, and to populate the database. This will accomplish a number of goals: I'll create data to work with, I'll learn more about interacting with the database, and I'll obtain some important early metrics on the database performance.

I start by creating the application. Specifically, I fire up Visual C++ 5.0 and choose **New...** | **Projects** | **MFC AppWizard (exe)**. I work my way through the AppWizard, creating an SDI application with database support, but without file support. We don't need file support as we won't be serializing data to disk, all our storage will be in the database itself. Next I identify the data source, and I can then connect to the skeleton database I created on SQL Server with the Database Designer. Visual C++ takes care of the network connection; I just have to identify the right tables.

The next question is whether to open each recordset as a dynaset or a snapshot. This is a big topic that Microsoft spends a lot of time describing. The short story is that a snapshot may have better performance, but at the cost that there are certain operations which will cause a very large temporary file to be created on the client side. This temporary table is the 'snapshot' itself. Further, the snapshot won't automatically track changes in the database — that is, one module might change the database and other modules won't know until they requery. Ultimately, I'll need to spend some time figuring out where I can use snapshots and where I can't; for now I just choose dynaset. I make a mental note to come back to this issue.

> As an aside, my mental notes aren't what they used to be, so I now use a log. My personal log is a perfect-bound notebook. It is important not to use a spiral bound notebook, as I want to discourage myself from ever tearing out a page. I find again and again that I have to go back to find some seemingly inconsequential note that only later reveals itself to be significant.

Using dynasets isn't a day at the beach. They can be substantially slower than snapshots, and if the table they are opening is large, they may time out. I discover quickly that I want to be very careful about my **WHERE** clause — without specifying a subset of the data, the dynaset builds a huge in-memory cursor on the server, and that can dramatically slow down the entire system.

Timeouts are a problem over a network, even the fastest network can have 'bursts of slowness' and ODBC connections can be finicky about response time. The easiest way to solve this is to call **SetLoginTimout()** on the **CDatabase** object. This method takes one parameter: the number of seconds to wait before timing out. There is a second method, **SetQueryTimout()** which will set the amount of time ODBC will wait before assuming a query has timed out. Mike Blaszczak points out that, "compared to connection times, query execution times are more dependent on query complexity and less dependent on network traffic." While my queries are not particularly complex, they will at times return large sets of data and that can slow down the response time as well.

Next, the AppWizard asks what COM support I require, and I accept the defaults. This will leave me with an application with some infrastructure (should I need it later), but with minimal overhead. The rest is pretty straightforward, and I take the defaults until I get to the last screen, where it is time to review the classes MFC will provide. I click on the view class to confirm that MFC will derive my view from **CRecordView**. I click Finish, and AppWizard assembles my files.

My first task is to create a simple form to build jobs and phone number lists. I'd like to be able to set some of the parameters, but I certainly don't want to add all the phone numbers by hand! My dialog looks like this:

This allows me to fill in the important information about the job, and click Populate Job. When I do that, MFC calls the **OnPopulate()** method I attached to the button using ClassWizard:

*This book was written in real-time, as the project developed. Code discussed is shown in the state it is in **at this stage of the project**. This is before serious testing and debugging begins, and I expect there are any number of problems that will be rectified as I go along. All code is shown to demonstrate my thinking and the implementation of my design; it is **not** intended as an example of the finished product.*

The first thing to do is to make sure the recordsets are open and a database connection is in place. I then enter a **try** block so that I can catch any database errors and take corrective action (for now, that involves nothing more than resetting the button).

```
void CCallServerView::OnPopulate()
{
    if (!m_pJobSet->IsOpen())       // the job record set
        m_pJobSet->Open();

    if (!m_pCallSet->IsOpen())      // the call record set
        m_pCallSet->Open();

    try
    {
```

Next, I disable the Populate Job button, but I'll re-enable it later on when the work is done. This will provide feedback so that I can tell when the function is working, and when the work is completed.

Then I set up a number of simple parameters. I capture the current time in a **CTime** variable named **now**. **StartTime** and **EndTime** are declared to be **CTime** objects as well, and they are initialized to times held in member variables that are filled from the dialog box. Thus, when I enter a start month of 'April' and a start date of '4', this gets assembled into April 4th, 1997. We also get the hour from the dialog box, but the minutes and seconds are forced to zero.

```
    m_Populate.EnableWindow(FALSE);

    UpdateData();
    CTime now = CTime::GetCurrentTime();
    const int yr = 1997;
    const int min = 0;
    const int sec = 0;
    const int dst = 0;
    int theTilt = FRONT_TILT;
    char buffer[12] = "";

    CTime StartTime(yr, m_StartMonth, m_StartDate, m_StartHour,
                                               min, sec, dst);
    CTime EndTime(yr, m_EndMonth, m_EndDate, m_EndHour, min, sec, dst);
```

Along the way, we get bitten by the new **RFX_Date()** bug. ClassWizard does not initialize the **CTime** fields in **CRecordset** objects, and this causes MFC to throw an exception when these fields are prepared during record edits. I fix this by adding my own initialization to the recordsets' constructors, for example:

```
    m_EndDate = CTime::GetCurrentTime();
```

This fills the **CTime** object with the current date and time and fixes the problem. You can read more about this in the MFC Knowledge Base article Q155721.

```
    if (m_Front.GetCheck())
       theTilt = FRONT_TILT;
    else
       theTilt = BACK_TILT;

    m_pSet->AddNew();
    m_pSet->m_AudioID = 1;
    m_pSet->m_CallID = 1;
    m_pSet->m_FlowID = 1;
    m_pSet->m_CustomerID = m_Priority;
    m_pSet->m_Priority = m_Priority;
```

```
        m_pSet->m_DateEntered = now;
        m_pSet->m_DateModified = now;
        m_pSet->m_JobID = m_JobID;
        m_pSet->m_Start = StartTime;
        m_pSet->m_EndDate = EndTime;
        m_pSet->m_Throttle = m_Throttle;
        m_pSet->m_Tilt = theTilt;
        m_pSet->m_RetryPolicyID = 1;
        m_pSet->m_WhoModified = "Jesse";
        m_pSet->m_WhoRequested = "Jay";
        m_pSet->m_ParentJobID = 0;
        m_pSet->Update();
```

In the above code, the option button that populates the member variable **m_Front** determines whether or not the job tilts towards the front. With that decided, I generate a new job record using a mixture of entries from the dialog and some fixed values.

```
        for (long i = m_Lower; i < m_Upper; i++)
        {
            if (i % 100 == 0)
                ShowProgress("Added: ", i - m_Lower);

            CString thePhoneNumber("617");
            _itoa(i, buffer, 10);
            thePhoneNumber += buffer;
            m_pCallSet->AddNew();
            m_pCallSet->m_JobID = m_JobID;
            m_pCallSet->m_StartTime = StartTime;
            m_pCallSet->m_EndTime = EndTime;
            m_pCallSet->m_NumberAttempts = 0;
            m_pCallSet->m_PhoneNumber = thePhoneNumber;
            m_pCallSet->m_Status = 1;
            m_pCallSet->Update();
        }

        m_Populate.EnableWindow(TRUE);

        m_pSet->Close();
        m_pCallSet->Close();
    }                                           // end try
    catch (...)
    {
        m_Populate.EnableWindow(TRUE);
    }

    return;
}
```

In the **for** loop, I iterate through phone numbers from the starting number to the maximum phone number provided in the From: and To: edit boxes. Thus, if I enter 4491000 and 4492000, the system will create phone numbers 6174491000 through 6174492000. These are added one by one via the calls to **AddNew()** and **Update()**. Each call to **AddNew()** creates a new empty record; each call to **Update()** fills that record with the values provided in the intervening lines.

I find that without any optimization at all, working over my 10Mbps local area network, I can add about 6,000 phone numbers per minute. I start experimenting with creating about twenty thousand phone numbers, and in a few days I'll bring that up to two million.

Building the Queue

To prepare for the interprocess communication, I decide to focus next on adding call objects into (and getting them out of) the call queue. In time, it will be the client machines that retrieve call objects from the queue, but for now I focus on getting the record locking working on the server alone.

This is a pretty straightforward exercise except for one thing: we'll want to lock the queue as briefly as possible. The scheduler will certainly *not* want to lock down the queue and only then start computing which calls to add. It fact, it doesn't even have the time to update the database while adding the calls to the queue. After all, the client machines may well be trying to get records *out* of the queue while all of this is going on, and they'll be blocked waiting for the queue to be unlocked.

To solve this, the scheduler will build up a linked list of call objects that it will provide to the queue all at once. The queue need do nothing more than take calls off of the list and add them to its own internal list — a very quick operation.

This brings up the question of just how many calls to pass in. The queue will know how many it needs, so the scheduler will pass in the largest number possible (that is, the size of the entire phone list) and the queue can take what it needs. By examining how many it got back, the scheduler will know how many were taken, and thus how many to replenish.

I decide to implement the queue as a subclass of a linked list. MFC offers the class **CTypedPtrList**, which is almost perfect for our needs. The **CTypedPtrList** utilizes templates to create a type-safe list. The queue will store pointers to call objects and will keep its own internal synchronization device, a **CMutex** object, to handle thread synchronization:

```
class CCallQueue : public CTypedPtrList<CPtrList, CCall*>
{
public:
    static CCallQueue*    Instance      ();
    virtual               ~CCallQueue   ();
    virtual int           AddToEnd      (CTypedPtrList<CPtrList, CCall*>& theList,
                                         CDatabase* theDatabase);
    virtual void          GetFromFront  (int howMany, CTypedPtrList<CPtrList,
                                         CCall*>& theList);
    virtual CCall*        GetFromFront  ();
    bool                  Invariants    ();
    void                  SetDoc        (CCallServerDoc*);
```

```
protected:
    CMutex              m_theMutex;
    int                 m_sizeQueue;
    CCallServerDoc*     m_pDoc;
    int                 CountQueue      ();

private:
    static CCallQueue*  theCallQueue;
    CCallQueue          (CCallServerDoc*);
    CCallQueue          ();
};
```

There are a number of things to notice about this class declaration. First, the derivation: this class derives from **CTypedPtrList**, which in its parameter list requires the base class (**CPtrList**) and the type of object it will store, in this case **CCall***. The base class is parameterized because you can create a **CTypedPtrList** based on either a **CObList** or a **CPtrList**. The former is for holding lists of MFC-derived objects — that is, objects derived from **CObject**.

The **CCall** class is not derived from MFC's 'master' base class, **CObject**, because we don't need to serialize these objects. Object persistence will, in our case, be handled by the database.

I declare a private static member called **theCallQueue**, and the public static method **Instance()**. This is the implementation of the singleton pattern I used extensively in the last chapter. This ensures that there will be only one **CCallQueue** object for the entire process, and that is why the constructors are private.

The synchronization object is **m_theMutex**. Here's how this is used. There are three member functions that actually manipulate the list: **AddToEnd()**, and the overloaded method **GetFromFront()**. Each of these will lock the list, and when the lock is acquired it will manipulate the list. For example:

```
int CCallQueue::AddToEnd(CTypedPtrList<CPtrList, CCall*>& theList,
                                               CDatabase* theDatabase)
{
    ASSERT(Invariants());
    CSingleLock theLock(&m_theMutex);
    int ctr = 0;

    if (theLock.Lock(WAIT_TIME))
    {
        for ( theList.GetHeadPosition(), ctr = 0;
              !theList.IsEmpty() && m_sizeQueue < MAXQUEUE;
              m_sizeQueue++, ctr++ )
        {
            AddTail(theList.RemoveHead());
        }
```

```
        theLock.Unlock();
    }

    ASSERT(Invariants());
    return ctr;
}
```

The **CSingleLock** object created by the second line of the function will hold a single synchronization object, in this case a **CMutex**. A **CMutex**, in turn, is an MFC object used for synchronizing access to a precious resource, in this case the list. We ask for the lock in the **if** statement, passing in a constant of how many milliseconds we want the lock to wait before timing out. The default is **INFINITE** — that is, it never times out (a risky business!).

When the lock is acquired, we iterate through the list passed in by the scheduler and add each call object to the queue's internal list. As each call object is added, it is removed from the list passed in. When we are done, we unlock the mutex and return.

Use of mutex objects is fairly expensive, but every object that might be corrupted by multithreading must be secured by some kind of lock. There are a number of counters in the application, and it would be very expensive to wrap each in a lock statement. Fortunately, Win32 supplies thread-safe increment and decrement methods. For example, when I want to increment the line manager's count of receivers, I can call:

```
InterlockedIncrement((long*) &m_nReceivers);
```

As you can see, I pass in the address of the counter object, cast as a pointer to **long**. This method is guaranteed to increment the variable **m_nReceivers** in a manner that's thread-safe, and thus protects me from this value being corrupted if the thread is interrupted.

The calls to **ASSERT(Invariants())** may well be new to you. **Invariants()** is a member method I add to every class I create, and it simply tests whether those things that we believe *must* be true about the class are, in fact, true. Every method begins and ends by **ASSERT**ing the 'invariants'. (The constructor checks them at the *end* of construction, while the destructor checks them at the *start* of destruction.) This is a way of creating a contract saying that while any given method may put the object into a transitory state, at the conclusion of each method the object will be valid. Of course, 'validity' is defined in whatever way I think is appropriate for each class, but regardless of the definition, the **Invariants()** method will test that validity.

It is up to the programmer to determine what aspects of the class are invariant. For many classes it will be invariant that a particular pointer is not null. For others it will be that a value is within a reasonable range. The more invariants you can identify for your classes, the safer your programming, and the likelier it is that you can catch problems before they explode in your face.

I run some quick tests, checking that we can get tens of thousands of numbers into and out of the queue with very fast response times. Before going on to systematically benchmark the performance, I turn my attention to getting it working across processes, and then across the network, using DCOM. Rather than tackling DCOM alone, however, I decide to spend a day with a DCOM expert. Since that's a week or two away, I turn my attention instead to something I can treat pretty much in isolation: making and receiving calls.

The Fundamentals of Placing Calls

I am eager to start working with the Visual Voice components because it is the area of implementation about which I am most anxious. I would like to test our theory that using the Visual Voice components will dramatically simplify the interaction with the Dialogic Cards, and getting this working will help us think through a number of related issues, including how the Visual Voice components will be controlled by the call flows.

The heart of this application is the audiotex interaction — the Interactive Voice Response (IVR) system. It is this sub-system that will interact with the customer, and it represents the bulk of the user interface for the first version. Jay has high expectations about how this will perform, and I want to see how hard it is to work with the Visual Voice components.

I needn't have worried. In the end, it turns out that the only difficult part of getting the Visual Voice code working is getting my head around what they are trying to do! Visual Voice offers three approaches: their ActiveX control, a class library, and a DLL.

The ActiveX control has a lot of appeal, but it's targeted at Visual Basic programmers, and isn't a good choice for use in a multithreaded C++ application. The support folks at Artisoft strongly suggest that I use the class library or the DLL. Since the DLL is in C, and the first thing I'd want to do would be to wrap a class library around the DLL interface, I turn to their class library. If it's at least as good as what I can write, and it's free, why not use it?

The bad news is that their documentation is targeted squarely at the Visual Basic programmer. In fact, as far as I can tell, their entire class library documentation consists of one paragraph. If you look up **Developing Visual Voice Applications** and open the **Visual Voice's Class Library Interface** section, you'll see that Visual Voice offers this as the sum of their C++ documentation:

> The Visual Voice Pro 3.0 Class Library Interface is a C++ class library
> representation of Visual Voice Pro's Voice Control. C++ developers will find this
> interface a very natural way to use Visual Voice. To use the class, add to your
> C++ project the files **Cvoice.cpp** and **Cvoice.h**, located in the
> **\Vvoice32\Dllapi** directory and link with **Vvoice32.lib**, located in the

same directory. Then use the class as you would the regular Visual Voice method, property and event (virtual function) interface. For a complete multithreaded C++ sample application, see **\Vvoice32\Dllapi\Multi\Multi.cpp**.

While I might have liked a little more help, there is actually more here than meets the eye. It turns out that the class library does follow the ActiveX control quite closely, and while I have some objections to how they implemented their sample program, it was enough to get me started. Their technical support was surprisingly helpful as well, and with just a couple of quick calls I've got the system making calls and answering when I call in.

Here's the trick: the class library is entirely encapsulated in their single **CVoice** class. This class provides a wrapper around their DLL, and so between the documentation for the ActiveX control (which tells you how the class methods are used) and the DLL documentation, I was able to get my brain around what I had to do.

I derived **CCaller** from **CVoice**, which provides dozens of methods, although only a handful of them are virtual. It is these virtual functions that afford you the required flexibility in your derived classes. Not surprisingly, the virtual methods are those that respond to events — **OnLineDropped()**, for example, or **OnRingDetected()**. Otherwise, your class simply calls methods in the base class as required.

Calling and Multitasking

The code for making a single call would be very simple, but I want to add multitasking. MFC offers a number of ways to create a multithreaded application, but since my threads will be 'worker' threads (that is, they will have no user interface), the preferred method is to call **AfxBeginThread()**.

AfxBeginThread() takes as parameters a pointer to a global method (a thread procedure), and a second **DWORD** that you can use for anything you like. Since I want my thread procedure to have access to the member variables of my **CCaller** class, I decide to make it a static member method, **PlaceCall()**, and pass it the **this** pointer as the second parameter to **AfxBeginThread()** — static member methods have no **this** pointer of their own. Thus my call to **AfxBeginThread()** looks like this:

```
AfxBeginThread(CCaller::PlaceCall, (LPVOID)this);
```

This call invokes my static method:

```
static UINT CCaller::PlaceCall(LPVOID pCaller);
```

The parameter **pCaller** will be the **this** pointer of the **CCaller** class that invokes the method; this gives us a tie back into the invoking object. Thus, when a **CCaller** object decides to make a call, it will call **AfxBeginThread()** and pass in its static member method **PlaceCall()** and its own **this** pointer.

When a **CCaller** object receives a call, its **OnRingDetected()** method will be called. In this case it must again spawn a thread and pass in a pointer to itself:

```
void CCaller::OnRingDetected()
{
    AfxBeginThread(CCaller::ReceiveCall, (LPVOID)this);
}
```

This lets **ReceiveCall()** run in its own thread (just like **PlaceCall()**), but provides the necessary link back into the calling object. Why have the object spawn a thread? It can't carry on in the main thread doing anything else, so why bother?

My original idea was to create these calling objects in their own threads. I'd create both a calling object and a receiving object, and assign the right one to a port depending on whether I was placing or receiving calls. But who would receive word of the incoming call and make the decision? Someone needed to own the outer thread, and that someone needed to detect the incoming call. There was no clean way to do that without having an object that manages the port. The right thing was to create the array of *calling* objects in the line manager, all in the same (controlling) thread. However, I certainly didn't want all 48 calling objects on any given machine to be answering calls within the same thread, so I had each spawn a thread when it had work to do, and then when the thread ends the object simply resumes waiting in the outer thread.

This raises a tricky issue: What if the object was told to make a call while it was receiving a call? The simplest way to handle this is to create a pair of Boolean flags: **m_receivingCalls** and **m_makingCalls**. These are set as the object changes state. To make sure these are thread-safe, I protect them with a mutex as well.

This is a significant departure from the original architecture, in large measure dictated by my emerging understanding of how Visual Voice works. Modifying the design on the fly is problematic: it is very likely that as I patch up one change to the design, I'll introduce new problems in other areas. I'm wary as I move forward, and make a mental note to come back to this design once it settles down.

In this new design, the line manager's job is to keep track of how many calling objects the calling machine has alive, and what 'state' they are in (waiting for calls, handling an incoming call or making outgoing calls). The line manager also keeps track of how many lines must be kept open for receiving calls. To do this, the line manager keeps a list of callers:

```
CTypedPtrArray<CPtrArray, CCaller*> myCallers;
```

The document keeps track of how many lines are to be kept open (it would get this information from the call server). The line manager tracks how many lines are *currently* in the process of handling an incoming call. With this information, it knows how many lines may place outgoing calls. For example, if the document says to keep 10 incoming lines open, and the line manager knows that four lines are currently handling incoming calls, then it knows that lines 0-13 must be kept open for incoming calls. This lets lines 14-47 place outgoing calls (assuming a total of 48 lines).

There is one caller object per port, so in our case there are 48 caller objects per machine. Each caller object can place calls or receive calls. Each caller object is responsible for knowing its own ID (so that it can ask the line manager what to do) and for keeping track of its own state. Each caller object can both place and receive calls.

When the caller is placing a call, its **MakeCalls()** method updates its own state flag (to indicate it is now making calls) and spawns the out-calling thread:

```
void CCaller::MakeCalls()
{
    CSingleLock theLock(&m_theCallingMutex);
    if (theLock.Lock())
    {
        if (!m_makingCalls)
        {
            AfxBeginThread(CCaller::PlaceCall, (LPVOID)this);
            m_makingCalls = true;
        }
        theLock.Unlock();
    }
}
```

The thread is a large, infinite loop that places a call and then checks to see if it should either shut down or switch over to receiving calls. Assuming it should continue making a call, it gets the next call to make, and then invokes the correct flow.

At this stage of development, flow management is stubbed out, and we always call the same phone number (my test number), but the actual process of calling and branching on user interaction is up and working. The critical line in the flow is the call to the caller's **Call()** method:

```
result = pCaller->Call(&ConnectResult, &len, timeOut);
```

The caller overrides this method (which is not virtual!) to extract the phone number and the calling policies from the call object and the policy objects, and then invokes its base class method:

```
return CVoice::Call(m_pCall->GetPhoneNumber(), pConnectResult,
                pConnectLength, CallTimeOut, fTranslateDialString);
```

The base class method in turn calls into the Visual Voice library, which calls into the Dialogic Driver and returns a call result. Note that since this is not virtual, it can't be treated polymorphically. In our case, this doesn't matter, as I never have a pointer to a **CVoice** object, but rather a pointer to my derived object, so I can still call my derived method.

As discussed in the design section, recognition of voice vs. answering machine is one of the trickier aspects of calling. Visual Voice will take care of implementing the call progress detection technology offered by the Dialogic card. In order to make this work I must initialize the calling object, set a 'Perfect Call' parameter, and load the correct line parameter file provided by Visual Voice.

Early testing is very encouraging. The system detects my voice with 100% reliability, and can detect my answering machine with equal fidelity. How this will translate to hundreds of phones, telephone companies, long distance providers and dozens of various answering machines remains an open question. I make a note that our test plans need to include extensive testing of the call progress analysis.

Once the fundamental IVR technology is working, it is time to begin thinking about how we'll control the flow of the conversation. While it may be acceptable to hard code the call flow interaction initially, ultimately we suspect the client will want to be able to create and edit these call flows without the assistance of a programmer. We need a technology that lets us take the description of the call flow out of the code and put it into a text file that can be manipulated by non-programmers.

Building the Flow Engine

We have decided to implement flow management using an embedded Tcl (pronounced "tickle") interpreter. Tcl is a small, lightweight and fairly powerful script engine originally developed for the UNIX environment.

In his white paper on scripting languages (*Scripting: Higher Level Programming for the 21st Century*, which can be found at http://www.sunlabs.com/people/john.ousterhout/scripting.html), John Ousterhout suggests that, "Scripting languages aren't intended for writing applications from scratch; they are intended primarily for plugging together components... [they] are often used to extend the features of components, but they are rarely used for complex algorithms and data structures... Scripting languages are sometimes referred to as glue languages or system integration languages."

That is exactly how we want to use Tcl in this application. Someone at Hypotenuse, probably a technician in Operations or a customer service representative, will write a simple Tcl script in a text editor. The application will read the script and execute it. We'll almost certainly want also to provide a stand-alone application that will read the script and validate that it does what the author intends.

To make this work, we'll extend Tcl to handle the calling primitives we'll need, such as 'go off hook' or 'dial'. These will become commands in the Tcl script, but Tcl will handle them by calling into routines we'll write in C++ (providing a C interface). The work itself will be done in the C++ program, invoking routines in the Visual Voice class library. The results will be reported back to the Tcl interpreter, which will continue working its way through the script.

Identifying the Primitives

The key task is to identify the primitives we'll need. Along the way we'll develop a series of flows which we hope will test the interpreter we're building, and will provide a starting point for the customer in building his own flows. To get us going, I look through the documentation for Visual Voice, identifying the various methods they provide. Many of these will have direct translations in our flow extensions.

The first obvious primitive is *Call*. The **Call()** method in Visual Voice takes two parameters: the phone number to call and the timeout value. The Tcl command will not need either of these parameters; the flow's job is to say what to do, but the C++ program will know the next phone number from the call object, and will get the timeout value from the policy object. The Visual Voice **Call()** method returns a number of possible outcomes (busy, connected, no answer, etc.) and we'll need to support nearly all of these.

A second primitive will be *PlayMessage*. This command will take a parameter indicating the identification of which message to play. There will be a number of related commands, such as *PlayDate*, *PlayCharacters*, *PlayFile*, and so forth.

Other important commands will include the ability to *PickUp* or *HangUp* the phone line. We'll also need the ability to capture touch-tones, and to set the range of acceptable touch-tones ("Please press 1 or 2, but not any other number."). The flows will also need to respond to various events, such as the line being dropped, or a ring being detected.

With these few simple commands and the inherent branching ability of the Tcl language itself, we should be able to build very powerful flows. To test this theory, we start with the initial flow Jay put together some months back as a preliminary system requirement:

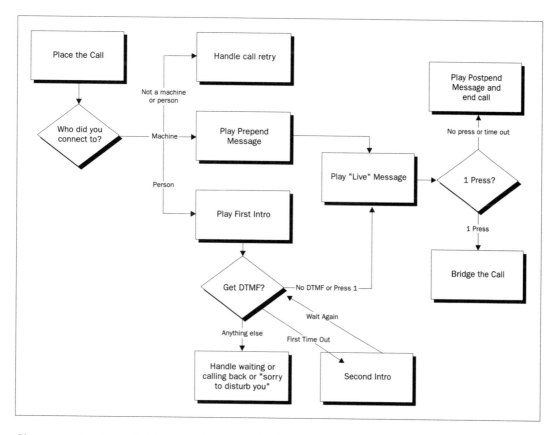

Close examination of this flow chart reveals that we can handle nearly all of it with the commands we've already identified. To place the call, we invoke **Call()**, passing in the next number. The return value from **Call()** will indicate whether or not we connected. If we connect to a person, we invoke the Visual Voice method, **PlayMessage()**, passing in the ID for the 'Prepend Message'. We then wait for a touch-tone or a timeout event. If we get a touch-tone, we call **PlayMessage()** with the ID for 'Live Message', and so on.

Steve and I spend half a day working through the issues. We look at the embedded interpreter, and the relationship between Tcl and C++. We'll need to provide a C interface to our methods, but that won't be difficult. The Tcl documentation assumes that the flow will be driving the interaction, and that C++ will just be used to create optimized commands. My perspective inverts that: the Tcl interpreter will be used to manage the flow, but the driving force will be the C++ program. That is consistent with how many folks use Tcl, and shouldn't represent much of a problem.

After a morning of 'getting our feet wet', and experimenting with writing simple flows, we break for lunch. Over Chinese food, we continue the conversation about how we'll integrate the Tcl interpreter into the client side machine. Suddenly, Steve realizes we've made an assumption that we'd better check: Td *is* thread-safe, isn't it?

This is a bad question to ask over lunch, as there is no easy way to check. Steve gets a worried look on his face as he begins to reassure me, and perhaps himself too, that he is 99% certain he read somewhere that Tcl is now thread-safe.

The issue we're worried about is this: what happens if we're in the middle of interpreting a flow when the thread gets interrupted, and then the second thread calls back into the interpreter? If the Tcl interpreter needs to maintain any kind of 'state', then it had better have a way to keep that state safe from the new thread, or it will get trashed as it 'starts over' in the second thread. When we return to the first thread, will that state be correct, or will it be trashed?

There is a sinking feeling I get in my gut when I realize I've done something dumb, and that feeling begins to grow when we get back to the office to research Tcl and threads. The Internet is a great place to get information, but the answer to this question proves elusive. We see lots of hints that threading is 'coming soon', a bad sign for us, but no conclusive proof that the current version *won't* support threads. Finally, we send some mail to one of the brighter stars in the newsgroup, Jeffrey Hobbs, who writes back:

> "Ousterhout has stated that he will make this... functionality possible, but [has] not stated exactly when. There have been reports that it works now, but can be fragile."

Bad news indeed. Confronted with the realization that we've wasted our time, and knowing that we are under tremendous deadline pressure this month, I'm momentarily tempted to 'make do' — to look for a quick fix. There isn't one that's worth serious consideration, however, and we realize it is time to set Tcl aside.[1]

Fortunately, we caught this quite early, and we've only wasted a day. Much of the work we did figuring out what Tcl had to do is reusable, and so overall it isn't a very significant loss. The big question is, what now? Visual Basic offers a potential solution, but I'm reluctant to start down that path. What I really need right now is to get things working. I decide to hard code the flow in C++.

Coding Flows in C++

Hard coding will get the product up and rolling quickly, and I can encapsulate the flows so that we can move to an interpreted solution later. It may turn out that we only ever need half a dozen flows, and hard coding them will have little practical cost and better performance characteristics. Or we may realize that we do need to write dozens of flows, in which case I can move to a different solution once we have more experience. In the interim, I can make forward progress without the digression into learning VBScript, and integrating it into my application.

---

[1] *Subsequent to this lunch, Steve decided to launch his own project to make Tcl reentrant. The result is the Tcl_r project, a reentrant Tcl for Windows 95/NT. He is documenting his progress at http://steverogers.com/projects/tcl_r/.*

It is time to go back to the customer. I talk with Jay to determine how many flows he anticipates there will ever be. We examine his flowchart and discover any number of issues we hadn't anticipated, but as we progress we agree that for quite some time there will be only four:

- Crisis call.

- Non-interactive call. Answer, play the message, hang up.

- Interactive call. Ask for a 1 press to identify the right caller.

- Interactive with call bridging. Same as three, but offer to connect the person to a third party (e.g. "Press 1 to be connected to your senator's office.")

This is a small enough number that I'm quite happy moving forward with hard-coded flows for now. These flows will be built into the client software and will thus be available to the client as required. We will, over time, want to convert these objects into text scripts stored in the database, but for now it is simpler, given the small number, just to code them right into the client as C++ classes.

In my code, branching among the flows is handled by simple **switch** statements:

```
result = pCaller->PlayFile("firstint.vox");

if (result < 0)
   pCaller->Log("Error %d in VoiceHandler. Exception!\n",result);

result = pCaller->GetDigits(sizeof(digits),digits);

switch(result)
{
case VV_R_MAX_DIGITS:
   digit = atoi(digits);
   switch(digit)
   {
   case 1:
      GotOneFromIntro(pCaller);
      break;
   case 2:
      CallBackLater(pCaller);
      break;
   case 3:
      WeWillWait(pCaller);
      break;
   case 4:
      SorryToDisturbYou(pCaller);
      break;
   default:
      IDidNotUnderstandYou(pCaller);
      break;
   }
   break;                              // end max_digits
```

```
   case VV_R_TIME_OUT:
      pCaller->Log("Error %d in VoiceHandler. Exception!\n",result);
      pCaller->Stop();
      pCaller->Hangup();
      break;
   case VV_R_RUNTIME_ERROR:
      pCaller->Log("Error %d in VoiceHandler. Exception!\n",result);
      pCaller->Stop();
      pCaller->Hangup();
      break;
   default:
      pCaller->Log("Error %d in VoiceHandler. Default tripped!! Exception!\n");
      pCaller->Stop();
      pCaller->Hangup();
      break;
   }
```

Much of this remains stubbed out. For now, any place I suspect I'll use exceptions I simply write a log entry. I'll put in most of the exception handling later, as the program shakes out and I approach a greater level of stability.

What is **pCaller**? Recall that **PlaceCall()** is a static method of **CCaller**. When this method is invoked, the caller object passes in a pointer to itself, and this pointer is stashed in **pCaller**. This points to the invoking **CCaller** object, and can call its methods (and access its private members!).

I begin by invoking the **PlayFile()** method of **CVoice**, which plays the contents of the named file in the default directory stashed away at the initialization of this object. I then call **GetDigits()**, passing in an array to fill and a number to indicate the maximum number of digits to get. Since I pass 1, this returns as soon as the person we've called presses any digit on his phone. I then **switch** on this digit, looking for one of the digits I requested. "If you'd like us to call back later, press 2..."

These **switch** statements branch to other methods within this flow object, and thus the structure of the object directly reflects the logic of the flow. There is a lot of work left to do to fully represent the flow as designed, but this is a good first test of the fundamentals, and I'm pleased to note that it is immediately able to place calls within the multithreading. I quickly ring my two test lines, and by switching between them I'm able to manipulate two independent incoming calls.

Splitting the Client from the Server

With all of this working, it is time to separate the client from the server, and to begin building the local call queue from which the local calling machines will draw their phone numbers.

In preparation for this change, I need a much stronger understanding of COM and DCOM. I decide to spend a day working on DCOM with an expert. My goals for the day are to determine whether DCOM offers a viable solution, and also to decide whether COM is easy enough to tackle early in the project, or if we'd be better off delaying until more things are working and tested.

We start by setting the calling program aside and getting simple client and server test objects talking with one another.

The Test Server

The **CSimpleTestServerforOle** object was created by asking AppWizard to generate an SDI application with support for ActiveX. The ODL file couldn't be much simpler:

```
[ uuid(65462545-B663-11D0-B356-0060977066A5), version(1.0) ]
library SimpleTestServerforOle
{
    importlib("stdole32.tlb");

    // Primary dispatch interface for CSimpleTestServerforOleDoc
    [ uuid(65462546-B663-11D0-B356-0060977066A5) ]
    dispinterface ISimpleTestServerforOle
    {
        properties:
            // NOTE - ClassWizard will maintain property information here.
            //   Use extreme caution when editing this section.
            //{{AFX_ODL_PROP(CSimpleTestServerforOleDoc)
            //}}AFX_ODL_PROP

        methods:
            // NOTE - ClassWizard will maintain method information here.
            //   Use extreme caution when editing this section.
            //{{AFX_ODL_METHOD(CSimpleTestServerforOleDoc)
            //}}AFX_ODL_METHOD
    };

    // Class information for CSimpleTestServerforOleDoc
    [ uuid(65462544-B663-11D0-B356-0060977066A5) ]
    coclass Document
    {
        [default] dispinterface ISimpleTestServerforOle;
    };

    //{{AFX_APPEND_ODL}}
    //}}AFX_APPEND_ODL}}
};
```

AppWizard creates a unique ID, and the right imports are created. We told AppWizard we wanted to support **IDispatch** by choosing Automation support, but we'll quickly change that to support the standard **IDataObject** interface. We'll use **IDataObject** to get the call objects across the wire when the time comes. This allows us to take advantage of DCOM's location transparency; we can distribute the server, the caller and the queue as we need to, and DCOM will serve up the objects transparently.

Passing *objects* around the network, rather than just data, allows us to encapsulate the object marshaling in the DCOM code. The rest of the system neither knows nor cares where the objects are or how they are transported.

AppWizard adds class factory initialization to the application's **InitInstance()** method:

```
m_server.UpdateRegistry(OAT_DISPATCH_OBJECT);
COleObjectFactory::UpdateRegistryAll();
```

However, we have to add a dispatch map for the **IDataObject** interface to the document class definition ourselves:

```
BEGIN_INTERFACE_PART(Data, IDataObject)
    STDMETHODIMP GetData(LPFORMATETC, LPSTGMEDIUM);
    STDMETHODIMP GetDataHere(LPFORMATETC, LPSTGMEDIUM);
    STDMETHODIMP QueryGetData(LPFORMATETC);
    STDMETHODIMP GetCanonicalFormatEtc(LPFORMATETC, LPFORMATETC);
    STDMETHODIMP SetData(LPFORMATETC, STGMEDIUM FAR*, BOOL);
    STDMETHODIMP EnumFormatEtc(DWORD, LPENUMFORMATETC FAR*);
    STDMETHODIMP DAdvise(FORMATETC FAR*, DWORD, LPADVISESINK, DWORD FAR*);
    STDMETHODIMP DUnadvise(DWORD);
    STDMETHODIMP EnumDAdvise(LPENUMSTATDATA FAR*);
END_INTERFACE_PART(Data)
```

These macros create a nested class called **XData** and a member of that class called **m_xData**. The **XData** class provides an implementation of the **IDataObject** interface, and the address of **m_xData** gives us a pointer through which we can call methods on the interface. It is **GetData()** that we care about at the moment, and for the first test we comment out its entire body and put in nothing more than:

```
MessageBeep(0);
return S_OK;
```

Thus, when the client tries to get data from the server, we'll know it works if it beeps!

The Test Client

We then write the client, which is represented at first by a simple dialog box in the same application with a button to get the next set of calls. This dialog creates an instance of our COM class and retrieves a pointer to its **IDataObject** interface.

The GetNext button just invokes the **GetData()** method. At the moment that will result in nothing more than a beep (from the other machine), but that will at least prove the connection across the network, and in time we can replace the implementation of **GetData()** with something more useful.

All the interesting work happens in the dialog's **OnGetNextButton()** method:

```
void CSimpleTestClientForOleDlg::OnGetNextButton()
{
    FORMATETC fe; STGMEDIUM stg;

    fe.cfFormat = CF_CALL;
    fe.tymed = TYMED_HGLOBAL;
    fe.lindex = GetDlgItemInt(IDC_NUMBEROFCALLS);
    fe.dwAspect = DVASPECT_CONTENT;
    fe.ptd = NULL;
    m_pdo->GetData(&fe, &stg);
    char* cp = (char *)GlobalLock(stg.hGlobal);
    GlobalUnlock(stg.hGlobal);
    ReleaseStgMedium(&stg);
}
```

Here we create a **FORMATETC** structure to describe what it is we want from the server. **FORMATETC** is designed to extend the traditional Windows clipboard format by allowing the programmer to describe the format of the data, what target devices might be supported, how much detail is provided (the *aspect*) and the storage medium used.

In the code shown, we declare **stg** as a variable of type **STGMEDIUM**. This is another structure, described by Microsoft as, "a generalized global memory handle used for data transfer operations." Its most important member is a **union**, the contents of which can be used to access various data transfer media, such as bitmaps, metafiles, global memory, files and so forth.

Getting back to the code, we next create a custom format identifier, **CF_CALL** (which is nothing more than a constant value of 2001 in homage to the HAL 9000), which serves as a signal to the server. **m_pdo** is a member defined to be a pointer to an **IDataObject**, that is, an interface pointer, through which we can invoke **GetData()**. This interface pointer was filled during the dialog box's initialization with a call to **CoCreateInstance()**, which you can see overleaf.

```
        hr = CoCreateInstance( clsid,
                               NULL,
                               CLSCTX_SERVER,
                               IID_IDataObject,
                               (void**) &m_pdo );
```

With this up and running, it was time to separate the server from the client and test out the client/server relationship. The **GetData()** method would now have to be a bit more complicated than simply beeping — it would need to stream the call objects into a memory buffer on the server side, and then de-stream them on the client side.

In the **GetData()** method of the *server* we'll again set up the **FORMATETC** and **STGMEDIUM** objects. Once we are ready to go, we'll tick through the call objects in the server queue and build an array in a globally allocated memory block:

```
    CallBlob* pcb;
    CCall* pCall;
    int i;

    pcb = (CallBlob *)GlobalAlloc(GMEM_FIXED, sizeof(CallBlob) * lpfe->lindex);
    if (!pcb)
    {
        return E_OUTOFMEMORY;
    }

    for(theTemporaryList.GetHeadPosition(), i = 0;
        !theTemporaryList.IsEmpty(), i < lpfe->lindex;
        i ++)
    {
        pCall = theTemporaryList.RemoveHead();

        (pcb+i)->m_CallID = pCall->GetCallID();
        strcpy((pcb+i)->m_PhoneNumber, pCall->GetPhoneNumber());
        (pcb+i)->m_JobID = pCall->GetJobID();
        (pcb+i)->m_StartTime = pCall->GetStartTime().GetTime();
        (pcb+i)-> m_EndTime = pCall->GetEndTime().GetTime();
        (pcb+i)->m_NumberAttempts = pCall->GetNumberAttempts();
        (pcb+i)->m_Status = pCall->GetStatus();
    }

    lpstg->tymed = TYMED_HGLOBAL;
    lpstg->hGlobal = (HGLOBAL)pcb;
    lpstg->pUnkForRelease = NULL;

    return S_OK;
```

On the client side, we'll receive this memory block and unpack the array, creating call objects as we go and stashing them away locally. This is still just proof-of-concept test code:

```
    m_pDoc->m_pdo->GetData(&fe, &stg);
    CallBlob* pcb = (CallBlob *)GlobalLock(stg.hGlobal);
    CCall* pCall;
```

```
   if (pcb)
   {
      CSingleLock theLock(&m_theMutex);
      if (theLock.Lock())
      {
         for(int i = 0; i < howMany; i++)
         {
            pCall = new CCall( (pcb+i)->m_CallID,
                               (pcb+i)->m_PhoneNumber,
                               (pcb+i)->m_JobID,
                               (pcb+i)->m_StartTime,
                               (pcb+i)->m_EndTime,
                               (pcb+i)->m_NumberAttempts,
                               (pcb+i)->m_Status );

            AddTail(pCall);
         }

         theLock.Unlock();
      }
   }

   GlobalUnlock(stg.hGlobal);
   ReleaseStgMedium(&stg);
```

We fetch the data through the pointer to an **IDataObject** interface held in the
document, passing in the format we want to use and an empty storage medium for the
server to fill. We then get a lock on the storage medium and unpack it, taking from the
array passed in the number of objects we expect to find. We'll need more code (not
shown here) to handle the case where the server gave back fewer records than we
expected.

All of this is pretty straightforward until we start thinking about multithreading. The code
we've considered so far is not thread-safe. We haven't prevented two threads from
accessing the same block of data and thus causing corruption. To solve this we must look
more closely at COM threading.

COM threading comes in two flavors: the **apartment model** and the **free threading model**.
The apartment model says that any objects created in a thread will be read only in the
context of that thread. The free threading model is pretty much like the threading we've
considered so far — any thread may touch any object, and one must use synchronization
objects to handle the interaction.

MFC support for DCOM threading is restricted to the apartment model. While this isn't
very difficult to use, I become increasingly uncomfortable with introducing this level of
complexity into the program at this stage. The benefits of DCOM over using the database
were always open to discussion, and I begin to reconsider. It isn't that managing the
threading will be difficult, I'm just not confident enough that I understand all the issues
necessary to tackle it at this time.

One of the greatest dangers to any software project is that it will be untestable. Specifically, a program is untestable when it can be in so many interdependent states that one can never practically test all the various permutations. By their nature, multithreaded applications are complicated. Client/server applications are complicated. Distributed objects are more complicated still. Telephony and Internet applications are inherently complicated. DCOM is new and thorny, and not yet 100% reliable.

I begin to wonder if I'm not taking on too much too early by trying to introduce DCOM into a multithreaded Internet and telephony application before I've got all the rest working. After some more thought, I decide to set it aside for a few days and think about plan B: What if I use the database for the queue?

The time spent on DCOM was not wasted. I now understand the path to distributed objects, and when the need is compelling, I'll return. For now, though, it is time to get the queue working within the database.

Managing the Call Queue in the Database

We'd thought about this before, of course, and I knew that there were significant advantages, along with a couple of potential disadvantages. The biggest disadvantage I wanted to acknowledge was that it might be slow: we'd be asking the database to do more work, and that could have a negative impact on performance.

*The biggest disadvantage I did **not** want to acknowledge is that my friends might laugh at me: "You did **what**?" I hate the sound of developers snickering.*

The real questions, though, were these: would it make the system more or less reliable? Would it be slower or quicker at runtime? Would it get us to market earlier or later?

One thing that occurred to me was that if performance was an issue, I could always move the queue out of the existing physical database and onto its own machine. After all, I'd be extracting calls into the scheduler before putting them into the queue, so there is no requirement that these be in the same database. Perhaps if I were getting too many hits against a single database, the right answer would be to create a second. In any case, we wouldn't know what the performance characteristics were really going to be until we set up the real server and put it under real load.

This brings up an awkward issue. I'm developing on a system that's rather different from the one the call server will eventually reside on. I'm using a Pentium Pro 200 with 128 MB of memory and a 4-gigabyte SCSI hard disk, which is certainly nice and fast, but the final system will probably have at least 512MB of RAM and maybe much more. It will certainly have a RAID (**R**edundant **A**rray of **I**nexpensive **D**isks). The idea of these is to 'stripe' your data across a number of disks giving you much faster access and, equally important, the ability to recover should any one of the disks fail.

I plan a date in the not-too-distant future to go to Hypotenuse and talk with Kevin, VP of technology, about what equipment we want to buy. He and I agree that early in the process I'll need to start testing on the real equipment rather than on the miniature system I keep in my home office.

Before setting out to get the call queue into the database, I decide to do a better job splitting up the server from the client. The right way to do that is to build a new client application, and then to migrate the existing client-based code. This takes a few hours but is well worth the effort; when I'm done I have a much cleaner set of files, client and server.

Source Code Control

At this point, with a new client and a new server, it is time to get them under source control. I bought the Microsoft MSDN Enterprise Edition: a terrific, if expensive, investment. One (not unpleasant) drawback is that they ship you an overwhelming number of CDs, and it can take a while to sort everything out. However, I found that amid everything else, it did include Visual C++ 5.0 and Visual SourceSafe, so that seemed like a good way to go for source code control.

Putting the files into SourceSafe is trivial: the source code control is fully incorporated into the Integrated Development Environment. I right-clicked on the project and chose **Add to Source Control**. It created the a Visual SourceSafe project and put all the files into it. I make a point of doing a 'checkpoint' check-in each time I make a substantial change to the project, so that I'll have the opportunity to 'roll back' to a safe starting point should I enter a cul-de-sac.

So, having created a new client and server and tucked them into source code control for safekeeping, I'm ready to tackle the idea of moving the queue into the database. The first trick is to get the call objects into the database from the server, and to do this I need a new table. This table's fields will be identical to those of the call table, except that the Call ID field will be a simple integer rather than an auto-numbered field — that is, I'll want to keep the call objects' Call IDs intact. I don't want the queue table to create new Call IDs when calls are entered into the queue.

Rethinking the Distribution Algorithm

I'm afraid this forces an issue that has been raging for some weeks: exactly what should be the interaction among the queue, the dispatcher and the scheduler? The essence of the problem is that the scheduling algorithm we created during design was elegant, but far too complicated. Because we now know that phone lines will be going into and out of service as we hold lines open for incoming calls, the existing distribution algorithm becomes even more complicated, as it must constantly recalculate the number of available lines.

You'll remember that we discussed computing the number of calls that must be made and distributing these over the available lines by the computed ratios. I'm increasingly uncomfortable with this approach and decide to go back and think about it again.

My first simplifying assumption is that we will never overbook. Assuming the system is never overbooked allows us to say that as long as we call the required minimum number of calls per job over any given short period of time, we'll be sure to have the resources to finish every job in time. That short period is probably something like ten or fifteen minutes. Assuming Jay doesn't care what the distribution of calls *within* a ten-minute segment is, we can greatly simplify the algorithm. Here it is:

- We compute the minimum number of calls that must be made in the next ten minutes for each current job. Note that this computation does *not* care how many lines are currently available, it just says, "Here's the number you must call for this job in the next ten minutes to stay on schedule."

- We start a timer every ten minutes, and the first thing we do is to fill the queue from one job until we've put in this minimum number. We then go on to fill the queue from the next current job, one by one until all have had their minimum number put in the queue for that ten minutes. Remember that we've assumed we're not overbooked, so we'll always complete these calls before the ten minutes is up.

- During the remainder of the ten minutes, we iterate through all the current jobs, adding a few calls from each, as space becomes available in the queue. Because we only top off the queue periodically, and because we keep the queue fairly small, we are able now to add a few more calls and yet have the queue available for handling the minima again at the ten minute interval.

- The number to add will be based on the priority. I've changed the meaning of priority to this: if your priority is 5, we add five calls each time that it's your turn to be added. If your priority is 1, we add one call, and so forth. Again, this supports relative priority without requiring that we know what resources are currently available. We round robin, filling the queue until the ten-minute timer kicks in and then we start over, filling the required minima.

There are several nice features of this revised algorithm:

- It is far simpler than the one we had before
- It is easier to manifest in code
- It is order-independent
- It doesn't rely on knowing what resources are currently available

One question remains — How many calls should we have in the queue at any given moment? The answer is fairly simple: we want a queue big enough that it will never empty and small enough that it is responsive to changing priorities. This, I estimate, ought to be thrice the total number of ports ever available on the system. This number can actually be dynamic. The call manager will always know how many machines are attached (they register with the call manager when they come on line), so it can compute the queue size by multiplying the number of machines by the number of lines per machine (48, minus those held out for incoming calls) and then by tripling that number. Thus, if there are five machines attached, we'll want a call queue of 5 * 48 * 3 or approximately 720 calls.

The scheduler will periodically grab the queue, fill it, and then sleep for a while. But how will the scheduler know how many to add to fill the queue? The queue needs some way to report on its size. The problem is that the scheduler will be interacting with the queue using ODBC, and there is no clean way to establish the size of a table using ODBC. We could open a recordset on the queue and iterate through it, counting until we hit **EOF()**, but that is ugly and expensive. What we need is a clever hack!

I create a new table, **QueueCounter**, which has only one field, queue size. The scheduler will call:

```
INSERT INTO QueueCounter (theCount) SELECT COUNT(CallID) FROM Queue
```

This establishes the size of the queue. It will put the size into the **theCount** field in the **QueueCounter** table, which can then be read by requerying a recordset on that table. This call is quick because all the work is done at the server.

This does bring up a tricky part of ODBC. You call this SQL statement by issuing an **ExecuteSQL()** call against a **CDatabase** object. If there is a snapshot-type recordset open against this database, the system tries to pull the entire table across the network to the **temp** directory on the client in order to update that recordset. This is a bad thing. The trick is to open the recordset as a dynaset, which leaves the table where it belongs: on the server.

We want to have those tables which are used often and which change only infrequently to be snapshots, for performance. The remaining tables will be dynasets so that we can make **ExecuteSQL()** statements against them. Therefore, we will not share database objects among recordsets; each **CRecordset** will have its own **CDatabase** object. Later, when things stabilize, we'll look to optimize by sharing some, but for now they each get their own.

The scheduler will begin its work by computing the distribution of the jobs and determining from which job each call should be added. For now, we'll just add calls from the call table without regard to the proper distribution. Once this is working, we'll come back and figure out how to distribute the calls.

I have taken the expedient of talking directly to the database recordsets. On reflection, it would be better to talk to the **CCallQueue** class. Even if **CCallQueue** were nothing but a wrapper for the database calls, this would better encapsulate the queue management. Such a design would simplify the scheduler, and would make it easier to back out later and enhance the queue, taking the responsibility for queue management back out of the database.

I make a note that this is a flaw in the implementation. The design is clean, but the implementation didn't follow it closely. I'll need to come back to this and tidy it up before we go to V1.

```
bool CScheduler::Run()
{
    // figure out the proportions
    GetCurrentJobs(); // which jobs qualify for running

    if (!m_pDoc->m_DBQueueSet.IsOpen())
        m_pDoc->m_DBQueueSet.Open();

    if (!m_pDoc->m_callSet.IsOpen())
        m_pDoc->m_callSet.Open();

    if (!m_pDoc->m_QCtrSet.IsOpen())
        m_pDoc->m_QCtrSet.Open();

    CDatabase* pDB = m_pDoc->m_QCtrSet.m_pDatabase;
```

As you can see in the above code, the first task in using the SQL database directly is to make sure all the recordsets are open. Then, we get the pointer to the database used by the **QueueCounter** recordset, which in turn points to the **QueueCounter** table, and is open as a dynaset.

```
    CString strCmd1 =  "DELETE FROM QueueCounter";
    CString strCmd2 =  "INSERT INTO QueueCounter (theCount)
                                    SELECT COUNT(CallID) FROM Queue";

    ASSERT(m_pDoc->m_DBQueueSet.CanUpdate());
    ASSERT(m_pDoc->m_DBQueueSet.CanAppend());

    for (;;)
    {
        if (m_pDoc->bShutDownServer == 1)
            break;

        try
        {
            pDB->ExecuteSQL(strCmd1);
        }

        catch(CDBException& e)
        {
            Log("DB Error: %d",e.m_nRetCode);
        }

        catch (...)
        {
            Log ("Unknown exception trying to execute %s",strCmd1);
        }
```

```
    try
    {
       pDB->ExecuteSQL(strCmd2);
    }

    catch(CDBException& e)
    {
       Log("DB Error: %d",e.m_nRetCode);
    }

    catch (...)
    {
       Log ("Unknown exception trying to execute %s",strCmd2);
    }
```

We prepare the two required SQL statements for execution. The first thing to do is to empty the current contents of the table, and then we'll want to insert the new count. We put the execute statements into **try** blocks and make the calls.

```
    m_pDoc->m_QCtrSet.Requery();
    int currentCount = m_pDoc->m_QCtrSet.m_theCount;

    // Create the local list before giving to the queue
    while (currentCount < MAXQUEUE && !m_pDoc->m_callSet.IsEOF())
    {
       m_pDoc->m_DBQueueSet.AddNew();
       m_pDoc->m_DBQueueSet.m_CallID = m_pDoc->m_callSet.m_CallID;
       m_pDoc->m_DBQueueSet.m_PhoneNumber = m_pDoc->m_callSet.m_PhoneNumber;
       m_pDoc->m_DBQueueSet.m_JobID = m_pDoc->m_callSet.m_JobID;
       m_pDoc->m_DBQueueSet.m_StartTime = m_pDoc->m_callSet.m_StartTime;
       m_pDoc->m_DBQueueSet.m_EndTime = m_pDoc->m_callSet.m_EndTime;
       m_pDoc->m_DBQueueSet.m_NumberAttempts =
                                    m_pDoc->m_callSet.m_NumberAttempts;
       m_pDoc->m_DBQueueSet.m_Status = m_pDoc->m_callSet.m_Status;
       m_pDoc->m_DBQueueSet.Update();

       Log("Added callID: %d to queue\n",m_pDoc->m_callSet.m_CallID);
```

In the lines above, we **Requery()** the database to pick up the new count that results from these calls, and we set the local variable **currentCount** based on this result. It is now a trivial job to extract that many call objects from the call table, and to insert them into the queue using **AddNew()** and **Update()**. Note that we do *not* have to lock the table or manage the threading; all of this is handled by SQL Server. Similarly, we don't have to sweat the details of the interprocess communication; this is managed by the ODBC connection.

```
    m_pDoc->m_callSet.Edit();
    m_pDoc->m_callSet.m_Status = csEnqueued;
    m_pDoc->m_callSet.Update();
    m_pDoc->m_callSet.MoveNext();

    currentCount++;
    }
```

```
        Sleep(MILLISEC_IN_SECOND * SEC_IN_MIN * MINUTES_BETWEEN_SCHEDULER_RUNS);

    } // end loop

    return true;
}
```

Finally, we update the call table to reflect that these objects are now in the queue. We then sleep a predetermined number of minutes to allow the clients undisturbed access to the queue and to reduce the traffic both on the network and at the database itself.

Getting Calls from the Queue

We are now ready to consider the client side of this architecture. In an ideal world with no network latency, we'd just pull calls off the server's queue. However, because it can take a while to fetch a queue across the network, we'll cache some calls locally, in what we're calling the local call queue.

The first decision was to maintain the break between the **CCallQueue** and **CLocalCallQueue**. The **CCallQueue** class inherits from **CTypedPtrList** and is a managed list of call objects. **CLocalCallQueue** is derived from **CCallQueue** and handles the specific requirements of the local calling machine, delegating to its base class the actual queue management itself.

Thus, **CCallQueue** implements

```
    virtual CCall*   GetFromFront   ();
```

but this is overridden in the derived class. You might wonder, now that the main call queue has been shunted off into the database, why I'm bothering to maintain these as separate classes. I'm trying to keep my options open: I may still move the queue back out of the database at a later date, in which case the **CCallQueue** class will have far greater responsibility than it does now. Since this is working, I see no need to collapse these two classes, even though having them separate serves little purpose at the moment.

This is another reason to make sure I wrap the calls to the database in the **CCallQueue** class, as I discussed earlier. If I maintain the **CCallQueue** class, interaction with the server and with the database is fully encapsulated. Rather than collapsing the two classes into one, the right thing is to migrate the database code from the scheduler out into the **CCallQueue** class on the server side. For now, the base method implementation is pretty simple, and as generic as I can make it:

```
CCall* CCallQueue::GetFromFront()
{
    ASSERT(Invariants());
    CCall* pCall = 0;
    CSingleLock theLock(&m_theMutex);

    if (theLock.Lock(WAIT_TIME))
    {
        if (!IsEmpty())
        {
            pCall = RemoveHead();
            m_sizeQueue--;
        }

        theLock.Unlock();
    }

    else
        Log("Get from front locked out!\n");

    ASSERT(Invariants());
    return pCall;
}
```

It locks its synchronization object, removes a call from its list, unlocks the synchronization and returns the pointer to the call to whoever asked for it. The **CLocalCallQueue** uses this method, but adds the requirement that after each call is removed, the queue is checked to see if it has dropped below the low water mark:

```
CCall* CLocalCallQueue::GetFromFront()
{
    CCall* pCall = CCallQueue::GetFromFront();

    if (pCall)
        CheckRefill();

    return pCall;
}
```

Note that we check whether we get back a valid **pCall** object. It is an open question what to do if there are no calls to make. Certainly that is not an error, but the design is silent on how to behave. Should we sleep for a while? Should we wait to be signaled that there are calls to make? I will return to this section of code once we better understand what *should* happen in that situation.

The call to **CheckRefill()** is where all the interaction with the database will happen. The method begins by synchronizing, both so that we won't hit the queue while it is being used by another method, and so that we won't try to check for refilling in two threads at once.

```
void CLocalCallQueue::CheckRefill()
{
    CSingleLock theLock(&m_theMutex);
    if (theLock.Lock(WAIT_TIME))
    {
```

Next, we look for the difference between the low-water mark and the amount we currently have in the queue. This number will be negative or zero until it is time to refill the queue. Once this number goes positive, we'll want to get some more call objects.

If we do need to fill the queue, we'll **Open()** or **Requery()** the **m_DBQSet** recordset that represents the queue table in the database. This should never be empty, so we will throw an exception if it is. (Currently we just log the error.)

```
    int howMany = MIN_LOCAL_CALL_QUEUE - m_sizeQueue;

    CCall* pCall;
    bool failed;
    if (howMany > 0)
    {
        if (!m_pDoc->m_DBQSet.IsOpen())
            m_pDoc->m_DBQSet.Open();
        else
            m_pDoc->m_DBQSet.Requery();

        if (m_pDoc->m_DBQSet.IsEOF())
            Log("Exception! CheckRefill. DBQSet is EOF!\n");
```

This done, we begin filling the local queue to twice our minimum size. This reduces thrashing. If the low water mark is at 96, we'll fill up with 192 call objects so that we won't need to do this too often.

```
    while (m_sizeQueue < (MIN_LOCAL_CALL_QUEUE * 2) &&
                                        !m_pDoc->m_DBQSet.IsEOF())
    {
```

After caching the current record inside a **CCall** object, we try to delete the record from the queue. If this throws an exception, it will be due to another calling machine deleting the object after we read it, but before we could delete it. There is no inexpensive way to get an exclusive lock on the table, and many calling machines may have overlapping recordsets. This bit of code manages the synchronization so that no two end up with the same call object in their local queue. If the exception *is* thrown, we know that someone else has deleted it, so we toss the **pCall** object and try again. If the exception is not thrown, then we did delete it, and thus we may safely add this **CCall** object to the local call queue.

```
        failed = false;
        pCall = new CCall(m_pDoc->m_DBQSet);
```

```
        try
        {
            m_pDoc->m_DBQSet.Delete();
        }

        catch(...)
        {
            delete pCall;
            failed = true;
            Log("Unable to delete %d\n",pCall->GetCallID());
        }

        if (failed)
            continue;

        if (m_pDoc->m_DBQSet.IsEOF())
            break;

        m_pDoc->m_DBQSet.MoveNext();
        AddTail(pCall);
        Log("Added %d\n",pCall->GetCallID());
```

We increment our count of how many objects are now in the local call queue, and if we need more call objects we continue to iterate through the loop. When we are done, we unlock the mutex and return.

```
            m_sizeQueue++;
        }                                // end while
    }                                    // end if howMany

    theLock.Unlock();
    }                                    // end if lock
    else
    {
        Log("CheckRefill locked out!\n");
    }

    return;
}
```

Since we fill the local queue with calls so that every line should get at least two calls before we refill, and since we assume the average call will take a full minute, this should represent about two minutes' worth of calls. Thus, each calling machine will hit the database about every two minutes.

This code is robust, was easy to write and appears to have very acceptable performance characteristics. Equally important, it uses the same ODBC connections and architecture as the rest of the project, and thus greatly simplifies testing. I am ever more convinced this is the right way to go, and I set aside the DCOM code with a plan to revisit it either immediately before or immediately after version one is ready.

Testing the Calling Client

The calling client can now make multiple calls at a time. It can also handle incoming calls while managing outgoing calls. The test for this is straightforward: I set the system to hold one line open for incoming calls, and to start calling a test *Flash•Call*. I have the outgoing calls ring my test lines, while I call in on another line. Other than requiring 7 extra phone lines in my home office, this presents no problem. Our local phone company is quite amused when I ask them to add seven POTS (Plain Old Telephone Service) lines in addition to the lines I have. I think they're afraid I'm a bookie.

The next trick is to test its ability to work against the database while the server is running. To do this, I extend the client's user interface so that I can shut off its out-calling when I need to. Thus, it will get all ready to make the call but not actually dial. I also want to be able to toggle various levels of logging, so I go back to the call client's form view and tinker:

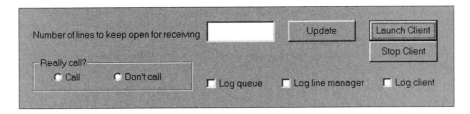

By choosing **Don't call**, I can turn off the actual outgoing calls, and watch the progress in the logs. I can also set the number of lines to set aside for receiving by entering a number in the edit box and pressing **Update**.

I fire up the server, which immediately fills the queue table, and then I fire up the client and let them both rip. The client counts down its local call queue until it falls below its (artificially low) low-water mark, and then it grabs calls from the queue table. Sure enough, the scheduler code on the server notices and fills in the queue at its next run.

This appears to work well, but of course at the moment I'm only testing one client against one server. Ultimately, I'll need to get a number of clients running on various machines, and have them all talk to the same database.

Building the Database Queue

Now that the system can make and receive calls, and add calls to the queue on the server, and get them off on the client, it's time to implement the new algorithm for adding to the queue. As you may remember, the steps are these:

- Establish which jobs are current
- Determine the minimum number to call for each job in each 10-minute period

- Add to the queue to satisfy the minima

- Once the minima are satisfied, add in proportion to priority

All of this will be accomplished in **CScheduler::Run()**, which begins by calling **GetCurrentJobs()**. This function, which I'll detail later, identifies the jobs that match the search criteria of starting before the current time and ending after the current time. Following that, the scheduler opens the queue table and the counter, which just holds the value telling how many call objects are currently in the queue.

```
bool CScheduler::Run()
{
    bool ProcessJobs = GetCurrentJobs();

    if (!m_pDoc->m_DBQueueSet.IsOpen())
        m_pDoc->m_DBQueueSet.Open();

    if (!m_pDoc->m_QCtrSet.IsOpen())
        m_pDoc->m_QCtrSet.Open();

    CDatabase* pDB = m_pDoc->m_QCtrSet.m_pDatabase;
    ASSERT(m_pDoc->m_DBQueueSet.CanUpdate());
    ASSERT(m_pDoc->m_DBQueueSet.CanAppend());
```

Next, the timer is initialized to the current time. This will be reset every ten minutes (or whatever value is set in **MINUTES_BEFORE_FILLING_MINIMUMS**). Once **ITERATIONS_BEFORE_CHECKING_JOBS** resets have been performed (the default is three, so this is after 30 minutes), I check to see if the list of jobs has changed. This is a temporary solution; in the long run, the job manager will notify the scheduler when there is a change.

```
    CTime timerStart = CTime::GetCurrentTime();
    bool FillingMinimums = true;
    int TimeCounter = 0;
    int grandTotal = 0;  // for debugging

    // Keep filling the queue until you are shut down
    for (;;)
    {
        if (m_pDoc->bShutDownServer == 1)
            break;

        CTime now = CTime::GetCurrentTime();
        CTimeSpan elapsed = now - timerStart;

        // Every ten minutes go back to filling minimums
        // Every thirty minutes recheck what jobs to run

        if (elapsed.GetTotalMinutes() > MINUTES_BEFORE_FILLING_MINIMUMS)
        {
            timerStart = CTime::GetCurrentTime();
            FillingMinimums = true;
```

```
            Log("Resetting timer, *** filling minimums\n");

            if ((++TimeCounter) == ITERATIONS_BEFORE_CHECKING_JOBS)
            {
                ProcessJobs = GetCurrentJobs();
                TimeCounter = 0;
            }
        }
```

I check to see if there are jobs to process; if not, I'll sleep for some minutes and then start over. Assuming there *are* jobs, I move to the beginning of **m_CallList**, which is a list of **CCallTrack** objects that was created by the call to **GetCurrentJobs()**.

CCallTrack objects are responsible for keeping track of where we are in the scheduling of a job. They keep track of whether we have covered the minima in any block of time, and they know the relative priority of the job and how much time it should be allocated. The **CCallTrack** object is a sort of 'staging post' between the call table and the queue table, and collaborates with the scheduler to ensure that every job is given sufficient representation in the queue.

```
    if (!ProcessJobs)
        Sleep(MILLISEC_IN_SECOND * SEC_IN_MIN * MINUTES_BETWEEN_JOB_CHECK);
    else
    {
        int currentCount = ResetQueueSize(pDB);

        POSITION pos;
        pos = m_CallList.GetHeadPosition();

        ASSERT(pos != NULL);
        CCallTrack* pTrack;
        pTrack = m_CallList.GetAt(pos);
```

The **CCallTrack** pointer is initialized, and it's time to check to see if we have room on the queue to add new calls. Assuming that we do, I begin iterating through my list of **CCallTrack** objects:

```
        while (currentCount < MAXQUEUE)
        {
```

The first check is to see if it's time to move on to the next job. We will do so if we are filling minima and we've already added enough calls for this job. If that's true *and* we're at the end of the list of **CCallTrack** objects, then we're done filling minima and it's time to start filling by priority. **ResetCallListCounters()** walks the list and sets all the counters to zero so we can keep track of how many calls have been added to the queue and in what quantity.

```
            while (FillingMinimums && pTrack->GetCount() >= pTrack->GetMin())
            {
                if (pos == NULL)
                {
```

```
                    FillingMinimums = false;
                    Log("*** filling by priority ***\n");

                    ResetCallListCounters();

                    pos = m_CallList.GetHeadPosition();
                    pTrack = m_CallList.GetAt(pos);
                    ASSERT(pos != NULL);
                    break;
                }
                else
                    pTrack = m_CallList.GetNext(pos);
        }
```

Next, if we're not filling minima, it's time to check to see if we've filled enough for this job based on its priority. Similarly to the code immediately above, we go on to the next **CCallTrack** object if we can, otherwise we reset and iterate through the entire list again:

```
        while (!FillingMinimums &&
                            pTrack->GetCount() >= pTrack->GetPriority())
        {
            if (pos == NULL)
            {
                ResetCallListCounters();
                pos = m_CallList.GetHeadPosition();
                ASSERT(pos != NULL);
                pTrack = m_CallList.GetAt(pos);
            }
            else
                pTrack = m_CallList.GetNext(pos);
        }
```

If the current **CCallTrack** object has no calls left, it is time to move on to the next call track:

```
        if (pTrack->GetTotal() < 1)
        {
            Log("Job %d finished, skipping...\n",pTrack->GetJobID());

            if (pos == NULL)
            {
                ResetCallListCounters();
                pos = m_CallList.GetHeadPosition();
                ASSERT(pos != NULL);
                pTrack = m_CallList.GetAt(pos);
            }
            else
                pTrack = m_CallList.GetNext(pos);

            continue;
        }
```

Note that here, and throughout the code, **Sleep()** *is used as a placeholder. In the final version I will go back and use event objects to block the thread as required. I find it easier to stub this out with* **Sleep()** *until I fully understand what the resume conditions are.*

Having chosen an appropriate **CCallTrack** object, we take the identified call object from the right job (based on minima or priority) and add it to the queue. **pTrack**'s increment operator updates the count and therefore decrements the number of calls remaining for that job:

```
m_pDoc->m_DBQueueSet.AddNew();
m_pDoc->m_DBQueueSet.m_CallID = pTrack->m_callSet.m_CallID;
m_pDoc->m_DBQueueSet.m_PhoneNumber =
                               pTrack->m_callSet.m_PhoneNumber;
m_pDoc->m_DBQueueSet.m_JobID = pTrack->m_callSet.m_JobID;
m_pDoc->m_DBQueueSet.m_StartTime = pTrack->m_callSet.m_StartTime;
m_pDoc->m_DBQueueSet.m_EndTime = pTrack->m_callSet.m_EndTime;
m_pDoc->m_DBQueueSet.m_NumberAttempts =
                               pTrack->m_callSet.m_NumberAttempts;
m_pDoc->m_DBQueueSet.m_Status = pTrack->m_callSet.m_Status;
m_pDoc->m_DBQueueSet.Update();

++(*pTrack);     // Increases count and decrements total left to do

if (FillingMinimums)
{
    Log("Added callID: %d", pTrack->m_callSet.m_CallID);
    Log(" jobID: %d", pTrack->m_callSet.m_JobID);
    Log(" min: %d, count: %d total: %d\n",
            pTrack->GetMin(), pTrack->GetCount(), pTrack->GetTotal());
}
else
{
    Log("Added callID: %d",pTrack->m_callSet.m_CallID);
    Log(" jobID: %d", pTrack->m_callSet.m_JobID);
    Log(" Priority: %d, count: %d total: %d\n",
      pTrack->GetPriority(), pTrack->GetCount(), pTrack->GetTotal());
}
```

Next, I update the call object in the database to indicate that this call is now in the queue:

```
pTrack->m_callSet.Edit();
pTrack->m_callSet.m_Status = csEnqueued;
pTrack->m_callSet.Update();
```

The final step is to get the next call from the **CCallTrack** object's list. If there isn't one, we get the next call track. If there's no next call track, it is time to reset all the **CCallTrack** objects and loop through again:

```
                    if (pTrack->m_callSet.IsEOF())
                    {
                        Log("Exception! Call Set exhausted prematurely!\n");

                        if (pos == NULL)
                        {
                            ResetCallListCounters();
                            pos = m_CallList.GetHeadPosition();
                            ASSERT(pos != NULL);
                            pTrack = m_CallList.GetAt(pos);
                        }
                        else
                            pTrack = m_CallList.GetNext(pos);
                    }
                    else
                        pTrack->m_callSet.MoveNext();

                    currentCount++;
                    Log("GrandTotal: %d\n", grandTotal++); // side effect!
                }              // End while queue is too small

            Sleep(MILLISEC_IN_SECOND * SEC_IN_MIN *
                                           MINUTES_BETWEEN_SCHEDULER_RUNS);

        }                      // End if process job
    }                          // End for ever loop

    return true;
}
```

Helper Functions

I said as I began discussing **CScheduler::Run()** that I'd return to discuss
GetCurrentJobs(), and that's what I'll do now. **GetCurrentJobs()** iterates through
the jobs that match the search criteria of starting before the current time and ending
after the current time. If it finds such a job, it creates a **CCallTrack** object. This object
keeps a recordset on the call table with the correct search criteria, and it also keeps track
of how many calls must be made per time interval (the minima), how many we've made
so far, and so forth:

```
bool CScheduler::GetCurrentJobs()
{
    PurgeCallList();
    bool foundJobs = false;
    CTime now = CTime::GetCurrentTime();
    CString today = now.Format("%b %d %Y %I:%M%p");

    CString filter = "start < '";
    filter += today;
    filter += "' and enddate > '";
    filter += today;
    filter += "'";
    m_pDoc->m_JobScheduleSet.m_strFilter = filter;
```

```
    if (m_pDoc->m_JobScheduleSet.IsOpen())
        m_pDoc->m_JobScheduleSet.Requery();
    else
        m_pDoc->m_JobScheduleSet.Open();


    CCallTrack* pCallTrack;
    bool ok;


    while (!m_pDoc->m_JobScheduleSet.IsEOF())
    {
        pCallTrack = new CCallTrack(m_pDoc->m_JobScheduleSet.m_JobID);
        ok = pCallTrack->Initialize();

        if (ok)
        {
            Log("ok\n");
            m_CallList.AddHead(pCallTrack);
            foundJobs = true;
        }
        else
        {
            Log("...Rejected!\n");
            delete pCallTrack;
        }

        m_pDoc->m_JobScheduleSet.MoveNext();
    }

    return foundJobs;
}
```

The goal of **GetCurrentJobs()** is to throw away the current list of **CCallTrack**s and rebuild the list based on current conditions. A **CCallTrack** is created for every current job. Each of these **CCallTrack** objects is then initialized:

```
bool CCallTrack::Initialize()
{
    CJobSet theJobSet;
    theJobSet.m_strFilter = m_callSet.m_strFilter;
    theJobSet.Open();
    m_total = theJobSet.m_theCount;

    // If you get here, you are current
    // First, how many days will you run
    CTime now = CTime::GetCurrentTime();
    CTime end = theJobSet.m_EndDate;
    CTime start = theJobSet.m_Start;
    CTime todayStart(start.GetYear(), start.GetMonth(),now.GetDay(),
                     start.GetHour(), start.GetMinute(), start.GetSecond());
    CTime todayEnd(end.GetYear(), end.GetMonth(), now.GetDay(),
                   end.GetHour(), end.GetMinute(), end.GetSecond());
```

```
        if (todayStart > now || todayEnd < now)
        {
            theJobSet.Close();
            return false;
        }

        CTimeSpan theSpan = end - now;
        int totalMinutes = theSpan.GetTotalMinutes();

        if (end > todayEnd) // spans more than today
        {
            int AdditionalMin = GetAdditionalMinutes(theJobSet.m_Start,
                                                theJobSet.m_EndDate);
            CTimeSpan todaySpan = todayEnd - now;
            totalMinutes = todaySpan.GetTotalMinutes() + AdditionalMin;
        }

        m_min = ( ( (m_total / totalMinutes) + 1 ) * SCHEDULE_BLOCK );
        m_Priority = theJobSet.m_Priority;
        m_Tilt = theJobSet.m_Tilt;
        m_Throttle = theJobSet.m_Throttle;
        m_JobID = theJobSet.m_JobID;
        theJobSet.Close();

        return true;
    }
```

The **Initialize()** method sets up the variables we must track, such as minima and how many numbers we've called. Its most interesting aspect is that it starts by looking for jobs that are *not* eligible to run right now. It does this by taking the start time held in the job record and comparing the time of day with the current time of day. If this is not eligible to run now, it will return **false**.

If the job *is* eligible to run now, it also looks to see if the job spans additional days. If so, it passes the date to **GetAdditionalMinutes()**, which is a helper function that computes how many minutes the job will run over the elapsed days.

Finally, **Initialize()** computes the minima by dividing the total number of calls to make by the total minutes available to make them in, and then multiplying that number by **SCHEDULE_BLOCK**. Right now, **SCHEDULE_BLOCK** is set to ten. In other words, we schedule in blocks of ten minutes.

If we make this **SCHEDULE_BLOCK** too small, we'll thrash; if we make it too large, we run the risk of not finishing one of the jobs. Ten minutes is a good balance: we'll fulfill the minima needed in the ten minutes, and then we'll go on to call by priority. If we've not overbooked, this should work perfectly.

Assuming **Initialize()** returns **true**, **GetCurrentJobs()** adds the new **CCallTrack** object to its list of similar objects, and when the list is complete it returns to **CScheduler::Run()**. Assuming some jobs were found that are eligible to run now, **ProcessJobs** is set **true**.

While this code is somewhat complex, it is only complicated in direct proportion to the complexity of what we are trying to accomplish. In short, these three functions manage the entire job of creating the right mix of calls for all the current jobs, ensuring that all contracted calls are made and that no one is called twice or left out.

Next Steps

The next development step is to spend a bit more time on the call flows, making sure that we can add jobs to the database through the receiving flows. Shortly after that I plan to tackle the Internet front end. There is plenty to do, but with just a few weeks of work I've demonstrated to my own satisfaction that all the tricky parts are entirely manageable.

How is the design holding up? A mixed answer. It certainly is not true that the design was written in stone and I had nothing more to do than fill in the blanks and connect the dots. On the other hand, the extensive design accomplished earlier in the project has greatly foreshortened the development effort. Even as I learn and adjust the design, I'm doing so in a well understood context, and that makes all the difference.

```
= false;

Time();
= now.Format("%b %d

er = "start < '";
oday;
' and enddate > '";
today;
'";

bScheduleSet.m_strFilter =

JobScheduleSet.IsOpen()

JobScheduleSet.Requery();

pDoc>m_JobScheduleSet.Open();

llTrack* pCallTrack;

l ok;

hile
pDoc>m_JobScheduleSet.IsEOF()
{
pCallTrack = new
allTrack(m_pDoc>m_JobScheduleSet.m_
bID);
ok = pCallTrack>Initialize();

if (ok)
{   Log("ok\n");
m_CallList.AddHead(pCallTrack);
foundJobs = true;
}
else
{   Log("...Rejected!\n");
delete pCallTrack;
}

pDoc>m_JobScheduleSet.MoveNext();
```

```
run
CTime::GetCurren
CTime end = theJobSet.
CTime start = theJobSet.
CTime todayStart(start.GetYear(),
start.GetMonth(), now.GetDay(),
start.GetHour(),
start.GetMinute(),
start.GetSecond());
CTime todayEnd(end.GetYear(),
CTime todayEnd(end.GetDay(),
end.GetMonth(), now.GetDay(),
end.GetHour(),
end.GetMinute(), end.GetSecond());

if (todayStart > now || todayS
now)
{   theJobSet.Close();
return false;
}

CTimeSpan theSpan = end no
int totalMinutes =
theSpan.GetTotalMinutes();

if (end > todayEnd) // 
than today
{   int AdditionalMinutes(the
GetAdditionalMinutes(the
t,
theJobSet.m_EndDate);
CTimeSpan todayS
now;   totalMinutes =
todaySpan.GetTotalMin
AdditionalMin;
}

m_min = ( ( (m_
totalMinutes) + 1
);   m_Priority = t
m_Tilt = theJo
m_Throttle = the
m_JobID = the
theJobSet.Cl

turn tru
```

CHAPTER SEVEN

Getting to Feature Freeze

Making Progress

Over the next few weeks I am able to make steady progress, both on the server side and on the client side. In early June I schedule a couple of days at Hypotenuse, with the goal of planning our hardware requirements and reviewing progress to date. The most important item on my agenda however, is to create a comprehensive feature list and to assign priorities to each of the features.

As we close in on the release date, it will be critical to know which features are *essential* and which are merely highly desirable. As it becomes necessary to trade away features in order to hit the schedule, we'll want to be sure that I'm spending my time on those aspects of the program without which we can't release the product, and not wasting time on nice-to-have but inessential items.

Some employers would be tempted to see this as the developer trying to cut back on what work he must do to fulfill the contract. Jay is perceptive enough to realize that, on the contrary, it is in *his* best interests that I develop only the most essential features. While it is true that many products never get past the first release, it is also true that far more products never get released at all. One reason so many products die in development is that they are killed by 'feature creep.'

As desirable but inessential features are added, the schedule takes a disproportionate hit. Not only does it take time to develop each new feature, but also testing becomes dramatically more complex. There is a combinatorial explosion of interrelationships, each of which must be tested. When you add a new feature, it impacts on all the existing features, and all these new interactions must be tested as well. Soon, the product bogs down in development, while the competition is releasing their new version with even more features. Suddenly you find yourself thinking, "Well, we can't go to market with *this*. We'll have to add a few more bells and whistles." This is the death spiral of new products.

It is nearly always best to get the minimal application out the door and into the hands of the end users. Give your customers a chance to see what you have, and let them provide the feedback. Again and again I come back to the idea that we need to ensure we have a *demand*-driven product and not a technology-driven product.

Prioritizing

In the first week of June, I drive down to New Jersey. We spend two full days building an outline of features and assigning preliminary priorities to each. We recognize right away that we will *not* be able to make the list comprehensive or definitive, but that it will be a good starting point. I capture the decisions in a simple outline, and then distribute it back to Jay and his staff as soon as we are done. They immediately begin adding and amending, but that is just fine. Over time the list will stabilize and it will guide development.

Scheduling Calls

One of the first features we discuss is scheduling. In many ways, the scheduler is the heart of this application. Jay's scheduling requirements are quite complex. Some jobs are back-tilted and some are front-tilted, and while we've discussed this quite a few times, this is the first time we've drawn pictures on a whiteboard to make sure we all understand how it will work.

Three related but different pictures emerge of how back-tilt jobs will be scheduled. Jay's vision is of a ramp, where the number of calls made increases steadily over time as we approach the deadline.

Kevin and I picture something more like rectangles whose areas represent their respective usage of the system. In Kevin's picture, we allocate more room to the larger jobs; in mine, we allocate size based on priority.

We consider accepting a simplification to make scheduling easier. Perhaps back-tilt jobs could fully utilize the system, to the exclusion of front-tilt jobs, sharing their access only among other back-tilt jobs? Front-tilt jobs must then be scheduled around the back-tilt jobs, and around one another. This brings up the issue of 'shuffling'.

The simplest scheduling algorithm we can think of is one where the system adds up the available port minutes, calculates the demand for access, and determines whether there are enough port minutes available to meet the demand. This simple approach quickly breaks down in the face of throttles. Here's an example:

Job	Start	End	Duration	Number	Throttle
A	12	2	2	50,000	0
B	12	3	3	40,000	?

For simplicity, let's assume the system can make only 30,000 calls per hour. The duration of this schedule is 12 to 3, or three hours. The system has time to make 90,000 calls, and since that's also the number we want to make, the jobs should fit. Suppose, however, that Job B is throttled to 15,000 calls per hour. Now we're in trouble. Job A only has two hours to fit in its 50,000 calls, so the best that Job B can do during this period is to make a total of 10,000 calls. While the system has *room* for Job B to make the remaining 30,000 calls in the final hour, it's not *allowed* to make more than 15,000 calls, and thus doesn't *really* have the room to finish.

We can solve this by dividing the number of hours each job has by the number of calls it must make, and ensuring that this minimal amount is available each hour — this is the algorithm we developed in the last chapter. In the example above, Job A would require 25,000 calls per hour, and Job B would require 13,333 per hour. The system would reject Job B, saying that it pushes the system over the 30,000 per hour limit. If both jobs were unthrottled, this would be unfortunate, as the system actually *does* have the resources to finish if it runs to the plan detailed above. It can run 25,000 of Job A and 5,000 of Job B in each of the first two hours, and then the remaining 30,000 of Job B in the final hour.

Shuffling

Can we solve this? Can we make the system smarter? This turns out to be a non-trivial exercise. Let's take another example:

Job	Start	End	Duration	Number	Per Hour	Throttle
A	3	6	3	40,000	13,333	15,000
B	2	6	4	50,000	12,500	25,000
C	12	4	4	60,000	15,000	none
D	12	4	4	30,000	7,500	none

There are a total of 180,000 calls to make in the period from 12 to 6. Since we have six hours, and we can make 30,000 calls per hour, it's just possible that the jobs will fit.

The tricky question is, can we *prove* we can do it, given the throttles on Jobs A and B? If I were doing this by hand (which is the right place to start), I'd note that I have four hours to run Job B, so I must schedule at least 12,500 calls per hour. I have 3 hours to run Job A, and thus want to schedule 13,333 per hour. I also need to schedule 15,000 per hour for Job C and 7,500 per hour for Job D. I'm overbooked from 2 to 4pm. (Between 2 and 3pm, for example, Jobs B, C and D will need to make 13,333 + 15,000 + 7,500 = 35,833 calls.) I must 'shuffle' some jobs out of the way.

I can push Jobs C and D around to *some* degree, but I really need to recognize that fact way back at 12:00, before the problem arises. Between 12 and 2, for example, I could finish Job D, and so by 2pm I would need to book only B and C, and they fit.

At 3pm, I'd need to schedule Jobs A, B and C, but their minima require a total of 40,833 calls per hour. I can make them fit if I push the remainder of Job B's calls out to the 4 to 6pm slot. If we run B at 15,000 from 2 to 3pm, then from 4 to 6pm it will have only 35,000 calls to make, and so can finish on time despite being throttled. The final schedule might look like this:

12 - 1	Job C	15,000
	Job D	15,000
1 - 2	Job C	15,000
	Job D	15,000 (finished)
2 - 3	Job B	15,000
	Job C	15,000
3 - 4	Job A	15,000
	Job C	15,000 (finished)
4 - 5	Job A	15,000
	Job B	15,000
5 - 6	Job A	10,000 (finished)
	Job B	20,000 (finished)

As you can see, we *are* able to schedule this within the throttled constraints, but only at the cost of doing some complex shuffling along the way. The system requires that we are able quickly to answer the question, "Will this fit?" Further, we must be able to answer the question, "Which job do I schedule for calls now?" at any given time.

I consider a number of allocation plans, the most promising of which is, "Find the job that's most constrained, and meet its needs first." Of course, the definition of 'most constrained' is subject to some interpretation. Is this the job with the smallest throttle? The fewest remaining minutes? The most calls to make?

Off and on for a few weeks, I rack my brains working on these problems. I conclude that there are really three distinct tasks I need to accomplish:

- Schedule the back tilt-jobs
- Compute if there are resources to take on a given job or set of jobs
- Schedule the next ten minutes of calling.

Jay and I agree that there are some things the system *must* be able to handle automatically, but there are others that for the interim we can use a human customer service person to manage.

My first strategy for solving this problem is to canvass the Internet. What we are trying to do certainly can't be unique. How different is this problem from that of filling a hotel, managing inventory for a manufacturing plant, or scheduling teachers, students and classes?

What I discover is that there are two types of resource available. First, there are academic papers on the theories of scheduling. Frankly, these are very esoteric documents and even understanding them would take longer than we have available to devote to solving this issue. Migrating that understanding into a design and then into code is way beyond our current time and ability.

The second resource is purchasable products. Unfortunately, while there are many scheduling packages available, these are end-product solutions, not programming engines. That is, it's certainly possible to buy something that will schedule your classes and teachers, or will help with inventory management, or even with booking hotel rooms, but there is nothing I've been able to find that serves the developer who is building such a product. I add to my 'to do' list the intent to return to the search, calling some of these resources and trying to track down a vendor who offers, ideally, a component that I can add to my program.

A Compromise

In the meantime, I need to make forward progress. Here's my fallback solution; we may be able to do better than this, but this is the minimum we can do. Each job will have a minimum number of calls it must make each hour, and this is simply the naïve average as computed above. For example, if we need to make 45,000 calls in three hours, the minimum for that job is 15,000 per hour. If each job makes this minimal number of calls every hour, it's guaranteed to finish on time.

Thus, when attempting to schedule a new job, I can add the minima per hour required by the other jobs that are running when the proposed job will run, and see if I have room for the new job's minimum number of calls. As noted above, this may cause me to reject some jobs I might otherwise take, but I can rest assured that I won't take any jobs I can't complete.

Rejecting a job will be defined as passing it to customer service. If the customer service representative realizes that by starting another job later, or by breaking it into two smaller jobs, they can fit the new job in, then this will be done manually.

Over time, the system needs to get smarter. We need to identify the types of reshuffling we're doing and incorporate them into the system so that they can be managed automatically. I anticipate a few things the system might want to recognize pretty early on:

- Are there hours I should make unavailable to all future jobs (due to back-tilt requirements, etc.)?

- Can I fit a new job if I compress an existing job into a shorter time span?

- Can I fit a new job if I break it up into two smaller chunks?

- Can I fit a new job if I break some other job up into two smaller chunks?

- Can I fit a new job if I make a minor change to the throttle of this or some other job?

There probably are many more things we could consider, but for the interim I'll code the 'minima' algorithm I've already developed.

How We Coded it for V1

To get us through V1, I decide to take a fairly simplistic approach to answering the question, "Will this new job fit?" Here are the steps:

- Gather the preproduction information from the customer

- Add the job to the database

- Check to see if there is room, and if so, set up all the calls

- If there is not room, pass the customer to customer service to see if we can reschedule

To check if the proposed job will fit, I get its start and end times. For every hour in the job, I query the system to find all existing jobs running during that hour and establish the minimum needed for each of those jobs. I add these minima together, and if the sum added to the minimum of the proposed job is less than a fixed maximum, then I'm okay.

An obvious problem with this solution is that jobs won't *run* at their minima, they'll run as fast as our resources allow. Thus, it's likely that we'll show many jobs as not fitting when they actually would have fitted in the end. We agree that if time allows, I'll make these simplifying assumptions to improve this code:

- No job will be running before 9am nor continue for more than one day

- All running jobs will use all available resources

Given these two assumptions, I may be able to accept some jobs that I would otherwise have turned down and passed over to customer service. I'm still quite unhappy about how crude the scheduling will be in V1, and this becomes a very high priority for the next release.

Back-Tilted Jobs

The problem of scheduling back-tilted jobs is even more complicated. The goal is to end the job at the latest possible moment. To schedule the job, we want to compute a starting time based on how many calls we need to make, how long each call will take, and how many lines are available. Computing the available lines is, however, a tricky business.

Once again I decide to go forward, for Version 1, with a reasonable guess. When scheduling back-tilted calls, we'll assume the system is otherwise completely empty. If we run into a scheduling conflict (which we surely will if any other jobs *are* already scheduled), then we'll kick the job out to customer service. They can shuffle jobs around and schedule the start time by hand. All of this may keep customer service busy at first, but we don't anticipate scheduling a lot of back tilt jobs, and we'll fix the back-tilt scheduling in the second version. We'll only have to live with this interim solution for a short while.

Good Enough Programming

The ego psychologist Donald Winnicott coined the term 'good enough mothering' to describe how children should be nurtured, but not smothered, by their mothers. That is, it should be 'good enough', but not so good as to overdo it. I am a big believer in 'good enough programming'. While we want to ensure that what we release is of the highest quality, that doesn't mean that we must implement every conceivable feature. We don't have to do it all, but what we do, we must do well.

In this case, we have decided to implement an interim solution to the scheduling problem. What do you do when you need to move forward, but suspect that you'll be changing the algorithm as you learn more, and as you continue to think it through? The answer is **encapsulation**. If we can constrain the impact and scope of scheduling to a limited portion of the software, then changing the algorithm should have no impact on the rest of the code.

As you saw in the previous chapter, the question, "What do I schedule to call now?" is encapsulated in the scheduler class. If the method of answering this question changes, only this class will be affected.

Getting to V1 on Schedule

During the month of June, I make progress on the top priority tasks, but it becomes obvious by the end of the month that there are holes in the specification. This is not uncommon. While we performed exhaustive analysis and design, sometimes it's only during implementation that you discover what pieces are incompletely conceived.

It is time for a short re-analysis and redesign session. This comes at a time when Jay is under enormous pressure to shorten the development cycle. The combination of the need for clarity and the pressure to cut features compels me to drive back down to New Jersey for a second round of prioritizing and clarification.

To give focus to the discussion, we solidify our release dates. We agree that we will plan to make the changeover from the old calling system to the new one by Thanksgiving. Having a completion date allows me to work backwards through our **drop-dead dates**, by which I mean something very specific: if we don't hit one drop-dead date, the subsequent date is unrealistic.

Given a delivery date of 11/25, I know I must be in beta by 11/4. In this phase of development, we will be using the new system, under load, as intended for release, but calling only 'friendly' users. I want no less than three weeks of beta testing to ensure that we have time to make last-minute corrections. However, we're not even *in* beta unless we think we've found and fixed all the critical and important bugs, and to do that we need to have subjected the code to **load testing**.

Load testing will take place at Hypotenuse, and will subject the system to large numbers of test calls using the real hardware, over the real network, interfacing to the real long distance carriers. Of course, this means they will need additional lines, as they must continue with their existing customers on the working production system.

This is when the rubber hits the road. I want a solid month of load testing. To be in beta testing by November 4, I need to ensure that Hypotenuse begins its load testing no later than 10/7 — a month earlier.

Still working backwards from the delivery date, in order to be ready for load testing by 10/7, I need time to do a solid month of in-house testing at Liberty Associates. That means I must begin my own testing in early September. I won't begin testing until all the features are in place and working, so we set our **feature-complete** date at September 9. We create this schedule in early July, leaving me with about 60 days of development time in which to complete the remaining features. To make sure I use this time wisely, I ask Jay to help me refine the feature list.

Despite our best efforts at a comprehensive analysis, there are many areas that are not yet specified. More importantly, Jay and his crew have implicit assumptions about what the software will do and how it will behave that we've not yet written down and committed to. I drive down to Hypotenuse to review these issues, and to take another stab at a comprehensive specification.

Assigning Priority to Features

The first item of business during my visit to Hypotenuse is to flesh out the feature list, and then to assign a value to each feature: how important is this feature to the first version? By understanding which of the features are required, and which are merely desirable, we reduce the risk of spending time and effort on the less important aspects of the service. We review our priority scale:

5 - *Sine Qua Non* (Without this, there is nothing). The definition of a 5 is: "Without this feature, we will *not* release the product." While it's tempting to give any number of features this value, the reality is that very few features really deserve it. The acid test is this: if this feature is not included, but all the other level five features are, will you really delay shipping?

4 - *Imperative*. The definition of 4 is: "I really want this to be a 5." A 4 is exactly like a 5, except that if you put a gun to my head, I will ship the product without it. We will hold up shipping for the want of a five; we'll ship without a four even if it hurts.

3 - *Very Important*. This is a feature we're willing to put some work and time into, but again, we won't hold things up if it turns out this must wait.

2 - *Nice to Have*. Put this feature in if you can do so quickly and inexpensively.

1 - *Only if it is Free*. Include this feature only if it has no impact on the schedule.

0 - *Not Even if it is Free*. This feature is specifically *not* desirable. We reserve this for the few features we've discussed and explicitly rejected.

Within this context, we evaluate the scheduling items as follows:

Feature	Value
System must know when to start calling a job	5
System must be able to stagger calls by time zone	4
System must be able to ignore time zone	4
System must be able to stop calling a job at a specific time	5
System must be able to stop based on time zone	4
System must be able to stop regardless of time zone	5
System must be able to stop based on an event	3
System must be able to compute schedule with reshuffling	4
Every job will at least trickle out during its entire scheduled time	3

System must know when to start calling a job just means we can schedule a specific start time for a job. It is hard to imagine the system without this feature, so of course it's a five. It is exactly this kind of 'obvious' feature that must be explicitly called out at this time so as to differentiate it, for example, from *System must be able to stagger calls by time zone*. While it is highly desirable that we can start the West Coast calls three hours after we start the East Coast calls, we *will* ship the product even if this is not working.

Of the 4s and 5s in this list, the only one I suspect won't make it into V1 is *System must be able to compute schedule with reshuffling* — as discussed above, this may not be fully developed by the time we roll out the first version.

The last feature — *Every job will at least trickle out during its entire scheduled time* — is interesting. In the event that we reshuffle the schedule, you can imagine that there are some jobs which won't actually make any calls during one or two hours of their scheduled time. This last feature says that no job ever drops to zero — that we always make at least some calls during the entire allotted time. This really is a matter of customer relations more than anything else, but can be an important consideration when scheduling. In any case, it's a 3 and so may not make it into the first version. It will be irrelevant, in any case, if we don't have reshuffling of jobs.

As a practical matter, knowing that reshuffling is a 4 and not a 5 frees me to turn my attention elsewhere. Dealing with scheduling in all its complexity was threatening to become a significant risk to the schedule. Since Jay has agreed that he would be willing to go to V1 without the ability to maximize his schedule, I can focus on those areas of the system that are most critical. As long as a human customer service operator can, by some mechanism, intervene in the system and manually reschedule as required, we're still better off shipping the product and automating the scheduling in a later release.

Other Priorities

We work hard to create a comprehensive list of features, so that I'm certain to work only on those that are of the highest priority. We agree that sign-up will be accomplished by a customer service representative assisting the new customer. Initially, customer service may need to access the database through a SQL Server front end, but quickly we'll add new tools, ultimately providing Web-based forms.

Interestingly, along the way I write a quick IVR application to accomplish sign-up for testing purposes. Once written, however, it becomes a potential tool for customer service, and I make a note to myself to fix it up as an alternative front end into the database. Whether we will provide access to this IVR customer sign-up system to the customer is an open question, but if nothing else it may be a convenient interface for customer service.

A major issue that's been outstanding for quite a while is what reports Hypotenuse requires for Version 1. Currently, Jay gets a number of canned reports from his old system, and clearly we'll need to design and implement many such reports for the new system over time. The issue at the moment is which of these he needs before we can go to the first version.

A second question is what real-time information Operations requires to run the system. This is difficult to answer in the abstract, but we agree in a subsequent meeting that most of what Operations needs can be achieved through SQL calls against the databases and logs.

Kevin argues that we can't go to V1 unless he can determine if the system is running properly, and whether jobs are tracking well. We agree that I will write a mechanism whereby the system will notify him, either by voice mail or by pager, when something significant goes wrong. Any time we try to make a call and can't get a line, or write to or read from the disk and can't access it; any time a VRU tries to talk to the server, or a server tries to talk to the VRU and they can't connect, we'll want to raise an alarm. To cut down on the number of false alarms, we'll try each of these things three times before calling for help.

> *VRU stands for Voice Response Unit, which is the name Hypotenuse gives to what I've simply been referring to as a 'calling machine'.*

To ensure that the system is tracking well, we'll want to produce a report of the current jobs. More importantly, we'll consider it an error condition when there is insufficient time to complete the minimum number of calls for any given job. Thus, if a job requires that 60,000 calls be made in the next hour, and there is only time to schedule 8,000 calls in the next 10 minutes, the job will signal a problem and a call will go out to Operations.

This indicates that there are some problems which aren't *fatal* to the system — they're certainly undesirable, but the system can keep running. These problems must be signaled to Operations on an emergency basis. This is an important design consideration in our error handling, and I make a note of its implications: that we can undergo certain significant failures and yet keep making calls, and that we must have a system rapidly to notify Operations of the problem.

Reports and Forms

To handle the reporting requirements, we need to provide reports to a number of constituencies. The customer needs to know how their job went, Jay and senior management need MIS reports, the Operations department needs real-time operational data, and customer service needs information on jobs past and future.

This need for reports is exacerbated by the interim solution to scheduling. A side effect of our decision to kick difficult scheduling issues over to customer service is that they now need better reports and forms so that they can analyze the situation and take corrective action. SQL will no longer do the trick.

There are a number of ways to approach this requirement. I could, of course, write custom forms and reports from scratch. This would be a nightmare, and there is surely no need to reinvent all the formatting and printing code this would require when other products already exist to do this.

Another possibility is to go with a third party database reporting product, such as Crystal Reports. Preliminary investigation suggests that can do what we need, so I decide to buy a copy and look more closely. Crystal Reports is a powerful program, but learning how to use it well will take a little time. More important, the result will be printed reports, and ideally we want the reports available on the intranet.

A third option is to build the forms and reports as web pages. This is clearly the right long-term solution, and I'm beginning to believe it's the right interim solution as well. Sometimes, the most expedient course is to do it right the first time.

Jay is very concerned about the deadline; he wants it faster, faster. At this point, he begins to increase the pressure to bring in more developers. I'm reluctant to expand the core development work, as the overhead of bringing someone up to speed may cost more than the benefit, so I look for places where a consultant can work independently. Writing reports and forms may be a clear example of such an opportunity.

It is my hope that if I can find a reliable expert in Active Server Pages and/or Crystal Reports, to whom I can explain what is needed and provide the specifications of the database, then he can work totally independently of my own efforts. This raises the question of how you go about finding such a person.

It's Not What You Know, It's Who Knows You

There is a common accusation that, "It's not what you know, it's who you know," which determines success. My experience is that this is true, but rather than seeing it as a problem, I view it as a natural result of the desire to hire people known to do good work. When I need to hire a consultant, I start by calling around the people I know. First, can they do the job? If they can, that's best for me, because then I know what I'm buying. If they can't, do they know anyone they'd vouch for who can?

A few Interchange alumni and I have formed The Digital Guild. The Digital Guild is a virtual company; an association of developers and designers who can provide consulting for one another, so that we can maintain the control we want over our own businesses while providing the breadth and depth of expertise that our customers require. The Digital Guild is very tightly controlled; it is our intention to knit together the very best developers and designers in the New England area.

I immediately contact the other Guild members to determine if any of them is available and has the necessary skills. One Guild member gives me the name of a first-class database developer: Cliff Gerald of Gamma Software, who has built Active Server Pages for him on a consulting basis in the recent past.

I make the call and talk with Cliff, who immediately impresses me with his professionalism. I explain what I'm doing and what I want to accomplish, and he feels confident his organization can meet my requirements. We discuss his day rate and how we might work together. I'm pleased to learn that he works with an estimate and a contract: two signs of a professional. I explain that we'll need to get him under non-disclosure, and he has no problem with that.

We arrange to meet early the following week to discuss specifics. He suggests I bring a couple of samples of what I want, and that we begin the relationship by having his company build a first example. His estimate is that we're looking at a few days of work to understand the problem and create the first report, but that subsequent reports will come more quickly. He also explains that the actual coding will be done by John Sequeira, a Gamma associate.

I explain up front that I don't so much want to buy the web pages, as I want to buy their knowledge and expertise. It is my intent that once they've delivered the pages, they'll also teach me about what they've done. I want this for a number of reasons, most important of which is that Jay can't afford to depend on yet another out-of-state provider. He needs me to fully understand what has been built, to support it and stand behind it, and to fully document my efforts.

Another reason I want Gamma Software to teach me, is that I need them to make themselves obsolete. Over time, I'll take over the development of many of these web pages, and I'm hoping to hire them to flatten my learning curve. Building web pages has never been easier — Visual InterDev is a powerful product — but there remain a lot of details and I need to get very smart, very fast. It is the knowledge transfer that makes them worth what they are charging me.

Designing the Reports

There are three reasons why producing an estimate is critical. First, the process of putting together the estimate forces issues into the open early in the process. Second, the estimate helps us focus on our priorities. And finally, an estimate establishes a professional and manageable relationship.

As I describe what I want to accomplish in the first meeting, the scope of the project immediately grows. I show Cliff the first two reports I have in mind.

The first is a summary report for the customer that will be sent at the end of each job via e-mail. This is a fairly straightforward report, and while it raises issues of how to interact with the database, it is unusual in that rather than displaying it as a web page, we want to mail it to the customer:

	MIS needed for Hypotenuse clients			Call #	Phone #	Time	Date	Result	Attempt #
	Report to be generated electronically at end of each job								
1	Time / Date of this report	xx:xx:xx am	xx/xx/xx	1	nnn-nnn-nnnn	xx:xx:xx am	xx/xx/xx	x	n
2	Time / Date this job started	xx:xx:xx am	xx/xx/xx	2	nnn-nnn-nnnn	xx:xx:xx am	xx/xx/xx	x	n
	Time / Date first attempts completed	xx:xx:xx am	xx/xx/xx	3	nnn-nnn-nnnn	xx:xx:xx am	xx/xx/xx	x	n
3	Time / Date all attempts completed	xx:xx:xx am	xx/xx/xx	4	nnn-nnn-nnnn	xx:xx:xx am	xx/xx/xx	x	n
4	Job number	nnnnn-nnnn		5	nnn-nnn-nnnn	xx:xx:xx am	xx/xx/xx	x	n
5	List number	nnnnn-nnnn		6	nnn-nnn-nnnn	xx:xx:xx am	xx/xx/xx	x	n
6	Audio number	nnnnn-nnnn		7	nnn-nnn-nnnn	xx:xx:xx am	xx/xx/xx	x	n
7	# of phone numbers dialed	n		8	nnn-nnn-nnnn	xx:xx:xx am	xx/xx/xx	x	n
8	Length of audio message (mm:ss)	00:00		9	nnn-nnn-nnnn	xx:xx:xx am	xx/xx/xx	x	n
9	% of calls completed on 1st attempt	n.nn%		10	nnn-nnn-nnnn	xx:xx:xx am	xx/xx/xx	x	n
10	% of calls retried	n.nn%		11	nnn-nnn-nnnn	xx:xx:xx am	xx/xx/xx	x	n
11	After all attempts made, total ...			12	nnn-nnn-nnnn	xx:xx:xx am	xx/xx/xx	x	n
12	% answered by human	n.nn%		13	nnn-nnn-nnnn	xx:xx:xx am	xx/xx/xx	x	n
13	% answewred by answering machine	n.nn%		14	nnn-nnn-nnnn	xx:xx:xx am	xx/xx/xx	x	n
14	% not answered	n.nn%		15	nnn-nnn-nnnn	xx:xx:xx am	xx/xx/xx	x	n
15	% busy	n.nn%		16	nnn-nnn-nnnn	xx:xx:xx am	xx/xx/xx	x	n
16	% operator intercept, or network not responding	n.nn%		17	nnn-nnn-nnnn	xx:xx:xx am	xx/xx/xx	x	n
17	% other	n.nn%		18	nnn-nnn-nnnn	xx:xx:xx am	xx/xx/xx	x	n
18	% of port minutes used midnight ET to 9 am ET	n.nn%		19	nnn-nnn-nnnn	xx:xx:xx am	xx/xx/xx	x	n
19	9 am to Noon ET	n.nn%		20	nnn-nnn-nnnn	xx:xx:xx am	xx/xx/xx	x	n
20	Noon to 3 pm ET	n.nn%		21	nnn-nnn-nnnn	xx:xx:xx am	xx/xx/xx	x	n
21	3 pm to 6 pm ET	n.nn%		22	nnn-nnn-nnnn	xx:xx:xx am	xx/xx/xx	x	n
22	6 pm to 9 pm ET	n.nn%		23	nnn-nnn-nnnn	xx:xx:xx am	xx/xx/xx	x	n
23	9 pm to midnight ET	n.nn%		24	nnn-nnn-nnnn	xx:xx:xx am	xx/xx/xx	x	n
				25	nnn-nnn-nnnn	xx:xx:xx am	xx/xx/xx	x	n
				26	nnn-nnn-nnnn	xx:xx:xx am	xx/xx/xx	x	n
				27	nnn-nnn-nnnn	xx:xx:xx am	xx/xx/xx	x	n
				28	nnn-nnn-nnnn	xx:xx:xx am	xx/xx/xx	x	n
				29	nnn-nnn-nnnn	xx:xx:xx am	xx/xx/xx	x	n
				30	nnn-nnn-nnnn	xx:xx:xx am	xx/xx/xx	x	n
				31	nnn-nnn-nnnn	xx:xx:xx am	xx/xx/xx	x	n
				32	nnn-nnn-nnnn	xx:xx:xx am	xx/xx/xx	x	n
				33	nnn-nnn-nnnn	xx:xx:xx am	xx/xx/xx	x	n
				34	nnn-nnn-nnnn	xx:xx:xx am	xx/xx/xx	x	n
				etc	etc	etc	etc	etc	etc
Legend: H = Human, M = Machine, B = Busy, N = No Answer, X = non working telephone, etc.									

We turn our attention to a second report. This is modeled after a report Jay currently receives about his daily polling:

MIS needed for Hypotenuse management	1	2	3	>	4	5	6	7	8	9	10	11	12
Report to be generated once a day, during overnight													
	1st job we did yesterday	2nd job we did yesterday	3rd job we did yesterday	etc >	Yesterday Wednesday 7/16/97	1 week ago Wednesday 7/9/97	Past 7 Days, 7/9/97 - 7/16/97	Past 30 days, 6/17/97 - 7/16/97	Year to Date 01/01/97 - 7/16/97	Past 12 Mos. 6/17/96 - 7/16/97	1 mo ago 6/1/97 - 6/30/97	2 mos ago, 5/1/97 - 5/31/97	3 mos ago, 4/1/97 - 4/30/97
1	# of jobs	1	1	1		n	n	n	n	n	n	n	n	n
2	# of phone numbers dialed	n	n	n		n	n	n	n	n	n	n	n	n
3	Avg # of phone numbers / job	n.n	n.n	n.n		n.n	n.n	n.n	n.n	n.n	n.n	n.n	n.n	n.n
4	Total port minutes used	n	n	n		n	n	n	n	n	n	n	n	n
5	Avg port-cycle time, start to start	n.n	n.n	n.n		n.n	n.n	n.n	n.n	n.n	n.n	n.n	n.n	n.n
6	Total connect minutes	n	n	n		n	n	n	n	n	n	n	n	n
7	Weighted Avg Cost per minute of phone time	$n.nn	$n.nn	$n.nn		$n.nn	$n.nn	$n.nn	$n.nn	$n.nn	$n.nn	$n.nn	$n.nn	$n.nn
8	Total cost of connect minutes	$n.nn	$n.nn	$n.nn		$n.nn	$n.nn	$n.nn	$n.nn	$n.nn	$n.nn	$n.nn	$n.nn	$n.nn
9	Cost of connect minutes / job	$n.nn	$n.nn	$n.nn		$n.nn	$n.nn	$n.nn	$n.nn	$n.nn	$n.nn	$n.nn	$n.nn	$n.nn
10	% of network utilized (ports min used ÷ ports min avail)	n.nn%	n.nn%	n.nn%		n.nn%	n.nn%	n.nn%	n.nn%	n.nn%	n.nn%	n.nn%	n.nn%	n.nn%
11	Avg length of completed call	n.n	n.n	n.n		n.n	n.n	n.n	n.n	n.n	n.n	n.n	n.n	n.n
12	Longest Completed call	n.n	n.n	n.n		n.n	n.n	n.n	n.n	n.n	n.n	n.n	n.n	n.n
13	Longest Port Cycle, start to start	n.n	n.n	n.n		n.n	n.n	n.n	n.n	n.n	n.n	n.n	n.n	n.n
14	% of calls completed on 1st attempt	n.nn%	n.nn%	n.nn%		n.nn%	n.nn%	n.nn%	n.nn%	n.nn%	n.nn%	n.nn%	n.nn%	n.nn%
15	% of calls retried	n.nn%	n.nn%	n.nn%		n.nn%	n.nn%	n.nn%	n.nn%	n.nn%	n.nn%	n.nn%	n.nn%	n.nn%
16	After all attempts made, total ...													
17	% answered by human	n.nn%	n.nn%	n.nn%		n.nn%	n.nn%	n.nn%	n.nn%	n.nn%	n.nn%	n.nn%	n.nn%	n.nn%
18	% answewred by answering machine	n.nn%	n.nn%	n.nn%		n.nn%	n.nn%	n.nn%	n.nn%	n.nn%	n.nn%	n.nn%	n.nn%	n.nn%
19	% not answered	n.nn%	n.nn%	n.nn%		n.nn%	n.nn%	n.nn%	n.nn%	n.nn%	n.nn%	n.nn%	n.nn%	n.nn%
20	% busy	n.nn%	n.nn%	n.nn%		n.nn%	n.nn%	n.nn%	n.nn%	n.nn%	n.nn%	n.nn%	n.nn%	n.nn%
21	% operator intercept, or network not responding	n.nn%	n.nn%	n.nn%		n.nn%	n.nn%	n.nn%	n.nn%	n.nn%	n.nn%	n.nn%	n.nn%	n.nn%
22	% other	n.nn%	n.nn%	n.nn%		n.nn%	n.nn%	n.nn%	n.nn%	n.nn%	n.nn%	n.nn%	n.nn%	n.nn%
23	% of port minutes used midnight ET to 9 am ET	n.nn%	n.nn%	n.nn%		n.nn%	n.nn%	n.nn%	n.nn%	n.nn%	n.nn%	n.nn%	n.nn%	n.nn%
24	9 am to Noon ET	n.nn%	n.nn%	n.nn%		n.nn%	n.nn%	n.nn%	n.nn%	n.nn%	n.nn%	n.nn%	n.nn%	n.nn%
25	Noon to 3 pm ET	n.nn%	n.nn%	n.nn%		n.nn%	n.nn%	n.nn%	n.nn%	n.nn%	n.nn%	n.nn%	n.nn%	n.nn%
26	3 pm to 6 pm ET	n.nn%	n.nn%	n.nn%		n.nn%	n.nn%	n.nn%	n.nn%	n.nn%	n.nn%	n.nn%	n.nn%	n.nn%
27	6 pm to 9 pm ET	n.nn%	n.nn%	n.nn%		n.nn%	n.nn%	n.nn%	n.nn%	n.nn%	n.nn%	n.nn%	n.nn%	n.nn%
28	9 pm to midnight ET	n.nn%	n.nn%	n.nn%		n.nn%	n.nn%	n.nn%	n.nn%	n.nn%	n.nn%	n.nn%	n.nn%	n.nn%

We discuss this for quite a while. It is Cliff's opinion that it will be very difficult to display a chart of this complexity over the Web: horizontal scrolling is difficult, and people tend to find it confusing. We can use frames to hold the headings and row names in place, but it's a bit complex for a first report. Further, we don't know how many columns are to the left of the divide; some days there will be only a few jobs to report on, but on other days there will be dozens.

We agree to divide the report in half. One page will display the report for the previous day, job by job. The second page will provide the information on the right of this sample report. We spend quite a bit of time defining how we'll approach the problem and I ask, "Is there a way to *display* segmented parts of this on the Web, but to *print* the whole thing?"

After some discussion, we agree that we'll unify the report for printing by using Crystal Reports. This is an important capability, and one that I'd like Gamma to explore and then teach me, as we'll want to do it a lot. They suggest that rather than having Crystal Reports do the actual printing, it would be a very powerful feature to have Crystal Reports create the report, and then 'print' to a **.pdf** file. This will allow Hypotenuse staff to print their reports over the Web from any system, without having to have Crystal Reports locally. Since this will only add a couple of hours to the schedule, and will only cost us the purchase price of the printer driver (estimated at a few hundred dollars), I authorize this additional feature.

After much discussion, Cliff understands what it is I want to accomplish, and promises a written estimate by the end of the day. I receive the estimate via e-mail and go over it in some detail. Since I have asked them to help Hypotenuse with setting up their web server and database, and since they want to build a data dictionary to make subsequent reports easier, the scope of the project has grown a bit since our initial conversations. Adding in the ability to interact with Crystal Reports, they now estimate that the first report will take approximately 10 days. This is at the high end of the amount we've budgeted, but it includes a day and a half dedicated to transferring their knowledge of how they did it, so that I can move forward with subsequent reports.

Further, their ten day estimate assumes that they will receive no significant support at Hypotenuse, but I know that Kevin and his staff are well prepared to do much of the work they've allowed for, and thus the schedule will be shortened by a few days. We have asked them for a total of three reports. We split Jay's original report in two, and the third report is a mailed message to the customer, summarizing the calls made in his job. My guess is that we'll get the first report completed, both for the Web and Crystal Reports, in about 7-8 days. We should be able to add the two other reports I care about with 2-3 days of additional work.

I am highly motivated to get them going on these reports, because time is getting short. Cliff sent me a message that's perfect for this time in the project: "You guys start writing code; I'll go figure out what they want."

The next step is to finalize the contract and approve the estimate, but more important is that I meet with Jay to iron out *exactly* what should appear in this first report. In our discussion we agree that on the Web, the report will be split into two sub-reports. The first will correspond to the left side of the original report, and will have five or six fixed columns, each one representing a job we did on the previous day. If we have fourteen jobs, then the first six columns will represent jobs 1-6, the second page will show 7-12, and the third page will show 13-14 with four empty columns.

The second sub-report will display aggregated results of all jobs during various time periods, such as the previous day, the same day in the previous week, the past seven or thirty days, and so forth. We also clarify some of the rows, redefining what some mean for the two reports. Finally, we agree that the printed report will draw this information back together into a unified presentation. Each web page will have a Print button, which will print the entire, aggregated report.

Once the estimate and contract are signed, I meet with Cliff again to talk through the final specifics of the modified report. We agree to stay in close contact so that I can monitor progress, and he is eager to assure me that if he gets the kind of help and cooperation I'm promising at Hypotenuse, they will easily do better than the time they estimated. To ensure this possibility, I immediately set up a conference call between Cliff, John (who will actually code the reports) and Kevin at Hypotenuse. Kevin brings in Kevin Tillbrook, who will actually implement much of the web technology at Hypotenuse Operations. We discuss what work will be done in each shop, and how John will receive access to the systems at Hypotenuse so that he can implement and test his reports.

Hardware

Kevin has agreed to assume responsibility for specifying, researching and purchasing the hardware. In my initial design I had envisioned that the system would run on a series of desktop Pentium machines. The need for absolute reliability has prompted Kevin to look for a more robust solution.

The goal is to provide a platform that will perform well under the anticipated load. The system must be able to sustain a variety of hardware and software failures, and yet continue to operate normally. We also want the system to monitor itself and to notify Operations when one of its components fails.

The disk systems are obviously crucial and are the most susceptible to failure. A RAID (Redundant Array of Inexpensive Disks) system provides the critical reliability we require. RAID level 5 allows a disk to fail without the system losing any data at all: the remaining disks can restore the lost data with 100% reliability.

In addition to media failures, the RAID system has to withstand cable failures, controller failures, power supply failures, cooling fan failures, cache data errors, bus data errors and complete shutdown of the host system without losing data in the cache that has not yet been committed to the disk array.

A catastrophic failure of the database server or the call server will cause the entire calling system to grind to an ignominious halt. To prevent this from ever happening, the servers need to be nearly 100% fault tolerant. In the event that either server fails, the system must switch to a backup system, and it must do so quickly and seamlessly so that no data is lost, and the calling platform as a whole can continue to operate. This is known as **transparent fail-over**. Since we have two servers, each running on its own Pentium, the servers can provide this seamless backup for one another.

The Database and Call Servers

After reviewing systems from dozens of vendors, Kevin chose the Data General 'Cluster in a Box'. Late in July, Data General configured and delivered a pair of dual processor Pentium Pro 200 Aviion 3600Rs, each with 512MB of ECC RAM. The entire set is mounted in an industrial-strength rack the size of a small refrigerator, about 4 feet tall by 2 feet wide. It is, as my daughter would say, wicked cool.

The RAID subsystem is a Clariion 2000 series RAID package. Clariion is a subsidiary of Data General and provides High Availability RAID systems for both UNIX and Windows NT environments. The system has its own UPS, hot-swappable redundant SCSI controllers, cache modules, 5 SCSI channels, redundant cooling fans and 3 hot-swappable power supplies. All buses and RAM are ECC (Error Correction Code) — used to dramatically reduce error rates and thus increase performance.

The Clariion RAID system allows for 'global hot spare' disks. The chassis containing the disks actually contains more than one logical disk volume. Having a global hot spare means that if any disk fails, the hot spare will automatically be assigned as the replacement disk, *without operator intervention*. This will minimize the amount of time any RAID volume will operate in a degraded state.

Operations will run FirstWatch by Veritas Software, Inc. FirstWatch will monitor various aspects of each system: it will continually check that all NT services and software applications are up and running. If FirstWatch detects a failure of any monitored component of either server, it will migrate all functionality from the failed server to the surviving server. Access to all data is shared between the two servers; this means that if either server goes off-line for any reason, the remaining server will assume operational control of the entire data set. The entire fail-over process take about 30 seconds from first detection of the failure until all of the services, applications and data are up and running on the remaining machine.

A benefit of this fail-over technology is that hardware and software upgrades can be accomplished without taking down the calling platform. A technician can initiate a controlled fail-over of one server, and once the fail-over completes, we can shut the downed server off and add new hardware and software. When the upgrade is completed, the server can be brought back on line, and the second server can be brought down. All of this is invisible to the calling software and the database; the system continues to work oblivious to the hardware upgrades.

The Calling Stations

In addition to ensuring that the servers are fault tolerant, the network itself must be highly reliable. If the network fails, the clients will be cut off from the server and within minutes they will be unable to make calls. To ensure maximum reliability, each server will have a pair of Ethernet Network Interface Cards (NICs), and the network will maintain multiple hubs. If we lose a hub or even an Ethernet switch, a large portion of the network will continue to function. Because the client responsibility is distributed across an arbitrary series of client machines, we can lose part of the network and continue to make calls; we may make fewer calls per minute, but all scheduled jobs will continue to go out.

To ensure that we experience only infrequent failures of the calling client machines, Kevin chose Cubix rack mounted systems. Each system can contain up to 8 individual Pentium PC's. Every Cubix system chassis has a hot-swappable redundant power supply and remote management features that include monitoring system status, controlling the keyboard and monitor, and the ability to restart any CPU.

The Internet Server will start out on a single-CPU Pentium Pro 200 system from Data General. This system uses a somewhat less robust, but adequate RAID controller from Mylex. All disks are hot-swappable, including the system volume. There are three redundant power supplies, as well as redundant Ethernet NICs. If and when appropriate, this system can be upgraded to a full 'Cluster in a Box', identical to the database and call servers.

We have chosen to start with a highly reliable infrastructure. The system is extensible: as our needs expand, we can add to it. If performance becomes an issue, we can upgrade from 512MB to a full 2GB of RAM per server. If we need to add servers, we can do so. If Internet access becomes a larger part of our service, we can upgrade the IIS machine. Finally, if absolute reliability and redundancy become mandated, we can create mirror sites in other cities.

This system is designed to provide mission-critical life and death reliability. We've thrown all the hardware we can against that goal, so the greatest vulnerability remains in the software. To ensure absolute reliability of the software I decide to contract a series of design and code reviews.

Feature Cutting

I believe it is imperative to get the first version out the door. Once that is up and running, we will be able to roll out new releases very quickly. I encourage Jay to be ruthless in cutting features, and he takes me up on this idea by agreeing to drop call bridging from the first release. This is a major cutback: we will not be able to say things like, "To tell your senator how you feel, press 1." More troubling, if we need to switch the caller to customer service, we will have to give them the 800 number and ask them to call back. We will fix this in the very next release.

While we believe this is a critical feature, we *can* go to market with a viable product without it. Cutting it saves us the time of developing it, and also of testing it. Jay believes this will significantly shorten our development and testing time, and has decided to push it off until V2.

When cutting features, our guiding principal is to look for those features which are not essential and which will take noticeable time either to develop or to test. If we do cut features, we want to make sure that we really are saving significant development or testing time, so that it is worth the price of going to market without the feature.

Along the way, Jay has often talked about limiting his customers' ability to constrain their scheduling. As ever, he has an analogy: "When you go to the cleaners, you don't say, 'Start cleaning the trousers on Tuesday at 9 a.m. and do the shirts before you do the jacket.' You say, 'I'd like these by Wednesday.' "

To give us the greatest flexibility, and to simplify the coding for the first version, we agree that customers will only be able to assign a limited number of start times: 9 a.m., noon, 3 p.m. and 6 p.m. Similarly, they'll choose from a limited set of end times. Finally, for the first version, we will not schedule jobs across days. If a job is too big to be handled in one day, we'll treat it as an exception and pass it to customer service.

The final significant feature we have decided to drop as a result of this discussion is the ability to call back and hear the message you've missed. While this feature is very appealing, it is not essential for the very first release, and cutting it simplifies the remaining work. For now, if the person isn't home, we'll play the message to the answering machine. Again, we believe we can add this feature quite quickly once we're up and running.

Design and Code Reviews

One of the few problems with working in a very small development group is that the developer can become isolated. There is little opportunity for other developers to review and comment on his work, and so it is easy for him to dig a very big hole from which he can not easily escape.

Surprisingly, this can often be the case in large development organizations as well. In some companies, the etiquette is to avoid changing anyone else's code without their permission. In more extreme cases, it is considered rude even to *read* someone else's code!

To avoid this kind of intellectual myopia, and to ensure that my code is as reliable as possible, I want another developer to review both the design and the implementation. The ideal candidate will know object-oriented design inside and out, will be an expert in C++, and will be compulsive about details. I know just the person. Steve has all these characteristics, and the added advantage that he is already up to speed on the design goals.

There is a trade-off here, because someone who's new to the design might be more objective. However, I made sure to subject the overall design to repeated reviews along the way, and it's now time to dive into the code. The benefit I obtain from Steve being up to speed overwhelms any downside of his being 'too close' to the design.

We schedule a series of design reviews. He will spend half a day reading through the code before we begin. I'm eager to hear what he has to say.

Rebuilding the Flows

Steve and I meet to begin our design reviews in preparation for my internal testing. We start by examining the call flows. These are the essential user interface to the system; the call flows dictate the user experience and they are the centerpiece of our most important use cases.

We identify the following incoming flows:

- Preproduction. This is how the customer launches a job.
- Recording per-customer audio. Customers record audio that will be used in all their interactive calls (listed in the diagrams below as *Play a long intro message* and *Play a shorter intro message*). They also record audio once if their account is set as 'always use same audio'.
- Account set up (not in V1).
- Demo set up. This allows salesmen to call into the system and set up a demo, which they can then run for prospective customers. In the demo they will call in, interact with the system, and then ring every phone in the customer's office, playing their demonstration message. These are very effective.

In addition, there are three flows for outgoing audio:

- Crisis
- Non-interactive
- Interactive

Since we've eliminated bridged calls for now, these are the only outgoing flows. The non-interactive flow is quite simple:

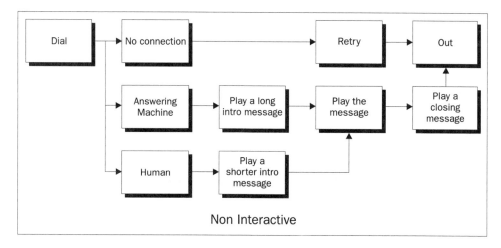

281

We dial the phone and connect either to an answering machine or to a human. The third path, shown at the top, is followed if we don't connect at all. If that happens, we handle the call according to the retry policy and recycle the port. If we connect to an answering machine, we play a standard ten-second message that's the same for all clients across all non-interactive calls. This is followed by the customer's message and then by our standard closing message, after which we hang up and recycle the port. Connecting to a human is the same, except that we play a shorter introduction.

Interactive calls are more complicated, because we need to ask for a button press. The recipient can press 1 to get the message, 2 to tell us to call back, 3 to ask us to wait for the correct person to come to the phone, or 4 to tell us we've reached a wrong number. Here is an excerpt of the flow chart:

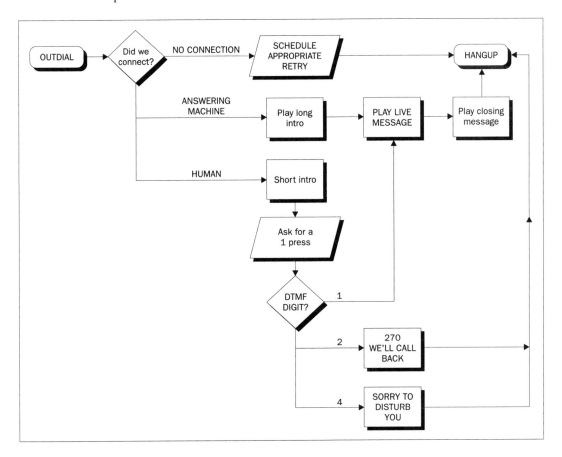

Calls passing through 'We'll call back' are marked for recall; those passing through 'Sorry to disturb you' are marked final and are not scheduled for recall. The recall schedule for 'We'll call back' is set by a policy, just like when to call back on a busy or no answer.

Preproduction Flows

Outgoing calls are pretty straightforward; preproduction is much more complicated. In essence, we only need to gather five pieces of information:

- Proper identification and authentication
- Which list do they want to call?
- Which flow do they want to use?
- When do they want to call?
- What do they want to say?

However, once we've factored in error checking and the sheer variety of customer requirements, preproduction is complex. Here are some excerpts from the flowcharts, the first of which shows an inbound call. We check to see if we know which number they were calling, and if it was the right number to enter a new job, we continue with this flow. Otherwise, we branch to another call flow.

Next, we ask for an account number, match the password, and make sure their account is authorized. We ask them to verify that we have matched the correct account ("This should be...") and then we are ready to begin processing their request. An excerpt of the logic appears overleaf.

From here, we go on to determine what phone list they want to use. We must check to see how many lists they have on file, and prompt them with the right request. Once we know what list they want to call, we recap their selection, reminding them of how many numbers are on that chosen list. The flowchart for this part of the interaction is on page 285.

After finding out what numbers they want to call, we must determine what flow the customer wants to use. Are the calls to be interactive or non-interactive? Is this a crisis or a routine job? All of this is encapsulated in the box that reads, "What kind of call are they making?" We're still ambivalent about how we'll determine this: will we ask them, or will it be decided by what kind of account they have? The issue is still being debated.

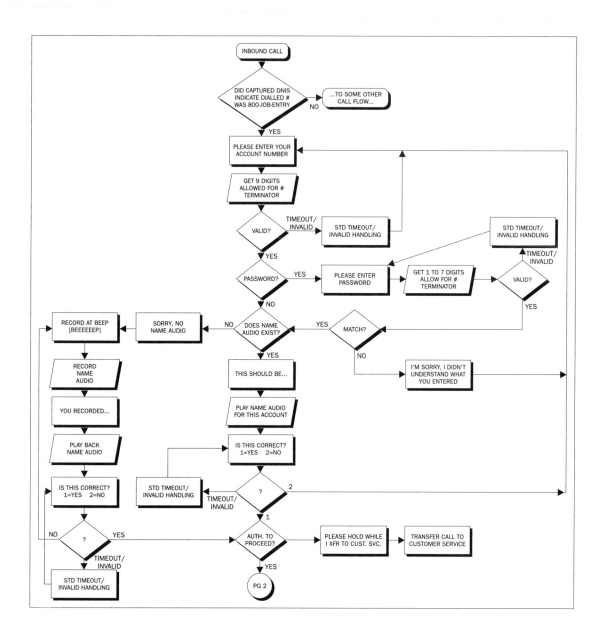

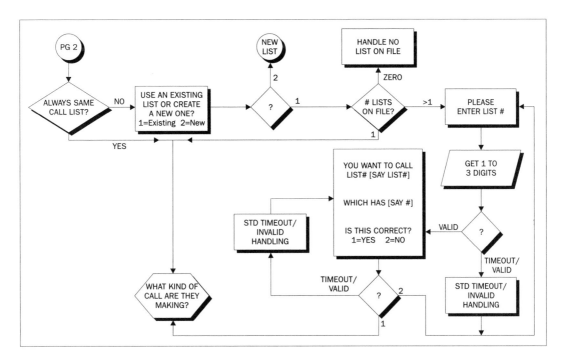

Depending on the flow they are using, we may allow the customer to schedule the call as either back-tilted or front-tilted. Part of the logic for scheduling a front-tilted job is shown on the next page. They must tell us the starting date and then pick a starting time. Note that this flow chart reflects our decision to offer only a limited set of start-time options. Once they've picked a start time, they can pick a time by which we must complete their calls. We then review their choices and ask them to confirm their requests.

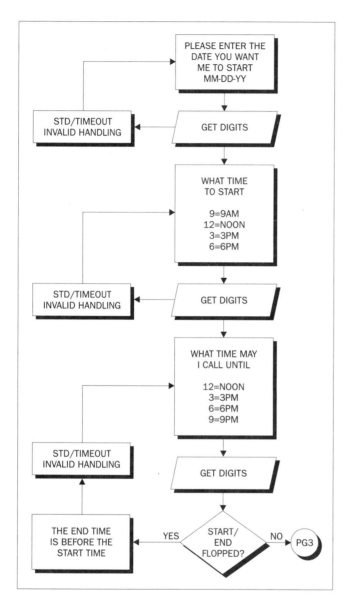

From here, we determine whether they are calling more than one time zone, and if they are, we ask if they want us to take time zones into account when calling. That is, if they've asked us to begin calling at 9 a.m., and we are calling the West Coast, ought we to call at 9 a.m. *Eastern* Time or 9 a.m. *Pacific* Time?

Once we know when to call, we need to know what to *say*. Once again, we check to see if they already have audio recorded, and if so which audio they'd like to use. In this case, they also have the opportunity to record new audio. Finally, we recap their request and then create the job and the calls.

Implementing the Flows

The implementation follows the flowcharts. While the logic remains linear, sequential and procedural, we use objects to effect the implementation. Each flowchart is implemented in a series of member functions of a class derived from **CScript**. The preproduction flow, for instance, is implemented in **CPreProduction**. Any work that will be shared among these objects is factored out into the base class.

For example, when the customer calls into the preproduction system, we answer the phone and ask them for their social security number (which doubles as their account number). We look up the number in the database, and if there is a password, we ask for that and see if there is a match. If so, we check in the database whether they are authorized to launch a job. Here's an excerpt of that code:

```
bool CScript::CustomerLogin(CCaller* pCaller, CCustomerRecordSet& crs,
                                                      int whichLogin)
{
    // Code detail removed...

        PlayString(pCaller, stringToPlay);

        if(!GetDigits(pCaller, AccountNumber, 9))
            continue;

        CString prompt;
        prompt.Format("CustomerID = \'%s\'", AccountNumber);
        crs.m_strFilter = prompt;

        if (crs.IsOpen())
            crs.Requery();
        else
            crs.Open();

        crs.m_Password.TrimRight();
        if (crs.m_Password.IsEmpty() && !crs.m_CustomerID.IsEmpty())
            break;

        // Please enter your password
        Play(pCaller, "demo indexed file.vap", DEMO_ENTER_PASSWORD);
        if(!GetDigits(pCaller, Password, 7))
            continue;

        // Test password and account number together
        if(!crs.IsEOF() && Password == crs.m_Password)
            break;

    // Code detail removed...

    if(VerifyLogin(pCaller, AccountNumber, ACCOUNT_NAME))
    {
        result = true;
        break;
    }
```

```
    // Error handling detail removed...

    return result;
}
```

As you can see, even leaving out some of the detail, there is no little complexity in playing the messages, gathering the digits, checking the validity, handling timeouts, and verifying the login.

Once the customer *is* logged in, we are ready to process his request. This logic is summarized in three function calls:

```
nWhichList = GetWhichList(pCaller, crs.m_CustomerID, alwaysSameList);
GetWhenToCall(pCaller, crs.m_CustomerID, alwaysCallNow, start, end,
                        divideByTimeZones, nWhichTilt, nIsCrisis);
GetWhichAudio(pCaller, crs.m_CustomerID, alwaysSameAudio, nWhichAudio,
                                            nAudioDuration);
```

Again, there's a lot of detail left out, but the essential logic is readily understandable. We start by calling **GetWhichList()**, passing in the caller object that's handling this incoming call, the customer's ID, and a Boolean value that's set by looking up the customer in the database to determine if he always calls the same list.

Similarly, we call **GetWhenToCall()**, passing in the caller, the customer's ID, whether the customer always calls immediately, and a number of parameters that will be filled by the function, including the start and end times, the tilt, and so forth. Finally, **GetWhichAudio()** determines which of the customer's prerecorded audio files he wishes to use, or whether he wants to record new audio.

GetWhichList() looks up the customer's account to see how many lists already exist. It then plays a message to the customer saying, "You have [n] lists. Which list would you like to use?" The customer enters the number and we validate it. Then we say, "You asked to use list [x] which has [y] phone numbers. If this is the correct list, press 1, otherwise press 2." And so on.

```
        for (;;)
        {
            // You want to call list # which has numbers on it.
            CString listReview;
            listReview.Format( "%s|I|%d,%d|NUMBER|0,%s|I|%d,%d|NUMBER|0,%s|I|%d",
                        plm,
                        PHONE_YOU_WANT_TO_CALL,
                        listChosen,
                        plm,
                        PHONE_WHICH_HAS,
                        sizeOfList,
                        plm,
                        PHONE_CORRECT_LIST );
```

```
            PlayString(pCaller, listReview);
            int myArray[2] = { 1,2 };

            if(!GetDigits(pCaller, digits, 1, myArray, 2))
               continue;

            break;
        }

        int okay = atoi(digits);
        if (okay == 1)
        {
            retVal = clrs.m_ListID;
            break;
        }
        else
            continue;
```

We continue on, gathering the information as we go, with the structure of the code closely following the logic as found in the flowcharts.

Reusability

To facilitate building reusable scripts, I develop certain routines that are owned by the base class, and utilized by the derived classes. For example, we need to ask the user to enter numbers in a variety of different circumstances. Sometimes we want to ask them to enter a known number of digits (e.g. "Enter 1 for the first option, 2 for the second."). Other times, we don't know how many digits there will be in the number ("For 12 noon, enter 12, for 3 p.m. enter 3, for 6 p.m. enter 6"). In this latter example, we may get a 12, a 3 or a 6. We don't know how many digits will be entered, but we *do* know the valid possibilities. Other times, we only know the maximum number of digits we can accept.

The **GetDigits()** method I added to **CScript** takes 5 arguments, three of which have default values. The first argument is a pointer to the caller that's interacting with the user. The second parameter is a **CString**, into which we'll put the user's response. Parameter three is the maximum number of digits we'll accept, while the fourth parameter is an array of integers. If we know the valid digits to check for, they are put into this array before **GetDigits()** is called. The final parameter tells the method how many values you've passed in the array. Thus, if you wanted to ask the customer to enter 3, 6, 9 or 12, you would code:

```
    for (;;)
    {
        // What time to start?
        Play(pCaller, sm, SCHED_WHEN_TO_START);
        int intArray[4] = { 3, 6, 9, 12 };
        if(GetDigits(pCaller, startBuff, 2, intArray, 4))
            break;
    }
```

This initializes **intArray** with four possible values, and passes the array in as the fourth parameter, and the number 4 (the size of the array) as the final value.

GetDigits() examines the value the customer enters and looks for an exact match in the array. Failing that, it calls **BeginsWith()**, which walks the array looking for a value that *begins* with the number received. Thus, if the user enters 5, we reject it because that can't be a valid value. If he enters 1, however, we keep going, hoping the next number will be a 2.

Finishing Preproduction

Once we determine what audio the customer wants to use, and what phone list, and when he wants to call, we're ready to recap. Assuming we have it right, we pass the request to **CreateTheJobs()**:

```
CreateTheJobs( pCaller,           crs.m_CustomerID,    nWhichList,
               nWhichAudio,        nAudioDuration,      nWhatPriority,
               nWhichRetryPolicy,  nWhichScript,        start,
               end,                nWhatThrottle,       nWhichTilt,
               divideByTimeZones,  nIsCrisis );
```

This method is responsible for creating the job in the database and then seeing if there is room in the schedule to accommodate this job. Before adding the job to the database, **CreateTheJobs()** checks to see if **divideByTimeZones** is true; if so it must break the job up into sub-jobs, setting the parent job ID to the original job number. It will then assign the job to the database based on the time zones we support. The phone list has a time zone field, so we can get the count of how many numbers we need to call in each time zone.

Once the job is in place, we call **IsThereRoom()**, which picks apart all the hours the job will run, and checks to ensure that there are enough resources to handle this job's minima, along with all the minima of all the other jobs we've already accepted.

If the job (or any of the sub-jobs) is rejected because there is not enough room, the job is left in the database, but a flag is set that the job has been rejected, and no calls are added to the database. The customer is passed to customer service to resolve the problem.

If the job is not rejected, **CreateCalls()** is called. This function runs in its own thread, reads the phone list and the job record, and makes call records in the call table for everyone who must be called during this job.

Designing the Interprocess Communication

At its heart, the calling software is a client/server application with a database back end. Until now, most of the interprocess communication has been mediated by the database. When the client needs to get phone numbers from the server, the server puts the numbers into the queue table in the database using ODBC, and the client in turn uses ODBC to get them out.

Nevertheless, there are still a few places where the client needs to talk to the server directly, most notably to handle a crisis. Here's what we want to have happen:

- The client receives a request for a crisis from a customer
- The client adds the job to the database
- The client notifies the server, "There is a crisis."
- The server immediately dumps its queue and rebuilds it with the calls for the crisis.
- The server notifies all the calling machines (clients) that there is a crisis
- The calling machines dump their local queues and refill, thereby getting the *Crisis•Calls*

In support of this, we want each client to 'register' itself with the server, saying in essence, "Let me know when there's a crisis." This follows the **observer** pattern as described in *Design Patterns*, and as discussed in Chapter 4. Note that each client is responsible for registering itself. Here, as elsewhere in the code, there is no omniscient managing class; responsibility is encapsulated in the client object.

Implementing this design on a Windows NT platform requires a protocol for interprocess communication. The obvious answer is COM.

The Philosophy of COM

COM is an integral part of Microsoft's strategic planning for the future. It provides a number of critical services and techniques, only one of which is to manage interprocess communication within a given machine. Using DCOM, this communication can be extended across the network, and ultimately across the Internet.

The goal of COM is to provide a *binary* standard for how objects communicate. The essence of this binary standard is that you can write COM objects in any programming language, and they are able to communicate with one another. This is a significant attempt by Microsoft to separate interface from implementation. Once you define a COM interface, you can implement it in (almost) any language you want. Initially, the implementation language of choice was C, but this has quickly migrated to C++ and Visual Basic.

291

There are a number of excellent books on COM and ActiveX, including *Professional DCOM* by Richard Grimes, *Professional ActiveX/COM Control Programming* by Li and Economopoulos, and *Inside COM* by Dale Rogerson. Each of these is prepared to take you through, in some detail, what it takes to write a COM application. In addition, Microsoft supplies not one, but two sets of tools for building COM applications: there are the Wizards for MFC, and there's the Active Template Library, with its own Wizards. The problem for me is that all of this is rather complex, and I want to do something fairly simple: I want one executable to be able to send messages to another across the network.

A Road Map and a Guide

To get me through the thicket of COM technology, what I need is someone to show me the shortest path. Here was my experience: I had read the first few chapters of half a dozen books on COM. I understood the underlying technology, but I still didn't get how to actually make two programs talk to each other. Something was missing in my understanding, and I was out of time: I needed this to work *right now*.

I spoke with Steve about this, and he proposed that we strip down the requirements to the bare bones of what we need, and then write it directly in C++, setting aside the macros and Wizards, which only hide the necessary workings of the system. Once again I suggested to Jay that an effective way to short-circuit the schedule would be to purchase expertise where we can. We agreed to buy up to three days of Steve's time to get this working. Steve and I started by designing, in detail, what we wanted to have happen.

Levels of Abstraction

When I teach C++ or the MFC, I am invariably asked for a cookbook. "Can't you just tell me, step by step, what I'm supposed to do?" I always answer the same way, "I understand why you want this, but here's why I don't provide a cookbook. If I tell you step by step, then you'll follow the steps, and the first time you want to do something different you'll be lost. If you set aside the procedures and the syntax, and focus instead on the underlying concepts, you'll be much better off." It's like the old proverb: "Give a man a fish and feed him for a day. Teach him how to fish and feed him for a lifetime."

Great theory. Once we got into COM, I was horrified to hear myself asking, "Can't you just tell me, step by step, what I'm supposed to do?" My concern about the complexity of the implementation was in the way of my understanding how to design my classes.

When you program, you're constantly moving among many levels of abstraction. COM adds a few more levels: there's the object and its interface, and then there's the implementation of the object, and the implementation of the interface. The relationship between the C++ classes and the COM objects and interfaces *need not be one to one*. Further, there are any number of ways to implement COM objects and interfaces, and the choice of implementation technique must be divorced from the overall design.

Implementing the IPC in COM

The server must provide two sets of services: those associated with the observer pattern, and those associated with handling a crisis. These cry out for two interfaces. An interface, to a COM programmer, is nothing more than a suite of related methods and the protocol for their use.

We agree that the server will present an interface to support the observer pattern. We call this interface **ICrisisRegistrar**. To create an interface in C++ we used an **abstract base class** — that is, a class with one or more pure virtual functions. Here's the C++ class that corresponds to **ICrisisRegistrar**:

```
interface ICrisisRegistrar : public IUnknown
{
public:
    virtual HRESULT __stdcall RegisterCrisisHandler(ICrisisHandler*,
                                        const IID& iid,
                                        void** ppInterface ) = 0;
    virtual HRESULT __stdcall RevokeCrisisHandler(ICrisisHandler*) = 0;
};
```

The keyword **interface** is defined to be a **struct** in **Objbase.h** (provided as part of the COM library). **struct**s are *exactly* the same as classes in C++ with two exceptions: inheritance is public by default (rather than private as in classes), and visibility is public by default (again, rather than private). Since I explicitly declare the inheritance to be public:

```
interface ICrisisRegistrar : public IUnknown
```

And I explicitly declare the access to be public:

```
{
public:
```

There is no difference at all. By convention, I use **struct**s when I intend to have nothing but a public interface (in the C++ sense); but this is purely convention. In any case, I always use **public** or **private** in my classes (and structures), as it is thereby self-documenting. This is even more important when using an alias such as **interface**, because Microsoft is always free to change this from **struct** to **class** and back.

Because both the methods of **ICrisisRegistrar** are pure virtual, this interface is abstract, which is precisely what we require. COM defines an interface to be a set of capabilities for the class (that is, a set of methods) manifested in a structure that is exactly equivalent to the virtual function tables that Microsoft's Visual C++ compiler produces (see Microsoft's Object Layout Specification).

ICrisisRegistrar offers two methods, the first of which is
RegisterCrisisHandler(). This method's purpose is to allow a client to register itself
for notification. The server needs to be able to call the registered client when there is a
crisis, so the client must pass *in* an interface pointer. The client passes in a pointer to an
ICrisisHandler interface, which the server will cache and use when it needs to notify
this client that there is a crisis.

ICrisisRegistrar will return an **HRESULT** to let the client know that it has
successfully registered, or that it has failed. This follows the convention that all COM
methods must return **HRESULT**s; they allow the COM subsystem to return an error code if
some part of the method call fails. If the client needs to revoke its registration — if the
client is shutting down, for example — it will call **RevokeCrisisHandler()**, and pass in
the same **ICrisisHandler** pointer it sent in to register. The server will use the pointer
as a key into the cache of **ICrisisHandler** pointers it will hold, so that it can remove
the correct one.

This works because interface pointers are unique, and so we don't need to add an
additional registration handle to differentiate among them. We can use the interface
pointer itself as a value to search for in the set.

The **ICrisisHandler** interface is itself as simple as an interface can be, consisting of a
single method to be called to notify the object that implements the interface that a crisis
has occurred:

```
interface ICrisisHandler : public IUnknown
{
public:
   virtual HRESULT __stdcall OnCrisis() = 0;
};
```

Getting Back an Interface

Not only must the client register with the server, but it must also be able to *contact* the
server when there is a crisis. This is the implementation of our design for crisis handling:
when a client receives a crisis job, it notifies the server, which in turn notifies all the
clients. For the client to notify the server, it will need to get a pointer to the
ICrisisHandler interface on the server — the very same interface as we have on the
client. We are reusing our design, and this reduces the complexity of the overall system.

The client *could* hang on to the **ICrisisRegistrar** pointer, and call
QueryInterface() on that interface to get the server's **ICrisisHandler** pointer when
it needs it, but at that point speed will be critical, and that's a bad time to start asking
for interface pointers across the network. Therefore, we want to get this interface when
we register, and cache it so we have it available when we need it.

This turns out to be quite efficient, because the client is already going across the network to register. We can piggy back on the registration with a request for **ICrisisRegistrar**, thus making only one round trip across the network.

RegisterCrisisHandler() takes two parameters in addition to the **ICrisisHandler** pointer. They're the same as the parameters you would find in calls to **QueryInterface()**, and they work in *exactly* the same way. When the client uses the **ICrisisRegistrar** interface to register, it asks for an additional interface; in the current design it always asks for **ICrisisHandler**. We've designed for future expansion at little additional development effort: despite this code, the client is quite free to ask for *any* interface the server supports.

Here's how it works. The client asks the server for **ICrisisRegistrar** (we'll cover how it does this in a little while). It uses that interface's **RegisterCrisisHandler()** method to register itself, passing in its own **ICrisisHandler** interface pointer. At the same time, it requests the *server's* **ICrisisHandler** interface pointer, which the client then caches to use when a crisis job comes in from a customer.

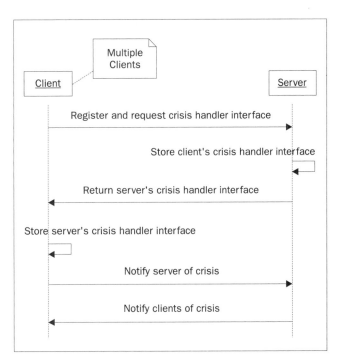

This technique of making a call that takes an action and also requests an interface pointer is a common idiom in COM. It is very efficient, and reduces traffic across the process boundary and across the network.

A Word on Naming Interfaces

We spend quite a bit of time talking about what to name the interfaces. The name will strongly influence how we think about the object and its interface; do we name the interface for its capabilities or for its role? If the former, then we'd have names like **IRegister** and **IHandleCrisis**. If the latter, then we get names like the ones we've used: **ICrisisRegistrar** and **ICrisisHandler**.

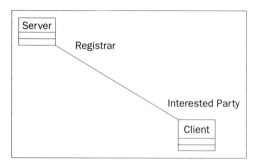

The interface is *not* the object. An object *presents* one or more interfaces. If you draw an object diagram, the interface is not a rectangle; it is the line between two rectangles. In a UML diagram, this line is labeled by the role the object plays in the relationship.

In this diagram, it is easy to see that 'Server' and 'Client' are objects, and 'Registrar' and 'Interested Party' are the roles played by the respective objects, so each of these roles would make good candidate interfaces.

How Does the Server Become a COM Object?

What does it mean for the server to present a COM interface? In the C++ code, there is no server object. The server is the executable running the scheduler. The entity that best represents the server itself is either the application object or the document, depending on your perspective. It is more convenient, and arguably a better conceptual fit, to use the document. The job of the document in this application is to encapsulate policy and state; this is a good place to manage the relationship with other objects.

This design is really a compromise with MFC. In fact, Steve has suggested that we create a Server object, and house that object in the document — the document would become nothing but an empty shell for the Server. The advantage would be that were we to decide to get rid of MFC, it would be cleaner and more obvious how to proceed. While I think this suggestion has a lot of merit, I'm comfortable leaving the document as is for now, and returning to this question once the product is up and running.

To make the server into a COM object, it must initialize the COM library. This is done in the **CCallServerApp**'s **InitInstance()** method, to ensure that the COM library is initialized each time the application starts up. Since this is an MFC application, we will let MFC manage the initialization.

```
if (!AfxOleInit())
{
    AfxMessageBox(IDP_OLE_INIT_FAILED);
    return FALSE;
}
```

The MFC and AppWizard provide a lot of support for COM, but because I'm adding the support later in the project, I must add many of these lines by hand.

We use OLE initialization because this application is written using MFC, and this is what MFC requires. The action on failure is to pop up a message box and exit the application. In time, we'll need to bring this in line with our failure notification routines. Once the COM library is initialized, the document is ready to register itself as a COM object. It does this in the constructor:

```
HRESULT hr = CoRegisterClassObject(
        CLSID_CallServer,      // Class identifier (CLSID) to be registered
        this,                  // Pointer to the class object
        CLSCTX_SERVER,         // Context for running executable code
        REGCLS_MULTIPLEUSE,    // How to connect to the class object
        &m_ClassObjectRegistration // Pointer to the value returned
                            );

if (FAILED(hr))
{
   AfxMessageBox(IDP_CLASS_OBJECT_REGISTRATION_FAILED);
   throw (new COleException);
}
```

As a COM object, the document must now inherit from **IUnknown**. You will read in many MFC books that MFC does not support multiple inheritance. What is really meant is that no object can inherit from more than one *MFC* class; it is perfectly safe to inherit from an MFC class and any number of other classes, so long as these other classes are not in the MFC inheritance hierarchy:

```
class CCallServerDoc : public CDocument, public IUnknown
{
// Attributes
public:

   HRESULT   __stdcall   QueryInterface   (const CLSID&, void**);
   ULONG     __stdcall   AddRef           ();
   ULONG     __stdcall   Release          ();
```

Class Objects

In the general case, when a client wants to create a COM object, it starts by creating the object's **class factory**, then asking it to create the object it really wants. This is accomplished by calling **CoGetClassObject()**, passing in the class ID of the class you want, along with the interface ID you are requesting (most commonly **IClassFactory**), and also a pointer to a pointer to an interface. **CoGetClassObject()** will then return the pointer to **IClassFactory** in your pointer to a pointer to an interface.

Once you have a pointer to the factory's **IClassFactory**, you can call **CreateInstance()** through that pointer, passing in the interface ID of the interface for which you want a pointer, and a pointer to a pointer to the interface, which

CreateInstance() will fill. You may do this repeatedly until you have all the interfaces you need. At that stage, you must be prepared to initialize the newly created object, if necessary, before using any of the interfaces you've received.

An alternative, and perhaps even more popular, route is to call **CoCreateInstance()**, passing the CLSID of the object you want to create and the IID of the interface you want returned. This hides the call to the class factory object, and is quick and efficient if you want only one interface from the class object.

In our case, we want to support the singleton design pattern — that is, no matter how often the class factory is asked, it will always return pointers to interfaces on the very same call server object. Because of this, we can merge the call server and its class factory into a single object (since the class factory is a singleton), which we implement in the call server document object. Thus, the client never asks for **IClassFactory**, but rather asks immediately for **ICrisisRegistrar**. As described above, the client then uses **ICrisisRegistrar** to obtain **ICrisisHandler**. While this will work, we may be asking for trouble down the road. If we want to interact with objects built in VB or Java, they will expect to create objects using **CoCreateInstance()**. We'll revisit this in the next release, and perhaps break out a class factory object after all.

Implementing Crisis Management

The server provides two interfaces: **ICrisisRegistrar** and **ICrisisHandler**. These may be implemented in any number of ways; we chose to implement them by deriving a concrete class, **CCrisisManager** from *both* interfaces:

```
class CCrisisManager : public ICrisisHandler, public ICrisisRegistrar
{
public:
   CCrisisManager          (CCallServerDoc& doc);
   virtual ~CCrisisManager();

   // Methods for IUnknown
   HRESULT __stdcall       QueryInterface          (const IID&, void**);
   ULONG __stdcall         AddRef                  ();
   ULONG __stdcall         Release                 ();

   // Methods for ICrisisHandler
   HRESULT __stdcall       OnCrisis                ();

   // Internal helper method
   void                    NotifyAllHandlers       ();

   // Methods for ICrisisRegistrar
   HRESULT __stdcall       RegisterCrisisHandler   (ICrisisHandler*,
                                                    const IID& iid,
                                                    void** ppInterface);
   HRESULT __stdcall       RevokeCrisisHandler     (ICrisisHandler*);
```

```
private:
    CCallServerDoc&         m_doc;
    static UINT             ImplementNotifyAllHandlers(LPVOID pMe);
    CCrisisHandlerSet       m_registeredHandlers;
};
```

Note that this class implements **IUnknown**, which it must do because both
ICrisisHandler and **ICrisisRegistrar** derive from it. The class also provides an
implementation of the pure virtual functions **RegisterCrisisHandler()**,
RevokeCrisisHandler() and **OnCrisis()**. The first two of these are from
ICrisisRegistrar, and the last is from **ICrisisHandler**.

This class is also responsible for managing the list of **ICrisisHandler** interface pointers
supplied by the clients. How should it store these? What we need is a set, and the
collection that comes closest to our needs in the MFC framework is a **map**. A map allows
you to store a value (the **ICrisisHandler** pointer) with a key. The key is used to 'look
up' the requested value.

In an array, the key is an integer, and the value is whatever you store in the array. In a
typical map, the key and the value are quite different. What we want is a set whose key is
also its value, so that, when asked to revoke an interface's registration, we can easily find
and remove the correct one.

We decide to create our own simple class, **CCrisisHandlerSet**, which will provide the
methods we need in the form we expect. This class will be implemented *in terms of* the
map through private inheritance. That is, it will inherit implementation, but not interface:

```
class CCrisisHandlerSet : private CMapPtrToPtr
{
public:
    CMapPtrToPtr::RemoveAll();
    CCrisisHandlerSet();
    ~CCrisisHandlerSet();

    // Add a new handler
    void Add(ICrisisHandler* newHandler)
        { SetAt( newHandler, newHandler ); }
    bool Remove(ICrisisHandler* handler)
        { return ( RemoveKey(handler) ? true : false ); }
    void NotifyAllCrisisHandlers();

public:
};
```

Note that this class provides only three methods in addition to its constructor and
destructor. **Add()** takes a pointer to an **ICrisisHandler** interface. It implements the
Add() method by creating a wrapper around the **SetAt()** method it inherits. In this
case it will use the **ICrisisHandler** pointer as both the key *and* the value.

Similarly, **Remove()** wraps the **RemoveKey()** method of the base class. Since the base class method returns a **UINT**, which is a **typedef** of an **int**, and we want to return a Boolean, we convert the returned value on the way out.

CCrisisHandlerSet also makes the **RemoveAll()** method public. The problem is that private inheritance hides all the base class methods. In this case, we have no need to override the method, so we simply move its declaration into the public section, thus 'publishing' it.

Finally, **CCrisisHandlerSet** provides **NotifyAllHandlers()**. This method will be used by the **ICrisisHandler** interface. It does its work by walking the map, calling **OnCrisis()** on each of the **ICrisisHandler** interfaces it is holding:

```
void CCrisisHandlerSet::NotifyAllHandlers()
{
    // Iterating all (key, value) pairs
    POSITION pos = GetStartPosition();
    void* pHandler;
    while ( pos )
    {
        GetNextAssoc(pos, pHandler, pHandler);
        HRESULT hr = ((ICrisisHandler*) pHandler)->OnCrisis();
    }
}
```

This is a classic example of 'implemented in terms of'. The **CCrisisHandlerSet** inherits the **GetStartPosition()** and **GetNextAssoc()** methods, and can use them without presenting them as part of its own interface.

GetStartPosition() initializes the **POSITION** object to the first record. Like all MFC iterators, **GetNextAssoc()** returns the *current* object and repositions **pos** to the *next* object. In this case, **GetNextAssoc()** returns the current key and value pair in the two pointers it takes as its second and third parameters.

The **NotifyAllCrisisHandlers()** method neatly encapsulates the responsibility of walking the list and calling **OnCrisis()** on each method. Creating a method that walks the list and calls a method on each object found can easily be generalized through the **visitor** pattern as described in *Design Patterns*. Typically, you'd implement the visitor pattern by creating a visitor object. If we had done this, **NotifyAllCrisisHandlers()** would have been renamed and rewritten to take a visitor object, or an object of a class derived from it.

When the client registers with the server, **CCrisisManager**'s **RegisterCrisisHandler()** method is invoked. As I said, this takes three parameters. The first will be a pointer to the client's **ICrisisHandler** interface. The second will be an interface ID, which we currently expect will be **IID_ICrisisHandler**, and the third parameter is a pointer to a pointer to **void**, into which we'll put a pointer to the server's own **ICrisisHandler**.

Here, we *will* generalize the solution, as the pattern for doing so is both well understood and inexpensive. We'll follow the pattern established by **IUnknown**'s **QueryInterface()** method. That means we'll accept as our parameters *any* interface ID and a pointer to pointer to **void**, to pass back the unidentified interface pointer:

```
HRESULT __stdcall CCrisisManager::RegisterCrisisHandler(
                                        ICrisisHandler* pHandler,
                                        const IID& iid,
                                        void** ppInterface)
{
    HRESULT result = S_OK;
    if ( pHandler )
    {
        try
        {
            m_registeredHandlers.Add(pHandler);
        }
        catch ( CMemoryException e )
        {
            result = E_FAIL;
        }
    }
    if ( SUCCEEDED( result ) )
    {
        result = QueryInterface(iid, ppInterface);
        if ( FAILED ( result ) )
        {
            RevokeCrisisHandler(pHandler);
        }
    }
    return result;
}
```

The first thing you'll notice is that registration is a two step process. If the client has passed in a handler, we try to add it to our map of handlers. The map object throws a memory exception if there is no room in the map, so we must be prepared to catch that.

> **Note that exceptions will not cross the process boundary, so we must catch and handle the exception here.**

Assuming we have a handler and it was added successfully, then we are ready to try to return the interface pointer they requested. We delegate this responsibility to **QueryInterface()**. If **QueryInterface()** fails (perhaps because they've asked for an interface we don't support), we must be certain to revoke the registration before returning.

Revocation of the registration, whether because registration failed or because the client has requested it, is quite simple:

```
HRESULT __stdcall CCrisisManager::RevokeCrisisHandler(ICrisisHandler* pHandler)
{
   m_registeredHandlers.Remove(pHandler);
   return S_OK;
}
```

Managing Reference Counts

The COM standard says that COM objects should unload when they are no longer in use. COM objects determine whether they are in use by maintaining internal reference counts. When the reference count on an object falls to zero, the object should unload itself (or allow itself to be unloaded).

Our implementation does not manage reference counts for the class objects, as they are implemented in the document objects of our application, and won't be unloaded until the program exits. The same can't be said for the proxy and stub objects that will handle the interprocess communication. It is imperative that their reference counts are managed properly and this is handled by the proxy-stub code.

Here is the protocol: if an object asks for an interface on another object, typically using **QueryInterface()**, the server will increment the reference count. When the client is done with the interface, it must call **Release()**. If a server offers an interface, then the accepting client must explicitly call **AddRef()** on that interface before using it, and **Release()** when it has finished.

Once the interface has been added to the collection of observers, its reference count must be incremented. When the interface is revoked, it will be removed from the server's collection, and at that point the reference count must be decremented:

```
void CCrisisHandlerSet::Add(ICrisisHandler* newHandler)
{
   SetAt(newHandler, newHandler);
   newHandler->AddRef();   // Only adds if SetAt() doesn't throw memory exception
}

bool CCrisisHandlerSet::Remove(ICrisisHandler* handler)
{
   bool removed = RemoveKey(handler) ? true : false;
   if ( removed )
      handler->Release();
   return removed;
}
```

Note that **SetAt()** will throw an exception if it fails, so we will never get to the **AddRef()** statement. On the other hand, **RemoveKey()** indirectly returns a Boolean value indicating whether the key was found, and thus, if we successfully remove the handler, we must be sure to call **Release()** on it.

This neatly encapsulates the reference counting and eliminates the concern that we may have to back out of a registration. By the previous logic, if we add the handler to the collection, we know we were able to register it and return the interface pointer that the client requested.

Handling a Crisis

Once the client has registered itself, if all has gone well, the client has a pointer to the server's **ICrisisHandler** interface, and the server has a map of pointers to **ICrisisHandler** interfaces on the clients.

As you saw earlier, the preproduction flow ends in the creation of a job and the creation and insertion of call records into the database. What we require is that once this completes, the calling machine will notify the server. The server must dump its queue, refill with the new jobs, and when that completes, notify the clients. The sequencing and timing is important, and we can't rely on simple **Sleep()** statements to get it right.

The Client

The client adds the new calls to the database in **CPreProduction::CreateCalls()**. This is a thread function, which means it operates independently of the calling machine's other threads. When this function is done, and just before it returns and ends the thread, it must inform the server that it has added a crisis. To understand how it does this, we need to take a quick look at the **CreateCalls()** method. The signature is this:

```
static UINT   CPreProduction::CreateCalls   (LPVOID ptheArgs)
```

All thread functions must return **UINT**, and accept either no parameters or a single 4-byte parameter cast to 'pointer to **void**'. In this case, however, I need to pass in three pieces of information: the filter string that will be used to select call records, as well as a pointer to the caller, and a Boolean indicating whether or not this is a crisis. It needs the pointer to the caller so that it can call methods of **CPreProduction**.

CreateCalls() is a method of **CPreProduction**, but because it is static, it has no **this** pointer and thus can't access other member methods. By passing in the **this** pointer, we can then use it to call other member methods explicitly.

The problem is that you can't pass three parameters into a thread function; you can only pass one. I create a small object named **CreateCallArgs**, which will hold these three arguments. Since the only object that will use this **CreateCallArgs** structure is the **CPreProduction** object, I declare the **CreateCallArgs** within the public section of **CPreProduction** itself:

```
struct CreateCallArgs
{
public:
    CreateCallArgs(CCaller& caller, CString& promptString, bool isCrisis) :
                                        m_caller(caller),
                                        m_promptString(promptString),
                                        m_isCrisis(isCrisis){}

    ~CreateCallArgs(){}
    CCaller& m_caller;
    CString& m_promptString;
    bool m_isCrisis;
};
```

Note that I use the keyword **struct** as a shorthand reminder to myself that this object has only a public interface and no private implementation. The constructor initializes the member variables, the destructor does nothing, and is really included only to show that it has nothing to do.

In a structure (as well as in a class), we want to pass the arguments to the constructor, rather than instantiating the object and then assigning the variables. It is the job of the constructor to create the **struct** or the class; to create a valid object. Avoid the mistake of creating an invalid object that you later intend to initialize. That is what constructors are for.

Having passed these arguments into **CreateCalls()**, I can test the **m_isCrisis** member, and if it is **true**, then I can invoke the **OnCrisis()** method in the caller by way of the **m_caller** member of the **theArgs** object I passed into **CreateCalls()**:

```
UINT CPreProduction::CreateCalls(LPVOID ptheArgs)
{
    CreateCallArgs* pArgs = (CreateCallArgs*) ptheArgs;
    CString& filter = pArgs->m_promptString;

    // ...create the calls

    if ( pArgs->m_isCrisis )
        pArgs->m_caller.OnCrisis();
}
```

The first thing I must do is cast the **ptheArgs** pointer from an **LPVOID** back to its real type: 'pointer to **CreateCallArgs**'. I can then extract the filter for the **CRecordset**. After the calls have been created, I test the member **m_isCrisis**. If it's **true**, I invoke **OnCrisis()** on the **CCaller** object passed by reference in the **CreateCallArgs** structure.

CCaller's **OnCrisis()** method calls the document's **OnCrisis()** method. This is reasonable, since the caller knows only to pass responsibility for handling the crisis on to the document. The document is the keeper of the policy, and it knows that in a crisis it must notify the server. Thus, **CCallClientDoc**'s **OnCrisis()** method might look like this:

```
void CCallClientDoc::OnCrisis()
{
    m_CrisisHandler.NotifyCrisisCoordinator();
}
```

The document knows that when its **OnCrisis()** method is called, the client has been handed a crisis and it must notify the server. It wants to do this by delegating responsibility to its **CCrisisHandler** object, which corresponds nicely to the **CCrisisManager** object on the server.

The problem is that this call is originating in the caller's thread, but the interface was originated in the main thread of the application. COM supports two threading models: free threading and the apartment model. MFC, unfortunately, only supports COM using the apartment model. This means that you can't directly use an interface pointer from any thread other than the one in which you received it. If you try, the interface pointer will be invalid and you'll cause an access violation.

There are two solutions to this problem. We can marshal the interface pointer across the threads or we can post a message across threads. We decide to get it working in two stages, first by posting the message, later by marshaling the interface. In the long run, marshaling will be a better solution, but posting will get us up and running right away.

Once again, the goal is to notify the main application thread to call the **CCrisisHandler**'s **NotifyCrisisCoordinator()** function. We do this by having the document get the application and call a method in the application, **OnCrisis()**, which in turn will *post a message* to the main thread. The new version of **OnCrisis()** looks like this:

```
void CCallClientApp::OnCrisis()
{
    PostThreadMessage( WM_NOTIFY_CRISIS_COORDINATOR, 0, 0 );
}
```

This message will be picked up in the application's message handler:

```
ON_THREAD_MESSAGE(WM_NOTIFY_CRISIS_COORDINATOR,
                             CCallClientApp::OnNotifyCrisisCoordinator)
```

This in turn causes the application's **OnNotifyCrisisCoordinator()** method to be invoked, *in the main thread*. This method, in turn, reaches through the document to grab the crisis handler and call **NotifyCrisisCoordinator()**:

```
CCallClientDoc::GetDoc()->m_CrisisHandler.NotifyCrisisCoordinator();
```

Finally, the **CCrisisHandler**'s **NotifyCrisisCoordinator()** method makes the call across the process boundary to the server.

The client's **CCrisisHandler** inherits from the abstract base class **ICrisisHandler**. It implements **NotifyCrisisCoordinator()** by using the **ICrisisHandler** interface pointer it got back from the server when it registered:

```
void CCrisisHandler::NotifyCrisisCoordinator()
{
    HRESULT hr = m_pCrisisCoordinator->OnCrisis();
}
```

The Server

When **OnCrisis()** is invoked, COM marshals the call across the process boundary, and in this case across the network. The implementation of **OnCrisis()** is in the server's **ICrisisManager** class:

```
HRESULT __stdcall CCrisisManager::OnCrisis()
{
    m_doc.SetCrisis(true);
    return S_OK;
}
```

The server takes no action except to set a flag in the document. As the scheduler runs, it frequently checks whether this flag is set. This polling is not very expensive, and *can't* be eliminated by using, for example, an event object. Since the thread is running, it is not possible to block on a synchronization object and await notification; we check the flag and keep going.

When the scheduler finds that the flag is set, it knows that a client has notified it that there is a crisis, and it can be guaranteed that the crisis and its calls are already in the database. This sequencing is important, and the order is maintained by the fact that the notification is not sent until both of these events are completed.

When the scheduler notices the crisis it dumps its queue, refills the queue by calling **GetCurrentJobs()**, and then calls **OnCallQueueFlushedForCrisis()** in the document:

```
if ( m_pDoc->IsCrisis() )
{
    m_pDoc->SetCrisis( false );
    FlushQueue(pDB);
    ProcessJobs = GetCurrentJobs();
    FillingMinimums = true;
    m_pDoc->OnCallQueueFlushedForCrisis();
}
```

Note that the very first thing it does is reset the **IsCrisis** flag; since this is the only place in the code in which this flag is to be read, the message is delivered and we can reset the flag.

Calling **OnCallQueueFlushedForCrisis()** at this point guarantees that the sequencing is correct; we've already flushed and refilled the queue. It's up to the document to know what to do once the scheduler has done its job. The document's **OnCallQueueFlushedForCrisis()** method wants to delegate to its **CCrisisManager** object the implementation of what to do, but it faces the same problem the client did: it's in the wrong thread. The solution is identical:

```
void CCallServerDoc::OnCallQueueFlushedForCrisis()
{
    AfxGetApp()->PostThreadMessage(WM_NOTIFY_ALL_CRISIS_HANDLERS,0,0);
}
```

This posts a message through the application, which the application will receive in the correct thread, and will pass to its member method **OnNotifyAllCrisisHandlers()**. This method, in turn, will tell the document's **CCrisisManager** to **NotifyAllHandlers()**.

```
void CCallServerApp::OnNotifyAllCrisisHandlers()
{
    CCallServerDoc::GetDoc()->GetCrisisManager().NotifyAllHandlers();
}
```

The **CCrisisManager** is now in the main application thread and can delegate to its collection the job of notifying all the registered handlers of the crisis:

```
void CCrisisHandlerSet::NotifyAllHandlers ()
{
    // Iterating all (key, value) pairs
    POSITION pos = GetStartPosition();
    void* pHandler;
    while ( pos )
    {
        GetNextAssoc(pos, pHandler, pHandler);
        HRESULT hr = ((ICrisisHandler*) pHandler)->OnCrisis();
    }
}
```

Once again, note that we are careful as to who has what responsibility and what knowledge. The scheduler knows to flush and refill the queue, and to let the document know it is done. It has no idea what the document will do with that information, so it does *not* call, for example, **m_pDoc->m_CrisisManager.NotifyAllHandlers()**. In the same vein, the document may not have the responsibility to actually notify the client machines, but the policy of what to do *is* in the document; it is just free to ask another object to do the work.

The calls to **OnCrisis()** are also marshaled across the network and resolved in the **CCrisisHandler** objects in the clients. Using the same pattern as the server side, the **CCrisisHandler** responds to the crisis by setting a bit in the client's document:

```
HRESULT __stdcall CCrisisHandler::OnCrisis()
{
    m_doc.SetIsCrisis();
    return S_OK;
}
```

This symmetry is not coincidental; it is essential to the architecture. This is design reuse, and makes the creation and maintenance of this code much easier.

When the client gets a call from its local call queue, it checks to see if this bit is set, and if so it dumps its own local call queue, reentering each call in the queue back into the database as a new and thus never tried call. It then calls **CheckRefill()**, which is the normal mechanism to see if the local call queue needs to be filled. Since it was just emptied, this will force a refill from the server, which is guaranteed to have the crisis, because we've controlled the sequence of events:

```
CCall* CLocalCallQueue::GetFromFront()
{
    CCall* pCall = 0;
    CSingleLock theLock ( &m_LocalCallMutex );
    if (theLock.Lock(WAIT_TIME))
    {
        if ( m_pDoc->GetIsCrisis() )
        {
            m_pDoc->ClearIsCrisis();
            while ( m_sizeQueue > 0 )
            {
                pCall = CCallQueue::GetFromFront();
                if (!pCall)
                    continue;   // locked out
                CTime now = CTime::GetCurrentTime();
                pCall->SetFinalResult(CRISIS_CALL, now, 0,0, DEFAULT_RETRY_POLICY);
            }
            CheckRefill();
        }
        pCall =  CCallQueue::GetFromFront();
        CheckRefill();
        theLock.Unlock();
    }
    return pCall;
}
```

Note that the call to **SetFinalResult()** near the center of this segment of code takes each call, changes its start time to now, and reenters it into the call queue, with its number of attempts set to zero. This ensures that the calls dumped out of the queue will be made in the normal course of events.

This design is symmetrical and clean; each object has a small and well-defined job to do, yet the interprocess communication is handled and the sequencing of events is ensured.

Getting it to Run

All of this was written without the help of Wizards or other tools; what we needed to do was fairly simple, and in this case the Wizards would just have gotten in the way. There is one thing left to do, however. We need a proxy and a stub to mediate the conversation across the network and across process boundaries.

The easiest way to do this is to create a **.idl** file. The MIDL compiler will spit out the code needed to build a DLL that both the client and server will use to bring in the necessary proxy and stub. Here is the **.idl** file for **ICrisisHandler**:

```
import "unknwn.idl";
[
    object,
    uuid(1D842B90-FFA2-11d0-B379-0060977066A5)
]
interface ICrisisHandler : IUnknown
{
    HRESULT OnCrisis();
};
```

The **.idl** file for **ICrisisRegistrar** is very similar:

```
import "unknwn.idl";
import "ICrisisHandler.idl";
[
    object,
    uuid(1D842B91-FFA2-11d0-B379-0060977066A5)
]
interface ICrisisRegistrar : IUnknown
{
    HRESULT RegisterCrisisHandler
        ([in] ICrisisHandler*, [in] REFIID iid,
                            [out, iid_is(iid)] void ** ppInterface );
    HRESULT  RevokeCrisisHandler([in] ICrisisHandler*);
};
```

Once the DLL is built, we put it where both the client and the server can find it, and Hey Presto! Interprocess communication.

Handling Exceptions

There are any number of places in the code that may throw an exception. We can get exceptions from the database, from the operating system, or within the custom code when resources are unavailable or something else goes wrong.

We've set a design goal that when we get an exception we'll try again a few times, and if the exception can't be resolved we'll report the problem and shut down gracefully. To do this, I must wrap every potentially dangerous function call in a **try** block, and must catch the exception in a **catch** statement. Further, I must keep track of how many times I've tried, and then when I've tried enough times, take appropriate action.

I'd like to encapsulate this code in an object. *Design Patterns* describes a **command** object, whose purpose in life is to de-couple the object that invokes the operation from the one that knows how to perform it. Thus, the object that wants to attempt a dangerous function need not know how to manage the retry policy.

I create a command object as an abstract data type; to do this I create an abstract base class called **CCommand**:

```
class CCommand
{
public:
    virtual bool Execute() = 0;
    CCommand();
    virtual ~CCommand();
};
```

Every derived class will override **Execute()**. The first place I identify a need for this capability is in the **CCaller** class. There are a number of Visual Voice methods that are candidates to throw an exception, including **Play()**, **PlayFile()**, **Pickup()** and so forth. I derive a **CCallerCommand** class from **CCommand**:

```
class CCallerCommand : public CCommand
{
public:
    CCallerCommand( CCaller* p,
                    void (CCaller::*pmf)(CString),
                    CString fileName,
                    CString error );
    CCallerCommand( CCaller* p,
                    void (CCaller::*pmf)(),
                    CString error );
    CCallerCommand( CCaller* p,
                    void (CCaller::*pmf)(CString, int),
                    CString fileName,
                    int index,
                    CString error );

    virtual ~CCallerCommand();
    bool Execute();
    void ImplementExecution();

private:
    CCaller* m_pCaller;
    void     (CCaller::*m_pmf0)();
    void     (CCaller::*m_pmf1)(CString);
```

```
    void     (CCaller::*m_pmf2)(CString, int);
    CString  m_fileName;
    CString  m_errorMsg;
    int      m_index;
    int      m_maxRetries;
    int      m_whichRoutine;
};
```

Note that this object offers three constructors, depending on the parameters to the
member functions we need to invoke. This class encapsulates both the retry policy and its
implementation. It also creates a table of methods to invoke, providing the correct
parameters to the method. Thus, it currently supports three pointers to member functions
of the **CCaller** class. **pmf0** takes no parameters, **pmf1** takes a **CString**, and **pmf2** takes
a **CString** and an **int**.

The constructor initializes the right pointer to member function and the necessary
parameters, as well as an internal counter that determines which pointer to member
function will be called. The **Execute()** method is overridden to encapsulate the retry
policy:

```
bool CCallerCommand::Execute()
{
    for (int i = 0; i < m_maxRetries; i++ )
    {
        try
        {
            ImplementExecution();
            return true;
        }
        catch (...)
        {
            CString logString;
            logString.Format("Exception caught: %s",m_errorMsg);
            log(UNKNOWN_ERROR, CCALLING_EXCEPTION_ERROR, m_pCaller>GetLineNumber(),
                                                                   logString);
        }
    }

    // If you get here, you failed more times than allowed
    CShutDownCommand sd(m_errorMsg, m_pCaller->GetLineNumber());
    sd.Execute();
    CFatalCallingException e(m_errorMsg);
    throw e;
    return false; // to appease MSVC
}

void CCallerCommand::ImplementExecution()
{
    switch(m_whichRoutine)
    {
    case 0:
        (m_pCaller->*m_pmf0)();
```

```
        break;
    case 1:
        (m_pCaller->*m_pmf1)(m_fileName);
        break;
    case 2:
        (m_pCaller->*m_pmf2)(m_fileName, m_index);
    }
}
```

It uses a helper function, **ImplementExecution()**, to **switch** to the correct pointer to member function to call. We could use inheritance to handle this, but the current method is simpler for a small number of options.

When it's time to attempt a dangerous method, such as **PlayFile()**, I create a **CCallerCommand** object and call **Execute()**.

```
CCallerCommand cmd( pCaller,
                    CCaller::PlayFile,
                    m_PrePendFileName,
                    "Can't play prependFile" );
cmd.Execute();
```

This cleanly tries the method a number of times and handles the failure if required. Note that handling the failure is delegated to the **CShutDownCommand** object, whose job is to bring the system to a halt cleanly after notifying Operations of the problem.

To support this, I create an abstract base class called **CCallingException**:

```
class CCallingException
{
public:
    CCallingException(CString error = "");
    virtual ~CCallingException();

    CString GetError() const { return m_error; }

protected:
    CString m_error;
};
```

From this class, I derive **CNonFatalCallingException** and **CFatalCallingException**. The threads that receive and place calls handle non-fatal exceptions by cycling the phone line and continuing; they handle fatal exceptions by cleanly shutting down the system:

```
try
{
    pCaller->ImplementPlaceCalls();
}
catch (CNonFatalCallingException * e)
```

```
    {
        CString s;
        s.Format("NonFatal Exception caught in PlaceCall. %s Hanging up...\n",
                                                    e->GetError());

        pCaller->Log( EXCEPTION,  RECEIVE_CALLS, s);
        pCaller->Stop();
        pCaller->Hangup();
        delete e;
    }
    catch(...)
    {
        pCaller->Stop();
        pCaller->Hangup();
        CShutDownCommand cmd("Unknown error",0);
        cmd.Execute();
    }
```

In this example from **PlaceCalls()**, the work of placing the outgoing calls is all implemented in the caller's method **ImplementPlaceCalls()**. Any exceptions thrown during the course of placing calls will be caught here. If the exception is non-fatal, we hang up the line and continue. If any other exception is caught, we shut down cleanly and notify Operations.

There is intentional redundancy in creating the **CShutDownCommand** object both here and when the fatal exception is thrown; eventually I'll be certain I'm catching every fatal exception thrown, and I'll move this code to where the exception is caught, rather than where it is thrown.

Are You Okay?

In addition to handling the exceptions that arise through normal processing, Operations has requested that we ensure that the calling machines and the call server are tested periodically. The goal is for each calling machine to poke the server and say, "Are you still okay?" and for the server, in turn, to poke each of the calling machines.

The cleanest way to do this is to piggyback on the observer pattern we already have put in place for crisis notification. Each client already has an interface pointer that lets it register with the server and send crisis messages; all we need do now is register as a client to test, and add the ability to ask the server, "Are you still there and still okay?"

Similarly, since the server already has the ability to tell each client of a crisis, it should be a simple matter to extend that to say, "Are *you* still there and still okay?"

If the server notes that a particular client is no longer responding, it can alert all the other calling machines to contact Operations by adding a new, special crisis to the database and using the normal crisis notification mechanism. This might, for example, call Operations and play a prerecorded alert message.

Unfortunately, if a calling machine notices that the server is no longer responding, it cannot use the normal crisis notification, but will have to insert a special set of calls into its own local call queue.

We separate notification from status checking. It is possible that any number of mechanisms will be used for notification. We may fire off a buzzer in the Operations department, make calls as described above, call a beeper, or take other action. We may do this in response to the "Are You Okay?" message, or in response to an exception being thrown in the normal course of running.

Into the Home Stretch

It is now late July. We are supposed to be at feature freeze by September 5. Jay asks me for an estimate of how much work remains. It is always very hard to put days to tasks, but I need a good 'to do' list at this point anyway, so I give him my best guess.

Between now and feature freeze we need to finish off the interprocess communication for both *Crisis•Calls* and self-testing. This represents another 2-5 days of work.

I still have some work to bring my code into conformance with the revised call flow charts; I estimate an additional 2-3 days of work at most. I will also have some involvement with the production of the reports; even though we are using a consultant, this will still eat a day or two of my time as we go forward.

A big unknown will be making the conversion from analog to digital. I have only analog lines in my house; Hypotenuse of course has digital lines. Artisoft assures me this will be trivial, but I'm budgeting for as much as three days.

It is the little jobs which *really* eat up the time; they are so small they are easy to miss. I know I need to make time for reading in a file of phone numbers and getting them into the database. I also have to tinker with my back-tilt algorithm, as well as with my code to sort and assign calls by area code. I need a day to finalize the throttling of calls, and another day to ensure I don't crush the central office in any given area code zone. I also need time to synch up the systems, transfer over the database schema and get it all working. I estimate 10-15 days for all of this. This nets out to a total of 12-20 days, and I have about 25 workdays remaining before deadline.

Based on these estimates, we should be fine. I'm less worried about the items on this list, than by what is missing — the things that will come up, but which we've not yet thought of.

Feature Freeze - Is It a Bug or a Missing Feature?

There is a story that a major release from a well-known software development firm shipped on June 35th. The joke is that they promised to ship in the first half of the year, so they redefined the calendar.

Feature freeze is an easy date to manipulate; you can leave out a feature and just call it a bug. After all, we have a whole month in-house after feature freeze for debugging. The problem is, who are you fooling? It is like cheating on your diet; ultimately your heart doesn't care if you tell yourself that you're eating yesterday's allotment; it will just stop beating and get your attention.

I have committed to completing all features for Version 1 by September 5. The month of September will be spent subjecting the code to exhaustive in-house testing preparatory to releasing the code to Hypotenuse for load testing during the month of October.

```cpp
= false;                                        CTime
Time();                          CTime::GetCur
   = now.Format("%b %d        CTime end = theJobSe
                              CTime start = theJobSe
                           CTime todayStart(start.Getie
er = "start < '";          start.GetMonth(), now.GetDay(),
oday;                       start.GetHour(),
   and enddate > '";        start.GetMinute(),
oday;                       start.GetSecond());
   = '";                       CTime todayEnd(end.GetYear(),
                            end.GetMonth(), now.GetDay(),
ScheduleSet.m_strFilter =   end.GetHour(),
                            end.GetMinute(), end.GetSecond());

                            end.GetMinute() > now || todayS

                               if (todayStart > now || todayS
JobScheduleSet.IsOpen()         now)
                                {   theJobSet.Close();
JobScheduleSet.Requery();               return false;
pDoc>m_JobScheduleSet.Open();
lTrack* pCallTrack;             }

l ok;                           CTimeSpan theSpan = end no
                                int totalMinutes = 
ile                             theSpan.GetTotalMinutes();
pDoc>m_JobScheduleSet.IsEOF()
                                if (end > todayEnd) //
    pCallTrack = new            than today
llTrack(m_pDoc>m_JobScheduleSet.m_    {   int AdditionalMin =
bID);                           GetAdditionalMinutes(theJ
    ok = pCallTrack>Initialize();
                                t,
                                theJobSet.m_EndDate);
    if (ok)                        CTimeSpan todaySp
    {   Log("ok\n");            now;    totalMinutes =
                                todaySpan.GetTotalMin
                                AdditionalMin;
m_CallList.AddHead(pCallTrack);
        foundJobs = true;       }

    }                              m_min = ( ( (m_t
    else                        totalMinutes) + 1
    {   Log("...Rejected!\n");   );   m_Priority = t
        delete pCallTrack;          m_Tilt = theJo
                                    m_Throttle = the
    }                               m_JobID = the
                                    theJobSet.Cl
m_pDoc>m_JobScheduleSet.MoveNext();
                                return true
m_pDoc>m_JobScheduleSet                   Jobs;
```

CHAPTER EIGHT

Delivering Version 1.0

Final Touches

As we enter the final weeks of implementation, my goal is to ensure that we have completed the requirements and that the system is solid and ready for testing. Early in August, I send Jay and Kevin a final specification of what we're building. Here's an excerpt:

Requirement	Notes
Customer can sign up for service	By talking with a customer service representative who will use SQL, or a web form (time allowing), or the IVR system.
Customer can give us phone numbers	Customer can send phone numbers via e-mail or FedEx. We'll run a validation program and then they will be batch-loaded into the database.
Customer can record audio	Customer can record per-job audio at preproduction time. Customer will have a special 800 number to call to record audio for interactive calls (these are the first and second introductory messages).
System can call on a schedule	Customer can specify (and system will implement) the ability to start and stop at specific times, and to take time zones into account.
System will support throttling	Customer service can add a throttle to a job, expressed as the maximum number of calls to make per hour.
System supports back tilt	Customer can specify a stop time, and the system will compute a reasonable start time.
System checks available resources	The system will ensure it has sufficient resources to call the 'minimum' number of calls per hour for each job scheduled, or will direct the customer to customer service.
Jobs have varying priorities	System supports a default priority per customer, which customer service can vary on a per-customer or per-job basis.

Requirement	Notes
Operational support reports	Operations can query the database to determine the current state of any calling machine, job or other process.
Failure reporting	The system will call out to Operations and report any failure of any machine.

My message to them goes on to explain each of these features in detail and to discuss the current status of their development. Attached to that memo is a to-do list, which I endeavor to keep up to date so they can track my progress in the final weeks.

Kevin and I are in close contact during this time. We need to ensure that his systems are tracking mine, so that when I deliver code, it will run on his hardware without difficulty.

Jay's analogy is this: On May 10, 1869, two great trains — the Central Pacific's Jupiter and the Union Pacific's No. 119 — met at Promontory, Utah to drive the final spike uniting the two lines in a transcontinental railroad. My code is the Union Pacific's track; Kevin's hardware is the Central Pacific's. Jay is standing in Promontory, holding a golden spike. If I end up in Kansas, and Kevin is in Montana, we're in big trouble.

That Knot in my Stomach

At this point in the development cycle, my entire life is given over to the project. For the past few months I've been working 10-12 hour days, and some weekends. Yesterday I explained to my wife that I would now be working longer hours. She just laughed.

I find myself thinking about the project even when I'm not sitting at the computer. It distracts me when I drive, when I shower, when I play tennis. I find myself jotting down notes while watching the news, and waking up at 5 a.m. to rush into the office to get something working. Unfortunately, it is also interfering with my time with the kids; they notice that I'm very distracted. There is nothing to be done but finish: the project can't be delayed, and it can't be denied. Lou Reed sings of heroin, "It's my wife and it's my life." I know how he feels.

This kind of pressure can cause you to make serious mistakes. You find yourself rushing to implement what appears to be a simple feature, but when it goes wrong you panic. You tear into the code, frantically trying to get it to work — you've got one eye on the debugger, and the other on the clock. Of course, in your rush, you forget to create a checkpoint in your source control system, and now you can't back out.

It is around now that I start making backups two and three times a day. I check in and out of source code each time something works. I'm beginning to manage this project the way a pilot flies a plane, always scanning for a place to land in an emergency.

The great danger, the one I wake up in the middle of the night worrying about, is the problem we forgot. What *did* we forget? What's going to pop up and shout "Boo!" right at the end, throwing us off track and into a ditch? Worry, worry, worry.

Sometimes I think I worry just so my customer won't have to. This time it isn't working; Jay is even more worried than I am. We'll both be fine when it's done, but the next couple of months won't be any fun at all. First we'll worry about code freeze. Then we'll worry that we'll find something terrible in testing. Then we'll worry that we'll find something awful when we put the code under load. Finally, we'll worry about the bugs we missed.

Implementing the Web Pages

It's mid-August when I travel to Gamma to review their progress. I am very impressed. With just a couple of days' work, they've already produced a great-looking report, and more importantly they *understand* the data and have built the infrastructure for any number of MIS reports.

Just as important, they've taken exactly the right attitude to the project: they've focused on the underlying technology and avoided the distraction of paying too much attention to the look-and-feel issues. Don't get me wrong; the screens look fine, but they're not over-polished. In fact, they're perfect for a rough-and-ready intranet:

MIS needed for Hypotenuse Management - Microsoft Internet Explorer

The Hypotenuse Intranet

Flash-Call® Management Reports:
Today is 8/15/97
Yesterday's Jobs for 8/4/97

H Y P O T E N U S E

Page 1 of 1   1 - 3 of 3 Jobs Total

	Job 2	Job 3	Job 5
# of phone numbers dialed	100	200	10
Total port minutes used	46475	60465	1848
Avg port-cycle time	288	163	47
Total connect minutes	17	31	2
Weighted Avg Cost/min.	$0.10	$0.10	$0.10
Total cost of connect minutes	$1.70	$3.10	$0.20
Avg length of completed call	0.63	0.6	0.22
Longest completed call	7	31	24
Longest Port Cycle			
calls completed, 1st attempt	16.15%	12.16%	10.26%
calls retried	37.27%	37.03%	0.00%
Of all attempts made, total:			
... % answered by human	15.53%	11.35%	23.08%
... % by answering machine	1.242%	2.703%	0.000%
... % not answered	10.56%	13.24%	7.692%
... % busy	30.43%	30.54%	66.67%
... % netw. not respond.	0.000%	0.000%	0.000%
... % other	42.24%	42.16%	2.564%

John explains that the only reason he is planning to use Crystal Reports is to accomplish the printing. We discuss an alternative, which is to export the data into an Excel spreadsheet. While the final printed result may not look quite as good, it will give Jay the ability to massage the data as he sees fit, as well as to print it. The downside is that Jay will need to have Excel installed on whatever machine he views the report, but this is a trivial issue, given how we'll actually be using these reports. On balance, the ability to manipulate the data outweighs the presentation quality issues, and I tell Gamma to switch over to Excel. They assure me that this will not add any development time, and may even simplify their job.

We then turn our attention to the code itself. Gamma has divided this work into two stages: data warehousing, and report generation.

In the **data warehousing** phase, we will summarize the day's data into a series of tables. It's these tables that will be queried for the reports. While the hardware is robust enough to allow us to query the active tables directly, data warehousing brings with it a number of advantages. First, the warehousing can happen late at night, which provides a load balancing effect on the overall system. Second, a complex report won't impede access to the database by the calling machines, because it's not touching the active tables. Third, introducing this level of indirection brings the advantage that we can change the underlying structure of the active tables without necessarily affecting the reporting code. Conversely, we could build new reports without changing the live data tables. Finally, when the reports do run, they are much quicker because the data has already been summarized and aggregated.

Building the Data Warehouse

The summary tables were defined in terms of the reports required. This makes sense: no table can be sufficiently comprehensive to support all possible requirements, so the tables were tailored to the *known* requirements. This provides enormous efficiency; each line item in the report corresponds to a particular column in the summary table, or can be derived from other columns in the summary table. These summary tables are populated by stored procedures, and the entire set of stored procedures is rolled up into a nightly batch process.

The stored procedures are nothing more than SQL statements stored in a file; it's exactly as if you typed the SQL statements directly. This is very similar to how batch files work under DOS, UNIX or Windows. For example, the first report, 'Yesterday's Jobs', needed summary data on each job run for a particular day. The table **rptStatsJob** was created to store these values:

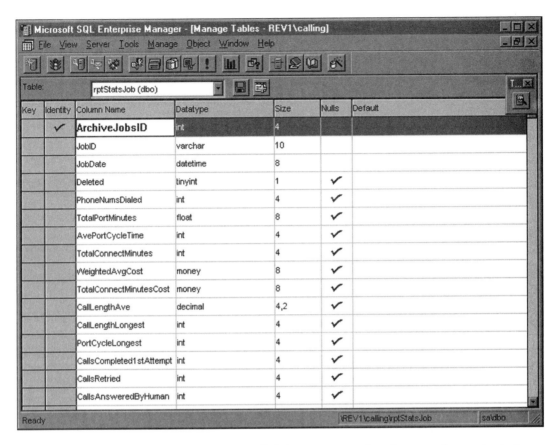

The second report, 'History of Jobs' was slightly more complex. It not only required the data to be summarized for all jobs for a particular day, but also for different days and ranges of days. For this report, we created a summary table for a particular day (**rptStatsDaily**), and another containing summaries for each of the date ranges (**rptStatsDailySummary**). The SQL statement to create the latter table is very straightforward; here's an excerpt:

```
CREATE TABLE dbo.rptStatsDailySummary ( ArchiveDailyID int IDENTITY (1, 1)
                                                          NOT NULL ,
                        CreateDate datetime NOT NULL ,
                        StartDate datetime NOT NULL ,
                        EndDate datetime NOT NULL ,
                        ...
```

Once the tables are completed, the stored procedures are run to populate the fields, based on the values in the active tables. First, local variables are filled using code like that shown on the next page.

```
    select @AnsweredOther = count(*)
                        from vCalls
                        where jobID = @jobID
                        and EndStatus NOT in (      0,   /* NEW */
                                                    1,   /* ENQUEUED */
                                                   10,   /* busy */
                                                   11,   /* not answ. */
                                             12,13,14,   /* operator/netw. fail */
                                                20,21,   /* ans. by human */
                                                   22 )  /* ans. by machine */
                        and startdate between @startd and @endd

    select @PortMinutes0000_0900 = sum(datediff(second, startdate, enddate)) / 60
                        from vCalls
                        where jobID = @jobID
                        and NumberOfAttempts > 0
                        and startdate between @temp_startd and @temp_endd
                        and endStatus > 1

        ...
```

Then the summary report fields are populated from these local variables:

```
    update rptStatsJob set PhoneNumsDialed =        @PhoneNumsDialed,
                        TotalPortMinutes =          @TotalPortMinutes,
                        AvePortCycleTime =          @AvePortCycleTime,
                        TotalConnectMinutes =       @TotalConnectMinutes,
                        WeightedAvgCost =           @WeightedAvgCost,
                        TotalConnectMinutesCost =   @TotalConnectMinutesCost,
                        CallLengthAve =             @CallLengthAve,
                        CallLengthLongest =         @CallLengthLongest,
                        PortCycleLongest =          @PortCycleLongest,
                        ...
```

Once the tables are complete, the job of accessing them and building the reports themselves is given over to Active Server Pages.

Active Server Pages

Active Server Pages provide a clean approach for server-side scripting and database access. They are a combination of server-side scripting code — typically VBScript or JScript — and inline HTML. The Active Server Page is interpreted, and HTML is produced that can be read on any compatible browser. No *client-side* script interpretation is required, though client-side scripting can be integrated into the final HTML page as well, if desired.

The ASP DLL (**asp.dll**) supplies the scripting environment, which is entirely object-oriented. ASP provides five high level objects: the **request**, the **response**, the **server**, the **application** and the **session**. Each of these objects, in turn, provides a series of methods and properties, as well as collections. For example, the request and the response object both provide the 'cookies' collection, which gives the programmer access to the cookies sent to and from the client. Our code is concerned primarily with the 'request' object, which contains five collections including the HTTP query strings and form variables.

The server-side scripting uses **Active Server Components** — COM objects that can be built in any suitable development environment, such as C++, Delphi or Visual Basic. ASP comes with a number of components, including the **ADO** components, which provide database access. ADO allows the developer to define a connection to any ODBC datasource, and to send SQL statements to that source. The result of the query is returned as a result set, over which the server side script may iterate. This is, not surprisingly, very similar to how things work with MFC's ODBC classes.

The ASP objects contain information both from the system and the person who is connected to the page. For example, to set the date, we ask the 'request' object for the 'form' object, and we ask the 'form' object for its **report_date**. From there we can determine yesterday's date, which is what this report requires:

```
<% ' ————— DETERMINE DATE OF REPORT ————— %>
<%
myReportDate = Request.Form("report_date")
Yesterday = MyReportDate

' If none is supplied, assume yesterday
If VarType(Yesterday) <> vbDate AND VarType(Yesterday) <> vbString Then
    Yesterday = DateAdd("d",-1,Date())
End If

StartDate = Cstr(Yesterday) & " 12:00AM "
EndDate = Cstr(Yesterday) & " 11:59PM "
DateRange = "'" & CStr(StartDate) & "' AND '" & Cstr(EndDate) & "'"
%>
```

The next step is to establish a connection with the database:

```
<%
' Define connection String and open connection to SQL Server DB
Set Conn = Server.CreateObject("ADODB.Connection")
Conn.Open Session("ODBC;DATABASE=calling;DSN=LocalServer;Uid=sa;PWD=;")
%>
```

Next, we define the SQL that we'll be sending to the server.

```
<%
szSQL = "SELECT 'Job ' + JobID as '', "
szSQL = szSQL & " PhoneNumsDialed as '# of phone numbers dialed', "
szSQL = szSQL & " TotalPortMinutes as 'Total port minutes used', "
szSQL = szSQL & " AvePortCycleTime as 'Avg port-cycle time', "
szSQL = szSQL & " TotalConnectMinutes as 'Total connect minutes', "

' ... (not all columns shown)

szSQL = szSQL & " FROM rptStatsJob where JobDate BETWEEN " & DateRange
%>
```

Now that we've defined the connection and what we want to send, we create a recordset using that information:

```
Set rs = Server.CreateObject("ADODB.Recordset")
rs.Open szSQL, Conn, 3
```

One interesting problem is that the database has a column for each row in our output screen. We need to read the recordset into an array, so that we can switch the row and column index as we loop:

```
<% for i = 1 to myCols -6 %><% ' Alternate Row color %>

<tr <% if i/2 = int(i/2) then
        %>BGCOLOR=#CCCCFF<%
    else
        %>BGCOLOR=WHITE<%
    end if%> >

<%
for j = 0 to myRows - 1  ' Now print the row, reversing row,column order
%>

<td>

<%=JOBS(j,i) & " "%> 

<%
next
next
%>

</table>
```

Putting it Together into a Report

When Jay browses to this page, he will choose which report he wants to see:

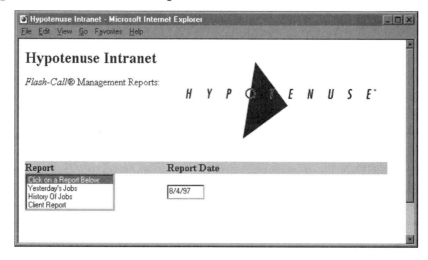

The two reports we asked Gamma to build first were originally conceived of as a single, integrated report. Their division of these reports made the breakdown of information cleaner, and provided a better display on the web page. You saw the first of these at the beginning of this discussion; this is the second, as seen through Internet Explorer:

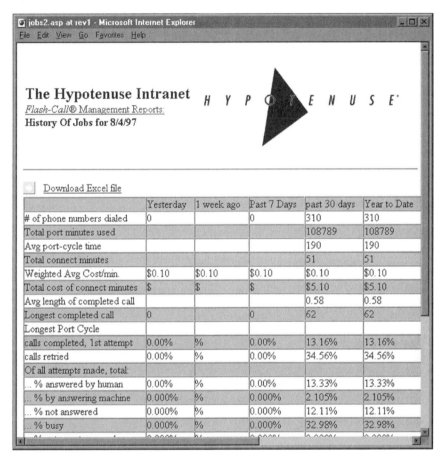

The ASP code for the 'History of Jobs' report was nearly identical to that used for the 'Yesterday's Jobs' report, because we reused the design of the data tables.

Printing the Report

To provide both printing and the ability to manipulate the data directly, Gamma created a custom COM component to produce an Excel spreadsheet from the database. The VB5 code used to create the component was straightforward, and appears on the next page.

```
'  ——————— Begin Class "ConvReport.ExcelGen" ———————

Const gREPORTPATH As String = "C:\Inetpub\reports\downloads\"
Const gDBPATH As String = "C:\data\reporting.mdb"

Public Function CreateFile(ByVal strReportName As String) As String

Dim strReportFileName As String
Dim strPrintFileName As String

strPrintFileName = gREPORTPATH & "historyt.xls"

Dim db As Object
Set db = New Access.Application

db.OpenCurrentDatabase (gDBPATH)
db.DoCmd.RunMacro ("mcrCreateExcelFile")
db.CloseCurrentDatabase

Set db = Nothing

CreateFile = ("<A HREF=file://" & strPrintFileName & ">History.XLS</A><BR>")

End Function
```

The **ConvReport** component contains one class: **ExcelGen**. This class is a **functor**. A functor is a design idiom of a class that provides a single method — that is, a class that can be used like a function, but that contains additional knowledge and state variables. The single method of this particular functor is **CreateFile()**. All this component does is call a simple macro called **mcrCreateExcelFile** in an Access 97 database, which creates a query like the one shown opposite. It saves this query as an Excel 97 spreadsheet in the **downloads** directory of the web server, and then returns a hyperlink to this file for display on the web page. The hyperlink allows the viewer to click and download the created file.

The **Crosstab** query serves the same purpose as the array transformation in our ASP code, and allows the spreadsheet to be saved with the date range columns running across the top of the sheet.

Row0	RowTitle	Yesterday	1 week ago	Past 7 Days	past 30 days	Year to Date
1	# of phone numbers dialed			311	311	311
2	Total port minutes used			108813	108813	108813
3	Avg port-cycle time			189	189	189
4	Total connect minutes			54	54	54
5	Weighted Avg Cost/min.	0.1	0.1	0.1	0.1	0.1
6	Total cost of connect minute			5.4	5.4	5.4
7	Avg length of completed call			0.59	0.59	0.59
8	Longest completed call			62	62	62
9	Longest Port Cycle					
10	calls completed, 1st attempt			13.5888501742	13.5888501742	13.5888501742
11	calls retried			34.3205574913	34.3205574913	34.3205574913
12	Of all attempts made, total:	0	0	0	0	0
13	... % answered by human			13.5888501742	13.5888501742	13.5888501742
14	... % by answering machine			2.26480836237	2.26480836237	2.26480836237
15	... % not answered			12.1951219512	12.1951219512	12.1951219512
16	... % busy			32.7526132404	32.7526132404	32.7526132404
17	... % netw. not respond.			0	0	0
18	... % other			39.1986062718	39.1986062718	39.1986062718
19	% of port minutes used:	0	0	0	0	0
20	... midnight ET to 9am ET	0	0	36.203394815	36.203394815	36.203394815
21	... 9am to Noon ET	0	0	10.2110961006	10.2110961006	10.2110961006
22	... Noon to 3pm ET	0	0	53.4954463162	53.4954463162	53.4954463162
23	... 3pm to 6pm ET	0	0	0.01010908623	0.01010908623	0.01010908623
24	... 6pm to 9pm ET	0	0	0	0	0
25	... 9pm to midnight ET	0	0	0	0	0

Following the production of the query, the Access97 macro outputs a spreadsheet containing the same data:

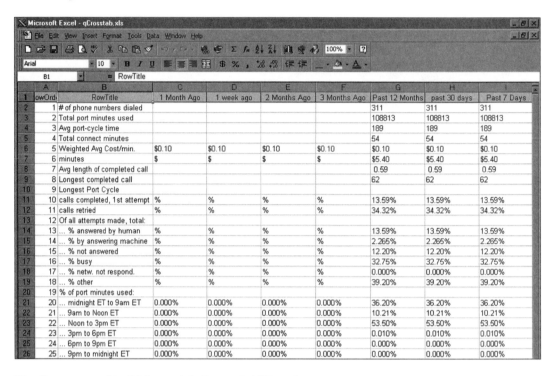

Finally, we use this fairly straightforward ASP code:

```
[produce page header]

<% Set myobj = Server.CreateObject("ConvReport.ExcelGen") %>

You may download a Excel spreadsheet version of this report here:<P>

<li><% = myobj.CreateFile(strReportname) %> (<% = Now() %>)

<% Set myObj = nothing %>

</HTML>
```

To produce this page on the Hypotenuse site:

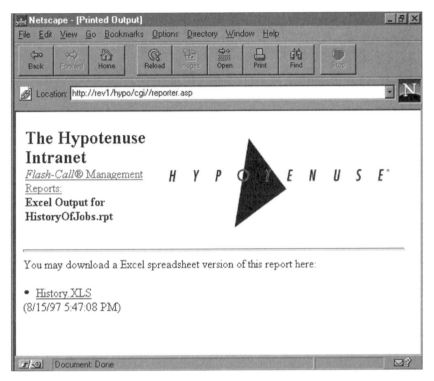

How Using Consultants Worked Out

Having Steve Rogers and Glenn Clarkson participate in the design as consultants was one of the better decisions I made during this project. Their contributions were enormous, and can't be overstated. Working as consultants freed them from any overhead of client or project management, allowing them to make their valuable suggestions without any distractions.

Gamma exceeded my expectations, and my expectations were very high. They were able to work in parallel with only the most minimal of supervision, which meant that every day they worked was a day shaved off the schedule. We were so happy with their preliminary work that we immediately asked them to go on to produce a number of additional reports.

Using consultants was successful because we were able to engineer a position where the pieces they needed to build were dependent only on work I'd already completed, and where none of my work depended on what they were producing.

Feature Cuts

At this point in the project, there is only one imperative: Get it done. However, it's one thing to say, "Get in the market. Get in the market. Get in the market," but it's quite another actually to make the hard decisions to drop features and stay on schedule. Remember our Rule Number One:

> **Features will yield to schedule and schedule will yield to quality. We will slip the schedule to ensure quality, but not to add features.**

The implication of this rule is not only that we won't *add* features, but also that when the schedule is threatened, we'll *cut* features. This is where the rubber hits the road. We've identified which features are essential to version 1.0 of the project, and now it is time to cut all the rest.

We try hard to cut to the bone, keeping only those features that are absolutely required for the integrity of the product. It's the right thing to do: it keeps us on schedule, it makes for a stronger product in the long run, and it hurts like hell.

What We Cut

There is a point in every project when my eyes mist over and I think back at the heady days of planning. We had such great plans, we would do it all. Everything goes to soft focus and that horrible song from the 1960s starts playing in my head:

> Those were the days, my friend,
> We thought they'd never end...,

Well, we'll always have Paris.

Snap. The fog clears, back to reality. To keep this project on schedule we've made some tough decisions along the way. I think they were the right choices, and we'll be in a great position to add these features into the second release and get them done quickly and cleanly, but for now they are on hold. These include:

- Call bridging
- Calling in to hear missed messages
- Advanced scheduling techniques
- *Snapshot*
- Signing up on the Web

- Launching jobs on the Web
- Least-cost call routing
- Adaptive scheduling
- Job management

Losing call bridging happened late in the process and it hurts the most. While the ability to bridge a customer's call to (for example) his senator is an important feature, more significant still is that for now we can't bridge a call to customer service. This is particularly painful because we've also lost some of the advanced scheduling techniques, which means that if there's anything that looks like a conflict in the schedule, we *must* involve customer service, and for now that means asking the customer to call back.

The second feature we cut towards the end of the project is the ability to call in to hear missed messages. We are concerned that some recipients may not hear the entire message clearly on their answering machines. We'll add this one back in the second version as well, but only time will tell us if it is used much.

We've cut *SnapShot* from the first version, along with some of the other reports we'd like to provide to customer service and to Operations. However, these will be very easy to add back, and the ability to work with Gamma means that we can add them in parallel with our other development work.

Adaptive scheduling is the ability for the system to modify its assumptions based on experience. For example, we tell the system to underschedule by 20% of its availability to allow us to stay on schedule even when we get a crisis call or a machine fails. It would be great if that number were automatically modified based on the system's accumulated experience over time. For now, that feature is on hold.

'Job management' is my shorthand notation for the ability to allow customers to schedule calls even when their audio or phone lists are not yet on the system. I call it this because it was intended to form a part of the responsibility of the job manager object, which we have not yet implemented. We actually cut this feature quite early in the implementation, realizing that we simply didn't need it in the first release.

On balance, I think we made the right decisions. We know what we've cut, and we've built a version 2 feature list, so that we can put these features back in quickly. More importantly, we have a solid design and a robust code base with well-encapsulated objects. This gives us the flexibility to add and remove features at will, without breaking the rest of the system.

How the Design Held Up

These final weeks are a good time to look back and see how the design held up in the implementation. One significant advantage of working alone or in a very small team is that the design becomes much more flexible. If changes are required, they can be incorporated as quickly as they can be validated.

In a larger team, there is much more resistance to changing the design. First, more people have to approve the changes. Second, and more importantly, changes will affect more people. This creates a greater rigidity, often before the design is robust enough to be treated that way. Like clay that hardens too quickly, your design becomes brittle and small changes can break it.

Design Follows Requirements

The revised feature set simplified the product, and the simpler requirements allowed for a streamlining of the design. In most cases the overall design didn't change, although at times there were areas I didn't implement because they just weren't needed yet. For example, the simpler queue I built into the database meant that I didn't need a dispatcher object. I didn't implement the flow manager on the client side, because the few flows we have are hard-coded as object modules. We set aside the job manager for the first release, because the modified requirement that all jobs must be absolutely ready to go before being added to the database gave the job manager much less to do.

Each of these design components is well understood and can be restored as features are added. Because these elements are well encapsulated, we should be able to plug them back into the working design without breaking everything else.

Some functionality that we originally thought would be encapsulated in a class is instead provided by a member function of an existing class. For example, the reporter object was replaced by the call object's member method, **SetFinalResult()**. Again, this is a direct result of the simplification of the product, and can be revisited as features are added.

Platform Decisions

There were a number of platform decisions made early on. As we near the first release, I can't help but review those decisions to see how they played out.

All Microsoft

The decision to go with an all-Microsoft solution has been vindicated many times over. Again and again, the implementation path was smoothed by complying with Microsoft's implicit assumption that MFC recordset classes would be talking with Microsoft SQL, and that the Visual InterDev tools would be working with Microsoft Internet Information

Server. While we certainly could have made tools from various vendors interoperate, the all-Microsoft solution was clearly the path of least resistance. To date, we've paid no significant price for this decision.

Visual Voice

When we considered how to manage the telephony aspects of the application, we considered three alternatives: the Dialogic API, the Visual Voice class library, and an application generator. Looking back, there is no doubt in my mind that we made the right decision here, too.

An application generator would not have saved us a significant amount of time, and would greatly have inflated the cost of the product, while at the same time imposing undue constraints on it. We would have been locked into a particular way of doing things, and extricating ourselves would have been expensive.

Writing to the Dialogic API may well have been fairly simple, but it would have introduced a more difficult learning curve at a critical point in the process. The Visual Voice library allowed me to smooth the learning curve and get the application working very quickly. However, late in July, I have a conversation with Jay in which I explain that I am still not 100% certain that we'll go to market with the Visual Voice components. He is nervous about this, but I assure him that even in the worst case, we were wise to start with Visual Voice and that at this point writing the code to talk directly to the Dialogic Card won't take very long. If nothing else, Visual Voice got us up and running quickly, and in fact I expect to continue with them for the long haul.

I'm really just jittery because there are a number of minor problems with the way Visual C++ 5 interacts with our current version of Visual Voice; I can't get the application to close down cleanly and there appear to be some memory management issues. This may well be because I'm doing something wrong. In any case, I have every reason to believe that within a week or two, all problems with the Visual Voice components will be resolved, as they've indicated that a new version is on the way.

I am scheduled to spend a day with Artisoft in late August, and I hope at that time to review their newest release, to upgrade my software, and to meet with their engineers to iron out the final issues. I am confident that there will be no problem going forward, but the final test will be on the digital lines at Hypotenuse, rather than the analog lines on which the product was developed.

The Programming Language

The decision to implement in C++ was 100% vindicated. At no time has the language gotten in the way. The one objection I continue to have with C++, however, is the absence of **garbage collection**. Java, and other languages that *do* have garbage collection, make memory management much easier, and avoid the pitfalls of stray pointers, memory leaks and so forth. Since the server and client must be able to stay up and running indefinitely, memory leaks are a significant risk; over time even small leaks will crash the system.

The testing period will shake out these issues, and I intend to subject both the client and the server application to the most rigorous testing, including extensive use of BoundsChecker. I've allowed a full week in my testing schedule for nothing more than getting the application to build without a single BoundsChecker error.

The Microsoft Foundation Classes certainly bring a lot of overhead, and given how little user interface there will be in the final product, it's arguable that in the next version I should strip MFC out of the application. That said, it would have been *far* more difficult to get to the first release without MFC, and I'm glad I used it. The support for the database, for a simple user interface, and for collection classes shortened the development cycle significantly.

The Overall Component Architecture

While many elements of the low-level design have changed, the overall component architecture has held up very well. The original diagram showed a dispatcher managing a queue outside of the server database. Other than merging this object into the main database, the component diagram is unchanged:

Before

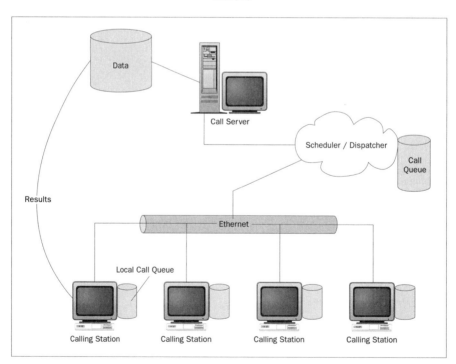

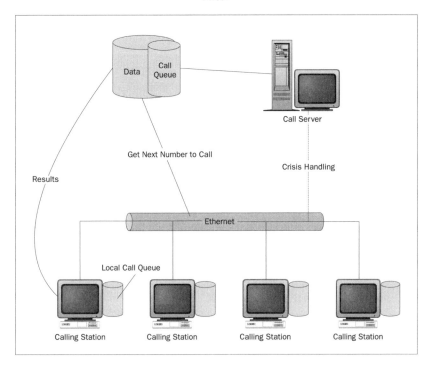

After

The Call Queue

The first and most significant departure from the original design had actually been anticipated and planned for from the very beginning. It would have taken a significant amount of time for me to learn COM to the point where I was happy to use it in an industrial-strength application, and I believed the time would be better spent creating a working version of the application. I put off implementing the call queue as a COM object, and decided instead to use a table in the database itself.

This turned out to have significant advantages beyond being a simple interim measure, and we decided to go at least to the first release with this modified architecture. In a stroke, this eliminated the need for a dispatcher object, and simplified the relationship between the database and the calling machines as well. In the current design, the only direct communication between the calling machines and the server is for crisis handling and checking that all machines are operating well. The routine management of getting numbers in and out of the database is handled for us by ODBC.

The Calling Machine Architecture

The original picture of the calling machine architecture is much more complex than the simplified calling machine we actually implemented for the first release:

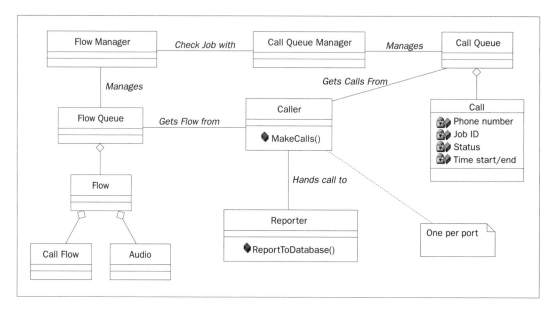

The flow manager and the flow queue disappeared with the simplified design. The caller talks to the local call queue, which is responsible for keeping itself full. The caller asks the call what job it is associated with, and from the job it gets the flow ID. Since the flows are hard-coded, the caller just instantiates a flow object directly. When the call is completed, the caller asks the call to report back to the database with the results. This reporting is handled in a low-priority thread, in which the caller tells the call to update the database.

While this is a significant departure from the original design, it followed naturally at implementation time. The original design set the overall perspective, and implementation details fed back into the design to simplify the first release.

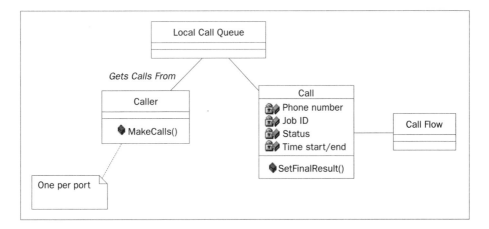

In subsequent releases, we'll want to implement scripted call flows, and that will cause us to reinstate the flow manager. I will take another look at breaking the call queue management out of the caller's set of responsibilities, probably reinstating the call queue manager at that time. I'm unsure about the reporter; while I like the division of responsibility, I think that the logical entity is well represented in the **SetFinalResult()** method of the call object, and I'm less inclined to break this out any time soon.

The Job Manager

A third major area of departure in the first release is one I've already mentioned: the complete elimination of the job manager. We agreed that for this release, no job will be added to the database that is not ready to run; thus there is no need for an object to 'validate' jobs. Furthermore, all preproduction work will be done through IVR; the customers will not launch jobs over the Web. Finally, crisis management will be handled by the client machine interacting directly with the call server, using COM. The design for the job manager remains valuable, however, and we certainly intend to revisit it in subsequent releases.

Evaluating the Changes

I couldn't be happier at how well these decisions played out. The design held up to these changes, we were able to adapt and simplify as we went, and none of these changes, however substantial, caused us to question the core design assumptions. In short, I consider the design to be a solid and robust success.

The proof of any design, however is in the implementation. If a solid implementation doesn't fall out of your design, the design is worthless, no matter how elegant it may be.

Implementing the Design

Looking back, the implementation followed the design quite well, and I'm convinced that the structure of the code was made more robust by having invested up-front in a substantial design effort. There were compromises made in the implementation as we accelerated the development schedule, but these decisions are well understood and have not undermined the fundamental integrity of the design. As we move forward in subsequent releases, pressure will be put on some of the components. As we generalize the flows, and increase the traffic, we may decide to go back and add some of the components that were simplified out of the current implementation. We'll be able to do that without breaking the core components, because we designed for these changes from the beginning.

Changing Horses in Mid-Stream

Just three weeks before feature freeze, I am invited by Artisoft to take a look at the beta version of Visual Voice 4.0, codenamed *Nile*. I sign their NDA (which they have waived for this book), and download the beta from their web site.

Normally, I wouldn't even consider changing such a fundamental part of a project at this late stage; the chances of disaster are simply too high. This time I decide to take a look, because the reasons for doing so are compelling. First, as I mentioned earlier, I have a number of minor but irritating ongoing problems with the **CVoice** class, which I hope they have solved in Release 4. Second, I have been trying for some time to buy a day of help from them, and they have requested I spend a week working with Nile before visiting them. Third, I know I can back out if I have to.

I start by backing up the entire system to both my Jaz drive and another computer. I then put a checkpoint into source control. Belt *and* suspenders (that's 'braces' on my publisher's side of the pond). Once the system is backed up, I install Nile. Even a quick glance reveals this will be a significant change. I start by looking up the class library in the help file. It says, "Visual Voice Pro 4.0 no longer includes C++ wrapper files for a class library interface." I get a terrible feeling of anxiety in the pit of my stomach.

Their new library is backwards-compatible with their previous API, and so we have the option of hanging on to their old class library implementation, which should continue to work. I have the option, therefore, of ignoring the changes they've made. However, they now suggest that C++ programmers use the VC++ 5.0 **#import** directive to import the Visual Voice control as a COM server. As before, they provide a sample program demonstrating how to do this, but not much more help than that.

The advantage of staying with what we have is that it is up and running. The obvious disadvantage is that I won't gain all the improvements they've made, and each time something doesn't work, they will surely be tempted to tell me to upgrade. I decide to bite the bullet and make the changes to use their new control.

Looking on the bright side, this is a great test for my design: how much has to change to accommodate their new architecture? I'm happy to report that only the **CCaller** class is directly affected, though there will be some minor ripples felt in the flows.

Using the Visual Voice ActiveX Control

I spend two hours trying to understand the new mindset. A page or two in the help file would make this much easier, but this is a beta release, after all. Finally, the light bulb comes on above my head. The idea is to convert my **CCaller** class so that it no longer derives from **CVoice** (which no longer exists) but rather from **CWinThread**. It will also get a new member variable: a pointer to the **IVoice** interface.

This has the enormous advantage that **CCaller** is no longer an invisible frame window, which always felt like a hack, even if it is a common and well documented MFC idiom. Now, **CCaller** is a thread in its own right, which simplifies both multithreading and also receiving messages. Further, because every calling object is a thread, implementing the apartment model is simple, and this keeps MFC happy.

The class constructor must call **EnableAutomation()**, but the bulk of the setup work will be done in **InitInstance()**. I integrate this with my own exception handling, pare out the sample application's DAO database initialization, and what I'm left with is the necessary work to initialize my caller object as a COM object. Here's an excerpt:

```
BOOL CCaller::InitInstance()
{
   long    lRc;
   BOOL    bRc;
   CString strSourceID;
   try
   {
      // ...
      lRc = CoCreateInstance(CLSID_Voice, NULL, CLSCTX_INPROC_SERVER,
                                       IID_IVoice, (void**)&m_pVoice);
      if (lRc != S_OK)
         throw lRc;

      // Connect the event sink to the Voice object.
      IUnknown *pUnkSink;
      ExternalQueryInterface(&IID_IUnknown, (void **) &pUnkSink);
      bRc = AfxConnectionAdvise(m_pVoice, DIID__DVoiceEvents, pUnkSink, TRUE,
                                       &m_dwAdviseCookie);

      pUnkSink->Release();

      if (!bRc)
         throw E_FAIL;
```

```
        // Instantiate the tracer object (one per thread)
        m_pTracer = new CVMTracer;
        ASSERT(m_pTracer);
        m_pTracer->CaptureVoiceManager();
        strSourceID.Format("Line %d", m_nLineNum);
        m_pTracer->SetSourceID(strSourceID);
        VMonTrace("InitInstance(), LineNum = %d", m_nLineNum);
        try
        {
            // Set the PhoneLine property
            m_pVoice->PhoneLine = m_nLineNum;

            // Initialize Voice object
            m_pVoice->Initialize();
            m_pVoice->PerfectCall = true;
            m_pVoice->TraceLevel = vvpUserDefined;

        // ...
        }
```

The caller's **InitInstance()** method is called when the thread is created. It attempts to create the Visual Voice object, and then it registers an event sink so that the caller can be informed when the object receives an event, such as a ring being detected. Next, it instantiates a voice tracer object so that I can track the progress of each call. The voice tracer class, **CVMTracer**, is supplied with Visual Voice to wrap their ActiveX control. Finally, I invoke a number of initialization routines in the voice object itself to set 'perfect call', which enables the voice control to provide me with high quality call progress analysis.

That turned out to be pretty straightforward. The next trick is to get the line manager to set the thread spinning and then, once the thread is going, to tell it to start making calls. The answer is to post a message to the thread; this way you don't wait for it to return, and the message pump ensures that the message isn't received before the object is initialized. Here's an excerpt from the modified line manager:

```
    for (i = 1; i < nLines+1; i++)
    {
        CCaller* pCaller = new CCaller(this, i, m_VRU, m_pDoc);
        BOOL bRc = pCaller->CreateThread();
        ASSERT(bRc);
        myCallers.Add(pCaller);
        pCaller->PostThreadMessage(WM_PLACE_CALLS, 0, 0);
    }
```

The new caller object is created, and then **CreateThread()** is called to set it spinning. The object is then added to the line manager's list of callers, and finally **PostThreadMessage()** is called. **WM_PLACE_CALLS** is a message I define, which will be caught by the caller object. To accomplish this, I add this line to the caller's message map:

```
        ON_THREAD_MESSAGE(WM_PLACE_CALLS, CCaller::MakeCalls)
```

When this message is processed, **MakeCalls()** is called. This sets up a **try** block, and calls a helper function that makes the actual calls:

```
try
{
    ImplementPlaceCalls();
}
```

This way, all exceptions can come back here to be handled properly. **ImplementPlaceCalls()** is responsible for working with the flow actually to place the calls. When it is time to ask Visual Voice to perform a service — to play a message, for example — it's a simple matter to use the interface pointer:

```
m_pVoice->PlayFile(FileName.AllocSysString());
```

The big advantage to their new design is that each **CCaller** object is a **CWinThread**. This creates a nicely compartmentalized approach to the various threads, and makes the entire system cleaner and more responsive.

A Day at Artisoft

Once I have this up, running and debugged, I arrange my day with the developers. Bright and early on a Thursday morning, I drive into East Cambridge to meet with the folks at Artisoft at their company headquarters. They are waiting for me in the conference room. I spend a bit of time explaining my architecture, and then we review my code. They are comfortable with how I'm using the control, though they make a few suggestions to improve my call progress analysis.

I talk with them about how their error handling works. It turns out that if the line is dropped, I'll only get a **vvpLineDrop** *exception* if the Visual Voice control is executing a method at the time. If my program isn't executing a Visual Voice method, I'll get a **LineDropped** *event* instead. The best way to handle this uniformly is to set a user-defined error (in this case, **myLineDropped**). When any Visual Voice method starts to execute, it checks to see if there is a user-defined error, and if so it immediately throws an exception. This effectively translates a **LineDropped** event into a **vvpLineDrop** exception. I can also set a flag which will signal the line drop and thus trigger an exception, even if I'm not about to call another Visual Voice method.

One of the outstanding issues for many weeks has been the conversion of my code from using analog lines, as I have in my office, to the digital T1 lines that Hypotenuse will be using. Analog signaling is quite different from digital, and the latter provides some capabilities, such as call bridging, that we will not even be able to test on analog lines.

Visual Voice manages most of these differences automatically; I need only make some minor changes in my code to enable the program to manage either analog or digital lines at runtime. The technicians at Artisoft walk me through the changes I need to make. On initialization, I will check the Visual Voice **.ini** file to see if we are in a digital or an analog world. If the former, then the new member variable **m_nTimeSlot** will be set to the line number. If the latter, **m_nTimeSlot** will be set to 0. That's about it; all the methods take the **m_nTimeSlot** variable as an argument, but if the variable is zero, it signals analog processing. Of course, I will need to update the **.ini** file on Hypotenuse's computers to reflect that they are using digital lines.

In a few cases, there are different events for digital and analog systems. For example, on analog lines, incoming calls are signaled by **RingDetected()** rather than **TimeSlotRing()**. It's a simple matter, though, to have **RingDetected()** call **TimeSlotRing()** with a time slot of zero, so that we can handle both possibilities in one place.

Call Bridging

While it won't make it into the first release, call bridging is a critical feature we'll be implementing soon. While I'm at Artisoft I ask them to walk me through what will be involved. It turns out to be pretty straightforward. Visual Voice supports the SC bus, which allows me to connect one outgoing line to another. The SC bus provides 1024 timeslots, or 1024 streams of data.

There are two types of SC bus devices: **network** and **resource**. Network devices move data between the card and the phone system. Resource devices are used to listen and speak, to play messages and so forth.

In short, the network device is the phone system, and the resource device is the Visual Voice control. Each device transmits data on one (and only one) timeslot at a time, and receives data in a similar fashion. It is possible for many devices to listen to (receive data from) the same time slot, so you can create one speaker and many listeners — this is how you'd enable many people to listen to the same 'on hold' music. While many devices can listen to the same time slot, only one device can *transmit* on any one time slot.

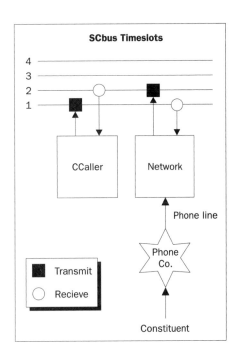

Our use case says that we call a customer, interact with them using voice messaging, and offer to connect them to a second recipient. For example, we could call a constituent and connect them to their senator. To accomplish this, we start with (for example) caller 1 registering to transmit on slot 1 and receive on slot 2. We then connect to a network device, having it *receive* on slot 1 and *transmit* on slot 2:

Thus, caller 1 and the network device (connected to the constituent) are in a *full duplex* conversation; they can both 'hear' and 'talk to' one another. Next, the caller registers a second line, so we've got one **CCaller** object controlling two time slots. The second line is talking on slot 3 and listening on slot 4:

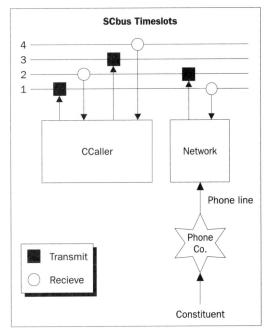

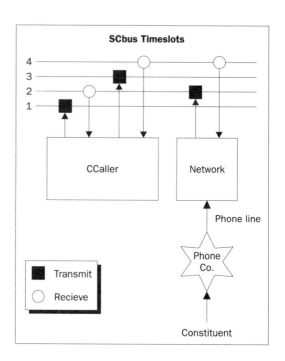

The caller then sets the network device so that it is listening on slot 4 as well:

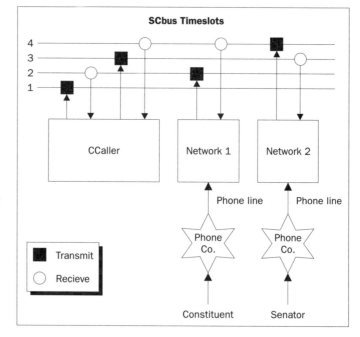

The constituent can now hear the progress of the call. The **CCaller** object connects to the senator's office, whose network device is now *listening* on slot 3 and *talking* on slot 4:

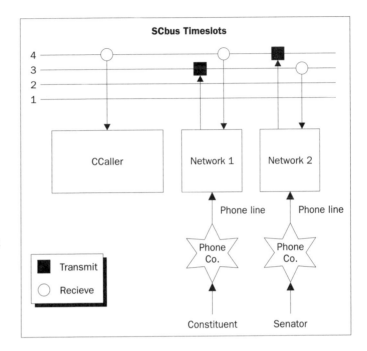

Thus, both Visual Voice and the constituent can hear the senator's office, but only the **CCaller** object can 'talk' to the senator. Once the **CCaller** object detects an answer, it is ready to bridge the call. It stops transmitting on slot 3, and sets the constituent to transmit on slot 3 instead.

Now the customer and the senator are in full duplex mode and can talk with one another. The **CCaller** object continues to listen for the end of the call (that is, either party hangs up), and when the line drop is detected, it tears down both connections.

This is really quite easy to do in Visual Voice. You register the timeslot to make the call to the customer. You then register a second timeslot and call **Dial()** to make the call to the senator's office, and **Route()** to change the customer to a half-duplex configuration to hear the progress. When you connect, you use **Route()** again to change the customer to full duplex. It's easier than it sounds!

WinkStart

When you pick up your phone at home, the phone company computer registers your request for a line, and before you can get the receiver to your ear, they've given you a dial tone. However, if you go off-hook to make 500 calls, all at the same time, the phone company comes unglued. It's as if every baby in the nursery started screaming for breakfast at the same instant. The net effect is that some of your lines won't have dial tones. Without a tone, your dialing sequence fails, and you waste a lot of time cycling through to try again.

What the phone company needs is for you to 'wink' the line — that is, to set a bit high and then low rather quickly. They will respond, when they are good and ready, with a bit signal of their own. By the same analogy, it's as if the baby burped, and then waited quietly for mom to find time to amble over and provide for its needs. The delay involved can be substantial, as much as 10 or 20 milliseconds. To a computer, that is lethargic in the extreme.

I had put off dealing with WinkStart for some time, hoping that Visual Voice would solve this problem. It turns out that they do. Before going off-hook, you call:

```
m_pVoice->Wink(nTimeSlot);
```

This causes Visual Voice to 'wink' the line — it goes off-hook, and then back on very rapidly. You then call

```
m_pVoice->Wait(sState, nTimeOut, nTimeSlot);
```

passing in the signal you are waiting for, how many milliseconds to wait before timing out, and the timeslot on which you want to wait (the same one you winked). This procedure allows you to wait for just the right amount of time. The network will come back when it's ready for you — no sooner, and no later.

This is similar to how you interact with the network to get the incoming dialing number (DNIS) or the ANI number, the digital equivalent to caller ID.

In short, some of the technology that Hypotenuse has long struggled with in previous versions of the software, and that I was quite worried about implementing, we'll get for free as part of the Visual Voice control's bag of tricks.

Design and Code Review

Before heading into testing, I contract with Steve for a day or two of his time to undertake a formal design and code review. Steve spends four hours reading the code and absorbing the design and we have our first session early in August.

The good news is that he sees nothing problematic in the design. The code seems pretty solid as well, "with," he says, "the possible exception of the Scheduler." Since that was my number one area of concern, I'm quick to agree. The scheduler has been evolving for some time, and though I've been tinkering with it — it now checks for *Crisis•Calls*, for example — I'm still not happy. It is better, but still not right. I take another look at the **Run()** method, and I immediately get a bad headache.

```
bool CScheduler::Run()
{
    // Build list of CallTrack objects with current jobs
    bool ProcessJobs = GetCurrentJobs();
    OpenRecordSets();
    CDatabase* pDB = m_pDoc->m_QCtrSet.m_pDatabase;

    ASSERT(m_pDoc->m_DBQSet.CanUpdate());
    ASSERT(m_pDoc->m_DBQSet.CanAppend());
```

```
CTime timerStart = CTime::GetCurrentTime();
bool FillingMinimums = true;
int TimeCounter = 0;
int grandTotal = 0;    // For debugging
int prevElapsed = 0;

// Keep filling the queue until you are shut down
for (;;)
{
   if (m_pDoc->bShutDownServer == 1)
      break;

   CTime now = CTime::GetCurrentTime();
   CTimeSpan elapsed = now - timerStart;

   // Every ten minutes go back to filling minimums
   // Every thirty minutes recheck what jobs to run
   if (m_pDoc->IsCrisis())
   {
      m_pDoc->SetCrisis(false);
      FlushQueue();
      ProcessJobs = GetCurrentJobs();
      FillingMinimums = true;
      m_pDoc->OnCallQueueFlushedForCrisis();
      timerStart = CTime::GetCurrentTime();
   }
   else
   {
      ProcessJobs = GetCurrentJobs();
      if (elapsed.GetTotalMinutes() >= MINUTES_BEFORE_FILLING_MINIMUMS)
      {
         timerStart = CTime::GetCurrentTime();
         FillingMinimums = true;
         // Log("Resetting timer, *** filling minimums");
      }
   }

   if (!ProcessJobs)
   {
      for (int i = 0; i < SEC_IN_MIN * MINUTES_BETWEEN_JOB_CHECK; i++)
      {
         if (m_pDoc->IsCrisis())
            break;
         Sleep(ONE_SECOND);
      }
      continue;
   }
   else    // There are jobs
   {
      int currentCount = ResetQueueSize();
      POSITION pos;
      CCallTrack* pTrack;
      pos = m_CallList.GetHeadPosition();
      pTrack = m_CallList.GetNext(pos);
```

```
// Walk the list of call tracks...

// const intMAX_QUEUE = 2 * NUMBER_PORTS *
                                MINUTES_BEFORE_FILLING_MINIMUMS;
while ( currentCount < MAX_QUEUE )
{
   if (m_pDoc->IsCrisis())
      break;
   ASSERT (pTrack->GetPriority() >= 0);
   ASSERT (pTrack->GetMin() >= 0);

   // If we've fulfilled the minimums or priority requirements
   // or if we have hit the throttle
   while (
         (FillingMinimums && pTrack->GetCount() > pTrack->GetMin()) ||
         (!FillingMinimums &&
                     pTrack->GetCount() > pTrack->GetPriority()) ||
         (pTrack->GetCount() > pTrack->GetThrottle())
         )
   {
      if (m_pDoc->IsCrisis())
         break;

      // Get the next one or restart
      if (pos == NULL)  // No more jobs? Reset them and get by priority
      {
         ResetCallListCounters();   // Set pTrack->GetCount() == 0
         pos = m_CallList.GetHeadPosition();
         FillingMinimums = false;
      }

      pTrack = m_CallList.GetNext(pos);
   }

   // If we're done with this job get the next one or reset
   // Total keeps track of how many left in list to call
   // Why check both? Is this just for safety?
   if (pTrack->GetTotal() < 1 || pTrack->m_pCallSet->IsEOF())
   {
      if (pos == NULL)
      {
         break;
      }

      pTrack = m_CallList.GetNext(pos);
      continue;
   }

   Log("Added callID: %d",pTrack->m_pCallSet->m_CallID);
   m_pDoc->m_DBQSet.AddNew();
   m_pDoc->m_DBQSet.m_CallID = pTrack->m_pCallSet->m_CallID;
   m_pDoc->m_DBQSet.m_PhoneNumber = pTrack->m_pCallSet->m_PhoneNumber;
   m_pDoc->m_DBQSet.m_CustomerID = pTrack->m_pCallSet->m_CustomerID;
```

```
            m_pDoc->m_DBQSet.m_JobID = pTrack->m_pCallSet->m_JobID;
            m_pDoc->m_DBQSet.m_StartDate = pTrack->m_pCallSet->m_StartDate;
            m_pDoc->m_DBQSet.m_EndDate = pTrack->m_pCallSet->m_EndDate;
            m_pDoc->m_DBQSet.m_NumberOfAttempts =
                                pTrack->m_pCallSet->m_NumberOfAttempts;
            m_pDoc->m_DBQSet.m_EndStatus = pTrack->m_pCallSet->m_EndStatus;
            m_pDoc->m_DBQSet.m_ConnectionDate =
                                pTrack->m_pCallSet->m_ConnectDate;
            m_pDoc->m_DBQSet.m_ConnectStatus =
                                pTrack->m_pCallSet->m_ConnectStatus;
            m_pDoc->m_DBQSet.m_LineNumber = pTrack->m_pCallSet->m_LineNumber;
            m_pDoc->m_DBQSet.m_VRU = pTrack->m_pCallSet->m_VRU;
            m_pDoc->m_DBQSet.Update();
            ++(*pTrack);    // Increases count and decrements total left to do

            pTrack->m_pCallSet->Edit();
            pTrack->m_pCallSet->m_EndStatus = ENQUEUED;
            pTrack->m_pCallSet->Update();
            currentCount++;
            pTrack->m_pCallSet->MoveNext();
        }    // End while queue is too small

        // Check for crisis every second
        for (int i = 0; i < SEC_IN_MIN * MINUTES_BETWEEN_SCHEDULER_RUNS; i++)
        {
            if (m_pDoc->IsCrisis())
                break;
            Sleep(ONE_SECOND);
        }
      }    // End if process job
    }    // End for ever loop
    return true;
}
```

I wrote this thing, and *I* can't tell if it works. You'd think I'd know better than to let this code grow to such absurd proportions that it is unreadable. Yet, just like turning up the heat on that slowly boiling frog, I added one bit of complexity after another, and only once it was done did I realize how ugly and convoluted it was. At this point, it is almost too overwhelming to try to sort it out. One of the wonderful things about a code review, however, is that you can't put it off any longer.

We slowly pick the function apart, challenging both the logic and the organization. When we are done, we have a much cleaner set of methods, each of which does one small thing. The entire algorithm is now much cleaner and easier to understand, and to debug:

```
bool CScheduler::Run()
{
    bool bProcessJobs = false;
    OpenRecordSets();
    CDatabase* pDB =    m_pDoc->m_QCtrSet.m_pDatabase;
    ASSERT(m_pDoc->m_DBQSet.CanUpdate());
```

```
        ASSERT(m_pDoc->m_DBQSet.CanAppend());
        ResetTimer();
        while(!m_pDoc->IsShuttingDown())
        {
            if (m_pDoc->IsCrisis())
            {
                FlushQueue();
            }

            if (!GetCurrentJobs())
            {
                SleepUnlessCrisis(MINUTES_BETWEEN_JOB_CHECK);
                continue;
            }

            ProcessJobs();
            SleepUnlessCrisis(MINUTES_BETWEEN_SCHEDULER_RUNS);
        }                                        // End for ever loop
        return true;
}
```

SleepUnlessCrisis() encapsulates an algorithm to sleep the required number of minutes, while checking for a crisis or a shutdown message every second. The tricky method is **ProcessJobs()**, which is responsible for adding the jobs to the queue:

```
void CScheduler::ProcessJobs()
{
    POSITION pos;
    CCallTrack* pTrack = GetFirstCallTrack(pos);
    int currentCount = ResetQueueSize();
    int passCount = 0;
    while ( currentCount++ < MAX_QUEUE &&
            HaveValidCallTrack(pos, pTrack, passCount) &&
            !m_pDoc->IsCrisisOrShutDown() )
    {
        m_pDoc->AddToDBQueue(pTrack);
    }
}
```

The logic is straightforward. Start by initializing the list of call tracks. If the queue isn't full, *and* you have a valid call track object, *and* it isn't time to stop to handle a crisis, then add this job to the queue and get the next one.

Once again, the difficult work here is handed off to another function, in this case **HaveValidCallTrack()**:

```
bool CScheduler::HaveValidCallTrack(POSITION& pos, CCallTrack*& pTrack,
                                                          int& passCount)
{
    int attemptNumber = 1;
```

```
      while (DoneUsingThisCallTrack(pTrack, passCount))
      {
         if (pos == NULL)
         {
            pTrack = GetFirstCallTrack(pos);
            passCount++;
            if (++attemptNumber > 2)
            {
               pTrack = 0;
               return false;
            }
         }
         pTrack = m_CallList.GetNext(pos);
      }
      return (pTrack != NULL);
   }
```

The logic in this small method is also clear. If you're done with the current call track, try to get the next one. If you are at the end of your call tracks, then wrap around to the beginning and get the first one. Keep track of how many times you do that. If you go through the entire list twice, then there are no valid ones, so return false.

This time, the interesting work is done in **DoneUsingThisCallTrack()**:

```
   bool CScheduler::DoneUsingThisCallTrack(CCallTrack* pTrack, int& passCount)
   {
      if (ElapsedTime() > MINUTES_BEFORE_FILLING_MINIMUMS_AGAIN)
      {
         passCount = 0;
         ResetTimer();
      }

      int min = pTrack->GetMin();
      int throttle = pTrack->GetThrottle();
      int priority = pTrack->GetPriority();

      int maxThisRound = min + (priority * passCount);
      int max = maxThisRound;

      if (throttle != 0)
         max = throttle < maxThisRound ? throttle : maxThisRound;

      if (pTrack->GetCount() > max || pTrack->GetTotal() < 1)
         return true;
      else
         return false;
   }
```

First of all, we check to see if enough time has passed to start filling minimums again. If so, we reset everything, setting **passCount** to zero and calling **ResetTimer()** to reset the timer. In turn, **ResetTimer()** will call **ResetCallListCounters()**, which will set the counters to zero. Whatever the **passCount**, we then check to see how many you are allowed to add for this round. In the first round, that will be the minimums. In subsequent rounds, it will be the minimums plus (**priority** * <whatever round we're in>). The net effect of this is that we add by priority each round after the minimums are completed.

Each method has taken on a small job, rendering the remaining methods much easier to understand, and thus to test.

Reviewing the CRC Cards

Now that the product is written, it is time to go back and build CRC cards based on the objects we've implemented. Once these are written, they become documentation for the objects and an opportunity to revisit our use cases and see how they play out.

Here are just a few of the CRC cards I put together based on the objects as they exist in the source code.

CCallClientDoc	
Responsibilities	_Collaborations_
Manages system-wide state	CLineManager
Manages ports	CLocalCallQueue
Owns local call queue	CCaller

CLineManager	
Responsibilities	_Collaborations_
Manages collection of CCaller objects	CCaller
Implements allocation of line policy	

CCaller

Responsibilities	Collaborations
Manages Visual Voice Control	IVoice
Manages flows	CScript

IVoice

Responsibilities	Collaborations
Manages Dialogic Card	
interactions	

CCall

Responsibilities	Collaborations
Responsible for characteristics	CJob
of a single call	Database
Records result of a call attempt	

CScript	ABSTRACT DATA TYPE
Responsibilities	Collaborations
Provides common interface for all flows	

CPreproductionScript	Parent: CScript
Responsibilities	Collaborations
Manages interaction for preproduction	

Each CRC card provides only the most essential information. On the back of each is a short description of the class. Collectively, these descriptions are part of the data dictionary of the overall project.

Reviewing the Use Cases

These short responsibility lists are enough to understand what each object does and to evaluate its role in each of the use cases. We revisit the principal use cases to ensure that the final implementation is sufficient to deliver on these requirements. The first task is to identify those use cases that will not be supported at all in the first version. Of those which will be supported, we identify those which will be handled outside the system. The remaining use cases are the core of the first version, and will be examined in some detail:

- A potential customer calls and talks with a salesperson to gather more information.

  Supported, but outside the system

- In a conversation with a salesperson, the customer decides to sign up.

  Customer service will enter the record using the database directly or using Web pages built by Gamma.

- A potential customer logs in to the Internet to sign up.

  Not supported in V1

- A potential customer calls into our phone mail system to sign up.

  Not supported in V1

- The potential customer needs more information or clarification.

  Supported in customer service

- An existing customer calls in, chooses phone numbers and audio, sets the date and time and other calling criteria and starts a job.

  Working

- An existing customer prerecords audio for future use.

  Not supported in V1

- A customer uploads a set of phone numbers for use with an upcoming job he has already scheduled.

  Not supported in V1

- A customer calls to cancel a job scheduled for the next day.

  Supported by customer service

- A customer calls in an emergency cancellation of a job already in progress.

  Supported by customer service

- A customer calls in a *Crisis•Call*. The audio and phone list have already been selected, the calls are to begin instantly.

  Working

- A customer has scheduled a job to begin now, but the audio is not yet available.

  Not possible in V1

- A customer needs to send us phone numbers but doesn't have access to the Internet, so he sends a list on a disk via Federal Express.

  Supported by customer service

- A customer needs a detailed report of everyone called, differentiating between those who answered, those where a message was left on an answering machine and those which couldn't be reached at all.

  Working

- The owner wants to know whether he has enough lines to handle every emergency.

  Working

- Operations wants to be certain the system is secure.

  Working

- Operations wants proof the system is reliable.

  Working

- The manager of Sales wants to know if he can sell a job calling 250,000 people in the first week of May.

  Supported by customer service

- A customer wants to deliver one message to registered Democrats and a different message to everyone else on his list.

  Not supported in V1

- A customer wants to offer the recipient of his call the opportunity to bridge the line to someone else.

  Not supported in V1

- We place a call and get a person on the line and play the appropriate messages.

  Working

- We place a call and get a machine and play the appropriate messages.

  Working

- We place a call and think it is a person but it is a machine. We do the right thing.

  Working

- We place a call and think it is a machine, but it is a person. We do the right thing.

  Working

- We place a call and get a busy signal and reschedule.

  Working

- We place a call and get an operator intercept for a number no longer in service. Cancel the call.

  Working

- We place a call and get a ring but no answer, call back later.

  Working

- A call recipient returns our call and asks never to be called again.

  Supported by customer service

- We place a call, deliver the message and report the result to the customer.

  Working

While there are a conspicuous number of use cases that didn't make it into V1, on reflection we do support the important use cases. Further, just about everything listed as *Not supported In V1* can be added quickly and easily to V2, and just about everything listed as *Supported by customer service* can be added by writing simple web pages.

Our final step is to walk through each of the working use cases, applying the CRC cards to see how they play out. Here is just one of them:

"An existing customer calls in, chooses phone numbers and audio, sets the date and time and other calling criteria, and starts a job"

I pick up the **IVoice** card and call out, "Ring detected." I then pick up the **CCaller** card and say, "I'm receiving calls, so I need the preproduction flow." Someone hands me the **CPreproductionScript** card and I say, "First, I need to know if you are a valid caller and allowed to start a job. I inherit this ability from **CScript**." I pick up **CScript** and say, "I check the login and validation."

I continue through the scenario, switching between preproduction and the script card until I've taken all the information from the caller. Along the way, I pick up the **CJob** card to create a job, and the ODBC card to manage my interaction with the database. ODBC isn't a class in our system, but it is a logical entity to which we delegate some of the responsibilities. I find having a CRC card for it very helpful, it crystallizes what I expect ODBC to provide.

Each area of responsibility appears to be well-defined and clean. No object, other than **CCaller**, has more than one thing to do. Still, I'm troubled by the fact that **CCaller** does appear to have two significant areas of responsibility: managing the **IVoice** object, and also managing the call interactions. I'll have to leave this as is for the first version, but I will return to it once version 1 ships. At that time, it may make sense to divide the object into two smaller objects, each with a single area of responsibility.

Walking through the use case reveals much of the strength of the design. It gives me an opportunity to ensure that I understand how the objects interact, and this will provide a solid basis on which to test the system.

As often happens, this use case begs the creation of others. How, for example, did the **CCaller** object spring into existence? How did it know it was supposed to be answering calls rather than making calls? We create more use cases to cover the set-up and tear-down scenarios, and test those with the CRC cards as well.

Transition

The use case review has offered a tremendous opportunity to review the state of the project and to clear the decks for testing. We are virtually code complete, we have a solid and sustainable design, and on balance, frankly I'm quite proud of how it all turned out.

In the final weeks before handing the product over to Hypotenuse, I'll turn my attention to building test modules that will exercise each of the principal objects. Once I've proven that the objects are solid, I'll create test routines to test their interactions. By breaking the system down and testing each part, I can enhance my confidence in the overall system. Finally, I'll build integrated test routines to shakedown the entire system.

It is time also to turn to BoundsChecker to find the inevitable memory leaks, API failures and other minor, hard-to-find bugs that undermine the long-term integrity of the project. Finally, once I'm confident the system is robust and I've found and fixed all the bugs I can find, I'll hand the system over to Hypotenuse for load-testing.

At the end of 1997, I will add an additional bonus chapter, describing the rollout and delivery of the final product. This will be made available, at no charge, on the Wrox Internet site (http://www.wrox.com) as well as on the Liberty Associates Inc. site (http://www.libertyassociates.com).

Looking Back

It has been an exciting and challenging nine months. Chronicling the project for this book has forced me to focus on the process, and I've learned a lot along the way.

We started out with a vision: Jay's idea for his next-generation calling platform. We ended with working code that will transform his business. We have a solid design on which we can build additional features, and a robust code base that's flexible and extensible. Most important, we completed the project on time and on budget, and we delivered the features our customer identified as most important.

We did this with a small, tightly focused team. We followed a well-understood process, and annotated our ideas and our decisions using the UML notation. This allowed us to clarify our thinking and to communicate cleanly and unambiguously.

It would have been easy to grow the team, and along with it to add features and to complicate the first release. I'm convinced now, more than ever, that we took the right path. By keeping the team small, the feature list well trimmed and focused, and the time line short, we produced a working product in nine months and we didn't let the project spin out of control.

I have a buddy who is working on a project that is similar in many ways. They are building a mission-critical system for patients to notify their families in case of a medical emergency. Their requirements are different from ours, but the projects have a lot in common. Any comparison must be misleading, but I can't help but notice that they have a much larger staff, and a much longer time-line. My friend's quick estimate of the cost of that project is no less than 20 times the cost of this one.

As I said in the beginning, not every project can be done with a very small team. However, I'm convinced that small teams are more efficient, less expensive, more likely to succeed and more fun.

This book did not attempt to be a tutorial, but rather was a case study in the *application* of object-oriented analysis and design techniques, UML, design patterns, C++, COM and related technologies. As we worked, I realized that it needed a companion volume that showed *what* to do; a step-by-step tutorial in the process and the notation. As a result of that insight, I'm now writing a new book, *Beginning Object-oriented Analysis and Design using C++* to be published by Wrox Press early in 1998.

Thanks

The end of a project is always a bittersweet time. A sense of accomplishment is mixed with the sadness that accompanies transition and change. You have collectively been an important part of this project. Because of your participation, a number of issues were clarified and documented in more detail than they might otherwise have been. Along the way, explaining what I was doing helped clarify my own thinking.

It is my hope that you found the project worthwhile and educational. If you have comments or suggestions, please don't hesitate to send me e-mail at jliberty@libertyassociates.com. Thanks again.

Jesse Liberty
October 1, 1997

```cpp
= false;
Time();
= now.Format("%b %d
er = "start < '";
Day;
' and enddate > '";
today;
*'";
ScheduleSet.m_strFilter =

JobScheduleSet.IsOpen())
JobScheduleSet.Requery();
pDoc>m_JobScheduleSet.Open();
lTrack* pCallTrack;
l ok;

ile
pDoc>m_JobScheduleSet.IsEOF())

pCallTrack = new
llTrack(m_pDoc>m_JobScheduleSet.m_
bID);
    ok = pCallTrack>Initialize();

    if (ok)
    {   Log("ok\n");

m_CallList.AddHead(pCallTrack);
        foundJobs = true;

    }
    else
    {
        Log("...Rejected!\n");
        delete pCallTrack;

    }

m_pDoc>m_JobScheduleSet.MoveNext();

    run
        CTime::GetCurre
    CTime end = theJobSet.
    CTime start = theJobSet.GetYea
    CTime todayStart(start.GetYea
    start.GetMonth(),now.GetDay(),
    start.GetHour(),

        start.GetMinute(),
        start.GetSecond());
        CTime todayEnd(end.GetYear(),
    end.GetMonth(), now.GetDay(),
    end.GetHour(),

    end.GetMinute(), end.GetSecond());

    if (todayStart > now || today
    now)
        {   theJobSet.Close();
            return false;

        }

    CTimeSpan theSpan = end no
    int totalMinutes =
    theSpan.GetTotalMinutes();

    if (end > todayEnd) // 
than today
        {   int AdditionalMin =
    GetAdditionalMinutes(theJ
t,
    theJobSet.m_EndDate);
            CTimeSpan todaySp
    now;    totalMinutes =
    todaySpan.GetTotalMin
    AdditionalMin;
        }

    m_min = ( ( (m_t
    totalMinutes) + 1
    );    m_Priority = t
        m_Tilt = theJo
        m_Throttle =
        m_JobID = the
        theJobSet.Cl
```

Fundamentals of Analysis and Design

This book is targeted at a number of people, with varying degrees of experience in the design and development of software. Some of you are professional programmers, perhaps with an extensive background in object-oriented development. Others are less experienced, but need to understand the process in greater detail.

To ensure that we all have a common understanding, this appendix will provide a quick background in object-oriented analysis and design, the fundamentals of software development and a quick overview of some of the technology used in this book. Most important, it will provide a road map to the process itself: what happens first, what follows and how we get from a great idea to working software to a finished product, without driving off into a ditch along the way.

This appendix can not hope to be a complete tutorial on these subjects. I have a new book, *Beginning Object-Oriented Analysis and Design* (due out early in 1998), which will provide a comprehensive tutorial, and which will act as a companion volume to this book.

Developing Software Start To Finish

The process of developing software is a black art to most people. They imagine that software development requires a fantastic mix of mathematical and analytical insight; programming must be a skill that few mortals can master. The dirty little secret is that programming isn't very difficult. With a few months of effort, any reasonably intelligent person can learn to program. It isn't all that hard, and for some of us it is great fun.

The trick in writing world class software is not in mastering the syntax of a particular language. Each language is just a tool, like a paintbrush or an awl; figuring out how to hold and manipulate the tool is the easy part. The hard part is in learning to express yourself once you've mastered the tool, and to express yourself effectively given the constraints of the real world: the goal is not just to make something beautiful, it is to make something *practical*.

The best developers go beyond their craft and see not just the code but also the business strategy the product serves. This book examines the *entire* process, from conceptualization through delivery.

Object-oriented Analysis And Design

Twenty years ago, the bulk of the work and skill in writing software was in the programming itself. This has so pervaded our thinking about software that it seems a tautology: of course the work in software development is in the programming, what else is there? Yet it is the thrust of this book that there are many other issues to consider. Writing the actual code is almost a trivial part of software development; certainly in many ways it is the easiest part.

This was not always the case. Thirty years ago structured programming didn't exist! Twenty years ago the microcomputer hadn't been invented, and we were all time-sharing on mainframes and refrigerator-sized minis. Even a decade ago skilled programmers spent their time making sure their code was small and tight and used as little memory as possible.

Great hackers not only knew the syntax of their programming language, they understood the memory configuration of their platform and the attributes and parameters of the hardware itself. Those were the days when the best programmers wrote in Assembler.

In the Eighties, we became aware that memory was getting cheaper, programmer time more expensive, and programs more complex. Methods were created to structure the software so that we could better maintain it. Programming languages such as C, which supported a structured approach, while not sacrificing performance, were very much in demand.

Today, memory is cheap, chips are fast, programmer time is expensive, and time to market is very short. We spend a lot less time worrying about optimizing memory usage, and a lot more time worrying about the complexity of the problems we're trying to solve. Building large complex systems requires a methodology. You simply can not build an enormously complex system without a plan; it would be like trying to build a skyscraper without a blueprint.

Object-oriented analysis and design is nothing more (and nothing less!) than a methodology for managing that complexity and ensuring that your programs will be sufficiently robust and flexible to withstand the rapidly changing *business* requirements behind your product. The demand that object-oriented analysis and design tries to meet is to build complex software quickly and reliably.

Mastering Complexity

It is a commonplace of pop-psychology that the human mind can hold seven ideas at one time (plus or minus two). Show most of us seven coins and we get it, show us nine and we just see a jumble, or we see groups of five and four, or three groups of three. Take a look at the picture on the left: you see three things. Now look at the picture on the right; you see a jumble of things. The picture on the left aggregates all the pencils into one idea: a box of pencils. The paper clips are bundled into a single concept, as are the dimes. Object-oriented programming builds on this understanding.

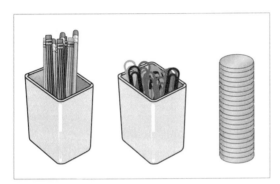 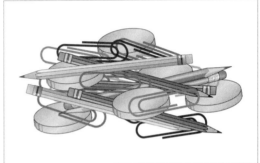

Millions of years of evolution have crafted our ability to find patterns and hierarchies in the world. We look at plants and we immediately and unconsciously begin to create taxonomies: trees and bushes, plants and flowers. We look at animals and we see mammals and fish. We look at mammals and we see horses and dogs, we look at dogs and we see hounds and terriers. We can't help it, it is what we do, it is part of being human.

Object-oriented programming builds on this inherent human tendency to classify. These hierarchies have tremendous survival benefit for us, they help us understand and predict the behavior of the things in our environment, and more important they protect us from being overwhelmed by the information we're constantly processing. If I can look at an animal and say "Oh, that is a kind of terrier," then with that single thought I learn a lot. I learn that as a terrier it will be small and yappy, that it is a dog and thus will be friendly if trained, that it is a mammal and thus bears live young, that it is an animal and thus breaths, that it is alive and thus moves and reproduces, that it is real and on this planet, and not a fantasy object, and so forth.

Think how much simpler it is to think 'terrier' than 'a real thing on the earth which moves and reproduces and bears its young alive and can be friendly if trained and is small and yappy'. I have to hold one concept (terrier) in my head rather than 8 (real, on-earth, moves, reproduces, live young, friendly-if-trained, small, yappy). This is the essence of object-oriented programming in a nutshell.

Closely related to our tendency to think of things as being in a hierarchy is our ability to create mental models. We model the solar system by showing a sun with nine balls around it. We model the atom by showing a nucleus with electrons swirling (or more recently clustering) around it. We model evolution by showing pictures of apes morphing into men. Object-oriented programming builds on the observation that when our model closely resembles the real world, it is more successful than when it is a few levels of abstraction removed.

Object-oriented vs. Procedural

In procedural programming, we thought of our programs as functions acting on data. If you were modeling a company's payroll, you might design a data structure with information about the employee's name, address, social security numbers and income, and then you would have functions to manipulate that data. These functions would be fed huge amounts of data and would process that data much as a machine processes raw materials.

The object-oriented programmer rejects this as an inadequate model of the world. When I think about the employees of a company I don't think of them as collections of data I can manipulate, but rather as entities, each of which has properties (age, salary, etc.) and capabilities (things I can ask this employee to do).

The advantage of the object-oriented perspective is that objects are tightly bound entities. Everything they can know (all their data) and everything they can do (all their methods) are tied together into a neat bundle. I can then think of them as a single thing; and that helps me simplify my model of the world. This is called **encapsulation**.

Object-oriented developers divide the world into providers and consumers. The provider of a class writes the class and makes it work. The consumer or client of that class uses objects of that class to get work done.

Providers and consumers talk to each other across an *interface*. The interface is the contract the provider offers to the consumer. The interface tells the client what the class can do. The details are invisible to the client. The power in object-oriented programming is that the consumer of the class does not want or need to know how the class works; he just wants to know what it can *do*. This is called **data hiding** and is a natural outcome of encapsulation.

There are two huge advantages to this approach. First, the client can ignore the details; thus he can concentrate on bigger and more important things. Second, and perhaps more important, the provider can change the inner workings of the class without breaking the client's program. Thus, as the class designer learns more, he can make his class better without forcing his clients to understand those details nor to recompile or, worse, to rewrite their code.

Encapsulation is one of the three pillars of object-oriented programming. The other two are **inheritance** and **polymorphism**. Inheritance is the ability to say that something is in an *is-a* relationship with another thing. A car *is-a* vehicle, a chimp *is-a* primate, a dialog box *is-a* window.

What do we mean when we say a dog *is-a* mammal? We mean you that everything you know about mammals will be true about dogs. If it is true that all mammals give birth to live young; then telling you that a dog *is-a* mammal tells you, implicitly that dogs give birth to live young. If a dog hatched from an egg, it wouldn't be a mammal.

When we say a button *is-a* window, we promise that anything you can do with a window, you can do with a button. That is a one-way promise. While all dogs are mammals, not all mammals are dogs. Similarly, while all buttons are windows, not all windows are buttons. A button can do everything a window can do, but not all windows can do everything a button can do.

We say the dog **class** (type) is **derived** from the mammal class, and we say that mammals are **base** classes for dogs. These terms, derived and base, are just shorthand to say that the derived type *is-a* specialization of the base type, and that the base type generalizes all the types derived from it.

This is powerful technique for managing complexity. It allows you to specialize functionality in derived classes (e.g. dogs specialize how mammals act and behave) and to generalize and factor out common behavior in base classes (e.g. mammals generalize the birth process of dogs, horses, cats, mules, apes, and so forth).

In software terms, this allows you to generalize how windows behave (draw, paint, move, etc.) but specialize particular window behavior (e.g. how buttons work).

The fact that buttons and dialog boxes and check boxes are all windows allows you to treat each of them as a window when you need to. Thus, you can tell a button, a check box, a list box or a dialog box to draw itself, and they all will.

Each of these window subtypes inherits the ability to draw from its window base type, but they each specialize their particular drawing routine. The part of your program that asks the various windows to draw doesn't need to know the details. It can have a window of any kind and tell it to draw itself, without knowing or caring whether this particular window is a button or a dialog box.

That ability to treat all windows the same and have them specialize their behavior based on their real type, is called **polymorphism**. *Poly* means many, *morph* means form. Thus you tell a window to draw and each of the many forms will behave appropriately.

Once again, we see object-oriented programming helping to manage complexity. Because you can ignore the details of how each window draws, you can focus on using the window rather than focusing on how it works. The client — that part of the code which needs the window to draw — can use the windows polymorphically, and the details are handled by the provider: the programmer who writes the individual window classes.

The Process

Object-oriented programming depends on two related but separate skills: **analysis** and **design**. Object-oriented analysis is a technique for examining a problem and understanding it. Object-oriented design is a technique for building a plan, a software architecture. These two, together, provide the necessary framework in which you can 'do' object-oriented programming.

Object-oriented analysis and design together are part of the overall process of developing software. The major steps along the way are:

Stage	Description
Conceptualization (also called Inception)	Figure out what you want to build
Analysis	Create a set of well understood requirements
Design	Create a plan or blueprint for implementation
Implementation (also called Construction)	Write the code
Testing	Make sure it works
Delivery	Get it into the hands of your consumers

Each of these stages has a particular goal and outcome. Typically these stages are not linear, you move among them and cycle through them, but each stage is at least conceptually discrete.

Conceptualization or Inception

The conceptualization phase is typically very short. The goal of this phase is to come to a common understanding of what the product is at a very high level of abstraction. This is often best understood in terms of how it will be used.

At this stage of the project, we think of the product as a 'black box' — that is, we don't examine in any detail how it works, but just how people (and other systems) will interact with it. We call these things which interact with our new system the **actors**.

A **use case** is a description of how an actor interacts with the system. In conceptualization we try to understand our most general use cases. Typically, the team involved with conceptualization is very small: ideally one person owns the vision of the product and the software architect's job is simply to clarify this vision and get it down on paper.

Elaboration

The elaboration phase consists of two activities: **analysis** and **design**.

Analysis

Analysis is for many people the most difficult challenge in the entire process. It is during analysis that the early conceptualization is fleshed out into a detailed requirements document. In analysis, all the hand waving stops, and the details of the interactions between the actors and the system are articulated.

In analysis, the user interface must be described in painful detail. The art of writing a good requirements specification is little appreciated; yet few are able to do it well. A good spec makes for a powerful contract between the customer and the software developer.

The analysis phase typically takes about 10%-20% of the life of the entire project. Depending on how complex the software is, and how well thought out it is before the developer becomes involved, this phase can last weeks, months or in some sad cases, years.

Design

Once the product requirements are well understood, it is time to plan how the software will work. This can be the longest phase of the entire product; and certainly is the phase which requires the most difficult and specialized skills. The software architect, or object-oriented designer, must form a bridge between the customer's requirements and the capabilities and attributes of the technology with which he will implement the product.

Good design is often broken into two phases: high-level design and low-level design.

High-Level Design

In high-level design, the architect thinks in terms of the component objects in the software without regard to platform considerations. That is, the architect determines what high-level objects will be required, such as an employee object, a calling scheduler and so forth, without thinking about what programming language will be used to implement these objects, what operating system the product will be run on, or what calling devices will be used.

In high-level design, we are interested in how the pieces fit together and how they interact. We focus on the class interfaces; specifically the public interfaces or contracts that the various classes will make with one another. Experienced designers often make use of **design patterns** at this stage of the development.

Design Patterns

You can't spend half an hour with a senior developer and not be warned never to reinvent the wheel. This is great advice — who wants to recreate a design that has been worked out by others dozens of time in the past? More important, the first time you work something out there is a high risk that it won't work correctly; using a well understood and well tested solution reduces the work and reduces the risk. The problem has always been, however, "How do I find out how this has been solved before?"

Companies created their own oral tradition of such solutions, but there was no easy way to find them, and it was easier just to recreate it than to search for these well understood solutions. Even when we did find a solution, it was difficult to explain what we had done, as there was no common vocabulary.

In 1995, Erich Gamma, Richard Helm, Ralph Johnson and John Vlissides set out to remedy this problem. They released a collection of well understood designs in the book *Design Patterns; Elements of Reusable Object-Oriented Software*. This revolutionary book undertook to provide simple, elegant, easily understood solutions to specific recurring problems in building object-oriented software.

In their preface they make the point that these solutions tend to evolve over time. By capitalizing on the work of others, not only can you save yourself that process, but you eliminate all the pain and suffering of going down the wrong paths.

Once you start looking for design patterns, you find them in more and more places. It is like staring at those 3-D pictures in the mall; suddenly you get it and the picture springs forth out of the background; clear and compelling. Design patterns can ensure that you are building robust and well designed programs.

Low-Level Design

In low-level design we translate the high level abstractions into a particular platform strategy. It is here that we think in terms of the particular implementation language, operating system, database and hardware.

We take the time to do the high-level design first, because we don't want to overly constrain our design by the capabilities and limitations of the implementing technology. In all likelihood the design will last longer than the particular version of the database or operating system we build on top of.

Implementation or Construction

When the design is sufficiently complete and understood, it is time to begin implementation. What is critically different in the implementation of an object-oriented program is that the implementation is both dictated by and constrained by the design. During design we created class interfaces; we now implement those interfaces. The interface is a contract among the various classes, and we are particularly reluctant to break that contract in implementation.

Transition: Testing & Delivery

Once the product is complete, and the features described in the analysis phase have been fully implemented, it is time to begin testing. The role of Quality Assurance (QA) is hugely important in the process — it is axiomatic that those parts of your software that you don't test, will surely break.

A fully tested product is ready for delivery. For some projects this means nothing more than transferring the software from the test system to the 'live' system. For other products this means distribution, either over the Internet, or in shrink-wrapped boxes at the local software store.

The Development Cycle

This process, from conceptualization through analysis, design and implementation is not as clean or as linear as this description would lead you to believe. In a healthy development environment you cycle through these phases as the project progresses.

Methodology

The specific techniques that help you accomplish your goals for each of these stages is called the methodology. Even identifying the stages and the right order of what to do first and what to do next, is part of the methodology.

Here's the scary part: there is no single right way. Until recently, there were many competing strategies. Three of the most prominent were created by Grady Booch, James Rumbaugh and Ivar Jacobson. Booch created the **Booch Method**, documented in his book *Object-Oriented Analysis and Design*. Rumbaugh and his colleagues created **OMT**, the **Object Modeling Technique**, documented in his book *Object-Oriented Modeling and Design*. Jacobson wrote *Object-Oriented Software Engineering* and is best known for conceiving of **use cases** — the systematic description of how people or systems will interact with the system you are building. There were a number of other methodologies created by other groups as well, each of which took a slightly different perspective on the *art* of object-oriented analysis and design.

Booch, Rumbaugh and Jacobson, known on the Internet as the Three Amigos, are now all at Rational Software. Together, they have released the **Unified Modeling Language** (**UML**) and soon they will release the much awaited **Rational Objectory**. Rational Objectory is an attempt to merge and build on their individual methodologies. The Unified Modeling Language is a technique for creating useful diagrams to understand the design as it evolves.

This book loosely follows the Rational Objectory model, but frankly I am not motivated to get any particular methodology exactly right; I tend to find my way through an eclectic assortment of proven techniques. This book has been reviewed by a number of experts in various methodologies, and they've helped me clarify my thinking and stay on track, but I resist jumping through hoops for the sake of form. The goal for me is to build a solid product, not to conform to a methodology. This book contains pointers to a number of resources which can help you learn the Rational Objectory model to whatever degree of conformance you find most comfortable.

Similarly, I use UML to illustrate the various use cases and object interactions. I believe you will find these diagrams to be self-documenting and not at all confusing. Once again, if you want to fully understand how to create your own diagrams, you will want to check the list of resources elsewhere in the book.

Tools & Techniques

A number of tools have been created to help both with the analysis and design process and with capturing the results in diagrams, and ultimately in code. For this project we used two principal tools: Rational Rose and CRC Cards.

Rational Rose

Rational Rose is software produced by Rational Software Corporation. It provides a powerful tool for creating UML diagrams, and is the commercial manifestation of the work done by the Three Amigos.

Rational Rose comes in many 'flavors', some of which will produce working code, others will read existing code, and so forth. I used the Rational Rose modeler version 4.0 to create most of the diagrams in this book. It is a great product, both for building models and for learning and understanding both UML and the process itself.

CRC Cards

Class - Responsibility - Collaboration cards were first described by Ward Cunningham and Kent Beck in an OOPSLA paper delivered in 1989. They were brought to a broader audience by Rebecca J. Wirfs-Brock and are often associated with her work. In 1995 Nancy M. Wilkinson wrote the wonderful book, *Using CRC Cards*.

CRC cards are nothing more than 4x5 index cards. On each card you write the name of the class, beneath the name you may want to write its subclasses and superclasses. The rest of the face of the card is divided in half, on the left side, you write the word *Responsibilities* and on the right side, you write *Collaborations*.

```
CLineManager

Responsibilities            Collaborations
Manages collection of CCaller   CCaller
    objects
Implements allocation of line
    policy
```

Finally, on the back of the card you write a brief description of the purpose of the class.

The advantage of using index cards, rather than electronic CRC cards is that they are 100% portable, they fit in your pocket. Further, as Wilkinson says, they are *anthropomorphic*. That is, you can pick them up and wave them in the air and easily see and feel exactly who is responsible for what behavior.

The disadvantage to using hand written CRC cards is that when you are ready to move the information back into another tool, such as Rational Rose, you must rekey all the details. CRC cards can be limiting in large projects as they don't scale well, but they are ideally suited for our project.

Relax

This book is not intended to be a tutorial, it is a case study. Along the way I'll explain what I am doing and why. You don't need to be an expert in object-oriented analysis and design, C++, patterns, or any other technology to enjoy or benefit from this book. The goal is not to teach how to do it, but rather to show how it was done.

```
= false;

Time();
= now.Format("%b %d

er = "start < '";
oday;
, and enddate > '";
oday;
"'";

bScheduleSet.m_strFilter =

JobScheduleSet.IsOpen())

JobScheduleSet.Requery();

JobScheduleSet.Open();

pDoc>m_JobScheduleSet;

llTrack* pCallTrack;
l ok;

ile
pDoc>m_JobScheduleSet.IsEOF())

pCallTrack = new
allTrack(m_pDoc>m_JobScheduleSet.m_
bID);        ok = pCallTrack>Initialize();

if (ok)
{    Log("ok\n");

m_CallList.AddHead(pCallTrack);
foundJobs = true;
}
else
{    Log("...Rejected!\n");
delete pCallTrack;
}

pDoc>m_JobScheduleSet.MoveNext();

run
CTime::GetCurre
CTime end = theJobSet.
CTime start = theJobSet.
CTime todayStart(start.GetYear(),
start.GetMonth(),now.GetDay(),
start.GetHour(),
start.GetMinute(),
start.GetSecond());
CTime todayEnd(end.GetYear(),
end.GetMonth(), now.GetDay(),
end.GetHour(),
end.GetMinute(), end.GetSecond());

if (todayStart > now || todayE
now)
{    theJobSet.Close();
return false;
}

CTimeSpan theSpan = end no
int totalMinutes =
theSpan.GetTotalMinutes();

if (end > todayEnd) // 
than today
{    int AdditionalMin =
GetAdditionalMinutes(the
t,
theJobSet.m_EndDate);
CTimeSpan todayS
now;    totalMinutes =
todaySpan.GetTotalMin
AdditionalMin;
}

m_min = ( ( (m_t
totalMinutes) + 1

m_Priority = t
m_Tilt = theJo
m_Throttle =
m_JobID = the
theJobSet.Cl
turn tru
```

RESOURCES

Books

C++

Effective C++
Scott D. Meyers
Addison-Wesley
ISBN 0201924889

Teach Yourself C++ In 21 Days, Second Edition
Jesse Liberty
Sams
ISBN 0672310708

COM

Beginning MFC COM Programming
Julian Templeman
Wrox Press
ISBN 1874416877

Inside COM
Dale Rogerson
Microsoft Press
ISBN 1572313498

Professional DCOM Programming
Richard Grimes
Wrox Press
ISBN 186100060X

Professional ActiveX/COM Control Programming
Sing Li and Panos Economopoulos
Wrox Press
ISBN 1861000375

Understanding ActiveX and OLE
David Chappell
Microsoft Press
ISBN 1572312165

Digital Telphony

Telecommunications Primer: Signals, Building Blocks, and Networks
E. Bryan Carne
Prentice Hall
ISBN 0132061295

MFC

Professional MFC Programming
Mike Blaszczak
Wrox Press
ISBN 1861000146

Object-Oriented Analysis, Design & Programming

Design Patterns: Elements of Reusable Object-Oriented Software
Gamma, Helm, Johnson, and Vlissides
Addison-Wesley
ISBN 0201633612

Object-Oriented Analysis and Design With Applications
Grady Booch
Addison-Wesley
ISBN 0805353402

Object-Oriented Modeling and Design
James Rumbaugh, Michael Blaha, William Premerlani, Frederick Eddy, William Lorensen
Prentice Hall
ISBN 0136298419

Object-Oriented Software Engineering: A Use Case Driven Approach
Ivar Jacobson
Addison-Wesley
ISBN 0201544350

UML Distilled
Martin Fowler with Kendall Scott
Addison-Wesley
ISBN 0201325632

Using CRC Cards: An Informal Approach to Object-Oriented Development
Nancy M. Wilkinson
Prentice Hall
ISBN 0133746798

Tcl

Tcl and the Tk Toolkit
John Ousterhout
Addison-Wesley
ISBN 020163337X

Web Programming

Instant ActiveX Web Database Programming
Alex Homer
Wrox Press
ISBN 1861000464

Professional Active Server Pages
Alex Homer, et al
Wrox Press
ISBN 1861000723

Magazines

C++ Report
SIGS Publications
http://www.sigs.com/publications/cppr/

The Journal of Object-Oriented Programming
SIGS Publications
http://www.sigs.com/publications/joop/

Microsoft Systems Journal
http://www.microsoft.com/msj/

Microsoft Interactive Developer
http://www.microsoft.com/mind/

Web Sites

Liberty Associates
http://www.libertyassociates.com/

Artisoft
http://www.artisoft.com/

Rational Software Corporation
http://www.rational.com/

Wrox Press
http://www.wrox.com/
http://www.wrox.co.uk/

```cpp
 false;
Time();
 = now.Format("%b %d

er = "start < '";
day;
' and enddate > '";
oday;
'";

ScheduleSet.m_strFilter =

JobScheduleSet.IsOpen())

JobScheduleSet.Requery();

pDoc>m_JobScheduleSet.Open();

lTrack* pCallTrack;
l ok;

ile
pDoc>m_JobScheduleSet.IsEOF())

        pCallTrack = new
lTrack(m_pDoc>m_JobScheduleSet.m_
bID);     ok = pCallTrack>Initialize();

    if (ok)
    {   Log("ok\n");
        m_CallList.AddHead(pCallTrack);
            foundJobs = true;
    }
    else
    {   Log("...Rejected!\n");
        delete pCallTrack;
    }

    m_pDoc>m_JobScheduleSet.MoveNext();


                    run     CTime
            CTime::GetCurre
            CTime end = theJob
        CTime start = theJobSet.
        CTime todayStart(start.GetYear(),
    start.GetMonth(), now.GetDay(),
    start.GetHour(),

        start.GetMinute(),
        start.GetSecond());
            CTime todayEnd(end.GetYear(),
        end.GetMonth(), now.GetDay(),
        end.GetHour(),

        end.GetMinute(), end.GetSecond());

            if (todayStart > now || todayE
        now)
        {       theJobSet.Close();
                return false;

        }

            CTimeSpan theSpan = end no
            int totalMinutes =
        theSpan.GetTotalMinutes();

            if (end > todayEnd) // a
        than today
        {       int AdditionalMin =
        GetAdditionalMinutes(theJ
        t,
                theJobSet.m_EndDate);
                    CTimeSpan todaySp

        now;    totalMinutes =
        todaySpan.GetTotalMin
        AdditionalMin;
        }
                m_min = ( ( (m_t
        totalMinutes) + 1 )
        );      m_Priority = theJo
                m_Tilt = theJo
                m_Throttle = the
                m_JobID = the
                theJobSet.Cl
                    eturn true
```

INDEX

C

Index

X

Z

```
= false;                                    run
                              CTime::GetCurren        CTime  
Time();                          CTime end = theJobSet.
= now.Format("%b %d           CTime start = theJobSet.GetYea
                                  CTime todayStart(start.GetYear(),
er = "start < '";              start.GetMonth(),now.GetDay(),
oday;                          start.GetHour(),
 and enddate > '';            start.GetMinute(),
today;                            start.GetSecond());
";                                CTime todayEnd(end.GetYear(),
                              end.GetMonth(), now.GetDay(),
ScheduleSet.m_strFilter =      end.GetHour(),
                                  end.GetMinute(), end.GetSecond());

                                  if (todayStart > now || todayS
JobScheduleSet.IsOpen())          now)
JobScheduleSet.Requery();         {    theJobSet.Close();
pDoc>m_JobScheduleSet.Open();          return false;

llTrack* pCallTrack;              }

l ok;                             CTimeSpan theSpan = end - now
                                  int totalMinutes =
ile                            theSpan.GetTotalMinutes();
pDoc>m_JobScheduleSet.IsEOF())

    pCallTrack = new                if (end > todayEnd) //
llTrack(m_pDoc>m_JobScheduleSet.m_    than today
bID);    ok = pCallTrack>Initialize();    {    int AdditionalMin =
                                  GetAdditionalMinutes(theJ
    if (ok)                      t,
    {    Log("ok\n");            theJobSet.m_EndDate);
                                      CTimeSpan todaySp
    m_CallList.AddHead(pCallTrack);    now;    totalMinutes =
         foundJobs = true;       todaySpan.GetTotalMin
    }                            AdditionalMin;
      else                       }
    {    Log("...Rejected!\n");
         delete pCallTrack;      m_min = ( ( (m_t
                                 totalMinutes) + 1 )
    }                            );    m_Priority = theJo
                                      m_Tilt = theJo
m_pDoc>m_JobScheduleSet.MoveNext();    m_Throttle =
                                      m_JobID = the
                                      theJobSet.Cl
m_pDoc>m_JobScheduleSet.             return true
bs;
```

Beginning Object-Oriented Analysis and Design with C++

Author: Jesse Liberty

If you've enjoyed this book, you'll get a lot from Jesse's new book, *Beginning Object-Oriented Analysis and Design with C++*.

Beginning Object-Oriented Analysis and Design with C++ takes an entirely practical approach to object-oriented software development. It teaches you, in a step-by-step tutorial, how to produce world-class commercial software, from conception through delivery. While *Clouds To Code* showed you what he did, in *Beginning Object-Oriented Analysis and Design with C++* Jesse teaches you what you need to know to do it yourself.

Beginning Object-Oriented Analysis and Design with C++ offers a working programmers' guide to the Unified Modeling Language, which is quickly becoming an industry standard. This is not an academic exploration of theory, it is analysis and design in the trenches, a nuts and bolts approach to developing robust, reliable, extensible and maintainable software.

The book begins with a fast paced overview of the entire development process. Jesse then takes each phase, from inception through elaboration and delivery and breaks it down into its component steps. The diagramming language is explained in detail, and he walks you through the entire process, providing tips, insights, warnings and details of what is required to build a robust design and implement it in C++.

Beginning Object-Oriented Analysis and Design with C++ assumes no prior programming experience, though it does assume you have read at least one solid primer on C++. It is written for programmers who want to build high quality commercial software that ships on time and on budget.

Professional DCOM Programming

Author: Dr. Richard Grimes
ISBN: 186100060X
Price: $49.95 C$69.95 £46.99

This book is for Win32 programmers taking up the challenge of building applications using the distributed component object model. There is a strong emphasis on the practicalities of distributed object design and use, and the text is also a complete examination of COM programming. The code is described and developed using Visual C++ 5, MFC and ATL.

Professional Visual C++5 ActiveX/COM Control Programming

Authors: Sing Li and
Panos Economopolous
ISBN: 1861000375
Price: $40.00 C$56.00 £36.99

"We believe that we can show you how to crack open COM and produce robust ActiveX controls to use now. It's our aim to show you the efficient route past all the pitfalls and dead-ends we've encountered and to help you succeed with the best methods. We've grappled with this technology since its inception and we know we can help you put solutions into practice. For some, it'll be the first time you've seen these new programming tools in action, but by the end of the book, you'll be using them to relieve some of your major development headaches"
Sing and Panos

This book is for anyone taking up the challenge of programming in the COM environment, using Visual C++, to produce industrial-strength ActiveX controls. You should be familiar with fundamental Windows development and using MFC. You will get the full benefit of learning how to develop professional controls for Win32 with the Active Template Library (ATL) included in Visual C++ 5

Professional MFC with Visual C++ 5

Author: Mike Blaszczak
ISBN: 1861000146
Price: $59.95 C$83.95 £56.49

Written by one of Microsoft's leading MFC developers, this is the book for professionals who want to get under the covers of the library. This is the 3rd revision of the best selling title formerly known as 'Revolutionary Guide to MFC 4' and covers version 5.0 of Visual C++.

This book will give a detailed discussion of the majority of classes present in Microsoft's application framework library. While it will point out what parameters are required for the member functions of those classes, it will concentrate more on describing what utility the classes really provide. You will learn how to write a few utilities, some DLLs, an ActiveX control and even an OLE document server, as well as examining Microsoft's Open Database Connectivity (ODBC) and Data Access Objects (DAO) strategies. At the very end of the book, you'll take a look at the features that the Microsoft Foundation Classes provide to make programming for the Internet easier.

There's a CD-ROM included which has the complete book in HTML format - now you can use any browser to read your book on the road.

WROX

Register Clouds to Code
and sign up for a free subscription
to The Developer's Journal.

A bi-monthly magazine for software developers, The Wrox Press Developer's Journal features in-depth articles, news and help for everyone in the software development industry. Each issue includes extracts from our latest titles and is crammed full of practical insights into coding techniques, tricks, and research.

Fill in and return the card below to receive a free subscription to the Wrox Press Developer's Journal.

Clouds to Code Registration Card

Name _____

Address _____

_____

_____

City_____ State/Region _____

Country_____ Postcode/Zip_____

E-mail _____

Occupation _____

How did you hear about this book?_____

☐ Book review (name) _____

☐ Advertisement (name) _____

☐ Recommendation _____

☐ Catalog _____

☐ Other _____

Where did you buy this book?_____

☐ Bookstore (name)_____ City_____

☐ Computer Store (name)_____

☐ Mail Order_____

☐ Other_____

What influenced you in the purchase of this book?

☐ Cover Design

☐ Contents

☐ Other (please specify) _____

How did you rate the overall contents of this book?

☐ Excellent ☐ Good

☐ Average ☐ Poor

What did you find most useful about this book? _____

What did you find least useful about this book? _____

Please add any additional comments. _____

What other subjects will you buy a computer book on soon? _____

What is the best computer book you have used this year?

_____

Note: This information will only be used to keep you updated about new Wrox Press titles and will not be used for any other purpose or passed to any other third party.

WROX PRESS INC.

Wrox writes books for you. Any suggestions, or
ideas about how you want information given in
your ideal book will be studied by our team.
Your comments are always valued at Wrox.

Free phone in USA 800-USE-WROX
Fax (312) 397 8990

UK Tel. (0121) 706 6826   Fax   (0121) 706 2967

Computer Book Publishers

NB. If you post the bounce back card below in the UK, please send it to:
Wrox Press Ltd. 30 Lincoln Road, Birmingham, B27 6PA

Supporting you on the web
http://www.wrox.com/

Fast download the source code to your book and collect updates on any errata

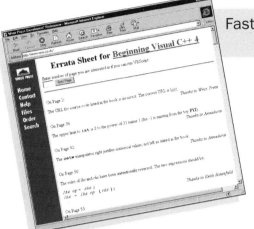

Preview forthcoming titles and test out some sample chapters

Get the full, detailed lowdown on any of our books - and read the reviews!

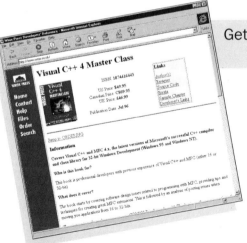

Sign-up for our free newspaper: "Developers' Journal" for Wrox activity, sample chapters and hot info on the industry

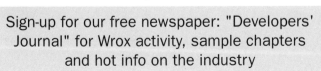

Drop into our mirror site at
http://www.wrox.co.uk